For Theory Building
in Archaeology

ESSAYS ON FAUNAL REMAINS, AQUATIC RESOURCES,
SPATIAL ANALYSIS, AND SYSTEMIC MODELING

STUDIES IN ARCHEOLOGY

Consulting Editor: Stuart Struever

Department of Anthropology
Northwestern University
Evanston, Illinois

For Theory Building in Archaeology

ESSAYS ON FAUNAL REMAINS, AQUATIC RESOURCES, SPATIAL ANALYSIS, AND SYSTEMIC MODELING

Edited by

LEWIS R. BINFORD

Department of Anthropology
University of New Mexico
Albuquerque, New Mexico

ACADEMIC PRESS New York San Francisco London

A Subsidiary of Harcourt Brace Jovanovich, Publishers

ACADEMIC PRESS, INC.
111 Fifth Avenue, New York, New York 10003

United Kingdom Edition published by
ACADEMIC PRESS, INC. (LONDON) LTD.
24/28 Oval Road, London NW1

Library of Congress Cataloging in Publication Data

Main entry under title:

For theory building in archaelogy.

    (Studies in archeology)
    "Most of the papers grew out of an advanced seminar
... conducted [by the editor at the University of New
Mexico]"
    Includes bibliographies.
    1.   Archaeology—Methodology—Addresses, essays,
lectures.   2.   Man, Prehistoric—Addresses, essays,
lectures.   I.   Binford, Lewis Roberts,   Date
CC75.F59   930'.1'028   76-58407
ISBN 0–12–100050–8

Contents

6   SEASONAL PHASES IN ONA SUBSISTENCE TERRITORIAL DISTRIBUTION AND ORGANIZATION: IMPLICATIONS FOR THE ARCHEOLOGICAL RECORD   251

David E. Stuart

PART III   Space: Its Organized Use and Analysis

7   A THEORETICAL APPROACH TO THE STUDY OF HOUSE FORM   287

Rosalind L. Hunter-Anderson

8   DUMMY DATA DISTRIBUTIONS AND QUANTITATIVE METHODS: AN EXAMPLE APPLIED TO OVERLAPPING SPATIAL DISTRIBUTIONS   317

Robert K. Vierra and Richard L. Taylor

PART IV Modeling and Monitoring Change in Relatively Complex Prehistoric Systems

List of Contributors

Numbers in parentheses indicate the pages on which the authors' contributions begin.

J. STEPHEN ATHENS (353), Department of Anthropology, University of New Mexico, Albuquerque, New Mexico

JACK B. BERTRAM (77), School of Australian Environmental Studies, Griffith University, Nathan, Brisbane, Queensland, Australia

LEWIS R. BINFORD (1,77), Department of Anthropology, University of New Mexico, Albuquerque, New Mexico

ROSALIND L. HUNTER-ANDERSON (287), Department of Anthropology, University of New Mexico, Albuquerque, New Mexico

L. B. JORDE (385), Department of Anthropology, University of New Mexico, Albuquerque, New Mexico

ALAN J. OSBORN (157), Department of Anthropology, University of New Mexico, Albuquerque, New Mexico

CHARLES A. REHER (13), Department of Anthropology, University of Wyoming, Laramie, Wyoming

RANDALL F. SCHALK (207), Department of Anthropology, University of New Mexico, Albuquerque, New Mexico

LAWRENCE GUY STRAUS (41), Department of Anthropology, University of New Mexico, Albuquerque, New Mexico

DAVID E. STUART (251), Department of Anthropology, University of New Mexico, Albuquerque, New Mexico

RICHARD L. TAYLOR (317), Department of Anthropology, University of New Mexico, Albuquerque, New Mexico

JOSEPH A. TAINTER (327), Department of Anthropology, University of New Mexico, Albuquerque, New Mexico

ROBERT K. VIERRA (317), Northwestern University, Evanston, Illinois

List of Figures

xi

List of Tables

General Introduction

LEWIS R. BINFORD

University of New Mexico, Albuquerque

Much has been written regarding the claims for a "New Archaeology," and there are arguments that attempt to assess the successes or failures of this alleged "movement." As far as I am concerned, however, much argumentative literature obscures the issues, at least those issues that I have tried to stress over a substantial period of time involving thought, research, writing, and teaching. I will not offer here an exhaustive critique of current debates, but I will point to certain differences between my views of archaeological science and the views of some of those who are generally lumped together with me as "New Archaeologists." In so doing, I will attempt to show that understanding is difficult to achieve, and that misunderstanding and confusion are common in the hands of struggling scientists.

The most commonly cited and debated point I have tried to emphasize is that to be productive, a scientist must operate with a self-conscious awareness of the ideas and assumptions by which he proceeds. I have suggested that facts do not speak for themselves; alleged inductivist approaches, which seek empirical generalizations, will not move us in the direction of explanation, and therefore understanding, of the facts observed. I have suggested that a self-conscious use of deductive methods is a prerequisite for scientific achievement. Since these suggestions appeared, there have been many attempted demonstrations and programmatic discussions of them. It is my impression that most of these have

1

been misleading or simply plain distortions of scientific method. Allow me to emphasize the point that scientific methods are designed to evaluate ideas. Science seeks to employ empirical materials in such evaluations. Thus, the problem that any scientist must understand is how one moves from ideas to facts or observations, and, in turn, how one may then relate the empirical findings back to ideas in an evaluative manner. Many who have been confused about these points tend to view empirical materials as sources or inspirations for ideas. This may be true in many cases, but the sources for ideas are not the concern of science directly; the primary concern is *only the evaluation of ideas once they have been advanced.*

At this point, the reader may justifiably ask questions regarding the kinds of ideas that scientists seek to evaluate. Are all ideas and concepts proper targets for scientific investigation? In one sense, the answer is yes, but in many important ways, it is no! The scientific method addresses itself to the evaluation of *theory.* The introduction of this term implies that all ideas and concepts are not aspects of theory, although all theory is essentially ideational and conceptual in character.

In moving between ideas about the world we live in and empirical observations of this world, the scientist must face a major problem: namely, what meaning is to be attributed to empirical observations? Only when observations have been given meaning can we discuss the nature of their relevance to ideas. That is, we can use only relevant empirical observations to argue the utility of our ideas. Relevance is established through arguments attempting to warrant that particular observations reliably and unambiguously inform us about certain conditions or states of systems or variables. Such arguments are always phrased in terms of the meanings given to observations and not simply in terms of the character of the observations themselves.

For instance, if we have the idea of a variable—for example, population pressure—we may immediately ask what empirical observations reliably and unambiguously inform us regarding the condition of this variable in different settings. Do we count numbers of archaeological sites, numbers of burials, numbers of broken pots, and so on, per unit of time? If we can advance a strong argument to support the contention that some class of empirical material reliably and unambiguously informs us about population pressure, we have provided meaning to that material through an operational definition of population pressure. In turn, we have simultaneously advanced a *convention* for assigning meaning to a specified class of empirical material. *A definition is not an hypothesis.* A definition specifies the relationship between a concept, word, or phrase, and a class of empirical or observational experience. On the other hand, an *hypothesis* asserts a relationship between two or more independently monitered variables said to be operative in the empirical world. When testing an hypothesis, the scientist must employ independent instruments to measure the multiple variables. He must have operational definitions of the variables stated in the hypothesis and, in turn, must specify the character of the anticipated interaction between the two or more classes of *defined* observational materials. Was the character of the observed interaction anticipated accurately by the hypothesis? If so, the ideas about the way in which the world works, from which the particular hypothesis was argued or deduced, can be said to have some utility.

Science is a method or procedure that directly addresses itself to the evaluation of cultural forms. That is, if we view culture as at least referring to the particularly human ability to give meaning expediently to experience, to symbol, and, in turn, view experience through this conceptual idiom, science is then concerned with evaluating the utility of the cultural tools produced.

Under these conditions, there is a paradox in that the scientist must use conceptual tools to evaluate alternative conceptual tools that have been advanced regarding the ways in which the world works. He never uses meaningless empirical material, only observations with alleged, and hopefully specific, attached meanings. There is no way out of this paradox: An evaluation of one set of ideas is dependent upon the accuracy of an assumed set of meanings, not currently under investigation, about what our observations meaningfully imply! This paradox is at the heart of the so-called "uncertainty principle," which asserts that we cannot prove anything positively; we may only negate hypothetical propositions. In any scientific argument, there are at least two types of tentative propositions: *hypotheses* deduced from ideas which we seek to evaluate, and *definitions* advanced as part of the argument that seeks to warrant the assertion that certain empirical materials may justifiably be used in evaluating the hypothesis. There is much confusion in the literature regarding different types of propositions and how they may be evaluated. Much of the recent discussion regarding scientific methods has failed to cope with this crucial paradox and has confused operational definitions with hypotheses.

For instance, James Hill's (1968) work is frequently cited as an example of hypothesis testing (see Watson, Le Blanc, and Redman 1971:37–45) and, therefore, as an example of the hypothetico-deductive method. I have not been able to find a single hypothesis in his work. (In all fairness, Hill does not make this error, only those who write about this work do so; he faithfully uses the term "proposition.") He addresses himself to a problem of identity. How do I archaeologically identify a storage room? He is concerned with warranting an *operational definition* for the concept "storage room." He is in no way testing an hypothesis regarding the expected forms of interaction between two or more variables, each operationalized independently for observational purposes. Hill's work is an excellent example of a strongly warranted argument that when certain observations are made and found to be congruent in rooms in sites of the American Southwest, one is justified in asserting that the room was used as a storage room in the past. The argument specifies the definiens of the concept "storage room." When one's experience matches the definiens, one is, by *convention*, justified in asserting that the room in question was a *storage room* in the past. Hill provides us with an operational definition for a concept that is useful in a restricted geographical and temporal frame. His work in no way allows us to understand (*a*) why he thinks such an operational definition is needed, (*b*) what ideas about dynamics would require the identification of storage rooms, or *(c)* how identifications, once they have been made, would be used in hypothesis testing.

In contrast, I might state as an example of an hypothesis that, other things being equal, dependence upon stored food will increase as the diversity of the subsistence base decreases in environments with less than 365-day growing seasons. Alternatively, other things being equal, dependence upon stored food will increase as the size of the consumer population increases in environments of less than 365 days of growing season. I will not attempt to argue the theory from which these hypotheses have been deduced; rather, they are simply cited as examples. Given these aforementioned hypotheses, we might view Hill's work as an attempt to operationalize an instrument for measuring dependency upon stored food. Some might argue that his operationalization—namely, the identification of storage rooms and perhaps the counting or measuring of storage room volume—is inadequate or ambiguous in that there are possibly other modes of storage or that things other than food may be stored in storage rooms. What I am suggesting is that, although one may offer strong support for the meaningful identification of some observed phenomena, this must remain merely an exercise or, at worst, a trivial endeavor, since the context of relevance in science for such attempts derives from the problem of operationalizing variables stated in hypotheses. Hill's work does not provide us with such a scientific context of relevance beyond some functional "understanding" of pattern variability in the archaeological record. Here Hill's work becomes unclear, since "understanding" is sought in the absence of theoretical relevance.

Aside from the confusion about hypotheses and definitions, there is a more general confusion about propositions and hypotheses. All propositions are not hypotheses. Many propositions are related to the evaluation of the adequacy and unambiguous nature of definitions. A classical, logical form of such a proposition is that all swans are white. Observations of black swans in Australia refutes the proposition. Has an hypothesis been tested? The answer is emphatically *NO*. Implied here is that the concept "swan" may be defined by criteria other than color, and, at one stage of our knowledge, we believed that white color was a powerful defining criterion of the concept "swan." Further observation shows that this is an unwarranted defining characteristic. Has such an observation refuted some theory regarding the pattern of interaction between color variables and other morphological or physiological variables? No, it has simply been shown that a particular incomplete definition of the concept "swan" is inadequate or ambiguous!

Let me draw another example from the recent literature, a work by Steven A. Leblanc (1973:199–214). Leblanc asserts that the logic used to evaluate a proposition has a basic form, and persons employing the proper form of logic, regardless of the content of the proposition, should not be subject to criticism, such as that of Flannery (1973:47:47–53). He also attacks the work of Tuggle, Townsend, and Riley (1972) and indirectly the work of Meehan (1968) as characterized by confusion converning "models" and "laws." In my opinion, neither understands the differences between definitions and hypotheses, and Leblanc is far from such an understanding. Leblanc further confuses the issue by attempting to argue that good science is dependent on the adherence to the proper logical form of evaluation regardless of the character of the proposition or its role in scientific argument! One does not advance science by spending one's time evaluating definitions simply because they exist. Who cares whether they are accurate or inaccurate if they are irrelevant? Relevance in science derives from the relationships between theory and hypotheses; propositions in hypothetical form generated in a theoretical void remain at best some form of empirical generalization. If our work misses this point, regardless of how well our procedures meet certain criteria of formal logic, we are not scientists. We may be logicians, Jesuits, or "law and order archaeologists," but we are not productive scientists simply because we adhere to a formal paradigm of reasoning. If we work only with existential propositions, such as "the size of a Bushman site is directly proportional to the number of houses on it"—an observation inductively summarized from direct experience—rephrasing it to read "the size of an archaeological site is directly proportional to the number of houses on it" does not constitute theory building. If we then proceed with good logic and method to evaluate the general accuracy of the statement, what has been evaluated beyond the existential accuracy of the proposition? Nothing necessarily has been evaluated. In short, we have perhaps proven a universal fact, but we have in no way validated any theoretical proposition. One does not build theory by accumulating universal facts or empirical generalizations, no matter how complex they may be. This is not to say that knowledge of such empirical relationships or forms of patterning may not be useful, but that their utility can be evaluated only with regard to (a) the degree to which they serve to inspire questions as to why the world is the way it appears to be and (b) the degree to which they may be useful in arguments of relevance attempting to relate concepts of theoretical interest to facts of the empirical world. Both of these criteria ask how they stimulate theory building, not how they help to evaluate theory or to provide us with theory directly. What I am suggesting is that polemic assertions that one is working "hypothetico-deductively" are meaningless when only propositions of an existential or definitional character are involved. Such a stance is a misguided inductive strategy. It results in, as Flannery (1973:51) has aptly phrased it, "Mickey Mouse laws."

It has been suggested that there is a procedure or third "paradigm" consisting of the evolutionary-systems "package" with a statistical–probabilistic wrapping (Willey and Sabloff 1974:196) that may prove useful in archaeology. This, of course, is not a new suggestion, and it is one that has met with crowning failure whenever it has been attempted—as, for example, in sociology. Statistical or probabilistic statements as to relationships between things are simply complex empirical facts. The only assumption one needs to make in order to project from such facts is that the system will remain unchanged, that things will stay as they are. These are *projections,* not *predictions,* since the latter require the specification of the conditions under which both stability and change will be manifest. Predictions require understanding of dynamics, not merely simple comprehension of patterning. In my opinion, evolution refers to the processes responsible for changes and diversification in organization; it does not refer to the products of evolution and the patterning that we may observe in these products when they are viewed temporally or spatially. The products, including patterning, are what we must explain with evolutionary theory. Statistical summaries and probabilistic statements about the patterning do not explain; they simply describe.

This form of criticism brings us to a discussion of what I view as an interesting phase of archaeological history: Archaeology–1976. I have argued, perhaps with some effectiveness, that the traditional paradigms of archaeology were inadequate, misleading, and essentially, a set of conventions for accommodating archaeological observations to a given cognitive map of man, the past, and cultural dynamics. By opening Pandora's box, by questioning the accuracy of meanings traditionally assigned to observations, and by insisting that we concern ourselves with the scientific task of evaluating ideas and concepts used in archaeology. The field was placed in a self-evaluative posture. Reactions have been varied but of essentially three forms. *(1)* There has been a rejection of the entire argument and an adherence (with tenacity) to traditional views (Flannery's [1973] old and new fogies). *(2)* There have been impatient and enthusiastic excursions into the application of "scientific" methods and rhetoric in the absence of any substitutive or original theory. Here we see an overemphasis on method or logic coupled with an apparent faith that the application of logical methods will result in the generation of theory (the law-and-order people of Flannery [1973]). In my opinion, this has been a return to an inductive strategy. *(3)* Finally, there are some who view the development of theory as the primary concern. This is a creative process for which there are no methodological rules to insure success. Given a theoretical vacuum left by the shaking of traditional archaeological ideas and conventions, we must seek new ideas, concepts, and their theoretical integration with reference to how the world works, why man behaves the way he does at different times and places, and how we may understand recognized patterns of changes and diversity in organized human behavior. Only to such theories may the scientific method be properly addressed. Thus, today's challenge is in theory building, and thus far little progress has been made, although many persons have seen the challenge and accepted it.

As I currently view this challenge, there are urgent needs for theory building on at least two levels. One level is what I refer to as *middle-range theory*. If one accepts observations made on the archaeological record as contemporary facts along with the idea that such facts are static, then clearly basic problems for the archaeologist include *(a)* how we get from contemporary facts to statements about the past, and *(b)* how we convert the observationally static facts of the archaeological record to statements of dynamics. Both of these problems pose the question of meaning. What meaning may we justifiably give to contemporary static facts regarding past dynamics? What conditions of dynamics, not available for observation, produce the forms and structures observable as static patterning in the archaeological record? In approaching this problem, we must develop ideas and theories (middle-range theory) regarding the formation processes of the archaeological record. Only through an accurate understanding of such processes can we reliably give meaning to the facts that appear, from the past, in the contemporary era.

It is interesting that, in the early days of the development of the science of geology, the focus of study was directed toward the elucidation of formation processes. What dynamic conditions produce what kinds of static effects? What remains in a geologic section can be reliably viewed as deriving from the operation of erosional processes in the past? Clearly such questions must be investigated through the study of contemporary facts, both dynamic and static. Early arguments in the field of geology centered around the validity of assumptions of uniformitarianism—that the same dynamic processes operative in the past are operative today. Obviously, such an assumption must be warranted to a high degree, since it is central to the development of meaningful arguments about the past that are deduced from contemporary observations on the geological or archaeological records. Without the development of a body of theory treating the relationships between statics and dynamics, and, also important, approaching this development with a deep concern for the degree to which uniformitarian assumptions may be justified, no real progress will be forthcoming.

I consider this the challenge to develop "middle-range theory"; I consider it middle range because I believe that we seek to make statements about the past in order to evaluate ideas we may hold about the conditions that brought about change and modification in the organization of dynamics occurring in past living systems. We seek understanding of the *processes* responsible for change and diversification in the organizational properties of living systems. In approaching this problem, we seek the development of general theory. The archaeologist must seek parallel development in theory relating to determined change and variability in processes resulting in the static facts remaining for our observation. Only with developments in both general and middle-range theory can the "scientific" method be appropriately employed. In the absence of theories and ideas for evaluation, discussion of appropriate scientific methods seems strangely misplaced.

Why do I suggest that the development of general and middle-range theory must proceed hand in hand? Simply because, in the absence of criteria of relevance, we may waste much time in developing middle-range theory concerning the dynamic significance of certain static facts that prove to be irrelevant to the evaluation of our ideas about the general determinant processes that promote change and diversification in living systems. The field must advance as a whole. Advances in middle-range theory divorced from general theory may prove to be a waste of time; similarly, advances in observational techniques or "field methods" may prove irrelevant once we have some idea of the kinds of data needed for evaluating our ideas.

In the following essays, we present *(a)* a variety of attempts to explicate, not so much scientific methods conceived of as a set of procedures, but the particular functions that scientific methods play in seeking understanding and explanation; *(b)* a number of provocative discussions aimed at the development of middle-range theory—namely, suggestions concerning the relationships between dynamics and their static by-products remaining for the archaeologist to observe; *(c)* papers treating a further complication arising from the operation of noncultural dynamics on archaeological remains that modify the statics away from their original patterns as derived exclusively from the dynamics of cultural system—in Schiffer's (1972) terms, "N-transforms"; and finally *(d)* a number of papers that address more general issues relating to both the evaluation of ideas advanced, as well as provocative suggestions concerning ideas not previously considered in seeking to understand the processes responsible for changes in dynamics of cultural systems.

The chapters in this book are the products of students and faculty of the University of New Mexico. Most of the papers grew out of an advanced seminar I conducted with graduate students and colleagues, which focused on the contemporary state of archaeology. Our aim in so doing was, hopefully, to isolate areas of research critical for advancing the field. The papers represent specific endeavors in that direction. We have attempted to integrate the diverse papers by means of cross referencing and in discussions of relevance as to how and why we viewed the subject covered as important and in need of study.

The organization of the book implies some opinions and convictions that may not be directly apparent in the context of the chapters. As has been suggested, most theory is at some point dependent upon the accuracy of uniformitarian assumptions—namely, that things were in the past as they remain in the present as far as conditions or processes are concerned. As far as man is concerned, such an assumption cannot be supported over the span of time with which archaeologists are concerned. Certainly, early populations of *Australopithecus* were not the same kind of creatures as modern man and, in turn, were probably not even capable of the kinds of behavior that we take for granted among ourselves. As I have pointed out many times, this means that *interpretations* of behavior from the products of early man (tools and artifacts) is likely to be a very risky business indeed. We may reasonably ask ourselves whether or not there are other classes of data remaining from the past which might better support *uniformitarian* assumptions. In short, are there not classes of data available to us for which a more reliable set of conditions might be projected into the past than for projections of human behavior per se? I answer with a resounding *yes*. I further reason that there are at least three domains of data that are archaeologically recoverable which, if developed theoretically, well might serve as excellent reference dimensions against which to view and evaluate different examples of hominid behavior relative to one another and to behavior of modern man as documented ethnographically. The first domain is ecological and respect to species with which man interacted in the past. For many species, examples are still available for direct observation concerning their behavior and qualities that might have been useful to ancient populations. Some of the species of aquatic shellfish, fish, and even some terrestrial examples are cases in point. We may evaluate these species today in order to determine their periods of availability, abundance, and utility to man under different conditions. Given such knowledge, we may then evaluate the actual patterns of use employed by ancient populations and the conditions under which we might expect variable usage. Such arguments are developed or eluded to in the chapters in both Parts I and II of this book. Additionally, I reasoned that, since most animals can be known anatomically, that is, we may know quite accurately the numbers of different bones in an animal of a given species form the past, we may study the frequencies of parts actually used, transported, or abandoned by ancient people as a direct measure of their economic and logistical sophistication and appropriate variable behavior in different settings. The first steps in our efforts toward a middle-range theory with emphasis on anatomical part frequencies is introduced in the chapter by Bertram and myself. Thus, the ecological and anatomical domains are emphasized in the chapters of Parts I and II in this book.

The third domain that I envisioned as having potential for theoretical development was that of space use. My original thoughts were simple. Human or hominid behavior always takes place in a spatial theater. The way in which this behavior is organized must be conditioned by certain relationships between the properties of alternative spatial organizations and the labor and social pressures operative during periods of organized behavior. If we could isolate even some of the constraints that are operative, within a dynamic system, on the character of spatial usage, we might well be able to analyze at least some aspects of past behavioral systems in structural terms rather than the more commonly emphasized formal or content categories of tool frequencies, types, and so on. The two chapters in Part III address themselves to this problem. One deals with the recognition of structural properties in the archaeological record, and the other treats the problem of middle-range theory building in the spatial domain.

In Part IV are three papers which seek to relate some aspects of systems organization meaningful to the static facts of the archaeological record or, conversely, some patterning in such facts to variables or states characteristic of past ecological interactions or systems functioning. These are important concerns, and much more work is needed in this area of archaeological theory building.

The term "new archaeology" has been much used. In the absence of progress toward usable theory, there is no new archaeology, only an antitraditional archaeology at best. I look forward to a "new archaeology," but what has thus far been presented under the term is an anarchy of uncertainty, optimism, and products of extremely variable quality.

In my opinion, the new archaeology was something of a rebellion against what was considered sterile and nonproductive endeavors by archaeologists. Rebellion cannot continue simply for rebellion's sake. The "stir" created in the 1960s has not resulted in many substantial gains. If we are to benefit from the freedom of nonparadigmatic thought that has perhaps resulted from our little rebellion, such benefits must be in the form of substantial new theory and knowledge of both the archaeological record and the relationship between statics and dynamics—archaeological formations processes. This book is an attempt to move in this direction. As such, we hope that some advance in the field has been accomplished and that, with this volume available, others will be to stimulated to address the difficult task of theory building and methodological development. If the argumentative environment of the 1960s stimulates only further argument, then the "new archaeology" will have been a failure, providing only social excitement in a relatively dull field.

REFERENCES

Flannery, Kent V.
  1973 Archaeology with a capital 'S'. In *Research and theory in current archaeology*, edited by Charles L. Redman. New York: John Wiley. Pp. 47–53.
Hill, James N.
  1968 Broken K pueblo: Patterns of form and function. In *New perspectives in archaeology*, edited by Sally R. and Lewis R. Binford. Chicago: Aldine. Pp. 103–142.
LeBlanc, Steven A.
  1973 Two points of logic concerning data, hypotheses, general laws, and systems. In *Research and theory in current archaeology*, edited by Charles L. Redman. New York: John Wiley. Pp. 199–214.
Meehan, Eugene J.
  1968 *Explanation in social science: A system paradigm.* Homewood, Ill: Dorsey Press.
Schiffer, Michael B.
  1972 Archaeological context and systemic context. *American Antiquity* **37:**156–165.
Tuggle, H. David, Alex H. Townsend, and Thomas J. Riley
  1972 Laws, systems, and research designs: A discussion of explanation in archaeology. *American Antiquity* **37** (1):3–12.
Willey, Gordon R., and Jeremy A. Sabloff
  1974 *A history of American archaeology.* San Francisco: Freeman.
Watson, Patty Jo, Steven A. LeBlanc, and Charles L. Redman
  1971 *Explanation in archaeology.* New York: Columbia University Press.

PART

I

Faunal Remains and the Archaeological Record

1

Adaptive Process on the Shortgrass Plains*

CHARLES A. REHER
University of Wyoming

Introduction

This paper outlines a framework for interpretation of archaeological materials from the Vore Site, a Late Prehistoric buffalo jump in the Black Hills of north-eastern Wyoming. The discussion that follows offers a set of assumptions and hypotheses that attempt to explain the role of the large, cooperative buffalo kill in adaptive process and cultural evolution on the shortgrass Plains. As such, the discussion is most concerned spatially with the Northwestern and High Plains (as shown by Wedel 1961:20; 1963), the western sector of the Plains stretching from southern Alberta and Saskatchewan to northern New Mexico and Texas, and chronologically with the period from about 1500 to 1800 A.D. Premises derived in this manner must be of general applicability to be theoretically useful, but their general quality will remain to be tested with other archaeological evidence. Explicitly theoretical research, by subsuming increasingly complex phenomena under fewer and fewer principles, provides the best avenue for moving toward an explanation of Plains prehistory, if such explanation is indeed an archaeological goal.

Culture is assumed to be most elegantly defined in terms of man's extrasomatic

* Excavations at the Vore Site were supported with a National Science Foundation Grant (GS 28641) obtained by George C. Frison of the University of Wyoming.

13

adaptation to his environment, a behavioral definition as put forth by White (1949, 1959:8). Adaptive decisions are formed by means of least-cost estimates of potential energy payoff among several alternative strategies (cf. Davenport 1960; Lee 1969; Gould 1969). If environmental (density independent) or demographic (density dependent) stress exceed tolerances of the cultural system, homeostatic mechanisms, such as the employment of buffering resource strategies, are no longer feasible; the system must undergo basic reorganization of its energy-extractive components or move in the direction of increased mortality and extinction.

Such fundamental reforming of thermodynamic relationships is referred to as evolutionary change and usually involves increasing the structural complexity and efficiency of the system (White 1949:367; Binford 1965). An evolutionary sequence can thus be abstracted from various characteristics of the organizational complexity of prehistoric groups, as they are reflected in the technological leavings of the archaeological record. Segments along a continuum from lesser to greater complexity can be categorized as "bands," "tribes," "chiefdoms," and so on, but this is not necessary and may in fact obscure significant ranges of variability within a particular category.

The research project charted here pertains most directly to aspects of subsistence behavior manifested in the organization of cooperative killing and butchering labor forces; such organization is assumed to have been mirrored in large part by sociological components of the cultural system (cf. White 1949:35; Steward 1955:36–37). Understanding the organization of killing and butchering activities should provide immediate insight into the nature of kinship systems, for example. Frison (1971:87) noted that a family level of organization was indicated by the small, separate processing features associated with the Archaic Ruby Site buffalo pound; each one of the large complexes of processing features evident at a Protohistoric Crow buffalo jump (Frison 1967:88–92) would have required the cooperation of several women and presumably reflect an affiliation such as the Crow matrilineal clan.

The Vore Site

The Vore Site is located on the Woodrow Vore ranch in Crook County, Wyoming, about 5 miles west of South Dakota and 33 miles south of Montana (Figure 1.1). The jump occurs in a large psuedokarst sinkhole feature on the rolling, grassy uplands between two forks of Redwater Creek, at an elevation of 3862 feet. Pine-covered hills and ridges begin within 3 or 4 miles to the north, south, and west and rise to elevations of over 6500 feet within 10 or 15 miles of the site area. The site is only 15 miles south of the lowest point in Wyoming (3125 feet), where the Belle Fourche River enters South Dakota. Numerous flowing streams, such as Redwater Creek, originate in the Bear Lodge Mountains (to the west) and other surrounding prominences, and there also occur several intermittent streams, springs, and small lakes within a radius of a few miles. The grassy flats,

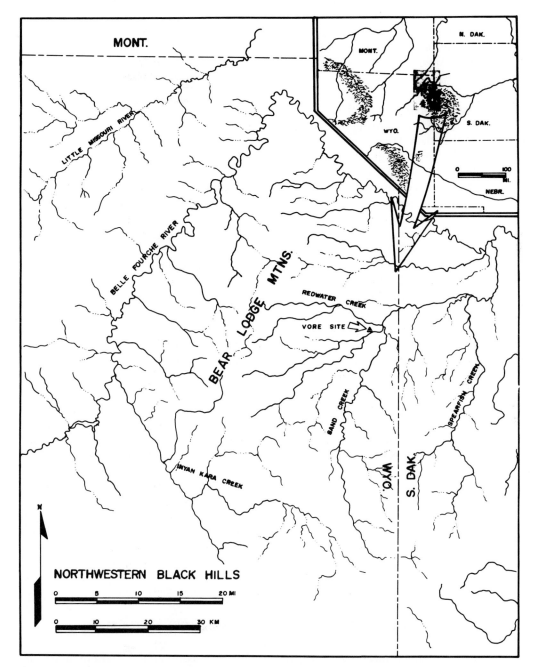

Figure 1.1 Map of the northwestern Black Hills showing Bear Lodge Mountains and Belle Fourche River and inset showing location of Vore Site area in part of the Northwestern Plains.

15

good sources of water, relatively low altitude, and nearby sheltered areas probably made this a very attractive area for prehistoric buffalo populations.

The sinkhole in which the site is located is about 125 feet in width with relatively steep sides about 50 feet high that would have provided a suitable jump-off at any point around the margins. The sink is formed in thick gypsum beds and red soils of the Triassic Spearfish formation, near the point at which the underlying Permian Minnekahta limestone slopes to the surface and then eastward to form the cave-bearing limestone plateau encircling the Precambrian granite core of the Black Hills (Thornbury 1967:297).

The site stratigraphy consists of at least 22 bone levels beginning about 4 feet below the surface and continuing to a depth of 17 feet in the flat-lying deposits at the bottom of the sinkhole. These bone levels range from a "one-bone" thickness to solid masses of bone 3 feet thick, and each level apparently extends horizontally from one side of the sinkhole to the other, about 90 feet (Figures 1.2 and 1.3). The sheer amount of bone encountered precluded large scale excavations in the time alloted, and the eight 7.5-by-10-feet excavation units, ranging in depth from 9 to 25 feet, represent at best a 10% sample. Bone levels are relatively thin and distinct in the upper and lower thirds of the site, while the central third consists of thick bone middens that separate into thinner levels only in certain areas of the site (Figure 1.4).

Cultural material recovered is all diagnostic of the Late Prehistoric Period (Mulloy 1958), and this is supported by radiocarbon dates of 1580 ± 140 A.D. (RL-349; 17 feet deep), 1750 ± 90 A.D. (RL-173; 9 feet deep), and "<230 years B.P." (RL-172; 5 feet deep). Thus, the upper portions of the site were laid down close to the inception of Historic times, although no material indicative of white contact was recovered. In addition, the deposits from about 12 to 20 feet of depth consist of finely laminated, varved sediments formed when the sinkhole contained a large pond; a preliminary attempt to refine site dating by correlating varve thickness with three-ring sequences indicated a probability that the bottom level may date closer to 1540 A.D.

Artifacts recovered describe the typical, relatively restricted assemblage found in most buffalo kills. They consist basically of two components—projectile points and butchering tools. The latter include chipped stone knives, a few large cobble choppers, and numerous bone butchering tools, such as have been described for the Glenrock jump (Frison 1970b:26). Retouch flakes from resharpening chipped knives occur quite frequently, and an occasional awl, end scraper, and bone or antler knapping tool are also found.

Adaptive Process on the Prehistoric Shortgrass Plains

Increasing utilization of the grassland biome is assumed to be synonymous with increasing dependence on meat. The degree to which buffalo were available for exploitation is the inverse of the degree of dependence on game and plant

Figure 1.2 An exposed bone level along a trench 7.5 feet wide and 40 feet long, Vore Site. Deeper excavation unit in center, at end of trench, is center of the site. Ground level is at top of photo, 4 feet above shelf on either side of trench.

17

Figure 1.3 Photograph of north wall of excavation unit N1, Vore Site. Thickest bone levels occur from 7.5 to 11 feet below ground. Varved sediments can be discerned below thickest bone (same profile is represented in Figure 1.4).

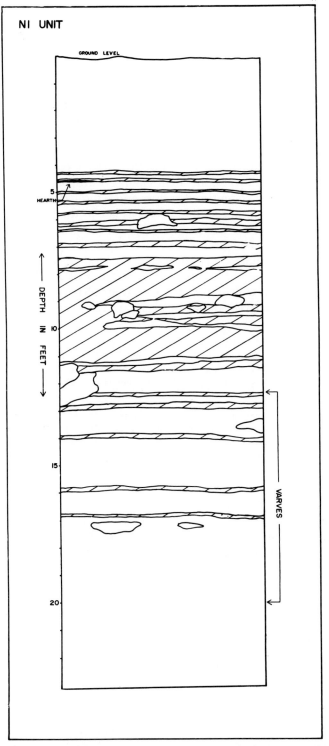

Figure 1.4 Schematic representation of profile of north wall of unit N1, Vore Site, showing early kills averaging intervals of 25 years followed by thicker bone levels and then by thin but relatively frequent bone levels in top part of profile.

resources from bordering mountain areas and from riverine and juniper-scarp enclaves. Such enclaves exist on the Plains with greater frequency than might be expected and were certainly utilized heavily on at least a seasonal basis (Wedel 1963; Reher 1971), but they cannot by themselves provide a secure basis for extensive occupation of the Plains area. Conversely, there is no evidence that the buffalo alone was entirely sufficient for a Plains adaptation; the Cheyenne, who were in the Black Hills during part of the time under consideration (Grinnel 1972:1–33), are typical of meat-dependent Plains groups, but they also ate 35–40 wild plant species, raided rodent seed caches, and hand-carried water to plots of corn on the North Platte and Laramie Rivers as late as the mid-nineteenth century (Grinnel 1972:250).

Nevertheless, when available, buffalo represented an option of high energy and protein potential that could attract agricultural and hunting–gathering groups from all points of the compass. The number of groups dependent to some extent on buffalo is truly impressive (e.g., Roe 1951:Appendix G), and such considerations are a recurrent theme in Plains study:

> When the reindeer, buffalo, and moose abounded, the Crees were then the peaceful possessors; the animals have disappeared and with them the ancient lords of the forest. Scarcely do we meet with a solitary hut . . . . For the Crees have gained the buffalo plains and they contend for them with the Black-feet, whose mortal foes they have become [Father DeSmet, 1845, Mandelbaum 1940:184].

> During Late Prehistoric times the western Plains and adjacent Mountains appear to have become attractive to several groups of sophisticated eastern farmers. It is tentatively suggested that the attraction may have been an increasing buffalo population which could be tapped by trapping and other communal techniques [Mulloy 1958:214].

It has been argued that stored meat products gained from large autumn kills were often necessary for periods when the intense Plains winter limited subsistence-oriented movement (Frison 1967:4, 34, 49; 1973:79). While probably not the case every winter, during an especially bad winter or series of bad winters, stores could represent the difference between starvation and survival. Again using the Cheyenne as an example, Grinnel states:

> Although making some provision against a time of scarcity as did most tribes of the buffalo plains, the Cheyenne yet often faced want . . . no matter how tempestuous the weather or how bitter the cold, if food was lacking, men were obliged to hunt. Often while out in the winter after buffalo, they were chilled to the bone by the bitter winds and were caught in blinding prairie snowstorms and obliged to camp for days, perhaps, without fuel, often freezing hands and feet. If the buffalo disappeared, the young men must make long journeys in search of them, and often their sufferings from fatigue, hunger, and cold were very great [1972:258].

The buffalo products gained from fall and winter kills were, therefore, a main "limiting factor" (Odum 1971:106; affecting human populations, and it is not unreasonable to assume human carrying capacity *(K)* can be defined in terms of buffalo available for such cooperative, storage-oriented ventures. It would, how-ever, be overly simplistic to then approximate K only in terms of buffalo num-bers. Given that such kills required the manipulation of several hundred animals, either in one jumping event or a series of pounding events, then there is a density threshold below which buffalo may have been present but not sufficient. Frison (1973:6) has noted, as a consequence, that there must be a "critical number" of animals in a gathering area and with anything less the probabilities of a success-ful kill rapidly decrease. We may also speak of the critical number of buffalo in a region, as it is the distribution of this macropopulation that determines the over-all probable group size to be found in a gathering area.

The concept of a critical number gives no indication of the exact number of animals that can be run into a pound or over a jump, only that too few can make cooperative kill ventures unfeasible. Thus, while the Gros Ventre may once have run three buffalo into a pound (Arthur 1974:103), it can be logically argued that they did not construct the pound and settle for the winter because they saw three animals, but that they did so only when the presence of these and numerous others made a series of communal kills appear feasible.

A further consideration in operationalizing some measure of buffalo for a carrying capacity model is the fact that buffalo numbers could fluctuate signifi-cantly in response to climatic variation. Harpending and Bertram (1975) have demonstrated that the logistics growth model, which assumes a relatively con-stant K, is so oversimplified as to be logically inconsistent for many problems. Defining K as a function of time with sinusoidal input based on stochastic climatic variation is a closer reflection of ecological reality. Investigation of the response of cultural systems to fluctuation of buffalo population will, thus, depend on defining the frequency and amplitude as well as other characteristics of such events.

The seasonal patterns of mobility, aggregation, and dispersion can also be attributed largely to seasonal variation in buffalo behavior and numbers in any area. These processes have been documented ethnohistorically, ethnographi-cally, and archaeologically, but one quickly realizes there is considerable differ-ence in the mechanisms and the seasonal mannerisms proposed. These have included fall aggregation and winter dispersion (Frison 1967, 1970b, 1971), in-tensive hunts in both spring and fall (Flannery 1953:53), and the fall as the "buffalo hunting season" (Ewers 1955:128). Arthur (1974) has presented consid-erable ethnohistoric documentation of aggregation and cooperative kill opera-tion throughout the winter on the Northern Plains and notes occurrences during most other seasons. Oliver (1962) records a pattern for historic equestrian tribes of summer aggregation and winter dispersion.

Frison's observations are based upon expectations of buffalo behavior and the resulting restrictions on the behavior of pedestrian hunters using Late Prehis-toric sites in Wyoming. The use of kills in autumn into early winter in these areas has been substantiated by age analysis of juvenile mandibles from kill site samples (Frison 1970a:30; Frison and Reher 1970; Reher 1970, 1973, 1974; Frison and

Wilson 1976). Arthur disagrees with this model and this evidence, and argues for use of kills throughout the winter as the basic pattern. Apparently, his contention is that, since ethnohistoric accounts describe kills throughout the winter, the analysis of archaeological materials must be erroneous.

The methodology of aging young animals through tooth eruption and wear is not new and is based on well-known paleontological and game management techniques. The fact remains that, if both calving season and kill operations are seasonally restricted, the teeth of kill site populations will fall into discrete age clusters (e.g., calves 6 months old, born the spring of that year; 1½-year-old animals, born the spring of the previous year; 2½-year-olds; 3½-year-olds; and so on). Arthur points to the small calf mandible samples at the Glenrock and Wardell Sites, but ignores the increasingly adequate samples from all older age groups, which demonstrate tight, discrete clustering of eruption and wear. There is no possibility that such repetitive, nonrandom clustering could be the result of sampling error. If killing activity occurs at other times of the year or extends through winter, this fact will be reflected in the kill site age structures. The kills in the main mass of the Vore Site, for instance, were laid down in most seasons. Analysis of mandibles from the Jones–Miller Site, a Hell Gap site in Colorado excavated by Dennis Stanford of the Smithsonian Institution, does, in fact, show usage from late fall through the winter (Reher n.d.b). As opposed to Arthur's line of reasoning, this does not alter the fact that autumn kills are still autumn kills.

Clearly, the historic and prehistoric information indicates a wide range of alternative strategies. At this point, it would be most constructive to seek general principles explaining all these strategies, rather than to perpetuate debate on the "real" season of intensive hunting. For instance, it is sufficient for the purposes of this chapter to propose that aggregational behavior was a function of buffalo productivity in all seasons. Seasonality is a secondary consideration, a consideration for refining the model in terms of specific areas and times, and need not be considered initially. The determinant effect of buffalo population upon mobility, group size, and other aspects of prehistoric organization is the principle that allows us to hypothesize where, when, and how we expect certain types of behavior to be manifested in the archaeological record.

Large communal kills represent the largest economically cooperative, socially integrated population segment during the yearly round. Regardless of the season, the size and duration of maximal yearly aggregation was a direct function of the buffalo available for such exploitation. Any social trend toward greater complexity over a span of years would also be a function of the state of buffalo populations. More formalized, institutionalized social structures would be expected to arise among groups aggregated every year while among groups averaging only one or two cooperative ventures in 10 or 20 years, such developments would not be anticipated.

Discrete categories, such as "bands" or "tribes," (e.g., Service 1962) have been common ways of treating complexity as conceived here. In this case, such a bipartate scheme would force us to obscure much of the relevant patterning remaining from the processes of culture change.

Documentation of a significant increase in effective moisture, such as that which occurred during the Little Ice Age (ca. 1500–1800 A.D.), is sufficient to infer a significant increase in buffalo carrying capacity (i.e., shortgrass productivity) and to predict an acceleration of the rate of cultural evolution. The rate and amount of cultural change should be proportional to the duration of the episode. Occasional or local buffalo "highs" should define an increase from family-level local groups to temporary aggregations of over 100 people (e.g., Frison 1967). Episodes of longer duration should witness more frequent aggregations, larger group size during the jumping season, and perhaps longer duration of the semisedentary behavior associated with the kills. These changes are not dependent on population increase among indigenous people but are reflected by mass migrations from nearby areas, especially among agricultural peoples. It is not clear whether such processes only result in more frequent and widespread association of groups on the order of 100 to 200 people, or if they can result in the group size of several thousand people that has been observed historically. Such development may have been dependent upon acquisition of the horse: The horse increases search radius and other characteristics of predation efficiency by several orders of magnitude; one can contend that the possession of even a few horses must have had a significant effect on cultural behavior.

When grass and moisture decrease, we can expect concomitant decrease of dependence on buffalo, less frequent integrative periods, and increasing dependence on buffering strategies. This undoubtedly happened time and time again over the last 10,000 years, if the characterization of the shortgrass ecosystem used here is appropriate. Archaeological and ethnohistorical evidence (e.g., Mulloy 1958:215; Grinnel 1972:13) describes large influxes of people who became fully nomadic in only two or three generations. Toward the end of a period of a few hundred years, either decreasing buffalo numbers or a large input from migrations (or, more likely, a combination of both) would bring these populations close to carrying capacity and, at some point, would produce stress upon the system. We are then immediately dealing with a situation that involves selecting for the evolution of more complex strategies that could more efficiently utilize remaining buffalo. However, such strategies would not remain viable if buffalo populations continued to decrease. Once again, it appears that the effect of the horse may have been to allow cultural development to reach a stage that was never possible with the use of pedestrian hunting methods.

These kinds of questions can be investigated through refinement and quantification of a theoretical model that can translate ecosystemic dynamics into the expected state of cultural systems; this, in turn, must be translated into terms that can be tested by reference to an archaeological sequence. It seems clear that, to investigate such a culture process on the Plains, the large kill site offers the appropriate context. Thus, the model that we are constructing here seeks to explicate the relationship between:

1. The distribution and organizational complexity of late Late Prehistoric Period groups using cooperative buffalo kills as part of the subsistence strategy; these factors are measured by means of the location, seasonality, and date of kill site components, the probable number of people involved, the frequency and duration of cooperative episodes, and various organizational characteristics of butchering labor forces, such as their size, amount of specialization, and the amount of common preparation and sharing of buffalo products. These, in turn, are reflected in kinship and other social forms.

2. They are in response to secondary productivity in the form of the distribution and density of buffalo populations available for cooperative exploitation. This is determined by extent, thickness, and frequency of bone levels in the kill site midden, number of animals killed, various aspects of population dynamics and morphological variation that provide information about survivorship and mortality rates and genetic fitness, and the integration of all of these variables with approximate carrying capacities.

3. These capacities are based on the net primary productivity of shortgrass, as measured by biomass and successional state (such data is necessarily gathered from literature on recent fluctuations and is inferred for the climatic situation associated with the Vore Site).

4. This productivity is a function of climatic fluctuation, as measured by effective moisture and temperature (moisture is especially important as a master limiting factor for the semiarid Plains); analysis of the Vore Site varve sequence and paleoclimatic literature serve to operationalize this measure.

The Shortgrass Ecosystem

Climate

In the last decade, research by Bryson and others (e.g., Baerreis and Bryson 1965; Bryson *et al.* 1970; Wendland and Bryson 1974; Bryson 1974) has demonstrated that climatic change can be caused by relatively rapid shifts in the seasonal position of various air masses, from one "quasi-stable" steady state to another. These, in turn, often reflect general, worldwide shifts in patterns of upper atmospheric circulation. Most climatologists agree these changes can ultimately be explained by the "forcing" input of solar energy in combination with other astronomical and atmospheric factors.

The processes leading to actual on-the-ground weather become exceedingly complex, and predictive theory relating parameters, such as annual precipitation, to higher-order phenomena is still being developed. Simple correlation of metereologic phenomena with the known sun spot cycle seems oversimplified (e.g., Bryson and Dutton 1961). It has also been argued that periodicities extracted from annual weather data are primarily a function of the techniques of harmonic analysis used (Mitchell 1964:192). Astronomical phenomena, such as the obliquity of the earth's axial tilt and eccentricity of the earth's orbit, contribute to small but significant differences in solar input and, therefore, in mean temperatures. These phenomena are known to vary in regular, periodic fashion (e.g., Vernekar 1972), and it seems likely that underlying harmonic components in climatic fluctuation have some basis in reality. In any case, the use of various time series analyses (e.g., Anderson 1958; Koopmans 1974; Yevjivich 1972) allows for the derivation of trigonometric functions that model and describe the frequency and amplitude of any series of climatic episodes.

The climate of the shortgrass region has been discussed in much detail elsewhere (e.g., Borchert 1950, 1971; Coupland 1958; Trewartha 1961; Collins 1969; Reeves 1973), and only a few brief points need be made here. The grassland biome, especially the western portion, has the most variable climate in North America. Overall, the region is semiarid, receiving an average of about 15 inches of precipitation annually. The town of Sundance, 15 miles west of the Vore Site, receives an average annual precipitation of 16.24 inches, and Colony, 30 miles to the north, averages 14.43 inches annually (Becker and Alyea 1964:9). Rainfall typically increases throughout spring and then drops off sharply during the summer. The dry Mild Pacific air mass dominates the shortgrass Plains during both the summer and winter, and this results in the low precipitation. Rainfall is the result of intrusions of Arctic or Tropical Maritime air masses. The steep rainfall gradient associated with the summer mean frontal position of Mild Pacific air marks the boundary between the shortgrass Plains and the Eastern Prairie, and is the primary determinant of shortgrass vegetation. Large droughts have characteristically afflicted the Great Plains about every 21 years during the time in which climatic records have been kept, extending truly arid conditions up the Western Plains and semiarid conditions east into the Prairie; the most severe droughts seem to occur during alternate droughts (Borchert 1971).

Prehistoric fluctuations in buffalo carrying capacity cannot be investigated before we define the relevance of the climatic scale with which we are working. A series of 4 dry years in one decade does not have the same results as a 100-year period of frequent below-average moisture. Substitute time series such as tree rings, varves, or actual precipitation values, can provide resolution on an annual scale, usually going back no more than several hundred years. As one moves further back in time, climate can usually only be stratified in terms of major episodes discernable, usually measured in hundreds or thousands of years. If such resolution, however, allows one to conclude that buffalo carrying capacity was relatively high or low, it is sufficient for the problems at hand.

Varves are thinly laminated bands of fine sediment laid down in relatively still bodies of water, such as ponds, lakes, and lagoons. Many different sorts of varves result from various depositional regimes and precipitates, but, in general, they consist of paired couplets with each couplet representing two basic seasonal regimes within one year's time (Anderson 1961). Varve thickness is known to be an approximate index of precipitation and temperature. Other more minor factors, such as evaporation, storminess, and changes in the drainage system, influence formation processes, but these cannot usually be recognized in ancient varve sequences (Anderson 1961:425).

The Vore varves may be somewhat unique in geological terms, for they occur in a sinkhole feature atop a slight knoll, and this feature is essentially a rain gauge that is 100 feet in diameter. It does not appear that many sources of possible error are a factor here, and Vore varve thicknesses are assumed to be a relatively accurate indication of past precipitation (Figure 1.5). At least 282 laminations representing 141 years contain the lowest five bone levels in the site strata. The five couplets associated with particular bone levels might include a larger error component, due to extra organic input, modification of the sinkhole sides by the site users, and so on. Analysis of the sequence with and without these particular varves, mathematical smoothing operations, and other techniques have indicated that such error is insignificant.

Radiocarbon dates and diagnostic characteristics of the artifact assemblage show that the Vore varves monitor the climate between about 1500 A.D. and 1650 A.D. The rest of the site sequence, above the varves, extends the time period under consideration to around 1750 A.D. Programs were written in APL-360 to run sliding correlations between the varve series and dated tree-ring series from the Missouri River and North Platte River basins (Schulman 1956). These techniques (based on Anderson and Kirkland 1966), indicate that the most probable starting date for the Vore varves is in the first decade of the sixteenth century, giving a probable date for the first bone level at around 1540 to 1550 A.D. (C_{14} date 1580 ± 140 A.D.). (This is discussed in more detail in Reher n.d.a).

Therefore, the Vore sequence encompasses almost all of the series of upswings in moisture that have been recognized collectively as the "Little Ice Age." This episode has been monitored in neoglacial activity (Richmond 1965:227; Porter and Denton 1967; Breckenridge 1974), in the application of the Blytt–Sernander sequence to North America by Baerreis and Bryson (1965:217) and on a refined scale by the O_{18} concentration in cores of the Greenland ice cap (Dansgaard *et al.* 1970). Power spectrum analysis of the Vore varves demonstrated a significant trend toward a 10-year periodicity; that is, peaks in precipitation tended to occur at 10-year intervals during the first part of the Little Ice Age. From historic sources documenting a drought cycle of about 20 years, it appears that above-average moisture occurred with greater frequency as well as with apparent greater duration and magnitude. Thus, the Vore sequence restricts us to an examination of the relationships of human behavior to essentially two scales of climatic variation—the series of annual to decennial episodes evidenced by the varves and the 150–200-year episode of increased effective moisture of which they are part.

Shortgrass Productivity

Effective moisture, as monitored by annual precipitation or some similar variable, is the main limiting parameter for the productivity of the High Plains.

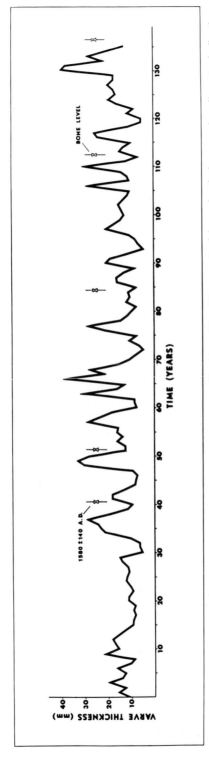

Figure 1.5 Graph of varve thicknesses from one column in N1 profile, Vore Site. Placement of bone levels in varved sediments, indicating trend for kills to occur after peak precipitation, are also shown. Time period represented is ca. 1500–1650 A.D. Mean thickness is 14.7 mm.

27

Vegetational response to historic droughts has been well documented (e.g., Ellison and Woolfolk 1937; Coupland 1958). Under such conditions, there are *significant* losses in grass biomass and basal cover as well as major successional changes. Using biomass as a rough indicator of carrying capacity and the historic droughts as analogies, it should be feasible to reconstruct these parameters under a given scale and set of climatic fluctuations.

On the annual to the decennial scale, shortgrass communities respond to occasional bad years with losses in plant height and some loss of biomass and basal cover. Under extended conditions of below-average moisture, increasingly significant effects accumulate. Losses in biomass and basal cover reach the order of from 70% to 90% (e.g., Coupland 1958:288), and major successional changes occur. Such losses are not replaced by species that are adequate for forage, and they can be equated with drastic reductions in carrying capacity. Cumulative effects in the hydrologic system, such as in stream-flow and soil moisture, accentuate the drought and increase the difficulty of recovery from such droughts. The rains return, however, and plant yields increase with relative rapidity to "normal" levels in 4 to 6 years.

Periods of extended above-average moisture lead to reciprocal major increases in biomass yield, and plant communities reach what is considered a postclimax stage. According to Coupland (1958:290), "in 1955 the calculated yield of a large section of the Northern Mixed Prairie was 237 percent as great as in 1944, even though the vegetation in that region had been considered to have fully recovered from drought by 1944." On a second-order scale, such as an episode of above- or below-average moisture of 100 to 200 years duration, the effects on grasslands should also be cumulative and more pronounced than those just discussed. Thus, during the series of relatively extended moist periods of the climatic sequence partially seen in the Vore varves, biomass could have been raised on the order of 200%, maintained there during most years, and perhaps increased beyond that. Increased basal cover and concomitant increased soil moisture would have sustained biomass over occasional dry years with fewer losses. During this period, one can infer an increase in carrying capacity of a magnitude seldom seen on the Plains.

The same cumulative interaction of these parameters means that it is probably highly erroneous to use historic droughts as driect analogs for the Atlantic or Altithermal episode, as done by Reeves (1973:1224). Although the series of droughts in the Atlantic may have been caused by the same circulatory mechanisms that cause historic droughts, they apparently occurred with much greater frequency, duration, and intensity (see Dansgaard *et al.* 1970: Fig. 6); taken as a whole, we are dealing with a different order of phenomenon altogether. Shortgrass biomass could easily have dropped to 10–20% of its former level, but unlike recovery during historic droughts, it would have been continually beaten back to even lower levels. This does not rule out local or less frequent fluoresces, for we are, after all, dealing with a period of 2000 years, but historic standards of fluctuation in carrying capacity should not be applied. Shortgrass communities under these conditions extend to the north and east, replacing drought stricken Prairie communities, and buffalo would behave accordingly. These extensions, however, could not begin to compensate for the incredible reductions in biomass on the Western Plains.

Buffalo Population

Exact data on buffalo population densities under varying climatic situations do not exist, to this writer's knowledge. Data given in McHugh (1958), primarily for national park herds, are equivalent to densities of from 648 to 3667 animals per 100 square miles, with most values tending to cluster around 1200 animals per 100 square miles. These animals are presumably maintained well below carrying capacity. Supplemental feeding and establishment of artificial water holes, however, are sometimes necessary; therefore, it is possible that they are not maintained in this manner. These densities, multiplied by the approximately 700,000 square miles of shortgrass Plains, indicate total populations of 4.5 million to 25.5 million animals, with a mean of about 8.5 million. Carrying capacities before, during, and after historic droughts (Coupland 1958:288) show forage requirements ranging from 12 acres per animal unit to 50 and 70 acres per animal unit. These values (assuming one a.u. = one buffalo unit) indicate a carrying capacity ranging from 37.5 million a.u. to 8.5 million a.u. to 6.5 million a.u. By these standards, the estimation of 40 to 60 million Bison on the Protohistoric–Historic Plains (Roe 1951, and others) supports the contention that the conditions were extremely optimal.

It is also difficult to deal in any exact terms with densities associated with the "critical number" of buffalo mentioned previously. The aforementioned carrying capacities permit rough calculations of the probability of the number of Bison occurring in a given gathering area (that area from which herds can be manipulated toward a kill site) as a parameter of this model. For example, in a gathering area of from 10 to 25 square miles, optimal carrying capacities of 12 acres per a.u. give a probability that 500 to 1300 animals could occur there (a table of predicted densities for any size gathering area and any stated carrying capacity can easily be calculated and entered into this stage of the model). A comparable density would seem to indicate that at least one of several alternative locales would contain sufficient buffalo to support a kill or series of kills.

These values are calculated on the assumption that buffalo were evenly distributed across the landscape; actually, they were not. Local conditions of grass, topography, and access to water could mean that, with almost any density, one area could contain large numbers of buffalo while another contained none. It is also probable that not every single buffalo in a gathering area was forced over a jump. It seems likely that probabilities of successful kills drop rapidly as buffalo populations decrease below average values. Intensive, widespread kills could occur only when population levels were well above average levels, since this requires replacement of animals killed. Further refinement and quantification of the thresholds of the model are needed; for the time being, we must be content with the less rigorous terminology of population "highs" and "lows."

Buffalo populations, with a generation span of only 3 years and very high mobility, should be quite sensitive to fluctuation in grass productivity on a decennial scale, such as the droughts discussed earlier. Under such conditions, one would expect higher mortality rates, especially among juvenile animals, to be reflected in irregularities in age pyramids (such as were found for the extinct *Bison* sp. population at the Casper Site; Reher 1974:121). The magnitude of the climatic perturbation and initial closeness of the population to carrying capacity should control the magnitude of this effect upon age structure and survivorship rates. Behavioral responses to drought probably include movements toward permanent water, foothills, and so forth. If these longer spans are significantly deviant from the mean of previous, similar spans (say a 200-year period with several severe droughts and, on the whole, deficient moisture), we would expect more drastic depression of survivorship rates and, thus, of population levels.

During a positive fluctuation on this "second-order" scale, we would expect increases in population levels, less irregular age structures, and generally higher fitness. If a series of relatively frequent moisture peaks occur, such as those that are probably associated with the Vore Site, the carry-over of grass and soil moisture would tend to damp the effects of a few intervening dry years. The next moisture peak would tend to pick up the growth curve of buffalo population and to accelerate it to a greater extent. Population size will continue to grow during the maturation period of the young animals, even if the adult population is approaching carrying capacity (Emlen 1973:288). Eventually, the combination of these factors means that population maxima occur shortly after the actual moisture peak and that maximum population levels of buffalo tended to extend well beyond the peak of the Little Ice Age.

If a climatic episode of "third-order" scale, that is, of up to several thousand years in duration, is sufficiently deviant, one must logically predict increasingly significant effects on indigenous Bison populations. Initial effects of widespread, frequent drought situations, such as existed during the Altithermal, should include greatly depressed survivorship rates and population levels, increasingly deviant age structures, and overall decreases in fitness. Given that moisture peaks occurred with much lower frequency, we would be dealing with extended periods during which the Western Plains area could not have supported viable buffalo populations. The carrying capacity values being used here are admittedly crude approximations, but they indicate only a few million buffalo, constrained during most years to riverine areas, montane situations, and new shortgrass areas to the north and east and with sporadic forays onto the High Plains after a number of good years.

In support of this contention, it is also clear that the effects on Bison populations during the Altithermal went beyond the depression of survivorship rates and so on and were more than just an intensification of the kinds of effects found during a moisture-deficient 100- to-200-year episode. During the Altithermal, the tolerances of the species as it then existed were exceeded, and stress of this severity resulted in evolution toward the smaller *Bison bison*.

Large mandible samples from kill sites represent the only remaining source for demographic data on Bison, and certainly the only source for most of the former extensive range of the species. Accordingly, we have been involved for a number of years in a program to reconstruct the population dynamics of animals exploited at these sites so that we can add demographic factors to the overall reconstruction of ecosystemic dynamics. By using age criteria developed by Frison and Reher (Frison and Reher 1970) and by refining paleontological techniques developed by Kurten (1953), we can operationalize measures of population dynamics for both modern and extinct forms (Reher 1970, 1973, 1974, n.d.b).

A small set of standardized measurements is sufficient to obtain data on individual sex and age and the season of the kill and to reconstruct life span, age pyramids, and approximate life tables and survivorship curves. All of these potentially provide information about the cumulative total of climatic events that resulted in the configurations and dynamics of a particular population. Age structure, as noted earlier, reflects fluctuation in annual mortality rates. For example, several lines of evidence suggested that the Casper *Bison antiquus* population was undergoing unusual stress, and concomitant irregularities in the population's age pyramid were observed (Reher 1974:120–122; Frison 1974). Approximate life tables and survivorship curves derived for kill site mandible samples are sufficiently discriminatory to differentiate between *Bison bison* from a marginal area, such as the Green River Basin, and *Bison bison* from a relatively optimum area, such as along the North Platte in east-central Wyoming (Reher 1973:102).

Successful response to environmental fluctuation depends on increased genetic variation, which, however, lowers overall fitness, since this implies the existence of individuals with nonoptimum genotype (Emlen 1973:75). Measures of certain aspects of tooth morphology and size thought to be genetically controlled have been tentatively shown to reflect the selective pressures operating on the population (Reher 1974:120). The difference between extinct *Bison* spp. undergoing stress towards dwarfism, for example, and healthy, viable *Bison bison* during the Little Ice Age is quite distinct (Reher 1974:Fig. 2.7; n.d.b). Continued refinement and comparison with other populations is necessary before this type of technique will be as useful as possible in specifying antecedent environmental conditions.

Given the assumptions presented thus far, the thickness and frequency of bone levels in a stratified site, the number of animals killed in each level, and similar evidence can be seen as a measure of the state of buffalo populations through time. This is possible only in an approximate sense, since we do not know how many nearby, alternative kill sites were utilized. However, the alternating cultural and sterile levels common to almost all buffalo kills, such as the Kobold Site (Frison 1970a), Glenrock (Frison 1970b), Wardell (Frison 1973), Boarding School (Kehoe 1967), the Gull Lake Site (Kehoe 1973), the Old Woman's jump (Forbis 1962), and the Bonfire Shelter (Dibble and Lorraine 1968), are certainly partially reflective of Bison fluctuations through time in the site area. The Vore Site provides a nice example here since it encompasses most of a known climatic sequence. Levels in the bottom of the site occur on the average of once every 25 years; then they increase in thickness and frequency toward apparent continual cropping of local herds; finally, they return to relatively frequent but discrete events (Figure 1.4). Adding all known kill site components together would provide, for all intents and purposes, a histogram of the amount of dependence on Bison (as has been recently done for Southern Plains sites by Dillehay, 1975, and for the Southwest by Johnson, 1974). Despite the fact that these groups probably employed kills in other areas and at other seasons, we could not provide a more appropriate example of the expected cyclical nature of buffalo populations and buffalo kills during the sixteenth, seventeenth, and early eighteenth centuries than that reflected in the Vore strata.

The effects of human predation on Bison populations are unclear, but they are potentially significant and cannot be passed over lightly. Human beings were the chief, most effective Bison predator, with the predation of wolves confined to culling only the very young and very old. We argued previously that predation that consistently removes hundreds of animals of prime breeding age must have had drastic local results (Reher 1974:123–124). Data on cooperative antelope kills in the Great Basin are not directly comparable, but Steward (1968:1972) notes that, after a kill, antelope populations in the vicinity were not suitable for another kill for as long as 10 years. Frison, however, has stated that "it does not appear possible, in terms of the methods used, that more than a negligible percentage of the total number of animals in a specific area could have been taken during any given year" (1973:6), and, at least initially, this may have been the case.

It can be argued that increasing human population and concomitant predation was, in a sense, "beneficial" to buffalo populations approaching carrying capacity in the Late Prehistoric to Historic period. Intensive predation in one area raises the carrying capacity for adjacent populations, in effect, by allowing them to donate excess numbers to the predated areas. Stresses accumulating from density dependent or density independent processes are, thus, temporarily alleviated. This too may have been a contributing factor in extending maximum population levels for some years beyond the actual maxima of carrying capacity. A whole series of complicated, feedback relationships between predator and prey will have to be understood in the final analysis of Plains prehistory.

Organization of Human Groups

Large kill and processing sites offer the best context for studying organizational parameters of nomadic Plains populations. The amount of meat obtained, for example, can be roughly calculated to give the approximate size of the group involved (cf. Frison 1967:34; Wheat 1972:121). Since preparation for a kill involved a special trip to a quarry to manufacture tool blanks and projectile points, identifying the source of these materials gives some indication of the number of groups that came together for the kill and of their territorial range. At the Vore Site, assemblages are almost entirely made up of comparable percentages of Spanish Diggings quartzite from east-central Wyoming, metamorphised shales and other materials from southern Montana, and what is probably Knife River flint from western North Dakota. From the widespread location of these quarries, it is reasonable to postulate an aggregate of at least three groups at the Vore Site. The North Dakota materials, especially, are suggestive of the range of the Cheyenne during the time period under consideration. From ethnohistoric references, however, it can be seen that it is impossible to restrict interpretations to one ethnic group. Grinnel (1972:39) has records of the Cheyenne, Arapahoe, and Gros Ventre together in one camp in one instance, and, in another case, a large camp on the Northern Plains contained Piegans, Blackfoot, Sarcees, and Plains Cree (MacGregor 1966:80).

The large middens of butchered bone, which are the most prominent feature of such sites, appear at best to be a confusing jumble, but it has been our working assumption that they are patterned by the organized butchering that occurred there and are potentially quite informative of organizational parameters of the site users. Computer storage and retrieval has proven to be the only feasible way of handling the thousands of bits of information represented by several tons of bone from a kill site. Preliminary work with multivariate statistics has demonstrated that the expected nonrandom patterning exists and can be attributed to the spatial organization of butchering activities (Reher n.d.a). Initially, simple patterns that reflect the involvement of several groups are discernable. Measurement of finer resolution, such as differentiating the amount of cooperation and specialization within or between groups, necessitates increasing control over the various factors that affect butchering processes at these sites (seasonality, the occurrence of previous kill on the same location, etc.). The Vore Site bone is currently being analyzed and should be especially valuable in correlating organizational parameters with a known climatic episode. In addition to evaluating the anticipated increase in organizational complexity and efficiency, it should be possible to specify the range of complexity achieved.

Processing areas are actually much more useful in terms of providing evidence for solving these kinds of problems. As noted previously, features at the Piney Creek processing area (Frison 1967:35, 88–92) consist of several complexes of large stone-boiling pits, stone-heating pits, and several anvil stones. Construction, maintainence, and operation of each of these complexes clearly required the cooperation of several women. Even if we did not know that this was a Crow Site, it would be apparent that we are dealing with processing labor and consumptive units beyond a simple family level of integration.

Other lines of evidence could be followed to establish the organizational complexity of population segments involved and to monitor an evolutionary sequence of these units through time. In combination with measures of associated environmental conditions, this would initially be sufficient to test a model like the one offered here. We make no claim that it has been developed beyond the most preliminary stages, but an approach like this is essential.

Conclusions and Implications for Archaeological Interpretations

If buffalo numbers did not commonly and regularly exceed the "critical number" necessary for maintaining cooperative kills, cultural systems would necessarily be quite responsive to annual or decennial variation in climate. Furthermore, we would expect maximum buffalo numbers (which supposedly did reach this prerequisite level) to be reached at least one buffalo generation (about 3 years) after a peak in effective moisture. The predictions of the model in this regard are verified by the initial Vore Site sequence. The five kills contained in the varved strata occur an average of 4 years (range of 3 to 7 years) after precipitation maxima (Figure 1.5). They also occur on an average of only once in 25 years (range of 17 to 35 years). Apparently, the critical number of buffalo necessary for jumping did not exist continually in the Vore Site vicinity during the sixteenth century and first half of the seventeenth century.

Adaptation to this sort of fluctuation during most of Plains prehistory would then be expected to take the form of *(1)* several associated local groups conducting fail to early winter jumps after increases in buffalo population, dependence on buffalo stores during bad periods of the winter, and smaller groups exploiting various game and plant resources during the remainder of the year; *(2)* far-flung scouting for possible alternative, localized buffalo increases to exploit by communal methods during other years, perhaps involving movements of several hundred miles (but perhaps less) and association with different local groups; *(3)* dependence on non-Bison, buffering resources even in the fall if relatively widespread drought made cooperative kills regionally unfeasible or if, for some other reason, sufficient buffalo could not be located; or *(4)* taking of deer and Big Horn sheep with cooperative kills in mountainous areas, such as is in evidence at the Dead Indian Creek Site (Frison, unpublished data; see also Frison *et al.* 1974:119; Smith 1970).

Without being able to control for the number of alternative kill locations utilized, it is not possible to state how often groups on the order of 150 people could aggregate, but this does not appear to have occurred every year. The essential characteristic of social organization would seem to be a requirement for built-in flexibility and extensive alliance networks allowing access to areas where communal kills were feasible. Any attempt at maintaining exclusive access to certain territories would eventually be disadvantageous; well-defined, institutionalized authority structures to control sustained production and communal preparation of stored meat products at very regular intervals would also be unnecessary. In this context, Frison has noted that, while Archaic kills clearly involved cooperative behavior, processing and distribution of meat took place at the family level (Frison 1971:86–87). A further consideration that cannot be discussed in detail here includes such factors as an expected region-wide homogeneity in stylistic variability of projectile points.

Behavioral response to a series of frequent moisture peaks that define a positive fluctuation in Bison productivity of several hundred years duration include *(1)* greater frequency and duration of aggregation of several local groups, perhaps including longer kill seasons and kill seasons at other times of the year than the fall; *(2)* probably an overall increase in group sizes during all phases of the yearly economic round; *(3)* large influxes of population from areas surrounding the Plains; and *(4)* increasing dependence on buffalo products and less tendency to utilize buffering strategies.

Concomitant with this, we would expect to find the evolution of more formalized, stable kinship, authority, and other structures for organizing larger butchering task forces. Increased efficiency in processing larger amounts of meat should be reflected in increasing specialization in both kill site and processing area. At some point in this episode, the beginnings of territorial exclusion, increased ethnicity and the associated heterogeneity of stylistic variation, and competition for resources would be likely. Flexibility of organization would still be a prerequisite for successful adaptation, but not to the previous extent. Such authoritative structures as did evolve would still not be permanent fixtures, nor would truly lineal kinship systems and sodalities seem to be viable. In this regard, Lowie described, with incredibly apt terminology, the "periodically functioning" police force of the Plains Indian and the fluid, nonexclusive nature of bilateral kinship and age-grade societies found among many Plains tribes (Lowie 1963:8).

Oliver (1962) has noted the examples of "cultural continuities" evidenced in Historic Plains groups, such as the reflection of more complex organization in groups of agricultural extraction. Within the paradigm incorporated here, it would be argued that the more important issue to be explained is the fact that, due to the deterministic effect of adaptation to the shortgrass ecosystem, both simple and complex groups were rapidly approaching the same level of integrational complexity.

If such extensive demographic and organizational shifts are the response to a 200- or 300-year increase in productivity, what, we may logically ask, is the response to a 2000-year period of frequently deficient productivity? From the evidence collected thus far, we would postulate widespread decreasing dependence on Bison, heavy reliance on mountain and riverine areas, and infrequent aggregation above even a multifamily level. During such a period, the buffalo that did exist would seldom be aggregated in the numbers necessary for systematic, cooperative kills. When such kills occur, they are not on the current Western Plains, but on the flanks of the Black Hills (e.g., Frison and Wilson 1976) and in other favorable, peripheral areas. It would seem the concept of an Altithermal hiatus in the Plains cultural sequence (e.g., Mulloy 1958:208–209) still has some merit, and also that communal buffalo hunting was not the "basic strategy" (Reeves 1973:1246) on the Plains during the Altithermal.

Whatever interpretations are ultimately supported by Plains archaeologists, the point to be made here is that they must be based upon the dynamic, periodically fluctuating nature of the shortgrass ecosystem. The reflection of these characteristics in human behavior will include the state of cultural systems as an equilibrium system responding to stochastic climatic input, and the rate of cultural change as a direct function of buffalo productivity. The state evidenced by widespread cooperative kills even may have been a relatively unusual event, if the entire sequence were known.

ACKNOWLEDGMENTS

The author wishes to take this opportunity to express his gratitude to Dr. Frison for permission to excavate the Vore Site and to utilize the material recovered as the basis for a doctoral dissertation. Computer programs to correlate the Vore varve sequence with tree-ring series and for power spectrum analysis were written for the APL-360 system by Lynn Jorde of the University of New Mexico. Roger Anderson of the University of New Mexico, Department of Geology, offered advice on the varve sediments. The ideas proposed here benefited from discussions with George Frison, Jim Judge, Lewis Binford, Henry Harpending, Lynn Jorde, and numerous friends and colleagues. Errors and overstatements are the responsibility of the author.

REFERENCES

Anderson, Roger Y.
  1961   Solar terrestrial climatic patterns in varved sediments. *Annals of the New York Academy of Science* **95**:424–439.
Anderson, Roger Y., and Douglas W. Kirkland
  1966   Intrabasin varve correlation. *Geological Society of America Bulletin* **77**:241–256.
Anderson, T. W.
  1958   *The statistical analysis of time series.* New York: John Wiley.
Arthur, George W.
  1974   An introduction to the ecology of Early Historic communal Bison hunting among the Northern Plains Indians. Unpublished doctoral dissertation, Department of Anthropology, University of Calgary, Alberta, Canada.
Baerreis, David A., and Reid A. Bryson
  1965   Climatic episodes and the dating of the Mississippian cultures. *Wisconsin Archeologist* **46**:203–220.
Becker, Clarence F., and John D. Alyea
  1964   *Precipitation probabilities in Wyoming.* Agricultural Experiment Station Bulletin 416, Laramie.
Binford, Lewis R.
  1965   Conceptual problems in dealing with units and rates of cultural evolution. *Anthropology UCLA* **1**:27–35.
Borchert, John R.
  1950   The climate of the central North American grasslands. *Annals of the Association of American Geographers* **40**:1–39.
  1971   The Dust Bowl in the 1970s. *Annals of the Association of American Geographers* **61**:1–22.
Breckenridge, Roy
  1974   The use of archaeology in dating quaternary deposits in the Upper Wood River area, Absaroka Range, Wyoming. In *Applied geology and archaeology: The Holocene history of Wyoming,* edited by Michael Wilson. Pp. 22–26. Geological Survey of Wyoming Report of Investigations No. 10.
Bryson, Reid A.
  1974   A perspective on climatic change. *Science* **184**:753–760.

Bryson, Reid, A., and John A. Dutton
    1961   Some aspects of the variance spectra of tree rings and varves. *Annals of the New York Academy of Science* **95**:580–604.
Bryson, Reid A., David A. Baerreis, and Wayne M. Wendland
    1970   The character of Late-Glacial and Post Glacial climatic changes. In *Pleistocene and recent environments of the Central Great Plains,* edited by W. Dort and J. K. Jones. Pp. 53–73. Lawrence: University of Kansas Publications.
Collins, Don D.
    1969   Macroclimate and the grassland ecosystem. In *The grassland ecosystem: A preliminary synthesis,* edited by R. A. Dix and G. R. Beidleman. Pp. 29–39. Range Science Department, Science Series 2. Fort Collins.
Coupland, Robert T.
    1958   The effects of fluctuations in weather upon the grasslands of the Great Plains. *Botanical Review* **24**:274–317.
Dansgaard, W., S. J. Johnsen, H. B. Clausen, and C. C. Langway, Jr.
    1970   Climatic record revealed by the Camp Century ice core. In *Late Cenozoic Glacial Ages,* edited by K. K. Turekian. New Haven: Yale University Press.
Davenport, W.
    1960   Jamaican fishing: A game theory analysis. *Yale University Publications in Anthropology* No. 59. New Haven: Yale University Press.
Dibble, David S., and Dessamae Lorrain
    1968   Bonfire shelter: A stratified Bison kill site, Val Verde County, Texas. *Texas Memorial Museum, Miscellaneous Papers* No. 1.
Dillehay, Tom D.
    1975   Late Quaternary bison population changes on the Southern Plains. *Plains Anthropologist* **19**:180–196.
Ellison, Lincoln, and E. J. Woolfolk
    1937   Effects of drought on vegetation near Miles City, Montana. *Ecology* **18**:329–336.
Emlen, J. Merritt
    1973   *Ecology: An evolutionary approach.* Reading: Addison–Wesley.
Ewers, John C.
    1955   The horse in Blackfoot Indian culture. *Bureau of American Ethnology Bulletin* No. 159. Washington D.C.: Smithsonian Institution.
Flannery, Regina
    1953   The Gros Ventre of Montana: Part I, social life. *Catholic University of America Anthropological Series* No. 15. Washington D.C.: Catholic University American Press.
Forbis, Richard G.
    1962   The Old Women's buffalo jump, Alberta. *National Museum of Canada Bulletin* No. 162:119–164.
Frison, George C.
    1967   The Piney Creek Sites, Wyoming. *University of Wyoming Publications* **33**:1–92.
    1970a The Kobold Site, 24 BH 406: A Post Altithermal record of buffalo jumping for the Northwestern Plains. *Plains Anthropologist* **14**:1–35.
    1970b *The Glenrock buffalo jump 48 CO 304. Plains Anthropologist* **15**(2) Memoir 7.
    1971   The Bison pound in Northwestern Plains prehistory. *American Antiquity* **36**:77–91.
    1973   *The Wardell buffalo Trap, 48 SU 301; Communal procurement in the Upper Green River Basin, Wyoming. Anthropological Papers* No. 48, Museum of Anthropology, University of Michigan.
    1974   *The Casper Site, a Hell Gap Bison kill on the High Plains.* New York: Academic Press.
Frison, George C., and Charles A. Reher
    1970   Age determination of buffalo by tooth eruption and wear. In *The Glenrock buffalo jump, 48 CO 304,* edited by George C. Frison. *Plains Anthropologist* **15**(2) Memoir 7, Appendix I.

Frison, George C., and Michael Wilson
  1976   The Hawken Site: A Paleo-Indian Bison kill in the Wyoming Black Hills. Unpublished
         manuscript, University of Wyoming, Laramie.
Frison, George C., Michael Wilson, and Diane J. Wilson
  1974   The Holocene stratigraphic archaeology of Wyoming: An introduction. In *Applied geology
         and archaeology: The Holocene history of Wyoming,* edited by Michael Wilson. Pp. 108–127.
         Geological Survey of Wyoming Report of Investigations No. 10.
Gould, Peter R.
  1969   Man against his environment: A game theoretic framework. In *Environment and cultural
         behavior Ecological studies in anthropology,* edited by Andrew P. Vayda. American Museum
         Sourcebooks in Anthropology. New York: Natural History Press.
Grinnel, George B.
  1972   *The Cheyenne Indians, their history and ways of life.* Vol. 1. Lincoln: University of Nebraska
         Press.
Harpending, Henry, and Jack Bertram
  1975   Human population dynamics in archaeological time: Some simple models. In *Population
         studies in archaeology and biological anthropology: A symposium,* edited by Alan C. Swedlund.
         American Antiquity **40**(2):82–91, Memoir 30.
Johnson, Paul C.
  1974   Late Prehistoric Bison utilization in Arizona. Paper presented at the 32nd annual Plains
         Conference, Laramie.
Kehoe, Thomas F.
  1967   The Boarding School Bison Drive Site. *Plains Anthropologist* **12** Memoir 4.
  1973   *The Gull Lake Site: A Prehistoric Bison drive site in Southwestern Saskatchewan.* Milwaukee
         Public Museum, Publications in Anthropology and History No.1.
Koopmans, L. H.
  1974   *The spectral analysis of time series.* New York: Academic Press.
Kurten, Bjorn
  1953   On the variation and population dynamics of fossil and recent mammal populations. *Acta
         Zoologica Fennica* **76**:1–122.
Lee, Richard B.
  1969   !Kung bushman subsistence: An input-output analysis. In *Environment and cultural behav-
         ior, ecological studies in anthropology,* edited by Andrew P. Vayda. American Museum Source-
         books in Anthropology. New York: Natural History Press.
Lowie, Robert H.
  1963   *Indians of the Plains.* American Museum Science Books Edition. Garden City: Natural
         History Press.
MacGregor, J. G.
  1966   *Peter Fidler: Canada's forgotten surveyor 1796–1822.* Toronto: McClelland and Stewart.
Mandelbaum, David G.
  1940   The Plains Cree. *Anthropological Papers of the American Museum of Natural History* **37**:154–
         316.
McHugh, Tom
  1958   Social behavior of the American buffalo *(Bison bison). Zoologica* **43**(1):1–40.
Mitchell, J. Murray
  1964   A critical appraisal of periodicities in climate. *Weather and our food supply.* CARD Report 20.
         Pp. 189–227. Iowa State University, Ames.
Mulloy, William
  1958   A Preliminary historical outline for the Northwestern Plains. *University of Wyoming Publica-
         tions* **22**(1).
Odum, Eugene P.
  1971   *Fundamentals of ecology.* Philadelphia: W. B. Saunders.

Oliver, Symmes C.
 1962 Ecology and cultural continuity as contributing factors in the social organization of the
       Plains Indians. *University of California Publications in American Archaeology and Ethnology*
       48:1–90.
Porter, S. C., and G. H. Denton
 1967 Chronology of the neoglaciation in the North American Cordillera. *American Journal of
       Science* **265**:177–210.
Reeves, Brian
 1973 The concept of an Altithermal cultural hiatus in Northern Plains prehistory. *American
       Anthropologist* **75**(5):1221–1245.
Reher, Charles A.
 1970 Population dynamics of the Glenrock *Bison bison* population. In *The Glenrock buffalo jump,
       48 CO 304,* edited by George C. Frison. Pp. 51–55. *Plains Anthropologist* **15**(2) Memoir 7,
       Appendix II.
 1971 A survey of ceramic sites in southeastern Wyoming. Masters thesis, University of Wyo-
       ming, Laramie.
 1973 The Wardell *Bison bison* sample: Population dynamics and archaeological interpretation.
       In *The Wardell buffalo trap, 48 SU 301: Communal procurement in the Upper Green River Basin,*
       edited by George C. Frison. Pp. 89–105. *Anthropological Papers* No. 48, Museum of An-
       thropology, University of Michigan, Appendix II.
 1974 Population study of the Casper Site bison. In *The Casper Site, a Hell Gap Bison kill on the
       High Plains,* edited by George C. Frison. Pp. 113–124. New York: Academic Press.
 n.d.a. Adaptive process on the Prehistoric shortgrass plains: Evidence from the Late Prehistoric
       Black Hills of Wyoming. Doctoral dissertation, in preparation, University of New
       Mexico.
 n.d.b Paleoecological reconstruction and the analysis of subfossil bison populations: The
       Jones–Miller Site extinct Bison sample. Unpublished manuscript, University of New
       Mexico.
Richmond, Gerald M.
 1965 Glaciation of the Rocky Mountains. In *The Quaternary of the United States,* edited by H. E.
       Wright and D. G. Frey. Pp. 217–230.
Roe, Frank G.
 1951 *The North American buffalo: A critical study of the species in its wild state.* Toronto: University of
       Toronto Press.
Schulman, Edmund
 1956 *Dendroclimatic changes in semiarid America.* Tucson: University of Arizona Press.
Service, Elman R.
 1962 *Primitive social organization: An evolutionary perspective.* New York: Random House.
Smith, Sharon K.
 1970 Preliminary report, Site 48 PA 551. *Wyoming Archaeologist* **13**(1):23–33.
Steward, Julian H.
 1955 *Theory of culture change: The methodology of multilinear evolution.* Urbana: University of
       Illinois Press.
 1968 The Great Basin Shoshonean Indians: An example of a family level of sociocultural
       integration. In *Man and Adaptation,* edited by Yehudi Cohen. Pp. 68–81. Chicago: Aldine.
Thornbury, William D.
 1967 *Regional geomorphology of the United States.* New York: John Wiley.
Trewartha, G.
 1961 *The earth's problem climates.* Madison: University of Wisconsin Press.
Vernekar, Anandu D.
 1972 Long-period global variations of incoming solar radiation. *Meteorological Monographs*
       12:1–21.

Wedel, Waldo R.
    1961   *Prehistoric man on the Great Plains.* Norman: University of Oklahoma Press.
    1963   The High Plains and their utilization by the Indian. *American Antiquity* **29:**1–16.
Wendland, Wayne M., and Reid A. Bryson
    1974   Dating climatic episodes of the Holocene. *Quaternary Research* **4:**9–24.
Wheat, Joe Ben
    1972   The Olsen–Chubbuck Site, a Paleo-Indian Bison kill. *American Antiquity* **37**(1) Memoir 26.
White, Leslie
    1949   *The science of culture, a study of man and civilization.* New York: Grove Press.
    1959   *The evolution of culture.* New York: McGraw–Hill.
Yevjivich, Vujica
    1972   *Stochastic processes in hydrology.* Fort Collins: Water Resources Publications.

2

Of Deerslayers and Mountain Men: Paleolithic Faunal Exploitation in Cantabrian Spain*

LAWRENCE GUY STRAUS
University of New Mexico

Introduction

Most current debate in the field of Paleolithic prehistory centers around the critical question of the nature of archeological subdivisions defined by lithic and bone tool assemblages. The debate often concerns the artifacts in and of themselves. Explanation of variability is, in general, reduced to the single dimension of assumed temporal change, even when strictly stratigraphic evidence cannot be brought to bear. But Paleolithic sites are not repositories for temporally standardized artifact assemblages that can be mined and interpreted like paleontological deposits. The artifacts abandoned on Paleolithic living floors and in midden fills constitute a part of the object set through which many of the interactions between individual cultural systems and aspects of their environment were mediated. Therefore, their kinds and frequencies of artifacts are clearly related to aspects of past human activities at each location and time, as well as to factors of differential abandonment and preservation. While representing important

* Field research in Spain during 1973–1974 was in great part supported by a National Science Foundation Dissertation Improvement Grant GS-40627 and by a National Science Foundation Graduate Fellowship. In addition, research in 1972 was made possible by grants from the Wenner-Gren Foundation for Anthropological Research (no. 2880) and from Arizona State University (no. 7805-806-15-8) (both the latter grants were to G. A. Clark), as well as by a Ford Foundation Travel Stipend (made available through Prof. Freeman).

potential sources of information on past behavior, artifacts, as agencies of systemic articulation, are difficult to interpret functionally in the absence of reliable data on the context of their use. Even in view of this vacuum of information on the operation of past ecological systems involving human activity, artifacts by themselves have been, nevertheless, given a paramount interpretive role as markers of temporal and "cultural" identity. This is neither explicitly justified nor always probable, in light of their certain and most frequent production for and use in the procurement and/or alteration of raw materials in particular situations.

What follows is a brief review of the current state of knowledge about the faunal remains for Paleolithic and Early post-Paleolithic occupations in one restricted region of western Europe. Hopefully, however, it serves to make a series of points that have more far-reaching theoretical relevance. Quantitative faunal data and information on the distribution of sites can provide powerful clues to the interpretation of Prehistoric adaptations. While faunal remains have often received some attention in Paleolithic analyses, this has generally been in the context of attempted reconstruction of gross climatic parameters and of dating the archeological strata.

By and large, the remains of fauna found in archeological levels are the result of an initial deposition as part of selective procurement and processing activities of man. Subsequent processes generally consist in the subtraction of parts of the record. Nonetheless, the faunal remains are a reflection (however dimmed) of an important class of past human subsistence activity. As such, they are direct products of man's patterned interaction with aspects of his particular environment.

Rather than being concerned with arbitrary, circular arguments about Paleolithic artifact "traditions," the purpose of this chapter is to investigate the evidence for changing faunal exploitation through time, as it relates to other germane aspects of human ecology, such as site density and location. The model providing the underlying basis of this study is that increased population density will result in significant changes in subsistence strategies. While the facts to be presented do seem to support this relationship, they do not constitute conclusive proof. However, the results of the exercise belie the utility of some of the speculative, universalistic criteria that are held out by archeologists as providing partial definitions for the various subdivisions of the Paleolithic (viz. supposed quantum behavioral changes among Middle, Upper, and post-Paleolithic time periods and among stage or "facies" divisions of these). While behavioral changes are never really "sudden" in the Paleolithic record (nor necessarily synchronous in different areas), some of the most interesting evidence of variability may not occur between subdivisions, but rather within them, either among different regions or simply among sites located in slightly differing habitats in the same area. Archeologists often forget that characterizations of change under one set of ecological circumstances, may not necessarily apply under others, even in neighboring areas at roughly the same time (e.g., southwestern France versus Cantabrian Spain).

The evidence that is presented here of a relationship between particular conditions of population increase and change in animal food procurement strategy (bipolar seasonal settlement pattern, single-species or biotope-set specialized hunting at particular locations, *and* increased diversification in the spectrum of resources consistently exploited at other sites) strongly suggests that such notions as "evolution" and "increased awareness of resources" have no explanatory power, per se. While the dimension of time remains important in terms of studying the evidence of processes of change, the dimension of space, as it includes settlement density and distribution, takes on greatly increased importance, once temporal attribution of cultural residues is controlled, preferably by radiometric means. In the light of the approach suggested here, explanation of aspects of artifact assemblage variability must be presented in terms of relationships with other relevant data sets, such as faunal remains. To test any idea about Paleolithic artifact function, it is necessary to go outside that class of data in search of confirmation. It is hoped that this study may provide the basis for further analysis and thought on the problem of behavioral variation and change in Paleolithic systems.

Background

Recently, Freeman (1973) published an important article on the mammalian faunas of Cantabrian Spain. Between the time of its writing and final publication, and subsequent to publication, there have become available many new quantitative data on fauna from the Cantabrian Paleolithic. While Freeman's interpretations and provocative conclusions were based largely on an exhaustive discussion of presence–absence data and some quantitative data principally from Cueva Morín in Santander, this discussion relies solely on calculations of minimum numbers of individuals per species for collections from 67 occupation levels throughout the region.

Much of this data stems from the dissertation on Guipuzcoan faunas by Jesus Altuna (1972), together with his studies of the Cueva Morín faunal assemblages (Altuna 1971, 1973). The second Cueva Morín study partially revises the first, which was used by Freeman (1973). In addition, classifications of the Altamira Solutrean (Altuna and Straus 1975) and of the El Conde Mousterian and Aurignacian levels (Altuna in Freeman 1975) have been made. Finally, during the course of my research on the Solutrean of Cantabria, I did preliminary calculations of minimum numbers of individuals for a number of Solutrean faunal collections, plus two Magdalenian and one probable Gravettian collection. The availability of all these new data justifies this further consideration of Cantabrian Paleolithic faunas, since they constitute a very substantial—if imperfect—information base from which comparisons can be made both among temporal subdivisions and among sites (and regions). This discussion, therefore, is a further contribution to the investigation of some of the ideas proposed by Freeman and, hopefully, will help promote both further discussion and investigation.

Cantabria Now and Then

Cantabria, as it is most inclusively defined, is that area of the northern coast of Spain composed of the modern provinces of Oviedo (Asturias), Santander, Vizcaya, and Guipuzcoa. Paleolithic occupation was apparently confined to the cave-riddled calcareous majority of this coastal strip and did not extend to western Asturias. Nor is there conclusive evidence of Paleolithic settlement of the Meseta del Norte south of the Cantabrian Cordillera in Burgos Province (Clark, Straus, and Fuentes 1975) (see Figure 2.1).

The region in question is about 350 km long (between the French border to the east and the Rio Nalón near the city of Oviedo to the west) by about 35 km wide. It is bounded to the north by the Cantabrian Sea (Bay of Biscay), to the south by the Cordillera (including the maximally 2600 m high Picos de Europa), to the east by the Pyrenees, and to the west by the low Cambrian and pre-Cambrian shield area of Galicia.

During glacial maxima, environments differed greatly from the present wet, equable, lush conditions of this coastal zone, with its (theoretical) climax vegeta-

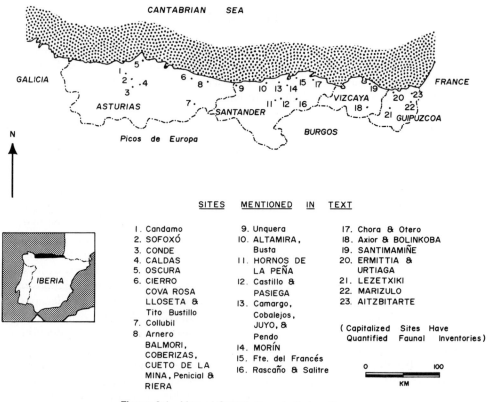

SITES   MENTIONED   IN   TEXT

1. Candamo
2. SOFOXÓ
3. CONDE
4. CALDAS
5. OSCURA
6. CIERRO
   COVA ROSA
   LLOSETA &
   Tito Bustillo
7. Collubil
8. Arnero
   BALMORI,
   COBERIZAS,
   CUETO DE LA
   MINA, Penicial &
   RIERA

9. Unquera
10. ALTAMIRA,
    Busta
11. HORNOS DE
    LA PEÑA
12. Castillo &
    PASIEGA
13. Camargo,
    Cobalejos,
    JUYO, &
    Pendo
14. MORÍN
15. Fte. del Francés
16. Rascaño & Salitre

17. Chora & Otero
18. Axior & BOLINKOBA
19. SANTIMAMIÑE
20. ERMITTIA &
    URTIAGA
21. LEZETXIKI
22. MARIZULO
23. AITZBITARTE

(Capitalized   Sites   Have
  Quantified   Faunal   Inventories)

0   100
KM

Figure 2.1 Map of Cantabria and site locations.

tion of dense oak–beech forest, despite its southerly latitude (c.43°N). Several glacial centers formed along the Cordillera (especially in the Picos de Europa), with regional snow lines of about 1500 m during stadial oscillations, where today there are no glaciers at all. Frost weathering was common even inside caves during these periods (see Butzer 1971a,b, 1973). Other evidence suggests conditions of marked seasonal aridity during some of the cold episodes, despite the coastal location. Palynological evidence suggests that, during glacial maxima, trees were scarce and confined to sheltered, moist spots, forming small woods and copses of pine with some supposedly thermophilous deciduous species. The results were mosaics of extensive open grass- and scrublands with scattered patches of woods (see Leroi-Gourhan 1959, 1966, 1971). These mid-latitude glacial environments provided abundant, rich pasture for grazing animals, such as horses and bovines, as well as both seasonal shelter and fodder for woodland-preferring cervids and suids. Interstadial periods saw the partial reforestation of parts of the region, and there was certainly frequent minor fluctuation in climate and vegetation as reflected by the propostions of trees and plants that are today typical of grasslands and alpine tundras. Information on the Late Pleistocene animal species and their biotope preferences is fully presented by Freeman (1973) and need not be repeated here.

The Collections

Before describing and interpreting the quantitative information on faunas, some details should be given concerning the collections. The Cueva Morín and Castillo beta collections have already been discussed by Freeman (1973), although the figures for Morín that I use here are taken from Altuna's original reports, including the upward revision of figures from Levels 17 and 8 based on results of the 1969 excavation. Attribution of levels excavated at the Cueva del Conde to the Mousterian and Archaic Aurignacian is now certain, as demonstrated by the excavator (Freeman 1975).

Attribution of the numerous collections listed as Solutrean is as certain as is possible with often old, at times inadequately labeled collections from excavations that are sometimes unpublished. Every effort was made to assure a correct, conservative interpretation, relying on all available published and unpublished information, as well as on interviews with several of the excavators of the sites in the four provinces. Attribution of Level E of Bolinkoba (Vizcaya) to the Gravettian is somewhat controversial, but it seems reasonable, since the one Solutrean point present is probably derived from the more clearly Solutrean Level D, due to known posthole digging in the site excavation (see J. M. de Barandiaran 1950; McCullough 1971). The nature of the El Juyo "Magdalenian III" faunal data is discussed at length later. While the entire question of the "lower Cantabrian Magdalenian" is in a state of flux at present and is under intense study, it is certain that there is evidence from at least the few sites with long, full stratigraphical sequences (e.g., Castillo) that this industry was interstratified between the Solutrean (with foliate points) and the Upper Magdalenian (with harpoons). This does not mean that some of the many isolated so-called Magdalenian III (or IV) assemblages are not simply Solutrean or Upper Magdalenian occurrences that lack classic fossil directors for reasons of Prehistoric site functional differences and/or partial archeological sampling. An example of the latter possibility is the case of the site of Tito Bustillo in Asturias, where an occupation originally thought to be Magdalenian III had to be revised upon the discovery of a harpoon fragment (see Moure 1974).

Stratigraphies and cultural attributions of the Guipuzcoan levels are outlined by Altuna (1972) in his work, but one of the sites, Lezetxiki, is rather controversial. Much of the stratigraphy was attributed to the Mousterian by its principal investigator, J. M. de Barandiaran, and a so-called Neanderthal humerus was found in the basal cultural stratum, Level VII. The taxonomic classification of this fossil and the designation of the level as Mousterian are clearly linked by circular reasoning based primarily on the archaic appearance of the lithic industry, which is, in fact, very rich in scaly retouched sidescrapers. As noted by Altuna (1972:136–138), Freeman has challenged the designation of Levels III and IV as Mousterian. In fact, these levels contain excellent, classic examples of Upper Paleolithic tool types, together with cruder looking sidescrapers and denticulates typical of Upper Paleolithic industries here and throughout Cantabria, despite their "Mousteroid" appearance (see Freeman 1975). Lezetxiki Level IV is probably Aurignacian, and Level III may be Gravettian. Level V has only very sparse remains. Levels VI and VII might well be Mousterian, but further study will be required before any firm conclusions can be drawn. The collections are only provisionally listed here as Mousterian.

Attribution of Levels II and III of Marizulo to the "Final Mesolithic" and "Tardenoisian" by Apellaniz and Marcan, as reported by Altuna (1972:187), may be subject to further revision. A C[14] date of 5300 B.P. in Level I (with Early Bronze Age ceramics) at least allows for the possibility that Level III could be roughly contemporary with the Late Azilian and Asturian.

Assignment of Level F of Urtiaga to the Final Magdalenian, based on the typological assessment of its 49 lithic tools (there are no harpoons) by J. M. de Barandiaran and de Sonneville-Bordes (1965), seems questionable now, due to a C[14] date of 17,000 B.P. from the base of this level (Altuna 1972:171). On this basis, I have included Urtiaga F among the collections from the Lower Magdalenian, a position also tentatively taken by I. Barandiaran (1973:221, fn. 107, 222, fn. 108). Nonetheless, this date is some 2000 years older than even those from each of the other Lower Cantabrian Magdalenian levels listed (El Juyo:15,300 B.P.; Altamira:15,500 B.P.; La Lloseta:15,200 B.P. [Crane and Griffin 1960; Clark 1971a]).

The only published Cantabrian Upper Solutrean date (from Aitzbitarte in Guipuzcoa) is 18,000 B.P. (Altuna 1972:414) but this is supported by a new date from Cueva Chufin in Santander (V. Cabrera and F. Bernaldo de Quiros, personal communication). The Gravettian has been dated as 19,300 and 20,100 B.P. at

Lezetxiki and Morín, respectively (Altuna 1972:410, fn. 1; González Echegaray, Freeman *et al.* 1973). Attributions of other collections identified by Altuna from the easternmost coastal Basque provinces are more straightforward.

Altuna (1972) presents his identifications of the very small faunal collections from Clark's tests in Coberizas, Balmori, and La Lloseta (all in eastern Asturias) in the form of number of remains per species, from which I have made rough estimates of minimum numbers of individuals where necessary. The first two levels are by definition Solutrean, due to the presence of one foliate point in each, and the last is probably "Magdalenian IV," according to Clark (1971a), due to the lack of harpoons and a C^{14} date of 15,200 B.P.

The Quantified Faunal Data

Table 2.1 presents the data in the form of minimum numbers of individuals. Percentages have been calculated for the species considered to be the principal big game animals. Percentages have not been calculated at all for the smallest of the collections (those with less than a total of five game animals from only a few species), since such calculations and the interpretation thereof would be particularly misleading. Judgments concerning the importance of particular species in particular collections should be based not only on an appraisal of their relative frequency, but also of their absolute number. The statistically insignificant collections are listed, but not otherwise considered.

Fauna of the Paleolithic Subdivisions

Mousterian

Large numbers of individuals were preserved in only three certain or possible Mousterian levels. The size of the faunal collections is not entirely a factor of the volume of sediments excavated in each case (see Table 2.1). The collection from Morín 17 has been recently revised by the addition of several animals, including boar, red deer, horse, steppe rhinoceros, ibex, and large bovines (Altuna 1973). As with the Castillo beta collection, horse, large bovines, and red deer are numerically by far the most important animals, and the former two certainly may have provided an overwhelming proportion of the usable meat weight. Only minimal information is available in the scattering of faunal remains from Morín 22, 16, and 15, although again deer, horse, and bovines are of about equal numerical importance.

The two lowest levels at Lezetxiki present a rather different picture from that of the Castillo and Morín collections. As opposed to the two central Santander sites, the Basque "Mousterian" site has very few (or no) red deer, whereas large bovines are overwhelmingly in evidence, even numerically. The Lezetxiki VI collection is unusual in that it has a large number of individuals from a wide

Table 2.1

Fauna from the Mousterian and Chatelperronian Levels

	Castillo beta[a] (Santander)	Morín 22[b] (Santander)	Morín 17[b,c]	Morín 16[b]	Morín 15[b]	Conde 6[e] (Asturias)	Lezetxiki VII[d] (Guipuzcoa)	Lezetxiki VI[d]	Morín 10 Chatelperronian
Cervus elaphus	16–45.7%		5–23.9%	1	1–20%			2–11.1%	1
Cervus sp.	7–20.0%								
Megalaceros sp.								1–5.5%	
Capreolus capreolus			1–4.7%		2–40%		1–16.6%	2–11.1%	
Sus scrofa			1–4.7%				1–16.6%	1–5.6%	
Large Bovines (Bos/Bison)	5–14.3%	2	6–28.6%	1	1–20%		4–66.7%	6–33.3%	1
Rupicapra rupicapra						1		2–11.1%	
Capra ibex	1–2.9%		1–4.7%					1–5.5%	
Equus caballus	6–17.1%	1	7–33.3%	1	1–20%	1		3–16.7%	1
Dicerorhinus kirchbergensis	1						1	1	1
D. hemitoechus		1	2						
Panthera spelaea							1	2	
P. pardus								1	
Felis lynx								1	
Meles meles								2	
Crocuta crocuta			1						
Ursus spelaeus								13	
U. spelaeus deningeri							6		
U. arctos								2	
Vulpes vulpes								2	
Canis lupus			1				1	2	
Lepus sp.								2	
Rodentia					2			4	
Pyrrhocorax graculus						1			
Approximate volume of sediments	50m³	.4	2.2	.5	.4	.1	70	40	.1

[a] Freeman 1973
[b] Altuna 1971
[c] Altuna 1973
[d] Altuna 1972
[e] Altuna 1975

48

variety of species, including many carnivores, both large and small. The many cave bears probably usually died naturally in the cave; they are numerous in all Lezetxiki strata. While very rare, both boar and alpine animals are present at both Morín and Lezetxiki. There is no clear indication of resource specialization, although, if both the horses and large bovines tended to prefer open grasslands or clearings, this biotope seems to have been particularly important to Mousterian hunters of both Santander and Guipuzcoa. The woods and mountain slopes were certainly not entirely ignored, but cervines and caprines did not take on the relative importance that they did during the Upper Paleolithic of western Cantabria and the Basque country, respectively.

Aurignacian

As noted by Freeman (1973), the unique Chatelperronian level in Cantabria (Morín 10) contained only three individual animals (one each of red deer, horse, and large bovine).

The Aurignacian is much better represented, especially with the Cueva Morín levels and structure (see Table 2.2). Once more, the number of animals per unit is not purely a function of sediment volume. Faunal remains were particularly dense inside the Aurignacian structure and in Morín Level 5 inferior, each having not more than 1 m³ of fill. As in the Mousterian collections, large bovines remain particularly important numerically, although there is only one in a Basque collection (at Aitzbitarte), compared with usually 2 or 3 each in the Cueva Morín collections. Another difference between the Basque sites and Morín is evident in the scarcity of alpine animals in the latter and their consistent representation in the former (especially Aitzbitarte). Caprines (especially chamois) are also strikingly important in the small collections from the Aurignacian of El Conde, located in the rugged Asturian uplands. Again, Lezetxiki has a large and diverse complement of carnivores, while Morín does include a few boar. Compared with the Mousterian collections, those of the Aurignacian seem consistently to have a good representation of red deer. However, there is no clear evidence of specialization, other than the three horses in Morín 8 that are associated with only a scattering of single individuals of four other species. Freeman's (1973) impression of continued "opportunistic" hunting, albeit with a generally somewhat widened spectrum of regularly hunted species, seems justified.

Gravettian

There are only five Gravettian levels with quantified data, but each of these has relatively many individual animals (see Table 2.3). Both Basque country sites (Lezetxiki and Bolinkoba) have particularly large numbers of alpine animals, and Lezetxiki continues to have many carnivores, suggesting that, while not inhabited by men, it may well have been a lair for various of these species at different times. For the first time, however, there are several carnivores (especially fox) in other sites, perhaps suggesting some consistent trapping, possibly for pelts. Compared with the Basque collections, those of Cueva Morín have particularly large numbers of cervines, as well as horses. Large bovines are few in number, but they are consistently represented in all the collections. One collection—that of the controversial Bolinkoba Level E—stands out. It has but one red deer. Half of its animals are alpine forms—mostly ibex (of which half, in turn, are juvenile). This seems to provide clear evidence of concentrated exploitation of the animals that probably preferred to inhabit the crags and steep,

Table 2.2

Fauna from the Aurignacian Levels

	Morín 9[b]	Morín 8[b,c]	Morín Aurignacian 0 structure[b]	Morín 7[b]	Morín 6[b]	Morín 5 inferior[a]	Conde 4[e]	Conde 3[e]	Conde 1[e]	Lezetxiki IVC[d]	Lezetxiki IVA[d]	Aitzbitarte (Guipuzcoa)
Cervus elaphus		1–14.3%	7–41.2%	5–55.6%	4–26.7%	10–40%	1	2–40%	1–16.7%	4–44.4%	2–25%	7–38.9%
Capreolus capreolus		1–14.3%	1–5.9%	1–11.1%	4–26.7%	6–24%				1–11.1%		1–5.5%
Rangifer tarandus										1–11.1%		
Sus scrofa		1–14.3%	2–11.7%									
Large bovines	1	1–14.3%	3–17.7%	2–22.2%	4–26.7%	3–12%			1–16.7%	1–11.1%	3–37.5%	2–11.1%
Rupicapra rupicapra			1–5.9%			1–4%	1	2–40%	3–50%	1–11.1%	1–12.5%	5–27.8%
Capra ibex			1–5.9%		1–6.6%	2–8%	1	1–20%	1–16.7%	1–11.1%	2–25%	2–11.1%
Equus caballus	1	3–42.9%	2–11.7%	1–11.1%	2–13.3%	3–12%						1–5.5%
Dicerorhinus kirchbergensis											1	
Panthera pardus					1						1	
Felis sylvestris				1	1							
Mustela nivalis											1	2
M. putorius											1	
M. erminea												1
Ursus spelaeus										4	3	
U. arctos												1
Canis lupus			1			1		1			2	1
Vulpes vulpes				1	1						1	
Lepus europaeus						1						
Rodentia										7	5	55
Insectivora											1	15
Approximate volume of sediments (m³)	.2	.6	.1	1.0	1.8	.9	.1	.1	.1	12	6	18

[a] Freeman 1973
[b] Altuna 1971
[c] Altuna 1973
[d] Altuna 1972
[e] Altuna 1975

rocky slopes surrounding Bolinkoba in the Sierra de Ambota. Lezetxiki, also located in the very rugged, mountainous Basque interior near Bolinkoba, has similarly high numbers (and proportions) of ibex and chamois, although they are combined with a number of cervines markedly higher than that of Bolinkoba.

Solutrean

Further apparent evidence of resource specialization is present among the numerous Solutrean faunal collections, with a basic difference in exploitation

Table 2.3

Fauna from Gravettian Levels

	Morín 5 superior[a]	Morín 4[a]	Bolin-koba E[b] (Viz-caya)	Lezet-xiki IIIA[a]	Lezet-xiki II[a]
Cervus elaphus	9–34.6%	10–41.6%	1–5.3%	8–25.8%	3–14.3%
Capreolus capreolus	5–19.2%	4–16.7%		1–3.2%	2–9.5%
Rangifer tarandus				1–3.2%	
Sus scrofa	1–3.8%			1–3.2%	
Large bovines	3–11.5%	2–8.3%	2–10.5%	3–9.7%	2–9.5%
Rupicapra rupicapra	1–3.8%	1–4.2%	3–15.8%	12–38.7%	8–38.1%
Capra ibex	3–11.5%	3–12.5%	11–57.9%	3–9.7%	3–14.3%
Equus caballus	4–15.4%	4–16.7%	2–10.5%	2–6.4%	3–14.3%
Coelodonta antiquitatis				1	1
Dicerorhinus kirchbergensis				1	
Elephas primigenius		1			
Panthera pardus				1	
Felis lynx		1			
F. sylvestris		1			
Crocuta crocuta	1			2	
Meles meles				2	1
Mustela putorius				1	
Martes martes				1	
Gulo gulo					1
Ursus spelaeus				7	2
U. sp.			2		
Vulpes vulpes	1	1	3	1	2
Canis lupus		1		2	1
Lepus sp.	1	1		2	
Oryctolagus cuniculus				1	
Castor fiber				1	
Rodentia	1	3	6	10	
Insectivora		1		2	
Approximate volume of sediments (m³)	.9	.8	6	32	30

[a] Altuna 1972
[b] Straus 1974a

pattern between the Basque and western Cantabrian regions becoming even clearer (see Table 2.4). Alpine creatures are particularly well represented as a set at Bolinkoba, Ermittia, and Aitzbitarte, while they are rare (or absent) in collections from Santander and Asturias (except Hornos de la Peña, which is located in particularly rugged upland country). Conversely, red deer, although present in

Table 2.4

Fauna from Solutrean Levels

	Alta-mira[e] (San-tander)	Hornos de la Peña[f] (San-tander)	Pasi-ega[g] (San-tander)	Morín 3[a]	San-tima-miñe[c] (Viz-caya)	Bolin-koba D[c]	Ermit-tia[b]	Aitzbi-tarte[b]	Caldas[d] (Astu-rias)
Cervus elaphus	20–48.8%	6–28.6%	12–60.0%	5–41.7%	7–43.7%	2–8.3%	3–15.0%	9–39.2%	6–54.5%
Capreolus capreolus	1–2.4%	1–4.8%	1–5.0%	3–25.0%	1–6.3%		1–5.0%	1–4.3%	
Rangifer tarandus	1–2.4%				1–6.3%		2–10.0%	1–4.3%	
Sus scrofa	2–4.9%						1–5.0%		
Large bovines	5–12.2%	2–9.5%	3–15.0%	1–8.3%	1–6.3%	3–12.5%		2–8.7%	
Rupicapra rupicapra	2–4.9%	6–28.6%	1–5.0%		1–6.3%	2–8.3%	4–20.0%	6–26.1%	
Capra ibex	2–4.9%	2–9.5%	2–10.0%	1–8.3%	3–18.7%	16–66.7%	8–40.0%	1–4.3%	2–18.2%
Equus caballus	8–19.5%	4–19.0%	1–5.0%	2–16.7%	2–12.5%	1–4.2%	1–5.0%	3–13.1%	3–27.3%
Elephas primigenius									
Panthera sp.									
Felis lynx							1		
Mustela nivalis								3	
M. putorius								1	
M. erminea							1	1	
Mustelidae indet.									
Martes martes									
Meles?						7			
Crocuta crocuta									
Ursus sp.	5		2			2			
Canis lupus				1			2		
Vulpes vulpes	2		2		1	6	3	1	
Lepus europaeus							1		
Rodentia	x			1	2	16	8	105	
Insectivora				1			3	67	
Phoca cf. vitulina	1								
Aves	2				x		x		
Pisces		1							
Approximate volume of sediments	12.5m³	3.8	1.4	.2	15	8	4.5	16	.5

Note: x = present; (n) = my estimate.

[a] Altuna 1971

[b] Altuna 1972

[c] Straus 1974a

all the levels, becomes of great importance only at western sites. This is especially true at El Cierro on the coast of Asturias, where there seems to have been great concentration on this single species, to the nearly total neglect of other animals. Even at the Vizcayan site of Santimamiñe, located near a rare strip of Basque coastal plain, red deer by no means seem to dominate the collection. While red

Oscura[d] (Asturias)	Cova Rosa[d] (Asturias)	Cierro[d] (Asturias)	Riera[d] (Asturias)	Bal-mori[b] (Asturias)	Cober-izas[b] (Asturias)	Cueto de la Mina F[d] (Asturias)	Cueto de la Mina E/3 + 4[d]	Cueto de la Mina E/1 + 2[d]	Cueto de la Mina E (undivided collection)[d]	C.M. "Solut." (undivided collection)[d]
7–58.3%	5–41.7%	21–75%	5–62.5%	(3)–60%	(2)–28.5% 1–14.3%	3–37.5%	8–53.3%	4–44.4% (1)–11.1%	6–60% 1–10%	2
		1–3.6%			1–14.3%					
2–16.7%	1–8.3%	2–7.1%					(1)–12.5% 1–6.7%		1–10%	
	3–25%				1–14.3%		(1)–12.5% 1–6.7%			
	1–8.3%	1–3.6%	1–12.5%	(1)–20%	(1)–14.3%		2–13.3%	(1)–11.1%	1–10%	3
3–25%	2–16.7%	3–10.7%	2–25%	1–20%	(1)–14.3%	3–37.5%	3–20%	2–22.2%	1–10%	
							1	1		
				1						
					1					
							1	1		
										1
								1		
			(1)							
			(1)			1	(1)	1		
				2	(4)	x		x		
				1	(3)					
						x	1 (1)	2		1
.9	4.2	2.5	2.2	.1	.2	.8	3.0	3.0	—	—

d Straus 1974b
e Altuna and Straus 1975
f Straus 1975a
g Straus 1975b

deer were very important at the Santanderine sites of Altamira and La Pasiega, many other animals were also hunted in substantial proportions, and, of these, bovines and horses were especially important relative to red deer in terms of their great usable meat weights. Despite the special exploitation of ibex and chamois in the Basque country, it is again only at Bolinkoba where such hunting was almost exclusively important—with apparent concentration on young ibex, as in the preceding gravettian occupation. Boar are still rare (although definitely present) among the Cantabrian sites, although small burrowing carnivores are increasingly well represented, especially in the Basque area.

Magdalenian III

The faunal collections presented here as "Lower Cantabrian Magdalenian" include those from the key site of El Juyo, near the city of Santander, previously published by Azpeitia (1958) and by Freeman (1973). From El Juyo, Trench I, Level IV, Azpeitia (1958:113) claims there was a "fairly large number of individuals of *Cervus elaphus,* certainly more than 50, though it is difficult—if not impossible—to be specific, since the majority of the pieces are very fragmented or isolated." (See Table 2.5.) Chiefly on the basis of this estimate, Freeman (1973:35,38–39) sees evidence for an important change in Paleolithic resource exploitation in Cantabria during the Lower Magdalenian. While there is undeniable evidence for a significantly increased exploitation of shellfish in the Cantabrian Magdalenian (and especially in the Azilian and Asturian), the aforementioned evidence of an *abrupt,* general shift to specialized red deer hunting in the Lower Magdalenian is, however, less certain.

In his discussion of the remains from Level IV at El Juyo, Azpeitia (1958:113,115) states that the mammalian remains studied numbered 112; of those—all of which are listed in detail—only 73 are of red deer. Of the red deer remains, only 52 are teeth (many being isolated incisors) or manible fragments with teeth, and Azpeitia's description in no way suggests that each of these was from a separate individual. Nor is that possibility at all provable or likely. Although the inventoried collection may be partially selected, it does include 11 pieces that are noted as being unidentifiable, while several others are listed as only tentatively identified. This is not simply a list of the finest pieces. Apparently on the basis of the study of these listed remains, Azpeitia reached his conclusions about minimum numbers of individuals (see Azpeitia 1958:101).

Based strictly on Azpeitia's list of remains from Level IV, and assuming the correctness of his tooth-age estimates for the red deer (granting him all the benefit of the substantial doubt), I have calculated the minimum number of individuals represented to be, in fact, about 20, at most. This is still a large number of red deer, considering the very small volume of Level IV in Trench I, but it is clearly not as overwhelming a figure as the "greater than 50" estimate employed by Freeman. The minimum number of red deer that can be recalculated from the raw counts (and age estimates of Azpeitia) is slightly lower also for

Table 2.5

Fauna from Lower Magdalenian Levels

	Juyo XI[c] (Santander)	Juyo X[c]	Juyo VII[c]	Juyo VI[c]	Juyo V[c]	Juyo IV[c]	Altamira[b]	Lloseta A[a] (Asturias)	Urtiaga F[a] (Guipuzcoa)
Cervus elaphus	6(4)	3(3)	7–8(4)	xxx(13)–81.3%	7–8(2)50%	50 + (20)80%	19–59.4%	(4)	17–38.6%
Capreolus capreolus						3(3)12%	2–6.2%	1	9–20.5%
Rangifer tarandus									2–4.5%
Large bovines			1(1)	4–5(1)–6.2%	1(1)–25%	—(1)–4%	4–12.5%		2–4.5%
Rupicapra rupicapra							2–6.2%		4–9.1%
Capra ibex							1–3.2%	1	9–20.5%
Equus caballus				8–10(2)–12.5%	3(1)–25%	7–8(1)–4%	4–12.5%		1–2.3%
Panthera cf. leo									1
Felis lynx									1
Mustela erminea									1
M. putorius									2
Ursus sp.									1
Vulpes vulpes									6
Lepus sp.									1
Rodentia								1	4
Insectivora									1
Pisces							x		
Approximate volume of sediments	1.1m³	.2	.4	.9	.1	.7	12.5	.1	22.5

Note: x = present; xxx = abundant; (n) = my estimate.

[a] Altuna 1972
[b] Straus 1975d
[c] Azpeitia 1958

Levels XI, VII, and V, whereas a figure of 13 has been calculated for Level IV, where Azpeitia gave no estimate. Estimates for the minimum numbers of large bovines and horses have similarly been altered in several cases on the basis of the published lists, and one bovine has been added to the Level IV summary, where Azpeitia estimated none, although remains thereof are identified as such in his inventory.

The other two collections listed here as Lower Magdalenian and Altamira and Urtiaga both have many red deer, yet the numbers differ in no way from those encountered in several Solutrean levels. In both cases, the woodland animals (*Cervus* and *Capreolus*) were probably equalled in economic importance by alpine animals (in the case of Urtiaga—a Basque Country site) or by open country forms (at Altamira on the Santander coastal plain). Undoubtedly, the evidence from Levels IV and VI of El Juyo does reflect a degree of repeated concentrated red deer hunting at this particular locality on the Santander coastal plain. Indeed, at the supposedly "Middle Cantabrian Magdalenian" of La Lloseta (which is, however, of almost exactly the same radiocarbon age as the El Juyo and Altamira Magdalenian III) on the Asturian coastal plain near El Cierro, all but 3 of the 54 faunal remains from Clark's tiny sample are of red deer. However, very similar degrees of selective exploitation of this species are apparent in the Solutrean level of El Cierro, and of ibex in Bolinkoba's Solutrean and Gravettian levels.

Upper Magdalenian

Prior to the publication of Altuna's (1972) new identifications, only one Upper Magdalenian faunal collection had been described quantitatively (Morín 2—by Altuna [1971]) (see Table 2.6). Although from a substantial archeological deposit, the Lezetxiki collection contains only one each of several species. The Urtiaga collection came from a very voluminous stratum and has correspondingly large numbers of animals—especially red and roe deer and alpine species (but very few open plains dwellers). The Aitzbitarte collection also seems to show approximately equivalent exploitation of both alpine and woodland resources. This is true as well in the old collection from the site of Sofoxó in

Table 2.6

Fauna from Upper Magdalenian Levels

	Aitzbi-tarte[b]	Ermittia[b]	Urtiaga D[b]	Lezetxiki I[b]	Morín 2[a]	Sofoxó[c] (Asturias)
Cervus elaphus	10–30.3%	3–12%	37–37%	1–16.7%	9–37.9%	6–25%
Capreolus capreolus	3–9.1%	1–4%	13–13%		2–8.3%	4–16.7%
Rangifer tarandus	2–6.1%	2–8%	7–7%		1–4.2%	
Sus scrofa	2–6.1%	2–8%	3–3%	1–16.7%	2–8.3%	1–4.2%
Large bovines	4–12.1%	1–4%	3–3%	1–16.7%	1–4.2%	3–12.5%
Rupicapra rupicapra	8–24.1%	2–8%	15–15%	1–16.7%	3–12.5%	4–16.7%
Capra ibex	2–6.1%	13–52%	20–20%	1–16.7%	3–12.5%	5–20.8%
Equus caballus	2–6.1%	1–4%	2–2%	1–16.7%	3–12.5%	1–4.2%
Felis sylvestris			1			
Mustela nivalis	8					
M. erminea	1		2			
M. putorius	1					
Meles meles	1		2	1		1
Ursus spelaeus	1		1			
Canis lupus			1	1		
Vulpes vulpes	3	1	18	1		1
Lepus sp.	2	1	3		1	
Rodentia	161	3	13	2	1	8
Insectivora	87	1	1		5	
Pisces						1
Approximate volume of sediments	16m³	5.3	45	14	7	(?)

[a] Altuna 1971
[b] Altuna 1972
[c] Straus (unpub.)

Asturias, tentatively classified by myself. Altuna (personal communication) has recently studied large collections from the coastal Asturias Upper Magdalenian site of Tito Bustillo, which indicate nearly exclusive hunting of red deer, especially adult females and juveniles. The fauna of the Santander mountain site of Rascaño, with both Lower and Upper Magdalenian levels, is heavily dominated by goat (Altuna, personal communication).

As usual, *Cervus* and/or *Capra* remain the numerically dominant species in the Upper Magdalenian. In both Lower and Upper Magdalenian collections, the low representation of both large bovines and horses is notable, in apparent contrast with the situation in most earlier collections, where open country species were quite important even numerically. Such differences seem independent of the rather marked fluctuations in proportions of arboreal and nonarboreal vegetation manifested in the pollen record of the Cantabrian Last Glacial.

While there exists little or no evidence of Lower Magdalenian hunting of boar or carnivores, the former is a consistent part of all the Upper Magdalenian collections, whereas many weasels were found in the Aitzbitarte level, and many foxes were found in the Urtiaga level. This is not unlike the evidence previously apparent in certain Solutrean collections.

Azilian

The six faunal collections now available from the Azilian and "Tardenoisian" periods manifest some clear differences from all the Upper Paleolithic collections (see Table 2.7). Horses and large bovines are now nearly entirely absent. This terminates an apparent trend toward diminishing importance that seems to have started in the Solutrean, although these presumably open country forms really seem only to have been numerically dominant in the Mousterian and in some Aurignacian levels. As usual, alpine forms tend to dominate the fauna of Ermittia, which is located on a cliff. Ibex and Chamois are fairly important as well in the Azilian of Aitzbitarte and Urtiaga, but, in the latter, there is clear evidence of very heavy exploitation of the woodland biotope set (the deer and boar). Boar are represented in all the collections available from the Early post-Paleolithic period (as they were in the Upper Magdalenian) and, in some cases, quite abundantly so. Chamois are absent, and ibex are very rare, not only in Morín 1, but also in the two "Mesolithic" levels at Marizulo, despite the latter site's mountainous location in the Basque country. There is a scattering of carnivore remains (especially mustelids, fox, and wolf) in each of the levels, except Morín 1. Altuna's (1972) listing of *Canis familiaris* in the Azilian of Urtiaga and in the "Late Mesolithic" of Marizulo and of sheep-goat in Urtiaga are, to say the least, intriguing, although not wholly unexpected.

Asturian

The Asturian mammalian fauna has been commented on at length by G. A. Clark (1971a,b). Quantified data from Clark's several small test pits are pre-

Table 2.7
Fauna from Azilian and "Tardenoision" Levels

	Morín 1[a]	Aitzbitarte[b]	Ermittia[b]	Urtiaga C[b]	Marizulo 3 "Tardenoisian"[b] (Guipuzcoa)	Marizulo 2 "Late Mesolithic"[b]
Cervus elaphus	5–45.4%	6–33.3%	3–23.1%	16–42.1%	3–33.3%	4–33.3%
Capreolus capreolus	1–9.1%	2–11.1%		9–23.7%	3–33.3%	3–25.0%
Sus scrofa	1–9.1%	1–5.6%	2–15.4%	5–13.2%	2–22.2%	4–33.3%
Large bovines	2–18.2%	2–11.1%	1–7.7%			
Rupicapra rupicapra		3–16.7%	1–7.7%	4–10.5%		
Capra ibex	1–9.1%	2–11.1%	6–46.1%	3–7.9%	1–11.2%	1–9.1%
Sheep/Goat				1–2.6%		
Equus caballus	1–9.1%	2–11.1%				
Rhinoceros sp.	1					
Felis sylvestris				1		1
Mustela nivalis		3				
M. putorius				1		1
M. erminea		1				
Meles meles			1	3		1
Lutra lutra					1	
Martes martes					1	1
Canis lupus		1		1	1	1
C. familiaris				1		1
Vulpes vulpes		1	1	3		
Lepus sp.				1		
Rodentia		79	2	19	1	1
Insectivora		39	2	4		1
Approximate volume of sediments	.4m³	16	4.5	12	5.3	4.5

[a] Altuna 1971
[b] Altuna 1972

sented by Altuna (1972) in the form of numbers of remains. Minimum numbers of individuals are not calculated. However, red deer is almost always the overwhelmingly dominant form, followed by boar, together with roe deer, some alpine caprines, large bovines, and a few horses. Together with the red deer, the Asturian is especially characterized by significant dependence upon limpets *(Patella)* and thermophilous topshells *(Trochocochlea)*. Real shell middens begin to appear in the Lower and Upper Magdalenian, composed principally of *Patella vulgata* and the cold-adapted periwinkle *(Littorina littorea)*. Possible effects of human exploitation on the limpet populations and shell size, as well as the possibility of shellfish "farming," are discussed by Freeman (1973) and require no further comment here, since further investigation will be necessary to test his hypotheses.

Preliminaries to the Interpretation

If is is possible to discern meaningful tendencies in these data, several interesting conclusions can be drawn that complement observations made by Freeman on the basis of more fragmentary information. Species considered here as primary big game animals include the cervines *(Cervus elaphus* and *Capreolus capreolus),* large bovines *(Bos primigenius/Bison priscus),* caprines *(Capra ibex* and *Rupicapra rupicapra),* boar *(Sus scrofa),* and horse *(Equus caballus).* Remains of mammoth *(Elephas primigenius)* and the various rhinoceros forms *(Coelodonta antiquitatis, Dicerorhinus hemitoechus,* and *D. kirchbergensis*—Merck's rhino) are very scarce and may not necessarily even represent animals actually hunted by men. They are usually represented by only a single or a very few molar (or tusk) fragments, which could have been picked up or even acquired from afar, although paleontological findings and two cave paintings of mammoth in the Santander area indicate that these beasts were at least present, if only in limited numbers, at some period during the Upper Paleolithic. Neither the mammoth and rhinoceros nor any carnivores, rodents, lagomorphs, or insectivores are counted here as primary game animals, although mustelids and fox certainly were hunted, undoubtedly for pelts. As suggested earlier, the many large cave bears and the few cave lions and cave hyenas may simply have died in the caves, which they, like men, preferred as shelter (albeit not simultaneously). Certainly the presence of some of the burrowing animals (especially rodents and insectivores) could also be fortuitous and not a product of cultural activity.

The number of individual animals per big game species per level obviously depends not only upon the contemporary local environment and the activities (and preferences) of the hunters and food processors of the period of occupation, but also upon aspects of archeological sampling. In order to allow for more meaningful comparison among levels, I have, for this reason, indicated a very rough estimate of the volume of sediments excavated from each level (see Tables 2.1–2.7). The practical definition of such "levels" by a variety of excavators— some of which were classified over a half-century ago—is highly variable, and excavation methods from site to site have ranged from pick and shovel work to the systematic use of small knives, brushes, and dental picks. Thus, strict comparability of the data cannot be assumed, although some of the earliest excavations (e.g., those of the Conde de la Vega del Sella) were conducted with impressive care. The presence of the remains of many animals may be largely due to a large excavation, from which preservation has been relatively complete. This seems to be the case especially with Altamira and Urtiaga. Despite its many deer, the Castillo Mousterian beta level faunal list seems somewhat impoverished, however, considering the vast area of the site and the great thickness of the defined level. The Oviedo collection identified by Zugasti (Freeman 1973) is clearly very incomplete and probably selected. Other collections (like those from El Juyo and several of the Asturias Solutrean levels) seem suspiciously impoverished, regardless of excavation size. These factors definitely bias any attempt to judge both "typical" patterns and the range of variation in big game exploitation in each major Paleolithic period. Problems of intersite activity differences, different carcass transportation and butchering practices, partial and different archeological sampling, and collection preservation all make the study of changing exploitation patterns and hunting strategies rather tenuous indeed.

An additional factor that further complicates comparison and the study of tendencies for change is the differing overall surroundings of the sites from which there happen to be quantified faunal lists for each Paleolithic period. Besides the imponderable variations in local ecology, the general topography (e.g., mountainous versus coastal plain) of a majority of the sites representing each period in the inventories could heavily influence the nature of the overall, average faunal picture in each case and, therefore, our perceptions of the hunting practices in each gross range of time. Thus, for example, the dominance of rugged Basque country sites among those representing the Gravettian certainly helps give the impression of heavy exploitation of alpine animals, which is not, however, true at the other two Gravettian levels (both at Cueva Morín). On the contrary, our average impressions of the Aurignacian and Lower Magdalenian faunas are strongly influenced by evidence from western sites (Morín with El Conde, and El Juyo with Altamira, respectively).

Changing Importance of the Big Game Animals

Cervus

All these justified warnings notwithstanding, the average numbers of animals per species per period do reveal some intriguing tendencies (see Figure 2.2). Even including the Castillo beta collection, the average number of red deer per level is very low in the Mousterian (less than five). It remains at the same low level in the Aurignacian collections but begins to rise somewhat in the Gravettian and in the Solutrean (6.2 and 7.1, respectively). In the Solutrean, there is what appears to be the first evidence of specialization in red deer hunting, to the near exclusion of other species (at El Cierro), with further evidence of sizable deer kills in Altamira and in the lumped Cueto de la Mina Level E collection. However, there is no way to tell over how long a period such numbers (about 20 in all cases) of deer were killed, since the strata in question are all fairly thick. The average numbers of red deer in Lower and Upper Magdalenian levels are dramatically higher (14.2 and 11.0, respectively), and they do seem to have been hunted almost exclusively at El Juyo, if the reported collections are at all representative of the contents of Levels IV and VI. This also seems to have been the case at Tito

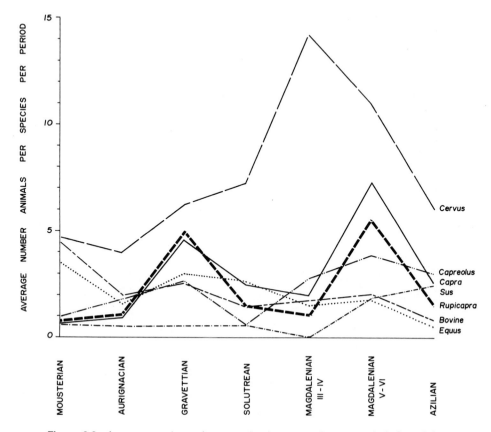

Figure 2.2 Average numbers of game animals per species per period: Cantabria.

Bustillo. Large numbers of red deer were also taken at Altamira and Urtiaga, but in combination with many other animals. The numbers of red deer in Azilian and "Tardenoisian" levels drops off to the Gravettian average of 6.2 per level.

In order to partially minimize the effects of differential excavation volume, the changes in animal frequency can be documented in terms of the proportion of each species of the total number of game animals per period (see Figure 2.3). The average percentage of red deer is at its lowest in the Mousterian (20.1%), increases somewhat in the Aurignacian (34.3%), and falls back to less than one-quarter in the Gravettian (24.3%). Red deer become proportionally more important in a dramatic fashion in the Solutrean—making up nearly one-half of the average collection (45.3%). This trend is further exaggerated in the Magdalenian III, where red deer reaches the zenith of its proportional importance at 61.8%. It falls sharply in importance in the Upper Magdalenian and post-Paleolithic collections (26.4 and 35.1%, respectively).

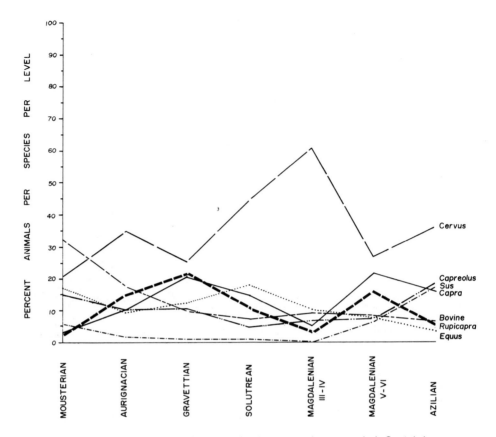

Figure 2.3 Percentage of game animals per species per period: Cantabria.

Capreolus

The tendencies in red deer frequency changes are *not* parallel to those of the other woodland-preferring animals, that is, roe deer and boar. *Capreolus* increases gradually in absolute numbers per period through the Gravettian, falling to practically nil in the Solutrean, and then increasing substantially to an average of 3.8 per level in the Upper Magdalenian and 3.0 in the post-Paleolithic. Although the percentage of roe deer is always low, it is lowest in the Solutrean (4.6%) and highest in the Mousterian (14.5%) and in the Azilian (17.0%).

Sus

The average absolute frequency of boar is extremely low, *decreasing* from .6 to 0 between the Mousterian and Lower Magdalenian, at which point it increases to 1.8 and 2.5 in the Upper Magdalenian and Azilian levels. The proportional representation of this rather dangerous, although meaty species increases even more dramatically in the two terminal periods from 0% in the Magdalenian III to 7.7% in the Upper Magdalenian and 16.5% in the post-Paleolithic.

Equus and Bos/Bison

Both horses and large bovines are most frequent on an average in the Mousterian (3.4 and 4.4, respectively). They both decline sharply in the Aurignacian, and they remain steady at relatively low figures until the Azilian, when they both drop off to an average of nearly nil (average of .5 and .8 per level, respectively). Proportionally, large bovines make up fully one-third of the composite Mousterian faunal assemblage. This percentage drops off steadily, reaching a low of 7% in the Solutrean; it increases to 10% in the Magdalenian III and falls again, finally, to 6% in the Azilian.

The proportional representation of horse is strikingly uniform, oscillating at around 15% from the Mousterian to the Lower Magdalenian, with the highest representation in the Solutrean—a tendency exactly opposite to that of the large bovines which were probably also open country dwellers. Horses have far lesser importance proportionally in the Upper Magdalenian and post-Paleolithic (7.6 and 3.4%, respectively).

Capra and Rupicapra

Finally, the two alpine game animals—the caprines—have completely identical patterns, both in terms of absolute and proportional representation. Both chamois and ibex are practically nonexistent in Mousterian levels but increase sharply through the Aurignacian to highs in the Gravettian (*Rupicapra:* 21.2%— average of 5.0 per level; *Capra:* 20.1%—average of 4.6 per level). Both decline in importance in the Solutrean (despite relatively large numbers in several Basque country sites), and they reach low figures in the Lower Magdalenian. They increase again to a peak in the Upper Magdalenian (*Rupicapra:* 15.5%—average of 5.5 per level; *Capra:* 21.4%—average of 7.3 per level) and finally decrease to moderate values in the post-Paleolithic. One reason for the apparent decline in alpine animals in the Lower Magdalenian may be purely artificial, due to the fortuitous overrepresentation of Santander coastal plain occupation levels in the available published sample for this period. The absolute and relative frequencies of the caprines and of red deer seem to vary inversely, perhaps due to gross climatic and resultant vegetational zone changes and/or to vagaries of my samples.

Rangifer

Reindeer are present neither in the Mousterian nor in the post-Paleolithic period. Both numbers and percentages of this animal remain completely insignificant (in sharp contrast to the great importance of reindeer throughout the Paleolithic of southwest France), except possibly in the Upper Magdalenian. Reindeer make up an average of a high(!) 4.2% of the big game taken in this period, there being an average of two individuals per level (chiefly because of the seven in the extensive Urtiaga Level D).

Carnivora

Among the carnivores whose remains are most likely to be present in the sites due to hunting by humans (though some could have died in burrows), mustelids and fox are almost totally absent from Mousterian and Aurignacian levels. There seems to be a slight increase (especially in fox) in the Gravettian. However, on an average, the importance of both mustelids and fox decreases in the Solutrean (except at Basque country sites, where they, together with the caprines, are very important). For reasons unknown, there are no carnivores in the El Juyo or Altamira Magdalenian III collections, although there are a few mustelids and a half-dozen foxes in the Urtiaga F collection. (Wolf is the only carnivore listed by Breuil and Obermaier [1935] for the Altamira Magdalenian, while several carnivore species are listed for the Solutrean. The *Canis* remains are now apparently missing.) There is a dramatic increase, however, in the numbers of these animals in the Upper Magdalenian, with the unusually high numbers of 18 foxes in the Urtiaga D collection and 11 mustelids in Aitzbitarte.

Lagomorpha

In distinct contrast to the Paleolithic of Mediterranean Spain, there are almost no rabbits (1 in the Gravettian of Lezetxiki) and a grand total of only 17 hares in the Cantabrian collections. Nearly half of the latter were found in the Upper Magdalenian.

Phoca

The early identification by Breuil and Obermaier (1935) of a seal in the Altamira Solutrean has been confirmed by Altuna (Altuna and Straus 1975). It probably represents no more than an accidental strandline carcass find, since it is represented by only one phalange. Another has recently been identified in the Upper Magdalenian of Tito Bustillo (Altuna, personal communication, 1975).

Pisces

As reported by Breuil and Obermaier (1935), there are remains of bony fish in the Magdalenian III of Altamira (16 large vertebrae exist in the collection today). I have also noted small numbers (1 or 2 each) of similar vertebrae in the Solutrean collections from Hornos de la Peña, Cueto de la Mina E/3 + 4, and in the

Upper Magdalenian of Sofoxo—a riverside site. In addition, there are single vertebrae in the Upper Magdalenian of both El Otero and La Chora (Santander) (Madariaga 1966, 1963). Recent excavations at sites like Rascaño, La Riera, Tito Bustillo have consistently revealed fish vertebrae in a series of Magdalenian and Solutrean levels.

Aves

There are remains of an eagle and a vulture in the Solutrean of Altamira (Altuna and Straus 1975), a scattering of unidentified bird bones in Cueto de la Mina E and F and in Santimamiñe VII, as well as many others in the Azilian and post-Azilian levels of the latter site (Altuna 1972). There is an eagle and a chough in the Ermittia Solutrean (Aranzadi and Barandiaran 1928), an alpine chough in El Conde Mousterian Level 6 (Altuna in Freeman 1975), and both jackdaw and raven in the Solutrean of Castillo (Vaufrey n.d.). There is an unidentified bird bone in the Upper Magdalenian of Otero (Madariaga 1966) and unenumerated remains of jackdaw, alpine chough, partridge, and grouse from unspecified level(s) at Hornos de la Peña (Altuna 1972). Finally, there were what were supposed to be bones of a "crane" in the Magdalenian of Altamira (Breuil and Obermaier 1935). These remains are unfortunately lost.

Mollusca

As noted earlier, there is no consistent evidence of more than very casual collecting of shellfish before the Magdalenian III, when some levels (such as those of El Juyo, La Lloseta, etc.) begin to resemble shell middens. This development culminated in the controversial "concheros" of the Asturian period some 8000 years ago (Clark 1971a,b). Nonetheless, the *preserved* Altamira Solutrean and Magdalenian III shellfish collections are of about equal size: about 300 *Patella vulgata* in each and about 75 *Littorina littorea* in the Solutrean as compared to about 120 in the Magdalenian. Such a large Solutrean molluscan collection is entirely unique among the preserved museum collections from this period, although both Obermaier (1925) and Vaufrey (n.d.) have claimed that limpets were "very abundant" or "abundant" in the Solutrean of Castillo, a mountainside site about 20 km from the present shoreline (and perhaps 25 to 30 km from the full glacial shoreline via the Rio Pas Valley).

Discussion

Two general conclusions can be drawn from the foregoing presentation of the data: *(1)* extreme caution must be exercised in interpretation and the development of generalizations from these sorts of observations, even if they present the quantitative illusion of scientific accuracy, due to the high likelihood of error or skewing introduced before, during, and after deposition of the faunal remains; *(2)* there is no overwhelming evidence of any sharp, widespread breaks in the record, either between the Mousterian and the earliest Upper Paleolithic levels or between specific pairs of culture–stratigraphic units within the Upper Paleolithic. No quantum jump in behavioral capacities is associated with that range of time some 35,000 to 40,000 years ago when the anatomical change between Neanderthal and modern forms of *Homo sapiens* presumably took place in northwestern Spain—at least judging from these data. (Actual significant human fossil evidence in this region is very sketchy. It is confined to the so-called Neanderthal humerus of Lezetxiki VII and the cranium of *H. sapiens sapiens* from the Camargo "Aurignacian," plus the child's mandible from the Typical Aurignacian of Castillo and the 2 cranial "cups" from the Lower Magdalenian of the same site [see Altuna 1972; Obermaier 1925].)

These facts indicate that changes in animal exploitation did take place in Cantabria throughout the Middle and Upper Paleolithic and post-Paleolithic, but these changes were gradual and not all simultaneous. There is also some evidence of subregional variation, especially between sites of the generally rugged, fully mountainous Basque country and those of the more topographically zonated areas to the west.

Specialization and Diversity

There is no clear indication of any trends in the average numbers of big game species represented in the collections of each period, although the period with the smallest average number of species (4.6) is, in fact, the Lower Magdalenian, with its possible concentration on red deer hunting. However, it must be recalled that such a conclusion is based almost solely on the data from one site—El Juyo. The period of greatest diversification would seem to be the Upper Magdalenian (7.5 species), while the rest (including the Mousterian) cluster fairly tightly around an average of 5.5 species per level.

Thus, while there is some evidence of single-species (or biotope-set) specialization or concentrated exploitation in many Upper Paleolithic levels, it does not seem generally that there was a corresponding restriction of the diversity of species hunted. In fact, the development of shellfish gathering, boar killing, small carnivore trapping (?), and perhaps some fishing and birding, from the time of the Solutrean and Lower Magdalenian on, indicates a definite *broadening* of the spectrum of exploited resources. These resources were all present earlier, but they were largely or totally ignored. Such a broad spectrum of exploitation, albeit with heavy emphasis on certain elements, differs somewhat from Freeman's (1973) notion of a change to "wild harvesting" in the Magdalenian III, which implies a narrowing of range.

While all the developments apparent in the available data are not completely parallel, it does seem that evidence of single-species or biotope-set (e.g., alpine caprines) specialization in at least many collections throughout the Upper

Paleolithic is generally with a broad spectrum of hunted game (frequently at the same levels). In addition, the Upper and post-Paleolithic witnessed a significant increase in the exploitation of species that are dangerous, small, hidden, and/or difficult to catch (e.g., boar, shellfish, mustelids, fox, and the wary, swift caprines). While the distinction between the Mousterian and Aurignacian collections is not overwhelming, it is worthy of note that, although they were diverse in composition, the Mousterian assemblages are generally dominated by the largest game animals (bovines and horses), and certainly the vast majority of usable meat came from these animals. At no time in the Upper Paleolithic is *Bos/Bison* numerically so important vis à vis the other game animals. On the contrary, elusive, dangerous, and small food resources are hardly, if at all, represented in the Mousterian, because these hunter–gatherers lacked knowledge, skill, technology, and/or "motivation" for their acquisition.

While the Aurignacian lacks evidence of marked specialization, exploitation of alpine species was clearly important, while, numerically at least, bovines and horses declined in importance. There also seems to be more indication of the hunting of small carnivores.

In the Gravettian, there is the first evidence of specialized hunting—of alpine animals at Lezetxiki and Bolinkoba.

There is evidence in the Solutrean of specialized hunting of red deer and alpine species at different sites. In addition, there was considerable hunting of foxes and mustelids and the first indications of both fishing and shellfish gathering of some significance (at least at Altamira), as well as some widespread taking of a few birds (or possibly the collection of their carcasses for the plummage).

The few Lower Magdalenian collections are either very diversified (Urtiaga and Altamira) or very restricted in composition (El Juyo IV–VI and La Lloseta), but, in all cases, red deer are very numerous. As is especially the case in other Basque Upper Paleolithic collections, the collection of Urtiaga F also has many alpine animals, mustelids, and foxes. Evidence for heavy exploitation of shellfish, particularly of two species, seems to really begin in this period (see Clark 1971a).

While red deer are generally important in most Upper Magdalenian collections, the faunal assemblages are often very diverse. Alpine animals are very important in the Basque country sites, as are mustelids and foxes. For the first time, boar are represented in all collections, generally by more than one individual. The Upper Magdalenian is unique in the apparently less than sporadic representation of hare, which were perhaps captured by traps.

The Azilian and so-called "Tardenoisian" seem generally marked by a decline of not only bovines and horses, but, to a certain degree, also of red deer. There is no clear evidence of specialized exploitation of single species. Boar finally seems to have become an important staple in the post-Paleolithic periods, however, and shellfish (including land snails) exploitation reaches its zenith. The coastal shell middens of the Asturian might possibly represent a seasonal activity pose of at least part of the Azilian, although this hypothesis requires further testing. There are C^{14} dates for Asturian residues of 8650 B.P. at both La Riera and Penicial

(Clark 1971a) and an Azilian one from Urtiaga C of 8700 B.P. (all Libby half-lives) (Altuna 1972).

Suggested Differences among Occupations

It is obvious that such gross generalizations and comparisons mask a great deal of variability among the occupations associated with each period. Ultimately, the most interesting studies will be those comparing particular occupations in terms of different activities performed during each period by various kinds of social units at different seasons or in different local environments. Such studies will require data of greater sophistication and comparability. Only a few rather subjective observations concerning functional differences among sites will be hazarded here.

Judging from factors such as size of sheltered area, frequency and depth of occupation levels, size and diversity of artifact and faunal collections, amounts of preserved *débitage,* and so on, it is clear that some of the sites were major multipurpose base camps, while others were ephemeral, specialized activity stations. It is beyond the scope of this chapter to probe this question in depth; however, there are certain indications in the faunal data alone. For example, while the collections of the moderately sized excavations at Altamira and Cueto de la Mina E have many red deer, they also have fairly large numbers of individuals from many other species, suggesting intense, long and/or repeated occupation with diverse hunting (and gathering, processing, manufacturing, and maintenance) activities. This also seems to be the case with the substantial Urtiaga levels, where once again there is evidence of heavy exploitation of both alpine and woodland biotopes. The fact that numbers of individual animals are never high at Cueva Morín is probably largely a product of the delicacy of excavation and the thinness of the defined levels, which were generally exposed over small surface areas. Many occupations appear remarkably restricted in the diversity of their faunal spectra, however. This is true at sites with both limited and large-scale excavations.

For example, red deer are not only very numerous, but also proportionally predominant at El Cierro (Solutrean)—75% of the total number of game animals—and at El Juyo (Lower Magdalenian)—over 80% in the two major levels—and at Tito Bustillo (Upper Magdalenian), and account for about 60% of the big game in several other Solutrean and Lower Magdalenian levels. Similarly, the alpine biotope set *(Capra* plus *Rupicapra)* seems to have been hunted to the near exclusion of other game at certain Basque country sites, especially Bolinkoba (Gravettian and Solutrean) and Ermittia (Solutrean, Upper Magdalenian, and Azilian). These sites may well have been specialized hunting camps, rather than major base camps. Certainly, the repetitive quality of substantial red deer hunting at El Juyo and of caprine hunting at the two Basque country cliffside sites suggests that these were established (possibly seasonal) loci for such specialized activities through time. Further analysis of occupation residues and further, more detailed excavations should help prove (or disprove) this hypothesis. Bibliographical information suggests that the Upper Magdalenian–Azilian site of Collubil, high in the mountains of Asturias, was almost exclusively an alpine animal hunting station (Obermaier 1925; González Morales 1974), and that the multilevel Magdalenian–Azilian site of Rascaño, located in very rugged Santander uplands, was a similar sort of station (Obermaier 1923). Recent excavations in the latter cave seem, to support this interpretation.

Seasonality

The question of seasonality is an important one, especially in view of the marked zonal quality of elevations between the nearby Cantabrian summits and shore. Very inadequate evidence, principally from red deer antlers, suggests that at least certain coastal sites were occupied in late winter–early spring during the Solutrean and Magdalenian. Even scantier evidence suggests the summer or fall occupation of at least one hinterland site (Castillo) during the Solutrean. Calculations of the supposed age at death of five reindeer from three Guipuzcoan Solutrean and Magdalenian sites by Altuna (1972:334–335), however, does not seem to support the hypothesis of seasonal movement of animals and humans between coastal and hinterland sites. At any rate, the hypothesis is probably more applicable to the western areas, where differences between coastal areas (low plains) and the interior (foothill ranges, intermontane valleys, and the Cordillera) are far more marked. It is certain that winters were far more rigorous in the interior hills than along the coast during the Upper Pleniglacial. Microclimatic differences even today are very striking, despite the short distance between the coast and the mountains. Such seasonal climatic differences in temperature, solid precipitation, frost, and so on would certainly have affected animal species upon which Paleolithic hunters heavily depended and would have also made the coastal sites more comfortable during the winter. While they are usually quite strategically placed high on cliff- or mountainsides, the hinterland sites are often very exposed, difficult of access, and sometimes quite small. During stadials, most of the upland sites would have been quite near mountain glacial centers. In contrast, most of the coastal sites are low, sheltered, and spacious and have good wintertime solar exposures. Being close to the sea, they would have profited from its moderating effects on winter temperatures and depth of snowfall, as is very noticeably the case even now.

With the onset of the Solutrean, the density of sites becomes great enough for the discernment of plausible evidence of patterned settlement locations. Sites in the Solutrean, Magdalenian, and Azilian tend to be located on the coastal plain at the mouth of the principal rivers that flow down from the Cordillera and upstream along these rivers where they break through the foothills in gorges to the coastal plain. Despite the effect of topographic irregularities, a repeated sort of bipolar settlement pattern seems to have characterized the placement of at least cave sites in the Late Upper Paleolithic, since caves are plentiful in all zones of the river courses. The repeated selection of caves on the coastal plain and others in the hills may well have had seasonal implications.

The numbers of Mousterian and Early Upper Paleolithic sites are too small for one to draw any plausible conclusions, either about seasonal movements or hunting strategies. Freeman's (1973) observation that Mousterian sites tend less often to be located toward the longitudinal (and altitudinal) extremes than Magdalenian sites should probably be considered with caution. Many of the Mousterian sites also have Upper Paleolithic levels. Several (e.g., Arnero, Unquera, Cobalejos, El Pendo, Morín, and Fuente del Francés) are, in fact, located on the coastal plain, often quite close to the present shore. Others (e.g., El Conde, Lezetxiki, Axlor, and even Castillo and Hornos de la Peña) are quite far inland, in surroundings that are mountainous and often quite high. Further site survey and site testing, such as is now being conducted in Asturias, will provide further evidence of settlement patterns at different periods, which is, at present, very fragmentary, especially for the earlier ranges of time.

Density of Habitation

One final set of data consisting of numbers of known sites per period provides further bases for the formulation of hypotheses concerning the changes in exploitation that seem to gain importance in the middle of the Cantabrian Upper Paleolithic (see Figure 2.4). I have gleaned all available references from the site report literature and have considered culture–stratigraphic attributions of the occupations made by the authors of numerous synthetic works (e.g., Clark 1971a; Freeman 1964; González Echegaray 1960; Jordá 1960, 1963; Moure 1974; McCullough 1971; Straus 1975c). These attributions have been "given the benefit of the doubt" when available materials were not available to make an independent judgment. Numbers of *sites* per period are presented, rather than numbers of *levels* since both the theoretical and practical definitions of archeological levels have been quite varied among the excavators in question. They can range in nature from major strata of a half meter or more in thickness to the very precisely defined lenses of Cueva Morín. Some clearly are composites of several superimposed occupation episodes, while others may come close to including the remains of just one such event. Enumeration of levels would, therefore, simply give a very false impression, and it would certainly bias the results of this coarse-grained exercise in estimating habitation density much more than the simple listing of numbers of localities employed as major sites in each gross temporal subdivision.

There is only one known Acheulean site in Cantabria (Castillo), together with one little-known, problematical site (La Busta) (Freeman 1964). Scattered surface finds of bifaces (e.g., near Peña de Candamo, Panes, Altamira, and Castillo) cannot be assigned to the Acheulean, since such pieces are also found in the Cantabrian Mousterian, and even in Upper Paleolithic industries. At the very most, there are 12 reported Mousterian sites, only one Chatelperronian site (Cueva Morín Level 10), 12 sites that have levels labeled Aurignacian *(sensu novo),*

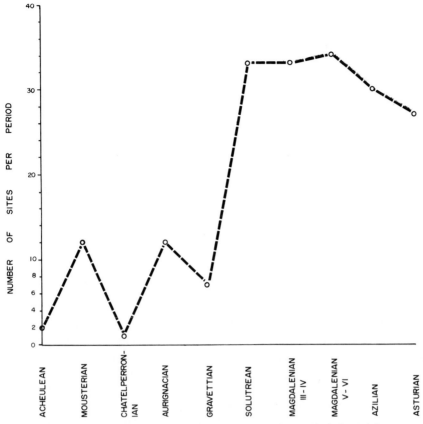

Figure 2.4 Number of archaeological sites per time period: Cantabria.

and only 7 that are labeled Gravettian (or Upper Perigordian). However, a few of
the levels labeled Aurignacian in the original sense in old references might be
Gravettian (or both Aurignacian and Gravettian). Since the collections are either
now lost or insignificant in size, a modern assessment cannot be made in some
cases. The shift of a few sites, such as Salitre, Hornos, and Camargo, from the
"Aurignacian" to the "Gravettian" sum (or vice versa) would not significantly
change the overall pattern, which, at any rate, provides only the roughest sort of
information.

   In contrast to the very low number and density of Lower, Middle, and Early
Upper Paleolithic sites, there is a dramatic change in the Solutrean to a relatively
high number and density of sites, which is sustained throughout the remainder
of the Upper Paleolithic and during the post-Paleolithic periods. There are 33
known Solutrean sites and also 33 sites that have been said to contain levels of the
so-called Lower and/or Middle Cantabrian Magdalenian (III and IV). Interpretation of these levels is difficult, since the Solutrean is essentially defined by the

presence of a class of diagnostic lithic artifacts, while the Magdalenian III–IV is basically defined by the *absence* of both the Solutrean foliate points and of the cylindrical antler harpoons of the Upper Magdalenian. The number of sites with levels attributed to the Upper Magdalenian, Azilian (with flattened harpoons), and Asturian (with cobble pics) remains both relatively high and remarkably stable: 34, 30, and 27 sites, respectively.

The impression of a dramatic increase in human habitation of Cantabria from time of the Solutrean on might be somewhat mitigated by the fact that remains of the earlier periods would tend to have been more easily destroyed and/or deeper and harder to find. However, on the contrary, the various Late Upper Paleolithic and post-Paleolithic periods were much shorter in duration than the Lower and Middle Paleolithic, and, therefore, theoretically there was much less time in which to produce and deposit archeological residues, assuming that the density of human habitation was indeed roughly equal throughout these periods.

The Relationship of Fauna and Tools

Although this is not the place to discuss this problem, it is noteworthy that the Solutrean lithic assemblages of Santander and Asturias, which are demonstrably associated with high proportions of red deer, greatly resemble the classic Cantabrian Lower Magdalenian of El Juyo, with many thick endscrapers, sidescrapers, notches, and denticulates (see González Echegaray 1960, 1971). In fact, the Solutrean site with the clearest indication of specialized red deer hunting (El Cierro) has the lithic industry that statistically most closely resembles that of the El Juyo industry—the type industry for the Lower Magdalenian (Straus 1975d). Perhaps it is not merely a coincidence that specialized red deer hunting in western Cantabria peaks during these two periods when the densities of sites (especially precisely in Santander and Asturias) seem highest. There is undoubtedly a functional relationship between the typical industries during these periods in these areas and the heavy exploitation of red deer (consistently together with bovines and horses in smaller numbers), perhaps related to some degree of increased population pressure. The relationship between these animals and important elements in the lithic tool assemblages is supported by the results of principal components analyses of the Solutrean artifact and faunal data (Straus 1975c).

On the other hand, the Solutrean industries of the Basque country, associated generally with high proportions of caprines, closely resemble Gravettian industries (Straus 1974a). Both have many backed blades and bladelets and burins—especially those on truncated blades—and, in terms of relative frequencies of tool types, are quite different from those of western Cantabria. These differences are particularly striking in the overall percentages of burins versus those of endscrapers. Gravettian levels in the Basque country are also associated with large numbers of ibex and chamois, undoubtedly due to the rugged topography of the surroundings of most sites. Once more, there seem to be some fundamental functional implications that transcend the archeologist-defined culture-stratigraphic units, at least in Cantabria. These relationships have yet to be fully explored and explained.

Conclusions

There seem to have been several critical and certainly interrelated developments during the course of the Cantabrian Paleolithic, but there were no absolute breaks or breakthroughs. Developments were not necessarily all parallel, simultaneous, or irreversible.

One development seems to have been a sharp increase in population density, coupled with the elaboration of a more apparently bipolar settlement pattern with seasonal implications in the middle part of the Upper Paleolithic period (i.e., ca.18,000 B.P.). In contrast with the Mousterian, there were increased multiple representations of important game species—especially alpine caprines and red deer—at least in the Gravettian. There was a decrease in the numerical importance of bovines. Specialization continued apace in the Solutrean and Lower Magdalenian, combined with the appearance of greater amounts of potentially usable meat in many of the levels, perhaps suggesting more intensive occupation.

While conclusions based on the calculation of potentially usable meat weights per species quite possibly misrepresent the actual diet, due to differential treatment in butchering and distribution and differential preservation, it is obvious that the presence of many red deer or ibex in a level does not usually mean that there was an overriding dietary dependence on these species. The small numbers of horses (usable meat weight about 180 kg [Freeman 1973]) and/or bovines (400 kg each) in even most Upper Paleolithic levels usually surpass or equal the numerically superior red deer (100 kg) or ibex (50 kg). Only in rare instances (El Cierro, El Juyo) is the numerically dominant species also the one that seems to have provided the most meat. While much time and effort may have been invested in the hunting of the single most frequently represented species, one bison would potentially equal four red deer or eight ibex in meat weight, for example.

Toward the end of the Upper Paleolithic, there were increasing tendencies to capture small burrowing and nocturnal fur-bearing carnivores, dangerous boar, birds, numerous but relatively small shellfish, and perhaps some large fish. The culmination of these tendencies is seen in the "Mesolithic" Azilian and Asturian periods, with evidence of a wide spectrum of food resource exploitation, including many shellfish and many species of mammals, especially red deer and boar. There is evidence of some subregional differentiation in the animals "preferentially" hunted (perhaps due to differences in overall topographies preferred by the animals) and of related differential frequencies of tool types between the Basque and western Cantabrian areas perhaps as early as the Gravettian, but certainly during the Solutrean. Future study will investigate the nature of interassemblage differences and similarities in terms of the paleoecology of each human occupation. Eventually, there should be far less concentration on the comparison of major blocks of time, somewhat arbitrarily and misleadingly established as "cultural" units of temporal systematics by modern-day prehistorians.

ACKNOWLEDGMENTS

I would like to thank Doctors J. Altuna, E. Aguirre, M. T. Alberdi, F. Borja Sanchiz, and C. Fuentes for advice and assistance in my preliminary classifications of several faunal collections. Any mistakes, however, are entirely my own. I especially wish to thank Dr. Altuna for his identification of the Altamira Solutrean collection and Dr. M. A. García Guinea, Director of the Museo de Prehistoria of Santander, for permission to transport it temporarily for study. I also owe much gratitude to Professors F. Jordá Cerdá, M. Almagro Basch, M. Almagro Gorbea, M. Grande, Srta. M. Escortell, and Father J. M. de Barandiarán for valuable information and permission to study collections that they either excavated or presently curate. Last, but not least, I acknowledge with warmest appreciation the encouragement and very considerable help of Father J. González Echegaray and Professor L. G. Freeman, whose 1973 article was the chief stimulus for this modest contribution to the subject of Cantabrian Paleolithic faunas.

REFERENCES

Altuna, J.
    1971   Los Mamíferos del yacimiento Prehistórico de Morín (Santander). In *Cueva Morín: Excavaciones 1966–1968,* by J. Gonzalez Echegaray, L. G. Freeman, *et al.* Santander: Patronato de las Cuevas Prehistóricas.
    1972   Fauna de mamíferos de los yacimientos Prehistóricos de Guipuzcoa, con catalogo de los mamíferos cuaternarios del Cantábrico y Pireneo Occidental. *Munibe* **24:**1–464.
    1973   Fauna de mamíferos de la Cueva de Morín (Santander). In *Cueva Morín: Excavaciones 1969,* by J. González Echegaray, L. G. Freeman, *et al.* Santander: Patronato de las Cuevas Prehistóricas.
    1975   Fauna from the Cueva del Conde. In *A contribution to the study of Paleolithic levels at the Cueva del Conde (Oviedo),* by L. G. Freeman. Unpublished manuscript.
Altuna, J., and L. G. Straus
    1975   The Solutrean of Altamira: The artifactual and faunal evidence. *Zephyrus* **26** (in press).
Aranzadi, T. De, and J. M. De Barandiaran
    1928   Exploraciones Prehistóricas en Guipuzcoa en los anõs 1924 a 1927. San Sebastian: Diputación de Guipuzcoa.
    1935   Exploraciones en la caverna de Santimamiñe: 3ª Memoria. Bilbao: Imprenta de la Excma, Diputación de Vizcaya.
Azpeitia, P.
    1958   Estudio de los restos paleontológicos de la Trinchera I. In *Memoria de las excavaciones de la Cueva del Juyo (1955–56),* by P. Janssens and J. González Echegaray. Santander: Patronato de las Cuevas Prehistóricas.
Barandiaran, I.
    1973   Arte mueble del Paleolítico Cantábrico. *Monografías Arqueológicas* **14.** Universidad de Zaragoza.
Barandiaran, J. M. De
    1950   Bolinkoba y otros yacimientos Paleolíticos en la Sierra de Amboto (Vizcaya). *Cuadernos de Historia Primitiva* **5:**73–112.
Barandiaran, J. M. De, and D. De Sonneville-Bordes
    1965   Magdalénien final et Azilien d'Urtiaga (Guipuzcoa): Etude statistique. In *Miscelanea en homenaje al Abate Henri Breuil. II,* edited by E. Ripoll Perello. Barcelona: Diputacion Provincial.

Breuil, H., and H. Obermaier
  1935 The cave of Altamira at Santillana del Mar, Spain, translated by Mary E. Boyle. Madrid: Tipografía de Archivos.
Butzer, K. W.
  1971a Communicación preliminar sobre la geología de Cueva Morín (Santander). In *Cueva Morín: Excavaciones 1966–1968*, by J. González Echegaray, L. G. Freeman, *et al.* Santander: Patronato de las Cuevas Prehistóricas.
  1971b *Environment and archeology: An ecological approach to prehistory.* Chicago: Aldine.
  1973 Notas sobre la gemorfología regional de la parte occidental de la provincia de Santander, y la estratigrafía de Cueva Morín. In *Cueva Morín: Excavaciones 1969*, by J. González Echegaray, L. G. Freeman, *et al.* Santander: Patronato de las Cuevas Prehistóricas.
Clark, G. A.
  1971a The Asturian of Cantabria: A Re-evaluation. Unpublished doctoral dissertation, Department of Anthropology, University of Chicago.
  1971b The Asturian of Cantabria: Subsistence base and the evidence for post-Pleistocene climatic shifts. *American Anthropologist* **73**:1245–1257.
Clark, G. A., L. G. Straus, and C. Fuentes
  1975 Archeological survey on the Meseta del Norte (province of Burgos, north-central Spain). *Journal of the Arizona Academy of Science* **10**:3–7.
Crane, H. R., and J. B. Griffin
  1960 University of Michigan radiocarbon dates V. *Radiocarbon* **2**:31–48.
Freeman, L. G.
  1964 Mousterian developments in Cantabrian Spain. Unpublished doctoral dissertation, Department of Anthropology, University of Chicago.
  1973 The significance of mammalian faunas from Paleolithic occupations in Cantabrian Spain. *American Antiquity* **38**:3–44.
  1975 A contribution to the study of Paleolithic levels at the Cueva del Conde (Oviedo). Unpublished manuscript.
González Echegaray, J.
  1960 El Magdaleniense III de la Costa Cantábrica. *Boletin de Seminario de Estudios de Arte y Arqueología (Vallodolid)* **26:** 69–100.
  1971 Apreciaciones cuantitativas sobre el Magdaleniense de la Costa Cantábrica. *Munibe* **23**:323–327.
González Echegaray, J., L. G. Freeman, *et al.*
  1973 *Cueva Morín: Excavaciones 1969.* Santander: Patronato de las Cuevas.
González Morales, M. R.
  1974 La Cueva de Collubil (Amieva, Asturias). Unpublished thesis, Departamento de Arqueología, Universidad de Oviedo.
Jorda Cerda, F.
  1960 El complejo cultural Solutrense–Magdaleniense en la region Cantábrica. *Primer Symposium de Prehistoria de la Peninsula Iberica (Pamplona).* Pp. 1–22.
  1963 El Paleolítico Superior Cantábrico y sus industrias. *Saitabi* **8**:3–22.
Leroi-Gourhan, Arlette
  1959 Résultats de l'analyse pollinique de la grotte d'Isturitz. *Bulletin de la Société Préhistorique Française* **56**:619–24.
  1966 Análisis polínico de la Cueva del Otero. In *Cueva del Otero (Excavaciones arqueológicas en España 53)*, by J. González Echegaray, Garcia Guinea, and Begines Ramirez.
  1971 Análisis polínico de Cueva Morín. In *Cueva Morín: Excavaciones 1966–1968*, by J. González Echegaray, L. G. Freeman, *et al.* Santander: Patronato de las Cuevas Prehistóricas.
McCullough, M. C. R.
  1971 Perigordian facies in the Upper Paleolithic of Cantabria. Unpublished doctoral dissertation, Department of Anthropology, University of Pennsylvania.

Madariaga, B.

    1963   Analisis paleontológico de la fauna terrestre y marina de la Cueva de la Chora. In *Cueva de la Chora (Excavaciones Arqueológicas en España 26)*, by J. González Echegaray *et al.*

    1966   Analisis paleontológico de la fauna terrestre y marina de la Cueva del Otero. In *Cueva del Otero (Excavaciones arqueológicas en España 53)*, by J. González Echegaray *et al.*

Moure, J. A.

    1974   Magdaleniense Superior y Aziliense en la region cantábrica española. Unpublished doctoral dissertation, Departamento de Prehistoria, Universidad Complutense de Madrid.

Obermaier, H.

    1923   Escultura cuaternaria de la Cueva del Rascaño (Santander). *Butlleti de l'Associacio Catalana d'Antropologia, Etnologia i Prehistoria* **1**:7–14.

    1925   *El hombre fosíl* (second edition). Comisión de Investigaciones Paleontológicas y Prehistóricas, Memoria 9. Madrid.

Straus, L. G.

    1974a Le Solutréen du Pays Basque Espagnol: Une esquisse des données. *Munibe* **26**:173–181.

    1974b Notas preliminares sobre el Solutrense de Asturias. *Boletin del Instituto de Estudios Asturianos* **82**:483–504.

    1975a El Solutrense de las cuevas del Castillo y Hornos de la Peña (Santander). *Trabajos de Prehistoria* **32**:9–19.

    1975b Posible atribución al Solutrense del yacimiento de la Pasiega. *Ampurias* **36**:217–223.

    1975c A study of the Solutrean in Vasco-Cantabrian Spain. Unpublished doctoral dissertation, Department of Anthropology, University of Chicago.

    1975d ¿ Solutrense o Magdaleniense inferior cantábrico?: Significado de las "diferencias." *Boletin del Instituto de Estudios Asturianos* **86**:781–790.

Vaufrey, R.

    n.d.   Castillo, Faune. Unpublished inventory (provided courtesy of M. F. Bonifay).

3

Bone Frequencies—And Attritional Processes*

LEWIS R. BINFORD AND JACK B. BERTRAM

University of New Mexico, Albuquerque

Every archaeologist must accept the following challenge: Archaeological observations are contemporary facts, and they are static facts. Our job is to make meaningful statements about the past from contemporary facts and to make meaningful statements about dynamics from static facts. In order to accomplish this, the archaeologist must have a strong body of theory—middle range theory—which guides him in making statements about dynamics from observed statics. In short, we must have a strong and well-founded understanding of the formation processes of the archaeological record. As if the transformation of statics into statements of dynamics were not difficult enough, this problem is further complicated by modifications in the statics which do not inform us regarding or even deriving from cultural dynamics of interest. We are all aware of the role of decay in modifying the original condition of the archaeological record.

Michael Schiffer (1972) has designated such distortions of culturally derived

* Research reported in this chapter was supported by a number of agencies. Much of the work with the Navajo was partially funded through the Doris Duke American Indian Oral History project. Ethnographic work among the Nunamiut Eskimo was supported both by the Wenner-Gren Foundation for Anthropological Research and by the National Science Foundation. To these agencies I am sincerely grateful. Most of the laboratory work and funds for student assistants came through the Grants and Fellowship Office of the University of New Mexico. For this aid, I am most indebted to Mr. Jerry Kasner.

statics arising from natural processes as "N-transforms," and he has commented on the role of the archaeologist to understand such processes and, at least in certain cases, to accomplish the accurate transformation of archaeological remains into statements of original conditions, unmodified by natural processes. Although this may not always be possible, most archaeologists would agree that the recognition of such distorting processes is clearly desirable. We want to be sure that the archaeological record is not simply accepted as a valid or accurate picture of the statics derived from culturally relevant processes or dynamics in the past. This problem seems to be particularly troublesome when it comes to the analysis of faunal remains. We all are aware that there are sites where fauna is not preserved, others where preservation is poor, and others where the preservation is good to excellent. In the latter situation, archaeologists generally accept the remains as an accurate reflection of the bones actually abandoned by men at the location.

We are concerned with the differential survival probabilities of anatomical parts. Interest in this problem stems from a belief that much information about the character of the logistics, seasonality, and site functions of Prehistoric hunter–gatherer adaptations is recoverable through comparative study of the patterns of differential anatomical part frequencies. Of course, such study must be conducted in the context of a strong body of theory regarding man's differential use of anatomical parts. Before such beliefs can be developed into methods, and theory can be operationalized for testing, we must be able to recognize and, if possible, correct for distortions in the archaeological record arising from the activity of agents such as soil acids, bone-gnawing dogs and other animals, and so on. The purpose of this chapter is *(1)* to further our understanding of the attritional processes that may modify a faunal assemblage, *(2)* to develop methods for their recognition, and *(3)* to offer suggestions as to how we may, upon recognition, accurately estimate the original condition of an assemblage. Two types of information were considered essential in addressing this problem: *(1)* well-controlled archaeological assemblages of bones remaining after the operation of a known agent of attrition on a population of bone of known composition; *(2)* measured characteristics of bones that are considered relevant in differentially insuring their survival when acted upon by an agent of attrition.

Description of the Controlled Populations of Bones: Data from the Nunamiut Eskimo

Data relevant to this problem were initially collected during the course of recent field work among the Nunamiut Eskimo. The Nunamiut keep dogs that are specifically fed—that is, they are tethered and are not free to scavenge general village debris. Three classes of data were collected among the Nunamiut:

1. There were collections of bones from the "Dog yards," where dogs were tethered, but we lacked specific information as to the actual population of bones

fed to the dogs. In these cases, we know that dogs, as agents of attrition, were active and we know what the faunal assemblage looks like after they had acted, but we do not know what the original population introduced to the dogs actually was in terms of part-by-part inventories.

2. There were data on the parts of caribou fed to dogs during the spring of 1971 and data recovered from dog-feeding areas for nearly the identical season on sites occupied prior to 1971. We were unable to obtain the "perfect" data for the total 1971 feeding record because the dogs were being continually moved around and tethered at areas that had not been cleaned of bones from earlier feeding (winter feeding of dogs). Therefore, a post-feeding pickup of bones was certain to include material not represented in the feeding data.

3. Finally, the perfect data were obtained for the feeding of nine dogs between June 24 and August 7, 1971. Following this record, the area where the dogs had been tethered (the area had been cleaned completely prior to the beginning of the feeding record) was cleaned of all bone fragments, providing a perfect measure of the effects of dogs as agents of attrition.

Table 3.1 summarizes the minimum number of individual caribou represented by each anatomical part from the "uncontrolled dog yard samples." Table 3.2, Record A, summarizes the minimum number of individual caribou represented by each anatomical part in the total 1971 feeding record—that is, what was actually fed to dogs during the spring of 1971—as well as the relative frequencies of parts recovered from dog-feeding areas on two residential sites from 1948 for nearly the identical period of the year as the 1971 feeding record. Finally, Table 3.2, Record B, summarizes the frequencies of anatomical parts fed to dogs between June 24 and August 7, 1971, and the bones remaining in the feeding area after the completion of the record. The latter are totally uncontaminated; that is, no bones were present when the record was started, and no bones were introduced that were not tabulated in the feeding record.

These data provide us with controls. The initial and most obvious conclusion is that dogs, as agents of attrition, do, in fact, modify the character of a faunal assemblage. This is well illustrated in Figure 3.1 where we compare the percentages of the number of individual animals represented by the parts actually fed to dogs with the percentages of parts surviving for observation after the dogs had fed on the bones. We note (Table 3.2, Columns 7 and 9) that 14 individual caribou were represented in the bones fed to dogs, while only 9 were indicated by the bones remaining after feeding. More important, however, is the fact that lumbar vertebrae were the most common part fed to dogs, while the pelvis was the most common part surviving after feeding. This observation points to another conclusion: The survival of parts after action by an agent of attrition is not necessarily indicative of the proportion of parts originally present. It would appear that different parts have different survival probabilities. This point is illustrated in the comparison of the frequencies of parts introduced and parts surviving for the vertebrae in Table 3.2 and in Figure 3.1. Action by an agent of

Table 3.1

Tabulation of Anatomical Parts Remaining in Dog-Feeding Areas at Anaktuvuk Village,
Representing Various Seasons of Feeding

	Period of accumulation											
	I Fall 1970 Sept. 17– Dec. 10		II Fall and winter 1970 Sept. 10– Feb. 28		III Winter 1971		IV Late winter 1971		V Early spring 1971		VI Late spring and mid- summer 1971 May 17–July 1	
	MNI	%	MNI	%	MNI	%	MNI	%	MNI	%	MNI	%
Antler	6.5	32.5	1.5	13.63	1.0	25.0	5.0	14.9	2.5	11.4	0.0	0.0
Skull	8.0	40.0	5.5	50.0	2.0	50.0	27.5	82.1	22.0	100.0	4.0	11.5
Mandible	16.0	80.0	6.5	59.1	2.5	62.5	29.0	86.6	12.5	56.8	34.5	100.0
Atlas	11.0	55.0	6.0	54.5	4.0	100.0	20.0	59.7	11.0	50.0	24.0	69.6
Axis	9.0	45.0	2.0	18.1	2.0	50.0	15.0	44.8	8.0	36.4	20.0	57.9
Cerv. V.	2.2	11.0	.4	3.6	.4	10.0	3.8	11.3	2.0	9.1	18.0	52.2
Thor. V.	.07	.3	0.0	0.0	.16	4.00	1.0	2.9	.2	.9	11.0	31.9
Lumb. V.	0.0	0.0	0.0	0.0	.37	9.3	2.25	6.7	.8	3.6	9.0	26.1
Pelvis	13.0	65.0	4.5	40.0	3.0	75.0	18.5	55.2	5.0	22.7	11.5	33.3
Ribs	.23	1.1	0.0	0.0	.47	11.7	1.16	3.5	0.0	0.0	.5	1.4
Sternum	0.0	0.0	0.0	0.0	.2	5.0	0.0	0.0	0.0	0.0	0.0	0.0
Scapula	9.0	45.0	6.0	54.5	4.0	100.0	33.5	100.0	7.5	34.1	10.0	28.9
Humerus P.	0.0	0.0	0.0	0.0	0.0	0.0	4.5	13.4	2.5	11.4	2.0	5.8
Humerus D.	20.0	100.0	11.0	100.0	3.0	75.0	28.5	85.1	17.5	79.5	17.5	50.7
Radio-Cub.	15.0	75.0	6.5	59.1	3.5	87.5	12.0	35.8	5.5	25.0	15.5	44.9
Radio-Cub.	8.0	40.0	2.0	18.1	2.0	50.0	6.0	17.9	3.5	15.9	9.0	26.1
Carpals	3.0	15.0	1.0	12.5	2.0	50.0	2.7	8.1	2.0	9.1	4.3	12.5
Metacarpal	9.0	45.0	8.0	72.7	1.0	25.0	7.0	20.9	4.0	18.2	0.0	0.0
Metacarpal	8.5	42.5	3.0	27.2	1.0	25.0	4.0	11.0	3.5	15.9	0.0	0.0
Femur P.	2.0	10.0	0.0	0.0	.5	12.5	3.5	10.4	1.5	6.8	0.0	0.0
Femur D.	2.0	10.0	0.0	0.0	.5	12.5	10.0	29.8	2.5	11.4	0.0	0.0
Tibia P.	3.0	15.0	1.0	9.1	.5	12.5	3.5	10.4	2.0	9.1	.5	1.4
Tibia D.	16.5	82.5	8.0	72.7	1.0	25.0	17.0	50.7	9.0	40.9	3.5	10.1
Tarsals	5.0	25.0	2.0	18.1	.5	12.5	4.7	14.0	3.5	15.9	3.0	8.7
Ast.	7.5	37.5	2.0	18.1	.5	12.5	5.0	14.9	3.0	13.6	3.0	8.7
Cal.	7.5	37.5	4.5	40.1	.0	0.0	5.5	16.4	3.0	13.6	3.0	8.7
Metatarsal	10.0	50.0	2.5	22.7	.5	12.5	6.5	19.4	5.0	22.7	4.0	11.6
Metatarsal	8.5	42.5	2.0	18.1	0.0	0.0	3.5	10.4	4.0	18.2	2.0	5.8
Phalange 1	1.5	7.5	.7	6.8	.85	6.2	2.2	6.7	1.4	6.4	.5	1.4
Phalange 2	1.5	7.5	.7	6.8	0.0	0.0	1.4	4.2	.8	3.6	.5	1.4
Phalange 3	1.5	7.5	.6	5.6	0.0	0.0	.5	1.5	.2	.9	.5	1.4
Mean date of sample	Oct. 6		Nov. 16		Jan. 6		Feb. 22		April 9		June 7	

80

Table 3.2

Tabulation of Spring and Summer Dog-Feeding Together with Summary of Anatomical Parts
Remaining after Action by Dogs

	Record A: Parts fed to dogs between May and June 1971 and parts surviving on 1948 sites for analogous period of the year						Record B: Parts fed to dogs between June 24 and August 7, 1971, and parts surviving at the same location on August 8, 1971			
	Feeding record Spring 1971		Spring dog-feeding area 1948 (Rulland)		Spring dog-feeding area 1948 (Morry)		Feeding record		Bones surviving	
	1	2	3	4	5	6	7	8	9	10[a] Survival
Anatomical part	MNI	%	MNI	%	MNI	%	MNI	%	MNI	%
Antler	11	57.8	4.5	69.2	5.0	31.2	0	0.0	0.0	—
Skull	13	68.4	5.5	84.6	5.5	34.4	0	0.0	0.0	—
Mandible	19	100.0	6.5	100.0	16.0	100.0	0	0.0	0.0	—
Atlas	13	68.4	2.0	30.7	5.0	31.2	4	28.6	3.0	75.0
Axis	12	63.1	1.0	15.4	5.0	31.2	4	28.6	2.0	50.0
Cerv. V.	12	63.1	1.0	15.4	2.3	14.7	8	57.1	3.0	37.5
Thor. V.	4	21.0	0.0	0.0	1.4	8.6	9	64.3	3.15	35.0
Lumb. V.	7	36.8	0.3	5.0	2.5	15.5	14	100.0	6.7	47.8
Pelvis	4	21.0	3.0	46.2	4.5	28.1	11	78.6	9.0	81.8
Ribs	1	5.3	0.1	1.6	.8	5.2	11.5	82.1	2.61	22.7
Sternum	0	0.0	0.0	0.0	0.0	0.0	2.0	14.3	.25	12.5
Scapula	3	15.8	2.5	38.4	0.0	0.0	5.0	35.7	2.5	50.0
Humerus P.	3	15.8	0.0	0.0	.5	3.1	0	0.0	0.0	—
Humerus D.	3	15.8	1.5	23.8	2.0	12.5	0	0.0	0.0	—
Radio-C. P.	4	21.8	2.0	30.7	3.0	18.7	0	0.0	0.0	—
Radio-C. D.	4	21.8	0.0	0.0	4.0	25.0	0	0.0	0.0	—
Carpals	2	10.5	.5	7.7	1.2	7.5	0	0.0	0.0	—
Metacarpal P.	2	10.5	.5	7.7	.5	3.0	.5	3.6	.5	100.0
Metacarpal D.	2	10.5	1.0	15.4	.5	3.1	.5	3.6	0.0	0.0
Femur P.	0	0.0	0.0	0.0	.5	3.1	2.0	14.3	1.0	50.0
Femur D.	0	0.0	0.0	0.0	1.0	6.3	2.0	14.3	.5	25.0
Tibia P.	1	5.3	.5	7.7	3.0	18.7	2.5	17.8	1.0	40.0
Tibia D.	1	5.3	1.0	15.4	1.5	9.4	2.5	17.8	1.5	60.0
Tarsals	2	10.5	0.0	0.0	1.0	6.3	2.0	14.3	.5	25.0
Ast.	2	10.5	0.0	0.0	1.5	9.4	2.0	14.3	1.0	50.0
Cal.	2	10.5	0.0	0.0	1.0	6.3	2.0	14.3	.5	25.0
Metatarsal P.	2	10.5	0.0	0.0	1.5	9.4	2.5	17.8	1.0	40.0
Metatarsal D.	2	10.5	.5	7.7	3.0	18.7	2.0	14.3	.5	25.0
Phalange 1	3.5	18.4	.12	2.1	.4	2.3	2.0	14.3	.37	18.5
Phalange 2	3.5	18.4	.12	2.1	.4	2.3	2.0	14.3	.25	12.5
Phalange 3	3.5	18.4	.12	2.1	.4	2.3	2.0	14.3	.12	6.0

[a] Survival percentage obtained by dividing Column 9 by Column 7.

81

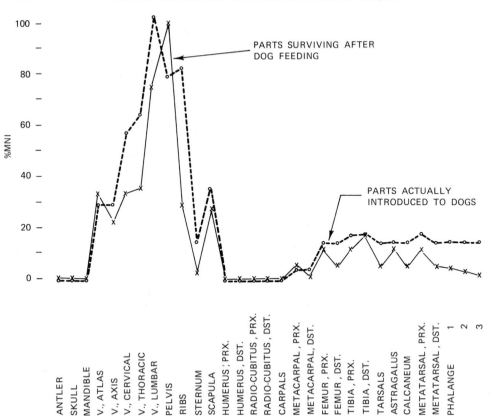

Figure 3.1 Graphic comparison between anatomical parts fed to dogs and parts surviving after dog feeding.

attrition may not only reduce the quantitative characteristics of a surviving faunal assemblage but may also change the structure, or the relative frequencies of the surviving parts.

Figure 3.2 illustrates the variability in the parts actually fed to dogs during the spring and summer of 1971 at Anaktuvuk village. Clearly, there are differences between the relative frequencies of parts actually subject to attrition by dogs. We note that, during spring, heads and upper neck parts are the most common parts surviving in dog-feeding areas, while, during summer, heads are absent, and lower vertebrae, ribs, and pelvic parts are more commonly present. These differences relate directly to the character of the population from which humans were selecting parts for use as dog food. During spring, a "fresh meat" population is the source of parts for use as dog food; during summer, a dried meat population is the source of parts from which selections are made for feeding.

In spring, large numbers of caribou are killed during the migration (May 10–20), and these are processed for storage. Two methods are employed: freezing in underground ice cellars and air drying on meat racks. It is from the latter stores that both Eskimos and dogs will obtain most of their food during the summer months when the main food animal, the caribou, is widely dispersed on the tundra to the north. During spring, when the animals are killed, consumption is largely of fresh meat. For dogs, this is frequently some by-product of the processing of parts for storage as well as parts that are not considered highly valuable for storage. For instance, the tongue and the head are not used for storage with the drying technique. Spoilage of the brain and tongue is rapid, and these parts are either consumed immediately or, in rare cases, frozen; however, even when frozen, the taste and texture is undesirably modified, and few heads or tongues are actually stored for summer use by humans. In spring, the caribou are generally suffering from poor nutrition, and animals that are killed in such a state are notably lean in the neck and front quarters, and the marrow in the front legs is qualitatively less desirable. Lean animals may be partially processed for drying or freezing; however, front quarters and necks are generally not processed in this manner. They are used as dog food. We may generalize that dog feeding during spring is conditioned by the judgments of the Eskimo regarding

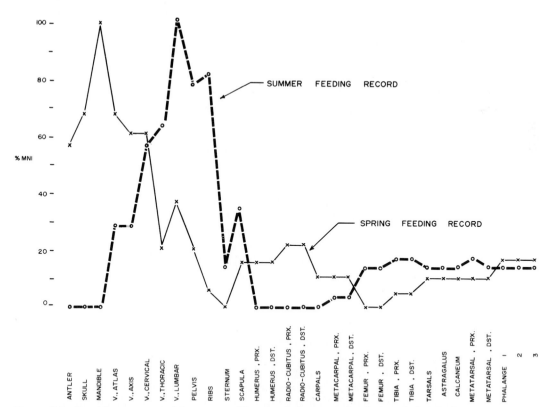

Figure 3.2 Graphic summary of frequency difference between anatomical parts fed to dogs during spring and summer.

the storage potential of different anatomical parts. Heads, necks, and front quarters are most commonly judged to be of low storage utility. In turn, we note a strong bias in the use of these parts as dog food during this season (Figure 3.2).

During summer, however, the picture is very different. All feeding is carried out from parts previously stored. In general, there are two basic tendencies in the pattern of human use of foods from stores: (1) Frozen meat is considered more reliable and of greater utility for human consumption. (2) Dried meat that was stripped from the bones at the time of processing is considered more desirable for human use than are parts that were dried with the bones. Such considerations determine the character of parts fed to dogs during the summer. There is a strong bias in favor of parts that were previously selected for drying with the bones remaining, and there is a minor bias in terms of parts that are the by-products of human consumption from frozen stores (these are the upper bones of the rear leg). Figure 3.3 illustrates the relationship between anatomical parts actually inventoried as dried meat on drying racks in Anaktuvuk village in 1971 and the summer dog-feeding records for the same year. It is clear that the character of the *population available for use conditions the pattern of actual use;* however, in addition, the character of the population available does not *determine directly the pattern of use for a specific purpose.* For example, there is a bias in dried meat dog feeding in favor of necks, lumbar vertebrae, and pelvis, while human consumption tends to favor ribs, sternum, scapula, and parts of the front leg.

This point is further illustrated by the data from the dog yards used from fall through spring (Table 3.1). In these data, we may assume that a constant agent of attrition has been at work (the dogs) and that variations in the actual frequencies of bone recovered from feeding areas will reflect, to some degree of accuracy, the differences in Eskimo feeding behavior across the seasons represented.

Given these arguments, regarding the use of heads and tongues in the spring and summer comparisons, we might anticipate that heads and tongues would be most common on fall sites (coinciding with the fall migration of caribou) and of decreasing frequency in populations accumulated after the fall migration and before the spring migration. Inspection of Table 3.1 shows that this is not the case and that, in fact, heads and mandibles are most common in the feeding area with a mean use date of February 22. Given some knowledge of the different contingencies affecting Eskimo decisions, this situation is understandable. At the time of the fall migration, animals are killed and cached on the tundra. This meat may remain in field caches (frozen) until as late as the following spring before it is introduced to the village for consumption. This strategy is interesting in the following manner: Approximately 350 animals are killed each year during the fall migration. This meat is destined for use over the period between October 15 and May 20, approximately seven months. The caching strategy is a labor-saving procedure in that the transport of all the winter stores into the winter village immediately after the fall hunt would necessitate a tremendous effort. Nevertheless, they would still have to make numerous trips out of the village during winter for purposes of (a) gathering firewood, (b) tending traps, and (c) monitoring the

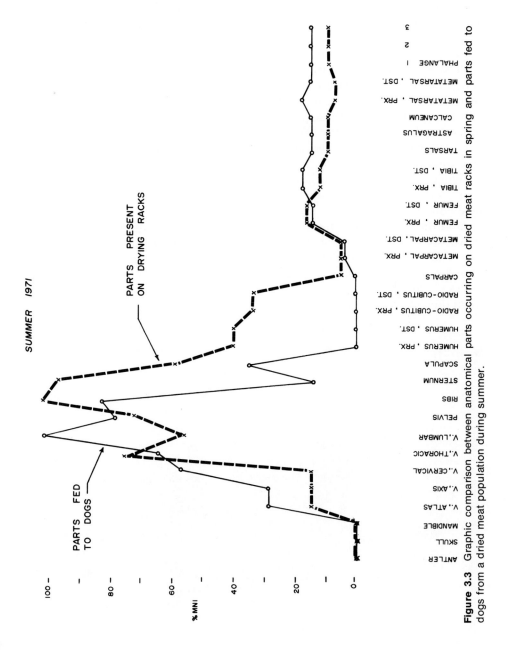

Figure 3.3 Graphic comparison between anatomical parts occurring on dried meat racks in spring and parts fed to dogs from a dried meat population during summer.

environment for game. By leaving the meat cached nearby or on the kill loca-tions, they can simply visit these caches regularly during the winter in conjunction with their trips out of the village for other purposes. In cases in which schedules are not exactly isomorphic, as, for example, when the need for meat, firewood, or trap checking occurs at different times, special trips may be made to the meat caches, but it is rare not to use such an opportunity to monitor the environment for game and/or collecting a little firewood. This strategy eliminates the labor investment that would accompany the transport of meat after the fall hunt, without eliminating any subsequent labor investment in mobility during the win-ter and early spring months. With the caching strategy, packing labor is simulta-neously scheduled with other tasks involving mobility throughout the period of consumption of stored meat.

Figure 3.4 shows meat caches remaining on the tundra shortly after the fall hunt. One should note that the meat is covered with the skin of at least one of the field butchered animals, and then the heads with the antlers attached are placed around the cache. These heads, with large antlers, serve several functions, the most important of which is as a cache marker, so that once snow accumulates the cache may be located. The clustered antler tips generally remain visible above the snow. In addition, the antlers are frequently used as supports for strings and pieces of cloth that tend to discourage ravens from feeding on the cached meat when they blow in the wind.

Figure 3.4 Photograph of meat caches on the Tundra in fall.

Thus, the value of heads at caches is not simply as alternative pieces of stored food, they are structural components of a temporary facility. This means that, as long as usable meat remains at the cache location, the heads will be used as markers. Only after the caches are exhausted will a decision be made to abandon the heads or to return them to the village to be used as food for dogs or humans. They will invariably be the last items removed from a cache. Thus, their rate of introduction into the village will be very slow during and immediately after the fall hunt and will increase as the winter wears on, finally showing a decrease in late winter and early spring, since by then the remaining caches are almost always at locations where the largest numbers of animals killed the previous fall had been cached. In early spring, if food stores are low, heads may be used increasingly as food for humans, while dogs may be fed parts that are even less desirable. If conditions are really bad, dogs may be fed the frozen carcasses of fur bearers (foxes, wolves, and wolverines) trapped during the winter and caribou parts of very little food utility remaining at cache-kill locations. Therefore the frequency of introductions of heads into dog-feeding areas during late winter and early spring will vary depending on the general condition of the Eskimo group as regards stored food, quite independently of the rate of cache exhaustion or the variability in the size of caches—factors that generally determine the rate at which heads are introduced as dog food during midwinter.

As a further example of the shifts in factors (contingencies) which differentially condition the manner and rate of use of different anatomical parts, we may compare this discussion of heads with the data on mandibles and on parts normally stored as dried meat—the scapula and the pelvis. Figure 3.5 illustrates the pattern of frequency variation for four anatomical parts remaining in dog-feeding areas across the full year, beginning in the fall.

In our experience, the scapula and the pelvis are parts that frequently dried with the bones remaining (see Figure 3.3 for their relative frequency in summer). In Figure 3.5 we note that these parts are very common in dog yards between late November and early March, with the scapula more common than the pelvis. On the other hand, between late June and late August, they are also common in dog yards. At this time, however, the scapula is more common than the pelvis. This pattern presents several questions: (1) Why is dried meat common in dog yards during the coldest period of the year? One would expect the use of frozen meat to be at a high point during this period. (2) Why is there a reversal in the frequency of the two parts monitored—scapula and pelvis—during the summer and winter?

During the period of fall hunting, considerable quantities of meat are dried on racks in the winter village. Most of this, particularly choice parts not containing bones, such as the tenderloin, is destined to be used as trail food by the men during winter trapping and hunting trips. However, the bulk of the meat will be used as dog food during the midwinter weeks of perpetual darkness. During this season, very few trips are made outside of the village, and just before the period of darkness, there is some effort to accumulate meat from the caches for use by the humans during this period. This meat is normally placed on the roofs of

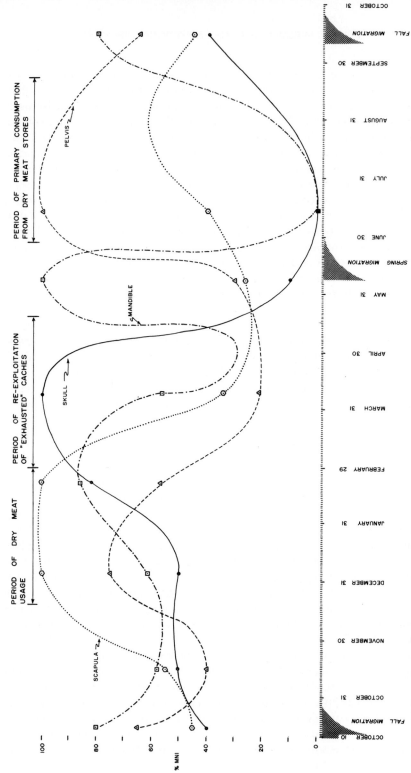

Figure 3.5 Comparison of frequencies for selected anatomical parts occurring in dog feeding areas at different seasons of the year.

houses and thawed inside for human use. Butchering takes place after thawing, inside the Eskimo winter houses. These parts are rarely fed to dogs; instead, the now frozen but previously dried meat remaining on the meat racks is used as dog food, and no effort is made to thaw this meat. In short, the dried meat represents a resource previously introduced into the village that requires no further processing for use as dog food during midwinter.

The question of the reversal of frequency of pelvis and scapula must be understood in terms of the nutritional cycle of caribou and of the differential usage made of anatomically identical parts depending upon the nutritional state of the animals at the time of butchering. In our discussions of spring and summer feeding, we noted that the front quarters are judged to be most responsive to poor nutrition. For these reasons, these are frequently abandoned at kills or otherwise not processed for summer use at the time of spring processing. During the summer, pelves are used more after since they are considered "better." However, as the season wears on scapula are used more often, although there is a bias against them in processing as well as feeding. On the other hand, animals killed in fall are in prime condition, and we note that scapula occur most often as dog food while the pelvis is less common. This reflects a shift in usage in which the scapula is more commonly processed for storage and the pelvis is now considered more appropriate for human consumption.

These examples of the shifting contingencies that condition human decision making illustrate a point that I have made repeatedly in previous works: The causes of variability in archaeological remains are multivariate and originate in dynamics that may be shifting in terms of conditioning factors. Traditional conventions for archaeological interpretation assume a single cause that is viewed in static terms (culture, or the ideas, values, or preferences of a "people"). Given this assumption, the traditional archaeologist confidently assigns meaning to observed variation among assemblages as evidence of differences in "culture" among "peoples."

As far as faunal assemblages are concerned, our data demonstrate two points. *(1)* The criteria of selection or "preference" within a single "people" is variable and conditioned by a number of contingencies. We note further that the character of the contingencies may be different in different contexts, such as biased selection of the same part, as is the case with dried meat usage in the summer versus the winter. Similarly, we note variations in the degree that parts vary as a function of independent selection versus "dependent" selection or appearing as a "rider" relative to another part. A good example is the mandible. At one time, its frequency is a function of the elapsed time from the period of availability of fresh meat in spring and fall. During the winter, it varies as a partial function of the frequency with which heads (skulls) are introduced. *(2)* As fascinating as such variability may be, it does not help very much in gaining a measured understanding of the effect that agents of attrition may have on a faunal assemblage. In the case of the dog yard material, we are holding the effects of agent (the dogs) constant and attributing observed variability to differences in the actual population of bones introduced to them. Since we do not know the actual composition of the populations of bone fed to dogs, we cannot measure the effect of dogs. In the one case in which we have both the inventory of parts fed to dogs and the counts of parts remaining after feeding, all the parts of the caribou are not represented, so that we are unable to measure the effects of dogs equally on all parts of the anatomy. Since we have never observed Eskimo feeding their dogs an entire caribou, control data of the type deemed necessary was sought in other places. During the course of conversation with Oswalt Werner, he pointed out that, in his opinion, the Navajo were a good potential source for the data needed. They were sheep herders and had animals with them, as opposed to the extended logistic-storage strategies of the Eskimo. As a result of this, we initiated some ethnographic work among the Navajo. What follows is a description of the data collected.

The Navajo: Data on Domestic Sheep

The following data were collected by a number of different persons. Oswalt Werner of Northwestern University had described and photographed butchering sequences. Martin Topper lived with the families at the site where our "archaeological" data were collected, and he arranged, on two occasions, for field parties headed by Mark Wimberly to collect bone and to interview informants. Subsequently, Binford visited the families and obtained information on food sharing, dog care, and variability in the selection of animals for butchering, as these facts may vary with the season.

Most important to the success of this project was the cooperation of John Percy, the owner of the houses and sites surveyed and the congenial informant for most of the behavioral information incorporated herein. Mr. Percy's houses are located "deep" in the Navajo reservation north of Tuba City, Arizona. There were five residents in each site to be described, and the numbers of dogs varied from 5 to 9 over the period covered by the bone samples. Mr. Percy tends a herd of approximately 350 sheep. In addition, he has several head of horses that are sometimes butchered for food during the winter.

We will describe the basic facts of butchering and food preparation prior to a description of the sites and the bone samples, since butchering and modifications during consumption have frequently been cited as affecting the relative frequencies of anatomical parts present archaeologically.

Navajo Sheep Butchering

The following description is based on information obtained from Oswalt Werner, of Northwestern University, who photographed the butchering sequences. Martha Ann Austin, a Navajo student, provided a description from her own recollections of butchering sheep when she was living with her parents. In addition, Martin Topper has interviewed extensively on this subject while living with a Navajo family. He observed in detail at least three butchering episodes. Mark Wimberly also observed the butchering of sheep, while he was in the field collecting the faunal material reported herein. In all of the accounts, there is remarkable agreement, indicating an extremely regular and patterned procedure for sheep butchering among the Navajo. The butchering sequence will be described in terms of the Navajo's conception of the various steps of the process.

1. *"Getting a big fat sheep"*
   a. The following is taken from an interview with an anonymous informant of the Bitterwater clan of Navajo living northwest of Tuba City, Arizona. "When he wants mutton, they butcher a sheep. . . . If he is hungry for mutton, and it only last them about a week . . . they try to go without eating mutton, . . . eating beans or potatoes. . . . If he is hungry . . . then you go out in the corral and look around and see which one you want. Grandpa goes out here and my grandma. Grandma says, kill this one and then grandpa says, no, that one is young or something, that other one is young, going to have babies . . . and then they choose another one, there is not very much fat on that one, and then you take another . . . feel his tail . . . and you feel his breast . . . fat . . . take him back down there to the house."
   b. When informants were asked directly how they choose a sheep for butchering, they consistently answered that they choose a "fat" sheep. However, the aforementioned demonstrates that age and reproductive condition are at least two additional considerations.

2. *"Cutting the throat"*
   The sheep is carried to the area just in front of the "butchering rack." This may be a frame constructed with two vertical poles set in the ground and a horizontal member tied across the top about 6 feet high. In summer camps, butchering may be done just outside the ramada when one of the corner posts may be used as a butchering rack. The sheep is placed on the ground on its side, and the four legs are brought together and tied so that the sheep cannot move. A small pan or bowl is then brought to the butchering floor, and a butcher knife is sharpened. After these preparations, the sheep is grasped by its nose, with the butcher kneeling behind the head. The head is drawn back and the throat is cut. An assistant is generally engaged to hold the wool back from where the cut is made and to hold the bowl or pan under the throat to catch the blood when the cut is made. After the animal is bled, the legs are untied. The head is not severed at this time; only the throat is cut.

3. *Butchering*
   An incision is next made through the skin along the sternum running up the neck to the point where the throat was cut. Then this cut is extended back across the abdomen to the tip of the tail. An incision is made up the insides of the front legs to the joint between the metacarpal and the distal end of the radiocubitus. The skin is worked back from the leg, and a cut is made through the carpals, severing the lower leg from the body. The lower leg remains attached to the skin. This is done on both sides. The rear legs are then treated in the same manner—incision along the inside up to the tarsals—the skin is worked loose, and a cut is made, generally below the tarsals, between the proximal end of the metatarsal and its articulation with the

tarsals. The lower leg is left attached to the skin. The skin is not cut in either case; only the bone articulations are. After the legs are freed, the skin is worked off around the neck and the sides of the body toward the vertebrae. At this point, the skinning stops, leaving the partially flayed skin attached to the body down the full length of the backbone. Next, the esophagus is pulled from the cut in the throat, and a knot is made in it so that the stomach contents will not drain out when the sheep is hung from the "butchering rack." Alternatively, this may be done before the skinning is started. Some Navajo generally cut off the head at this time by means of a cut made from the dorsal surface between the occuputal condyles and the atlas vertebra. Others prefer to remove the head after the animal has been hung on the butchering rack.

4. *"Hanging the sheep"*

A cut is then made between the large tendon running down the ventral surface of both rear legs attaching to the calcanium and the tibia. A rope or stout cord is inserted through this cut and thrown over the butchering rack. The sheep is pulled up on the rack, hanging upside down with the skin still attached along the backbone. Once the rope is secure, the final skinning begins. The skin is grabbed at the tail and worked off the body toward the neck. After the skin has been worked off about half-way down the body, it is grabbed at the back and pulled off the upper shoulders and neck. In cases in which the head was not cut off earlier, the final cut is made along the base of the skull freeing the skin from the body. The skin is then placed on the ground, wool side down. If the head has not already been removed, it is cut from the body at this point by means of a cut from the dorsal surface between the occuputal condyles and the atlas vertebra. The next step is the removal of the front quarters. An incision is made along the inside of the front leg at the point at which the meat is attached to the body. The leg is gradually cut from the rib cage, and the meat of the neck is cut off at the same time. Cutting close to the bone, the scapula and the trapezius muscle are removed up to the backbone. The other leg is cut free from the body in the same manner until the meat is worked up to the backbone. The knife is inserted under the muscle, and the two front quarters, attached by the trapezius muscle, are removed as a unit. These are then placed on the skin or hung over a line nearby.

The next step is to remove the band of breast fat by starting inside the cuts made for the removal of the front quarters and working the layer of fat off the breast down to brisket. A "V"-shaped cut is then made starting at the far end of the sternum cutting back toward the neck. Cuts are made along both sides through the cartilage between the ribs and the sternum plates. The sternum is removed as a unit together with the breast fat layer.

An incision is then made through the abdominal wall just to the rear of the diaphragm. This cut is only large enough for the hand to be inserted into the abdominal cavity. The hand is inserted, and the abdominal contents are worked loose from their attachments to the walls. Then the incision is extended rearward to the crotch.

The abdominal contents are gingerly removed as a unit: stomach and parts, intestines, spleen, and greater omentum. This is generally accomplished by two people who place the abdominal contents on the skin, where an assistant may begin cleaning these parts. The intestines are cleaned out, and the stomach is punctured and carried to one side where it is drained.

After this procedure, the contents of the thorax are removed: heart, lungs, liver, gall bladder, windpipe, and the diaphragm. All of these are used except the gall bladder, which is thrown away. These are placed on the skin for cleaning. The bladder is then cut out and thrown away. Kidneys may be left attached to the vertebrae.

The butcher now returns to the body hanging on the rack, and a cut is made with a knife along the dorsal vertebral spines, severing the tenderloin from the spines along the entire length of the thoracic vertebrae. The body is then twisted around on the rope so that the ventral surface is facing the butcher. The knife is inserted between the tibia and the tendon to which the rope is attached, and the tendon is severed on one leg. The body is now hung from only one leg. An ax may be procured, and a cut is made down into the pelvis severing one wing of the pelvis from the sacrum. The ax is used to hack along the edge of the vertebrae, breaking off the transverse processes of the lumbar vertebra down to the ribs. Chopping continues, holding the severed leg and attached abdominal muscles in one hand while chopping off the heads of the ribs with blows directed from inside the thoracic cavity until the entire rib slab is removed from the vertebrae. This procedure results in the removal, as a single piece, of the entire rear leg with one half of the pelvis attached and the muscles of the abdomen together with the complete rib slab. This is then hung across a nearby line or placed in a pile on the skin. Next the ax is used to cut the caudal vertebrae and sacrum from the other half of the pelvis. Once this is accomplished, hacking continues down along the vertebrae as was previously described until the complete vertebral column is removed as a unit. The other rear leg with attached pelvic half, abdominal muscles, and rib slab remains on the butchering rack. The rope is then taken down, removed from the remaining rear leg, and the final step in the initial butchering is completed.

A number of alternatives in the butchering have been noted; these include the use of a knife instead of an ax to cut the legs and rib slabs from the vertebrae. Similarly, the degree to which the secondary butchering may be done by a helper concurrently with the primary butchering just described depends on a number of factors. If butchering is being done in anticipation of entertaining guests, the vertebrae may be cut into three or four sections depending upon the size of the cooking pots. In general, the sections consist of a cervical unit, an upper thoracic unit, a lower thoracic–upper lumbar unit, and a lower lumbar–sacrum unit. In general rib slabs may be cut into three parts depending on the size of cooking pots. Dismemberment of legs is accomplished by breaking through the shafts of the long bones, whereas the vertebrae are generally cut into sections with an ax. A common practice is to store the blood in the cleaned stomach of the sheep. It may then be used later for a blood porridge.

Preparation for Consumption and Disposal

Consumption

There are several interesting facts regarding controls on body part destruction. The Navajo no longer crack long bones for the removal and consumption of bone marrow. The normal method of preparation for cooking is to cut the meat from the bones. Chunks are cut off for use in stew, whole muscles are sliced off and fried or put on the coals and roasted. Once the major meat has been removed from the quarters, the long bones are broken in half, midshaft, and the joints with articulated proximal-distal members are boiled for soup or cooked in a stew. Other anatomical parts are treated slightly differently. Ribs are frequently roasted and eaten without further preparation. Alternatively, they may be broken into half slabs and cut into units of three half ribs and placed in a soup. Vertebral parts are always boiled together with other ingredients for a soup. The head is prepared in several alternative ways. The most common method is roasting in a small "earth-oven." With this method, the head is singed to remove the hair and, today, frequently wrapped in aluminum foil prior to being placed in a small pit where a fire has been previously kindled. The head is then buried in the hot sand, and an additional fire is kindled on top. Upon removal from the pit, the normal method of preparation is to slice around the ears and then to cut the lips away from the bone, skinning back from the mouth toward the neck. Generally, as the skin is removed, parts are removed as they are exposed rather than skinning the entire head first. For instance, as the skin is worked back toward the jaw and the muscles exposed, the jaw is broken loose and cut from the skull by transverse cuts in the articulator socket of the ramus. The tongue is removed at the same time by cutting through the tongue along the hyloid, leaving the latter attached to the skull. After the jaw and tongue are removed, the eyes are removed. These are consumed as delicacies after the careful removal of the pupil. Finally, the skull is split from the top, normally with an ax, and the brain is removed for consumption. The muscles are then cut from the jaw, and everything remaining is given to the dogs.

Alternative methods of cooking the head are to steam it in a bucket with a tight cover or to boil it in a bucket. Whatever the method, except for the skinning prior to boiling, the treatment of the head is otherwise the same.

Deletion of Parts from Sites

Thus far, I have described only food consumption. The reader will recall, from the description of butchering, that the lower legs were removed with the skin. Informants confirm that this is a rather recent practice; it began only when there was a tanning specialist in the local community. Today, skins may be sold or traded to the tanner who prepares them for "sale" to tourists and for export to novelty shops in a variety of local cities. The tanner also prepares hides as sleeping mats for many of the local families. The "grease of the foot" is used by the tanner, and "he wants them with the hide." "In the old days, we ate the feet." The informant continued to say that feet were frequently roasted together with heads in the old days, and both activities were sometimes performed by the herders "out on the range." The procedure was to place the feet (unskinned) in a fire to singe off the hair. Once this was accomplished, the char was scraped off and the feet placed back in the bed of coals and covered. They may remain there for up to two hours before being removed for consumption. Today, feet are rarely eaten and are commonly left attached to the skin. This means that the phalanges and metapodial are being deleted from the site as a direct function of the number of hides being sent to the tanner. In the instances of butchering that we have observed, these were the only bones remaining on the hides.

In addition to the "normal" pattern of deletion from the site, meat may be distributed to relatives or used as "payment of debts." The details of this process will be taken up later when the specific sites are discussed.

Disposal

Most sites that we visited have a trash area near the hogan or ramada; however, most bones disposed of from the house are dumped near the door. The dogs, which are not tethered, fight over the bones and drag them off for consumption. Animal parts that go in the "dump area" tend to be parts that are discarded together with a liquid, the remains of soups, or they may be parts that were eaten as roasted meat within the house. The latter are periodically collected together with other nonedible trash and disposed of in mixed trash bulk. Dogs scavenge this area, but they do not clean it of bones as they do the specific dog-feeding disposals that occur outside the door.

In addition to this patterning in disposal, the roasting pit is generally located adjacent to the dump area, and the remains of heads are more common in the dump area, since heads are almost always roasted outside.

Summary

The Navajo keep domestic herds of sheep. They butcher their sheep at residential locations for their own consumption. Thus, all parts of the animal are initially present at the site. Butchering is a distinctive process, and we can expect some minor destruction of anatomical parts, particularly the transverse processes of vertebrae, as a result of it. Butchered meat is consumed locally, and the methods described indicate that no breaking of bones is carried out for the express purpose of marrow extraction or the rendering of bone grease. Some breakage occurs, however, in preparation of long bone joints for "soup bones" and in the preparation of ribs for inclusion in soups, as well as skulls in roasting. Aside from the acts of dismemberment, there is nothing in the process of consumption that should reduce the number of identifiable anatomical parts present at a site.

Contemporary practices result in some deletions from the site, particularly phalanges, metapodials, and occasionally radio-cubiti which are sent together with the skin to a tanner. In addition, meat distributions to friends and relatives occur from time to time. Parts distributed depend on the relationship between the giver and receiver.

Disposal occurs locally, and untethered dogs have free access to all the discarded bones. With the exception of possible deletions, differences noted in the presence of anatomical parts on a Navajo site relative to their anatomical frequency should be attributable to differential destruction of parts by dogs.

The Archaeological Remains

The cooperating Navajo family practices a seasonal movement between two permanently maintained houses. The summer site is normally occupied between April and September, while the winter site is occupied between late September and late April or early March. The winter site has been occupied for 7 consecutive years, and the summer sites has been in use for more than 10 years.

The Winter Site

During the winter of 1969–1970, five people occupied this site for approximately 6 months (September–April). During that time, the butchering and consumption of meat was from three sources.

1. Two horses (one adult mare and one colt) were butchered and used as a source of meat in a major distribution to relatives and guests associated with a social event. Ten families participated in the event, and all shared the meat from the two horses. In addition, some sheep meat was given away, primarily consisting of rib slabs and upper rear legs. The informants were uncertain as to the number of pieces that had been given away, but they estimated that five rib slabs and four hams had been distributed. Informants also commented that they had received similar cuts of meat from others as gifts but were uncertain as to the number received.

2. Sheep, butchered and dying on the site, were the second major source of material contributing to the archaeological assemblage. All informants agreed that the winter had been particularly severe and approximately 24 first-year lambs had died during the winter. In addition, 9 adult sheep died during the winter from a combination of old age and the severe winter. Informants estimated that 13 of the dead lambs were fed directly to the dogs. Of the additional 11 dead lambs, 4 died away from the site and their bodies were eaten by "wild animals." Seven were butchered for human consumption of the "choice parts," and the rest was given to the dogs. The 9 adult sheep who died were all butchered for human consumption. Eight prime adult sheep were killed and butchered specifically for meat in conjunction with the ceremonial feasts previously mentioned. A total of 37 sheep were consumed by dogs and humans on the site during the winter occupation of 1969–1970.

3. In addition to the aforementioned meat, some beef was purchased in supermarkets in Tuba City, Arizona. Informants estimated that five shopping trips were made during the winter. On two of these, some stocking up was done.

Cuts preferred were the cheaper ones (which generally contain bones), and, on two occasions, "several" soup bones were obtained from the butcher free of charge.

The Ethnoarchaeological Remains

The winter site was mapped, and the bones were collected by areas of the site designated by informants as "natural use areas." Each sample was bagged and returned to Albuquerque for study. Inventories were made for each sample by species and anatomical part, noting articulations and breakage patterns as well as evidence of butchering or dog gnawing. Remains of the horses, store-bought cuts of beef, and the sheep bones were recovered. It is interesting to note that the horses were represented by only the lower left leg; presumably, all other parts were distributed. Our concern is with the sheep bones recovered. Table 3.5 summarizes the inventory of recovered anatomical parts. This list is to be read as the minimal number of animals as a measure of survivorship of bones. That is, no attempt was made to match parts (see Chaplin 1971: 70–75) or otherwise to estimate the original number of individual animals present.

On the winter site, a minimum of 21.5 sheep are represented by mandibular elements. It should be noted that this is *less* than we know to have been present on the site during the winter of 1969–1970. The archaeological assemblage under-represents by some 41.9% the known population of animals present. In addition to this indication of attrition, examination of the percentages demonstrated that many parts of the anatomy are very poorly represented. Obtaining a mean value of the assemblage as a measure of its "fullness," the result is a value of only 20.6%. This means that the average bone represents only 20.6% of the bones that should be present, given the MNI estimate if complete skeletons had been the original condition of the animals represented. This low value is consistent with the contrast between the known number of 37 individuals as opposed to the 21.5 "archaeologically visible." Attrition on the bone assemblage is high, based on the known population initially present.

Age Structure of the Archaeological Population

Given the fact that mandibles represented the greatest number of individuals, these were tabulated in terms of patterns of tooth eruption. Table 3.3 lists the frequency of mandibles relative to differing patterns of tooth eruption, together with a scale of eruption times taken from Silver (1963).

Several points are interesting. First, all mandibles that had milk premolars were also characterized by molars *in the process* of eruption. No mandibles occurred with a molar in place without the presence of another in the process of eruption. This is a condition only characteristic of animals during the second half of their growth year. Since most lambs are born in March–April, this pattern is only characteristic of the period of the year between September and early March,

Table 3.3

Tabulation of Sheep Mandibles by Dental Pattern—Navajo Winter Site[a]

Dental pattern	Right	Left	Total	Age estimate of the pattern[b]	MNI
$D_2D_3D_4(M_1)$	2	5	7	less than 3 months	3.5
$D_2D_3D_4M_1(M_2)$	3	4	7	9–12 months	3.5
$D_2(D_3D_4)M_1M_2(M_3)$	1	1	2	18–24 months	1.0
$P_2P_3P_4M_1M_2(M_3)$	2	2	4	23–25 months	2.0
$P_2P_3P_4M_1M_2M_3$	9	7	16	adult greater than 2 years	8.0
$P_2P_3P_4M_1M_2M_3$	3	4	7	very old individuals	3.5

[a] (M) indicates tooth is erupting but not yet up to the height of adjacent previously erupted teeth.

(D_3D_4) indicates that the permanent teeth are in the process of pushing out the milk teeth.

D indicates milk premolars.

[b] Age estimates taken from Silver (1963:263).

exactly the period of the year during which we know that the assemblage accumulated.

Comparison of the age structure indicated through comparative tooth eruption and informant information as to the age of animals contributing to the faunal population is instructive. Informants estimated that, of the 37 animals known to have contributed to the population, 20 were "first-year lambs," that is, animals born the previous spring, 6–12 months in age. Thirteen were said to be prime adults (animals with all their teeth but not old), which would place them between 2 and 5 years of age. Four were old animals—"pets"—which are generally greater than 4 years of age. Figure 3.6 compares the age structure, as derived from mandibles and the expected numbers based on informant information.

Several points seem clear from these comparisons. Informants never mentioned animals being present that would have been less than 3 months in age, yet such animals are clearly indicated by the mandibles! Informants agreed that they generally abandoned their winter residence prior to the time of lambing. Animals born prior to or during a move of the flocks were apt to die more frequently than those penned and separated at the time of lambing. It would appear that at least a few births occurred prior to their move and that some new-born lambs died. More interesting, however, are the contrasts in the proportions of animals of different ages indicated by informants versus the structure visible from studies of tooth eruption sequences. Only 17.5% of the animals reported to have been killed or to have died at the winter site in the "first-year lamb" category are "visible" archaeologically, while 84.6% of the animals indicated as adult are represented archaeologically, if we place those between 18 and 24 months of age in the adult category; 87.5% of the old individuals are represented archaeologically. Clearly, the younger the animals, the less accurately they are represented in

Table 3.4

Comparative Data on Age Structure of the Navajo Winter Site
Sample by Dental Patterns and Informant Accounts

	Mandibles		Informants	
	MNI's	%	Numbers	%
0–6 months	3.5	16.3	0	0.0
6–12 months	3.5	16.3	20	54.1
12–18 months	0.0	0.0	0	0.0
18–24 months	3.0	13.9	0	0.0
24–48 months	8.0	37.2	13	35.13
more than 48 months	3.5	16.3	4	10.8

the archaeological assemblage. The age patterning indicates that attrition is not random with age, but, instead, it is patterned such that the younger the animal, the greater the rate of attrition.

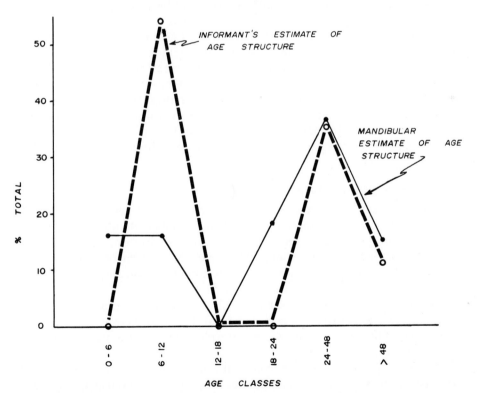

Figure 3.6 Comparison of the age structure of the Navajo winter sheep population as indicated by dental patterning and informant accounts.

The Summer Site

This location was occupied by the Percy family for approximately 6 months during the 1969–1970 period. Informants agree that they moved here prior to lambing and that all animals represented at the site were the remains of butchered animals selected as prime adult sheep. They suggested that, concerning patterns of consumption, disposal, and deletion of anatomical parts from the site, conditions were the same as those reported for the winter site. Dogs were present and had free range over the area where bones were disposed. The major difference in disposal concerned skins; fewer summer skins are sent to the tanner since, after shearing in the spring, the fleece has not recovered well enough for commercial use.

The summer site has been used for a longer period than the winter site and was not "cleaned" of bone from previous years; therefore, the number of individuals represented archaeologically cannot be directly compared to the number of butchered animals for the summer of 1970. Nevertheless, the age structure of the population should be unaltered by the lack of control since informants insisted that butchering during the previous summers had been similar to that of 1970, namely, only prime sheep were killed in summer residence.

Informants report that, during the summer of 1970, 11 sheep were butchered, and one old "pet" died of natural causes. Of the 11 selected for butchering, 8 were thought to be around 38 months old, 2 around 27 months, and 1 about 15 months in age. The "pet" was thought to be a little more than 72 months in age. Such a distribution yields a mean age for the death population of 37.3 months as compared to the value of 24 months obtained for the winter site. Also, in contrast to the winter site, informants indicate a unimodal age structure in favor of mature animals for the summer site while, on the winter site, a bi-modal age structure is present.

The Archaeological Remains

The inventory of recovered remains is summarized in Table 3.5. It is clear that there are more parts represented by substantial numbers in this assemblage than was the case for the winter site. The mean survivorship estimate is 34.9%, as compared to 20.6% for the winter. Similarly, the pattern of anatomical part frequency is different. For instance, on the summer site, the most common bone was the distal humerus; on the winter site, the mandible was most common, and the distal humerus was represented by only 32.6% of the animals indicated by mandibles. In short, there is a real structural difference between the recovered populations of bones from the two sites, as well as meaningful differences in their overall survivorship.

The age structure of the archaeological population was evaluated, as in the previous case, by a tabulation of mandibles for patterns of tooth eruption. Tables 3.6 and 3.7 summarize these data using the same techniques that were employed for the winter site.

Table 3.5

Anatomical Parts Recovered from Two Navajo Sites on which Bones
from Complete Animals Had Been Abandoned and
Subsequently Gnawed by Dogs

Anatomical part	Navajo winter site sheep[a]		Summer site sheep[b]	
	MNI	%	MNI	%
Horn cores	3.0	13.9	2.5	13.8
Skull (1)	16.5	76.7	11.0	61.1
Mandible	21.5	100.0	14.0	77.7
Atlas	4.0	18.6	5.0	27.7
Axis	4.0	18.6	5.0	27.7
Cerv. V.	3.7	17.2	8.3	46.1
Thor. V.	3.2	14.9	3.0	16.6
Lumb. V.	4.5	20.9	5.6	31.1
Pelvis (2)	9.5	44.2	13.0	72.2
Ribs	1.9	8.8	2.4	13.3
Sternum	.3	1.4	.2	1.1
Scapula	6.0	27.9	14.5	80.5
Humerus prox.	1.5	6.9	2.5	13.8
Humerus dist.	7.0	32.6	18.0	100.0
Radio-C prox.	7.5	34.8	12.5	69.4
Radio-C dist.	2.5	11.6	10.0	55.5
Carpals	2.7	12.6	1.8	10.0
Metacarpal prox.	2.5	11.6	5.0	27.7
Metacarpal dist.	2.5	11.6	3.5	19.4
Femur prox.	1.5	6.9	7.0	38.8
Femur dist.	2.5	11.6	3.5	19.4
Tibia prox.	4.5	20.9	8.0	44.4
Tibia dist.	7.5	34.8	13.0	72.2
Tarsals	3.6	16.7	4.0	22.2
Ast.	3.0	13.9	5.0	27.7
Cal.	2.5	11.6	5.0	27.7
Metatarsal prox.	4.0	18.6	4.5	25.0
Metatarsal dist.	2.5	11.6	5.5	30.5
Phalange 1	.87	4.0	.87	4.8
Phalange 2	.62	2.9	.62	3.4
Phalange 3	.37	1.7	.37	2.1

[a] $\Sigma = 640.0$
$N = 31$
$\bar{X} = 20.6$
[b] $\Sigma = 1082.9$
$N = 31$
$\bar{X} = 34.9$

The first point to note is that no individuals representing a pattern of tooth eruption for the second half of the yearly maturation sequence are represented in the mandibular sample. Of course, this is consistent with the fact that the site

Table 3.6

Tabulation of Sheep Mandibles from the Navajo Summer Site by Dental Pattern

Dental pattern	Right	Left	Total	Age estimate of pattern	MNI
$D_2D_3D_4(M_1)$	2	2	4	less than 3 months	2.0
$D_2D_3D_4M_1$	1	0	1	12–18 months	.5
$P_2P_3P_4M_1M_2M_3$	12	8	20	adult greater than 2 years	10.0
$P_2P_3P_4M_1M_2M_3$	1	2	3	very old individuals	1.5

was occupied only during the spring and summer months. Second, the major discrepancy between the age pattern of tooth eruption and the informants' information as to age structure (Table 3.7) is seen in animals of less than 3 months of age. It appears that informants did not inform us regarding the numbers of lambs that died during the first few weeks of life. This is almost certainly a function of the manner in which questions were phrased—always in terms of animals butchered for consumption. Figure 3.7 illustrates the relative fit between the age structure of the population as estimated by two independent sources of information.

It is clear that the fit between the two sources of information is very close. In fact, if the young lambs were omitted from the comparison, it would be nearly perfect.

Comparison between the Two Assemblages

These two samples provide an interesting set of contrasts. Table 3.8 summarizes some properties of the two assemblages.

General survival appears to be greater as measured by the mean percentage of anatomical parts surviving when the population is composed primarily of adult

Table 3.7

Comparison between Age Structure of the Summer Site as Indicated by Patterns of Tooth Eruption in Mandibles and as Estimated by Informants

Age classes	Mandibles		Informants estimates	
	MNI	%	MNI	%
0–6 months	2.0	14.3	0.0	0.0
6–12 months	0.0	0.0	0.0	0.0
12–18 months	0.5	3.6	1.0	8.33
18–24 months	0.0	0.0	0.0	0.0
24–48 months	10.0	71.4	10.0	83.3
48 months +	1.5	10.7	1.0	8.33

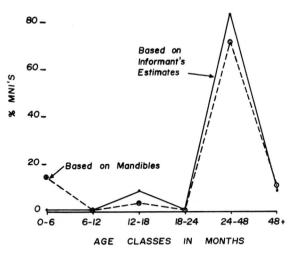

Figure 3.7 Comparison of the age structure of the Navajo summer sheep population as indicated by dental patterning and informant accounts.

Table 3.8

Comparative Data, Navajo Winter and Summer Camps

Dimension of comparison	Navajo summer camp	Navajo winter camp
Minimum number of individuals represented in faunal collection	18.0	21.5
Mean age of population as estimated by informants	37.3 months	24.0 months
Mean percentage of anatomical parts recovered	34.9%	20.6%
Number of lone bone splinters	188	212
Number of rib splinters		
Number of lone bone	61	17
articulator ends	126	108
Ratio: Long bone splinters / Long bone articulators	1.49	1.96
Percentage of adults in population (informants)	91.66%	45.94%

animals. Judging from the number of long bone splinters versus the number of articulator ends, either there were more individuals represented by long bone shaft fragments than articulator ends on the winter site or bones were broken up more extensively. The latter is unlikely, and the higher long bone splinter to articulator end ratio probably reflects the greater number of individuals reported to have been present on the winter site relative to the number "visible" in the archaeological assemblage.

Inspection of Figure 3.8 illustrates that, regardless of the factors conditioning the differential survival of parts on the two sites, the result is not a simple allometric relationship. When things have a greater rate of survival, as on the summer site, this rate does not reflect that pattern of survival on the winter site.

These two sites are considered by both the investigators and the occupants to be essentially identical, namely, that complete skeletons were being introduced to the archaeological record. No human behavior pattern, either butchering or consumption, was contributing to the actual deletion of parts from the assemblage that was visible archaeologically. On both sites, a constant agent of

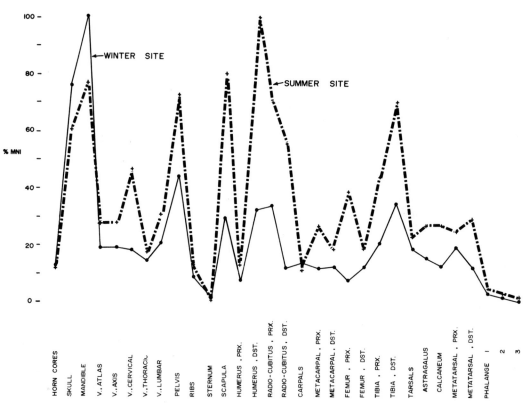

Figure 3.8 Inventories of anatomical part frequencies surviving on the Navajo summer and winter sites.

attrition was active: the same dogs who had equal and free access to all anatomical parts discarded on the site. Thus, as opposed to the Eskimo data in which the agents of attrition were held constant, but the parts made available to them were considered variable in terms of human decision making, *no such differences characterized the two Navajo samples.* The only difference between the two samples was in the age structure of the animals exposed to attrition through dog destruction. This observation led to the surmise that differences in the age of the animals exposed to a constant agent of attrition could condition the pattern of survival noted among different anatomical parts.

Summary of Empirical Findings and Hunches as to Causes of Differences among Anatomical Part Frequencies Noted from Assemblage to Assemblage

1. *Dogs may, in fact, modify the character of a faunal assemblage.* This conclusion is supported by the Nunamiut feeding record and by both Navajo samples. The marked divergence between the known anatomical inventory of the parts fed to the Eskimo dogs and the parts remaining for observation after the dogs were fed shows that their behavior may radically change the appearance of a faunal assemblage.

We may expect that dogs are not unique and that any gnawing agent may substantially change the original character of a faunal assemblage.

2. *One may not be able to recognize the "presence" of agents of attrition—such as dogs—through the simple comparison of patterns of bone survival.* This conclusion is warranted by a comparison of part frequencies among the samples from the Nunamiut dog yards (Table 3.1). We see that what survives is conditioned by the character of the assemblage subjected to attrition, as well as by the modifications that the dogs may make on an original population. In short, a faunal assemblage can be expected frequently to be the result of two or more "causes" of variation in interaction. When the latter situation holds true, the analytical task of "partitioning" the variance among interacting, but potentially independent, sources may not be easy.

3. *Even when the initial population is identical regarding anatomical parts, simple formal comparison of patterns of bone survival may not reveal the action of an agent of attrition.* In other words, when we know that complete skeletons characterized the initial population and that identical agents of attrition operated on this population, the patterns of bone survival may be quite different. We saw this in the Navajo comparisons.

4. Given these observations, we suggest that, since the only known difference between the two Navajo samples concerned the age structure of the initial populations, variations in the age structure of the initial population may well condition the character of the survival patterning manifested by an archaeological assemblage. This suggestion is not incompatible with a number of known facts. For instance, we know that the sequence of epiphysial union for different bones is

variable. Since epiphysial union is one aspect of a growth process, we may anticipate that other aspects, such as densification, may also be characterized by a
non-allometric pattern of development with increasing age. If the latter were the
case and if bone density itself conditioned survival probabilities, as has been
suggested by Brain (1969), then we might expect a range of variable survival
patterns depending upon the age structure of the initial population subjected to
an agent of attrition, all other things being equal.

Looking at Animals and Their Bones

Thus far, we have looked at bones in varying contexts in an attempt to recognize some of the factors that might condition variability in parts remaining on
archaeological sites where an agent of attrition was active. As we have noted, dogs
have demonstrable effects on the relative survival of bone, and the observed
survival rate is not directly proportional to the frequency of bone subjected to
dog gnawing. This means that we need to investigate some property of the bones
themselves that may condition their differential survival probabilities. The property judged most likely to monitor "survival probabilities" is bone density.

In addition, we have noted that, when the structure of a faunal population is
held constant (anatomically complete animals were exposed to dogs) and the
agents of attrition are held constant (the same dogs acted as agents), the population of bones surviving is different. The aforementioned conditions were met in
the comparison between the winter and summer Navajo samples, and it was
noted that the only difference between the two was in the age structure of the
animals fed to the dogs. From this observation, we suspect that bone density may
well vary non-allometrically with age, and, therefore, information on the character of bone density maturation is needed.

We must interrupt the presentation to relate some of the history of this research, since the sequence of work is reflected in the inadequacy of the controls
obtained. The field observations on faunal assemblages were made over the
period 1969–1972 for both the Navajo and Nunamiut cases. In the fall of 1971,
the first steps were taken to obtain the controlled anatomical data on sheep, and
the specimen of caribou was collected during the summer of 1971. During this
period, prior to the analysis of the Navajo data, it was assumed that changes in
density were an allometric function of age; therefore, one or two animals were
judged sufficient to provide the necessary controls. Despite the fact that all the
anatomical parts for two sheep and one caribou were available for study in the
winter of 1971, the laboratory analysis was not conducted; that is, no actual
measurements of density were made until the winter of 1973. As will be seen, the
results of this analysis demonstrated that the assumption of allometric maturation in bone density was false. After initial analysis, we were successful in obtaining an additional sheep of known age for study to help the situation; however, the
work with the Nunamiut Eskimo was completed, and there was no way to obtain
additional data on caribou.

The procedure employed in studying the bones was not ideal, as we will explain. The first two sheep butchered were studied first. The procedure was to boil the anatomical parts in an antiformin solution for 7 hours. Bones were then allowed to dry, and these were stored in the laboratory for density measurements some 2 years later. In 1973, when the actual measurement of density was undertaken, the bones were simply removed from storage, and each was weighed. Then the bone was submerged in a volumetrically scaled glass container, and the volumetric increase noted when the bone was completely submerged was recorded. Given weight and volume, density was then calculated as weight per unit volume measured in milliliters and grams. Comparison of the results obtained for the two sheep then available (one killed at 6 months of age and the other killed at 90 months of age) indicated that the rates of increasing density with age varied highly for different bones. About 2 months later, we were able to obtain an additional sheep of known age for study (killed at 19 months of age). This animal was butchered in analogous parts, boiled in antiformin solution, and allowed to dry for 3 days at room temperature. Then the weighing procedure was started, part of the sample was weighed, and we were interrupted. The next day, we returned to the task and were unable to locate the notebook in which the observations of the previous day were recorded. Therefore, we started all over again weighing the bones that had been weighed the previous day. Later that afternoon, we found the data sheets from the previous day's work. Much to our surprise, bones that had been weighed twice on consecutive days did not exhibit identical values! In fact, there appeared to be consistent differences in weights such that all bones weighed the previous day exhibited slightly higher values. We reasoned that this must be a function of differential humidity in the storage room. We took out the bones from the first two sheep studied and weighed them again. Comparison with weights obtained some 2 months earlier confirmed our suspicion that discrepancies between values obtained at two different times was consistent and directional with the time of measurement. These comparisons suggested that there was a long-term effect and a short-term effect of storage. The longer the bone had been stored, the greater was the decrease in weight between independent measurements; however, this was not a simple uncomplicated linear relationship, but one modified, or fluctuating, on a daily basis, presumably as a function of daily variations in humidity. In order to overcome these sources of measurement error, we dipped all the bones from all animals in tap water in a basket, allowing them to be submerged for 5 seconds, and then we placed them immediately in a poultry incubator at a constant temperature setting of 102°F. We let the bones stay in the incubator for 7 days to the hour and then weighed them as quickly as possible. Results appeared to be more standard; however, since an incubator is probably not a perfect dehumidifier and all bones simply could not be simultaneously weighed, there is probably some measurement error here.

While working on the problem of weights, we decided that submerging the bones in water was not a very accurate measure of volume since spongy bone would absorb more water and, therefore, register depressed values for volume.

Therefore, we melted paraffin, dipped each bone as quickly as possible into the molten wax, removed the bone, and allowed it to cool slowly under a heat lamp for a half hour. After this, we let the wax cool further at room temperature for an additional half hour and then removed any obvious lumps of wax with a pocket knife. Later, volumetric measurements were made in the graduated cylinders. Finally, density values were calculated as weight per unit volume in grams and milliliters. Table 3.9 summarizes the density data for the three sheep and the caribou studied.

Several conclusions are evident from inspection of the data presented in Table 3.9. In general, densities are higher for bones of animals of greater age; however, this increase is not proportional among different anatomical parts; that is, this increase is non-allometric. For instance, we note that the density of the third phalanges for the 6-month sheep is .66, and the density of the same part for the 90-month sheep is .78. This is a difference of only .12, while the value for the pelvis (actually the innominate) is 1.03 in the 6-month sheep and 1.71 in the aged sheep—a difference of .68. The overall pattern of changing density with age is summarized in Figure 3.9, in which it is clear that density does not increase allometrically in all parts.

This means that, given a density effect on survival, differences in the age structure of a faunal population may not only result in different overall rates of survival for bones given a constant agent of attrition, but that there will also be differences in the relative survival of various parts, resulting in different patterns of assemblage composition. We anticipated this condition during the observations of the Navajo data. For instance, if we imagine a constant agent of attrition operative on the bones of a population of young individuals, we might expect that the mandible, skull, and atlas and axis vertebrae would numerically dominate the surviving population of bones. On the other hand, if the same agent was active on a population of old individuals, we might expect the mandible, pelvis, distal humerus, and distal tibia numerically to dominate the surviving population—a different qualitative pattern.

Another interesting observation is that the overall distribution of bone densities for the adult caribou are generally lower than the densities of analogous parts in the 90-month sheep. If a constant agent were at work on a mixed population of equal numbers of sheep and caribou, one would expect sheep bones to tend to dominate the surviving population. In our opinion, the observed differences in density are not so much directly attributable to species differences as it is to body size differences among species. Animals with large bodies exhibit increases in the surface area of the articulator surfaces of weight supporting bones as a function of increases in overall body weight, all other things being equal. If this impression is correct, then survival of parts from large mammals should be less likely than survival of analogous parts from animals of smaller body size, all other things being equal. This supposition is at least partially supported by empirical data.

John Yellen (n.d.) observed that bones from small antelope tended to have a greater survival rate on !Kung Bushman sites that did their anatomical analogues from larger animals. Yellen attributed this to differential treatment by the

Table 3.9

Bone Density Estimates for Three Sheep of Different Ages and One Caribou,
Expressed as Grams per Milliliter of Volume[a]

| Anatomical part | Sheep | | | Caribou |
	6 months	19 months	90 months	2.5 years?
Antler	—	—	—	—
(1) Skull	1.32	1.49	1.64	1.49
Mandible	1.40	1.51	1.76	1.55
Atlas	.97	1.42	1.50	1.45
Axis	1.01	1.37	1.39	1.38
Cerv. V.	1.01	1.25	1.29	1.26
Thor. V.	.98	1.28	1.37	1.28
Lumb. V.	.98	1.38	1.44	1.35
(2) Pelvis	1.03	1.34	1.71	1.52
Ribs	1.00	1.14	1.15	1.07
Sternum	.58	.59	.62	.76
(3) Scapula	1.05	1.18	1.69	1.40
Humerus prox.	.70	.78	.87	.87
Humerus dist.	1.10	1.16	1.72	1.41
Radio-C. prox.	1.03	1.27	1.65	1.33
Radio-C. dist.	.85	1.04	1.52	1.36
Carpals	.76	1.09	1.41	1.19
Metacarpal prox.	.79	1.26	1.30	1.25
Metacarpal dist.	.94	.96	1.35	1.28
Femur prox.	.87	1.13	1.52	1.29
Femur dist.	1.00	1.07	1.21	1.14
Tibia prox.	.91	1.03	1.54	1.19
Tibia dist.	.87	1.15	1.69	1.46
Tarsals	.84	1.12	1.54	1.29
Ast.	.81	1.11	1.53	1.28
Cal.	.86	1.15	1.55	1.28
Metatarsal prox.	.86	1.25	1.36	1.33
Metatarsal dist.	.86	1.06	1.31	1.20
Phalange 1	.68	.71	.80	.90
Phalange 2	.68	.71	.80	.81
Phalange 3	.66	.68	.78	.76

[a] All values are means for analogous parts in a single animal. For instance, the value entered for proximal humerus is the mean of the observed values for both right and left sides.
  (1) is the value for the base of the occiput.
  (2) is the value for the acetabulum only.
  (3) is the value for the scapula head only.
The most dense element in the anatomy is the tooth. We could find no differences between mature maxilary and mandibular teeth.

Bushman, namely, that bones of the larger antelope were more commonly broken during the consumption process. This may well be true, but our guess is that, if this is so, the difference is related to bone density differences between the large and small animals. Thus, in Yellen's data, we may be seeing a compound effect of

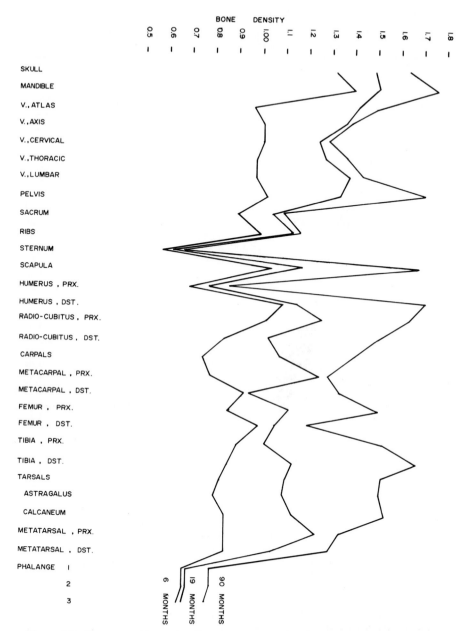

Figure 3.9 Summary of bone density measurements for three sheep of different ages.

greater breakage by Bushman as well as higher natural attrition rates for analo-gous parts from larger animals. (For Yellen's discussion, Yellen [n.d.: 52–53].)

The degree to which species can be expected to exhibit different overall patterns in bone density is only scantily indicated in the data available. For instance, a linear correlation between the density values for the caribou and the 90-month sheep yield a correlation coefficient of .74. A similar linear correlation between the 90-month sheep and the 6-month sheep yields a correlation coefficient of .71. This comparative result would lead one to suspect that age differences within a species may be at least as important a source of differential survival patterning as are the differences among the species represented. Given the fact that only two species have been studied, the domain of relevance of such a generalization cannot be specified; however, ungulates may well be the relevant domain.

Summary

Initial empirical study led us to the tentative conclusion that (a) survival probabilities of bones acted on by an agent of attrition vary with bone density; (b) also, when the agent of attrition was constant (the same dogs) and the structure of the initial population was constant (varying frequencies of complete skeletons), comparisons between controlled populations of bone showed that survival patterns were very different. The only known and suspected condition of relevance that was different between the two cases was the age structure of the initial populations. Therefore, we suggested that patterns of maturation in bone, as monitored by bone density, would show a non-allometric pattern of growth. If this were true, we would expect initial populations composed of animals of different ages to exhibit different survival patterning, all other things being equal.

Investigation of the actual anatomy of animals of varying ages showed that, in fact, bone density varied considerably with age and that the pattern of increasing density was non-allometric. A clear relationship between bone densities for animals of varying ages and the overall survival patterning among anatomical parts for populations of mixed age structure has yet to be demonstrated. If we can accomplish this, we will have offered an explanation for at least some observed and expected patterning in the survival frequencies of anatomical parts, and we may well be able to develop analytical methods of general utility to archaeologists.

Worrying about Dynamics

Thus far, we have presented a large body of data. Most of this is static information with only minor implications for dynamics. If we are to successfully develop a method that would let us attribute meaning to the variations in statics (differences in proportional frequencies among anatomical parts from one place to another), we must begin to explore the character of the dynamics that may bring variable patterning into existence. In this task, we must employ some facts that we know, some things that we suspect, and at least some relatively uninformed assumptions to develop a model of dynamics which, if correct, would let us anticipate the patterning thus far documented. What follows is an argument concerning the things we do not know but that we suspect to characterize the interplay of variables in the dynamics or transformation of a population of bones from one formal condition to another.

Some Things We Suspect but Do Not Really Understand in Detail

We suspect that, *(1)* all other things being equal, when bones are acted upon by an agent of attrition, their relative survival will be some function of their density, and *(2)* bones vary in their relative densities as a function of *(a)* the age of the individual from which the bones were derived and *(b)* the species of the animal from which the bones were derived; also, as a result of other research (see Sissons 1971), we may further anticipate that there will be some fluctuation in bone density in response to *(c)* the nutritional state of the animal at death.

We argue further that, all other things being equal, the relative survival potential of a bone will be some function of the strength of the agent acting upon the bones. There are at least three classes of such agents: chemical, physical, and biological. Under chemical attrition, we include bone destruction as a result of attack by soil acids, whether or not these are produced by microbes, leaching, or similar phenomena. Under physical attrition, we include cryoturbation, rolling, crushing by overburden, and so forth. We argue that the *rate of attrition* from all these agents depends on the porosity or density of the bone; porous bone dissolves more quickly, crushes more readily, or washes away more easily. Biological agents include gnawing by carnivores, primarily for fats and protein, and gnawing by rodents, primarily for minerals (we include destruction in the animal's digestive tract under the chemical classification). We note that biological agents also destroy less dense bone more readily and that the effect of a biological agent, as opposed to that of a chemical or physical agent, would be primarily in the "spotty" nature of its relevance. Carnivores are unlikely to attack compact bone, since there is little nourishment in its structure; however, if a carnivore were starving with only a compact bone available, the animal might attack it. Generally, however, we may expect attack of a compact bone by a carnivore to be due to the fact that the bones were actually containers of less dense and more nourishing matter, such as marrow. This type of bone is likely to be broken, but its destruction is improbable.

Rodent gnawing should have roughly the same effect, in that the less compact bone is more easily gnawed. Thus, while both rodents and carnivores, especially hyenas, are capable of destroying bone completely, the sequence of destruction on a large sample of anatomical parts is likely to be a simple function of density.

Modeling the Destruction of Bone: An Initial Description of Dynamics

We may write an equation that summarizes the destruction of a bone as a function of time. We expect that the rate of bone destruction is approximately inversely proportional to density and proportional to the ratio of surface area to volume (bone with more surface area is destroyed more rapidly):

(I) $$\frac{dD}{dt} = a\left(\frac{-S/V}{D}\right)$$

where S = surface area
V = volume
D = density

We also anticipated that the rate of destruction should be proportional to the strength of the agent (a) as measured by soil pH, size of jaw, mass of overburden, and so on, depending upon the context.

The surface–volume ratio is approximately constant for most bones, and, therefore, we can combine such effects with a as a constant in a first-order approximation assumed for the purposes of this argument to be a sufficient description (Equation II).

(II) $$\frac{dD}{dt} = \frac{-A}{D}$$

This equation has a solution.

(III) $$D(t) = \sqrt{D_0{}^2 - 2At}$$

where the positive root is relevant.

Since a bone at disappearance has density zero, we may write the relationship as follows:

(IV) $$D_0{}^2 = 2AT$$

Equation III gives the density during decay for any initial density (D_0). Figure 3.10 shows that bones of low D_0 disappear quickly, while bones of high initial density are, for a long time, essentially unaffected in their frequency. Thus at time t_1, bones of initial density H are completely decayed, bones of initial density G are

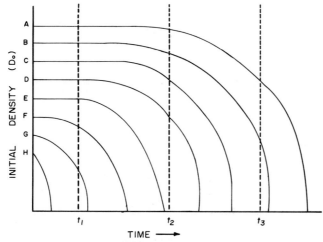

Figure 3.10 Graph of survival probabilities for bones of differing density at different times during an attritional process.

greatly reduced, and bones of initial density F are only slightly reduced. On the other hand, bones of initial density $A,B,C,D,$ and E are still very close to their original densities. These density changes would correspond to our observations had we excavated this site at time t_1.

If our excavation had encountered this assemblage at time t_2, we would have noted that bones of original density a are still very close to their original state, bones of initial densities $F,G,$ and H are completely decayed, and bones of initial density $B,C,D,$ and E are considerably modified.

Figure 3.11 shows that, whether we excavate the site at time $t_1, t_2,$ or $t_3,$ or at any other time, the relation of frequency surviving to density is a sigmoid function having asymptotes at $P = 0$ and $P = 1$ (we assume here a rescaling from percentages to a scale from zero to one) such that, for all density values of D_0 equal to or less than alpha (α), the survival is zero. Similarly, for all initial densities (D_0) equal to or greater than beta (β), the expected proportion surviving is 1.0 or 100%; that is, all survive. This is necessarily true for any decay function (A). Of course, it is conceivable (and likely in many archaeological cases) that the most dense bone in the assemblage had an initial density (D_0) less than beta (β). In such cases, no anatomical part would be represented in its original depositional frequency upon excavation. However, insofar as any bones survive their observed frequencies will be biased according to their original density.

Thus far, we have modeled our expectations in terms of agents that are continuously active. The analysis for gnawing destruction proceeds along rather different lines, we observe that some bones exist (adult teeth, for example) that may exceed the capacity to destroy exhibited by gnawing animals. We anticipate that the maximum bone density capable of being affected by a given animal will be a complex function of the animal's nutritional state and jaw power. Some animals, hyenas for example, probably are capable of reducing all or most of the

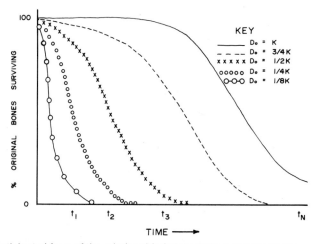

Figure 3.11 Anticipated form of the relationship between the survival of bones and bone density when acted upon by an agent of attrition.

bones in the anatomy of their prey, while small dogs are probably unable to exert sufficient force to destroy many of the more dense elements in a medium-sized ungulate form.

Nevertheless, we may anticipate the degree of destruction caused by a given agent to show essentially the same relations to density as would result from chemical or physical destruction (as modeled in Figure 3.11), all other things being equal. Unfortunately, "all other things are probably not equal." For instance, if we imagine that dogs are regularly fed previously disarticulated anatomical parts that have already been partically exploited for their meat by another agent (man), then the dogs would have equal access to all articulator ends at an initial condition of hunger. Under such a situation, we may anticipate that destruction may well occur as a function of density. On the other hand, picture a situation in which dogs are periodically fed or have access to complete and articulated bodies of animals. As the dog feeds, his hunger is abated and, by the time the articulator ends of a bone are exposed (are available) for consumption, the dog is no longer hungry and ignores or "wastes" this potential food. Under such conditions, we might expect destruction to proceed somewhat independently of density and to be related more to the relative exposure of a part or its placement in the anatomy relative to parts are high food value. In other words, the degree of articulation and association with meat may well bias behavior away from a predictable pattern directly related to density. It may not be possible to anticipate the behavior of the dog (or many other potential destructive agents) mechanistically, as was argued for agents such as soil acids, pressure, and so on.

In addition, our model of destruction assumes continuous action over time unmodified structurally by previous change. For instance, if soil acids cause a reduction in density, this does not modify the probability that the part will be further modified by soil acids. On the other hand, a gnawing dog may chew up bones as a function of their density; however, substantial destruction at point a in time almost certainly reduces the probability that there will be further destruction at a later time by the dog, all other things being equal, that is, assuming the absence of additional agents such as soil acids. On the other hand, if a gnawing agent partially destroys a bone as part of a depositional episode and other agents begin to operate, such as soil acids, and the archaeologist comes along and observes a survival population at an even later time, we may anticipate a major reduction in demonstrable relationships between the proportions of bones surviving and the density of bones as measured immediately after the death of an animal. That is, the "effective initial densities" would be different from the "initial densities" as estimated through the study of prepared skeletal material.

We may expect a further difference concerning dog hunger. A well-nourished animal may not destroy all bones of any density. This would mean, in our terms, that bones whose density was less than "alpha" may be expected to survive at levels greater than zero. Similarly, more dense bone may, in some cases, remain untouched depending upon the size and hunger of the agent; this results in a variable (beta) conditioned by hunger and size of the agent somewhat independently of the pattern of survival for bones of moderate density.

Despite these complications when dealing with gnawing agents as opposed to chemical or physical agents, we suggest that density related destruction and the resulting proportion of bones surviving in an archaeological site can be best anticipated by a simple curve, sigmoid in form, asymptotic at zero and one, and monotonically increasing. Further details cannot as yet be specified since we do not know the details of the distribution of the destruction function *(A)*. In addition, several weak (and relatively unimportant) assumptions were made—these will affect the result only in minor ways given our understanding of density related decay patterns.

Complicating Things with Our Suspected Understanding

Thus far, we have modeled a set of dynamics relating the progress of decay and, hence, proportional survival of bones of variable density under action by an attritional agent responsive primarily to bone density. As noted earlier, we observed that bone density is not a static condition of a species but is, in fact, variable with age, most likely with nutritional state, and possibly with other conditioning variables. This means that, before this model may be used in analysis, we must complicate the picture with several additional arguments.

The First Operational Argument: Taking into Consideration the Non-Allometric Densification of Bone with Changes in Age

As was noted in the description of the method of density determination, we found that density change with age for a single anatomical part is not a simple allometric pattern. Instead, some parts grow continuously throughout the animal's life, while other parts grow in spurts. Within this second class, there is further variability, in that some parts reach their maximum density after two growing seasons, some after three, and some parts, the distal tibia being a good example, seem to exhibit a densification spurt every year until the animal dies. This non-allometric pattern is critical to archaeological analysis of fauna. We can expect all but the oldest animals to have density changes with aging such that an error of 3 or 4 months in estimating the age of the animals subject to attrition can give rise to deceptive and dramatic differences in density. The result would be that an attempt to correlate survivorship of parts with density, uninformed as to the patterns of densification with age, would result in spuriously low correlations or none at all, depending upon the magnitude of the error in age estimation. This means that an age related reference dimension of density variation is crucial to any analysis that seeks to "reconstruct an original population from a surviving population.

We chose not to raise, kill, process, and measure a total sample of animals of variable age before attempting to develop an analytical procedure. Rather, we developed an age related frame of reference for density variation in sheep using the three animals previously studied (see Table 3.9). The values from the three animals were used to extrapolate density values for animals of ages not empirically studied. Furthermore, we argue that the trajectories indicated in the density values are, in reality, complicated by seasonal variations in density related to nutrition. Therefore, our extrapolation assumed a generally increasing trend of densification with age, overlaid by a damped sinusoidal component arising from seasonal variation in nutrition (Figure 3.12).

We do not have much empirical evidence of the character of the damping function, and it may well be complicated. For instance, one could argue that young animals are more subject to nutritional variance since, given rapid growth and densification, the magnitude of "delay" in growth due to poor nutrition would be some function of the actual rate of "potential growth." Thus, one might expect seasonal spurts in density change to be more marked prior to maturity. On the other hand, one could argue that nutritional variance might be less in immature animals since this variance is absorbed by the "mother" during the period of dependent feeding. If this were true, we would expect greater fluctuations in mature breeding females, less in adult males, and minimal effects in young animals receiving milk from their mothers.

Aside from these speculations, there is empirical support for the reduction of density in bone as a function of age and/or nutritional state (see Sissons 1971). For instance, when investigating seasonally correlated faunal remains among the Nunamiut Eskimo, informants claimed the ability to identify the season of kill from a simple inspection of the bones. We questioned them extensively and tested their alleged ability with known cases and found that they were reliably accurate in their estimates of season of kill made upon inspection of simple splinters of long bone. They claimed that spring bone was "chalky" in appearance, thin walled, and capable of being easily perforated with a knife point. In contrast, they characterized bones from fall killed animals as having a slick polished appearance and as being thick walled and very difficult to penetrate with a knife point. We reasoned that they were observing attributes of porosity and, using a simple method of a pipet and vegetable dye in water, dropped a single drop on a flat or convex surface of bones known to come from fall and spring killed animals. Measurements were then taken of the absorption diameter for the dyed liquid. Diameters were regularly and significantly larger on bones of spring killed animals. We took these results to indicate that there was an absolute reduction in porosity (and hence density) of long bone shaft fragments in caribou during spring—the period of absolute nutritional low in the Anaktuvuk Pass area of Alaska. Assuming this is true, we would expect an absolute reduction in bone density with nutritional cycling rather than a simple damping or slowing down of the rate of increasing densification. Furthermore, we might anticipate that the magnitude of such reductions would be a function of the magnitude of seasonal fluctuations in production and, therefore, vary geographically within a species.

These uncertainties are further exacerbated by the fact that even the three empirical cases available for extrapolation are all for animals killed in fall (November); therefore, if any inaccuracies exist (and they most certainly do) in our assumptions as to the character of the damping function, we may anticipate better "fits" for data derived from fall populations and less accuracy for spring and summer populations.

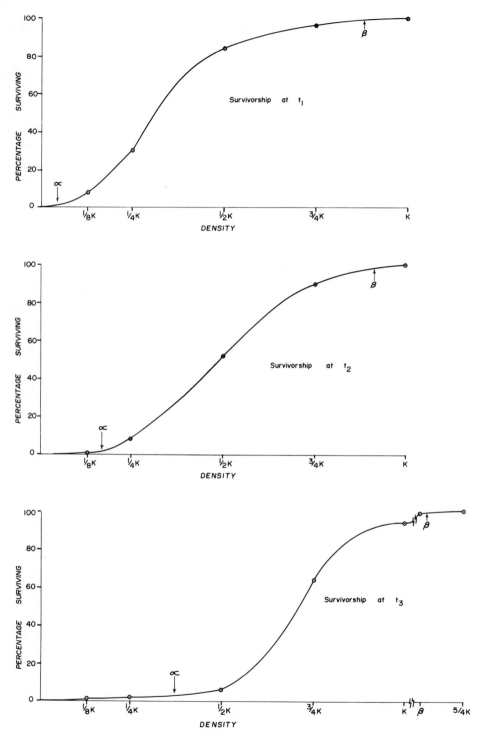

Figure 3.12 Anticipated survivorship curves for bones of different density at three different points in time during a decay process.

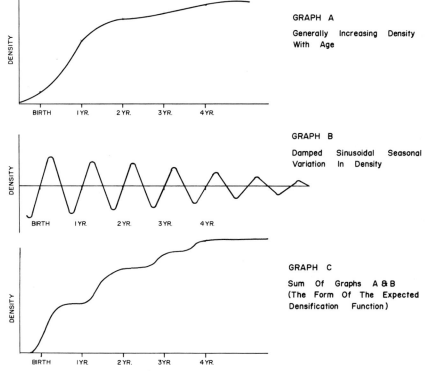

Figure 3.13 Model of changes in bone density with maturation and seasonal variation in nutrition.

No attempt was made to fit the densification curves to the sheep data, since these data are (and must remain so for the present) too sparse. The densification curves used in all further analysis are exemplified in Figure 3.14. This graph provides a direct reading of anticipated bone densities for any age between birth and 65 months of age. Clearly, what is needed is an empirical graph for each species to be studied. We chose to proceed with the development of an analytical method despite inadequate empirical data relative to the distribution of this important variable.

The Second Operational Argument: Approximating a Mathematical Form for the Survivorship Function

As we are presently unable to specify the precise mathematical form of the function relating survivorship to density, we must propose an approximation. For our purposes, we chose to approximate all possible distributions with the function:

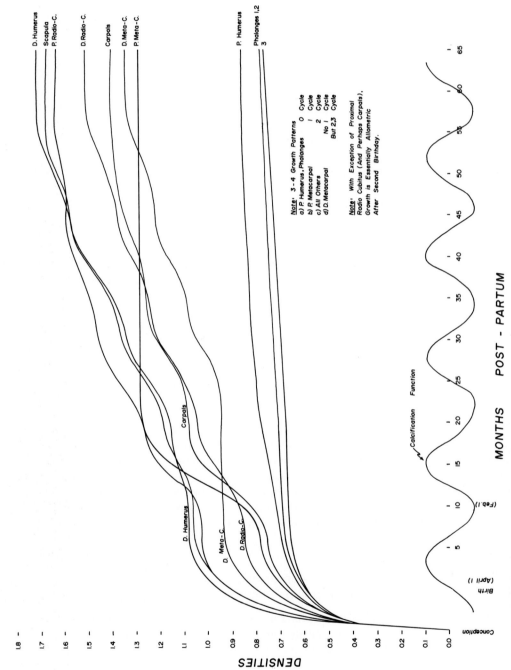

Figure 3.14 Interpolated pattern of density change with increasing age for selected parts of sheep.

120

(V) $F = P_1[\text{atan } (P_2) + \text{atan } (P_3 X - P_2)]$

F = the proportion surviving
X = the density of the element
P_1 = a proportionality constant
P_2 and P_3 = constants controlling the shape of the function

This arctangent function was chosen over several alternatives because it is simply analyzed geometrically, it requires few parameters, and it has the necessary asymptotic properties required by our argument thus far. The inflection point of F is the point where density $= P_2/P_3$ and where $F = P_1 \text{ atan } P_2$.

For those unfamiliar with analytical geometry, we note that the inflection point of this curve is the point at which F ceases to rise more rapidly or to accelerate with increases in density.

We note that the slope of the curve at the inflection point is given by:

$$\text{slope} = \frac{dF}{dX_{X=\text{inflect}}} = P_1 P_3$$

These values are interesting for several reasons. First, their computation makes possible the rapid sketching of the results of a given regression of Function V against data. Second, they constitute measurements in themselves regarding the details of density-related destruction of an assemblage—this is, of course, what is always implied by parameterization. Third, by inspection of these values, one can evaluate the degree to which the arguments presented fit empirical data.

The Third Operational Argument: The Problem of Variable Age Structure

An adequate evaluation of the arguments advanced thus far would be possible if we had concrete data that controlled for the age structure of the population of animals subjected to an agent of attrition, such that all animals were identical in age, and if the active agents of attrition were identical in their hunger and strength. Given these conditions, we would need only to plot the data and examine its conformity to our expectations for a survivorship curve with sigmoidal, monotonic form with asymptotic properties.

Obviously, we do not have such data. We are, therefore, forced to seek a means of evaluation that employs data that conforms to the conditions an archaeologist might face, that is, a heterogeneous population of animals regarding age, and a potentially variable matrix of attrition regarding the behavior of the agents. This means that, in the absence of the required data on the age structure of a population needed to determine the density values of relevance, we must apportion the variance of a survival population among several scales of density reflecting changes throughout the life of an animal. In short, we must proceed to the analysis with a goal of "predicting the age composition of the population acted upon" when we have reason to suspect that (a) only complete animals were subjected to an agent of attrition and (b) the only source of modification of an assemblage from the original state of a complete skeleton to a subsequently observed survival population was some agent of attrition. The prediction must, of course, exhibit some reasonable "fit" between observed survival frequencies and anticipated frequencies under some estimated age structure. We have three sets of data available with which to evaluate the procedure: the Navajo winter and summer occupations, where we know both (a) the seasons, relative to the season of birth, during which animals were killed, and (b) the age structure of the population subjected to dog gnawing. In these cases, the power of the agent may be assumed to be constant since the same dogs were responsible for both populations; however, their relative hunger is not known. Finally, we have one Eskimo assemblage known "before and after" attrition.

In order to make more explicit our reasoning in the development of a fitting technique, we will present an example of our expectations. Since we know that most ungulates are characterized by distinct seasons of birth and most births tend to occur in spring (in most places, in temperate settings during March and April), the animals that could be present in a population during any month of the year are roughly determined. For instance, most lambs are born in late March and early April. This means that, if we were to examine a sheep population in November, we might anticipate animals of 8 months, animals of 20 months (8 + 12), of 32 months [8 + (2)(12)], of 44 months [8 + (3)(12)], and so forth. On the other hand, if we examined a population during July, the ages of animals potentially present in the population would be quite different. We would find animals of 4 months, of 16 months (4 + 12), of 28 months [4 + (2)(12)], of 40 months [4 + (3)(12)], and so on. In other words, since births occur only at one time during the year, each month of the year has a different signature regarding the age of animals that could be present in a population at that time. In turn, this means that, if a human group (or another agent) kills animals at a given time of the year or during a given month, only animals of certain age mixes could, in fact, contribute to the death population, regardless of the bias for age that might be manifested in the behavior of the predator. Figure 3.15 summarizes this argument in terms of death risk. Given these expectations, we may develop models of the potential age structure present in populations of sheep (or other ungulates) during the different months of the year. As we have already seen, changes in bone density through a maturation sequence are correlated with age, and the changes among different bones are non-allometric. Therefore, the density profile of animals at various ages is distinctive and different from the same animals or from other animals at various ages. Therefore, we may design a *set* of equations, each of which is multiple in terms of a series of ages that could occur in a given month and differs in terms of different months. Demonstrations of a fit between data and any given set of equations should inform us of the month of death. Within any one set, the age classes that pivot, or account for the variance, should tell us something about the actual age structure of the death population.

We may now proceed to develop functions for our population, which is heterogeneous in age structure and may be biased in death risk by that structure.

We assume that Equation V represents the destruction of bones by dogs. Now,

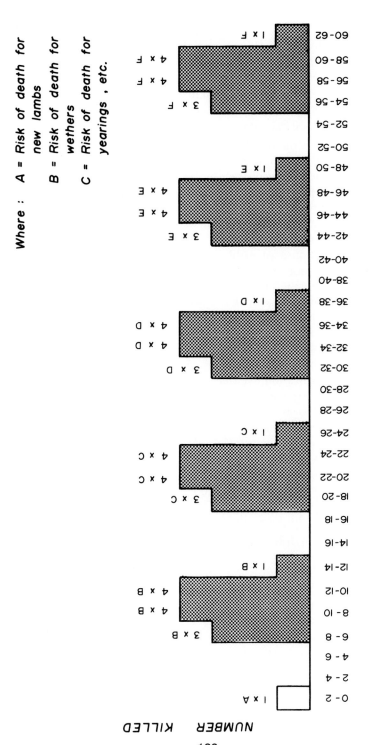

Figure 3.15 Distribution of "death risk" for a population of sheep being exploited during the weeks of late December and early January.

123

let X_{ij} be the initial density (D_0) of the ith faunal element for the jth age class, and let there by n age classes represented as elements fed to the dogs. We may rewrite Equation V as follows:

$$(VI) \qquad \begin{aligned} F = {} & P_1(\text{atan } P_2 + \text{atan } (P_3 X_{i,1} - P_2)) \\ & + P_4(\text{atan } P_2 + \text{atan } (P_3 X_{i,2} - P_2)) \\ & + P_5(\text{atan } P_2 + \text{atan } (P_3 X_{i,3} - P_2)) \\ & + P_{n+2}(\text{atan } P_2 = \text{atan } (P_3 X_{i,n} - P_2)). \end{aligned}$$

This function describes the number (F) of a faunal part that we would expect to survive after the dogs had done their damage. The parameters, $P_1, P_4, P_5, \ldots$ P_n, would similarly inform us of the number of each age class fed to the dogs (at present, we must accept the values as measures of this number—not necessarily equal to the real number). Notice that P_2 and P_3 appear in every term of the equation unchanged. This is the mathematical equivalent of the assumption that dogs eat lamb bones exactly as they eat mature animal bones—in terms only of density. This assumption is probably not true since small bones are often swallowed whole. This is not expected to affect the results, since lamb bones are generally low in density and would be eaten even if they were large.

We observe that, given a particular season of occupation, certain ages of sheep will *never* occur as contributors to the population subject to attrition (see Figure 3.15). On the other hand, other age classes will be represented in terms of a constant interval (birth $+ x$, birth $+ 12 + x$, birth $+ 24 + x = 3x$, etc.). Each of these age "sets" may be variable in terms of risk of death and, of course, in bone density. Given this realization, we may anticipate a mode of analysis employing several independent organizations of the basic function (F). Each organization would represent a different month or set of months relative to the average birth period for the species. Differences between results of different age structured regressions of Equation VI against data *should inform us of the most likely season of death for the population of bones being studied.*

The Fourth Operational Argument: The Problem of Nonlinear Regression

The function developed in Equation VI is nonlinear and cannot be made linear by transforming the variables by means of such methods as logarithmic conversion. It must be fitted against data using the techniques of nonlinear regression or nonlinear least squares. After several unsatisfactory attempts to write our own nonlinear regression program, we were fortunate in acquiring access to the BMD P3R Biomed—P program which solves nonlinear regression problems in a relatively efficient, accurate manner using the Gauss–Jordan algorithm (Dixon 1975; see also Hartley 1961; Jennrich and Sampson 1968).

We wish to point out that the statistical theory of nonlinear regression, especially its branch dealing with significance testing, is very new and poorly developed. We are neither prepared to discuss the statistical "significance" of our results, nor do we consider the topic very useful.

We take the pragmatic position that we are interested in accomplishing a description of complex surfaces in many dimensions; any equation that provides a good description and, hence, parameterization without outrageous implications is acceptable at this stage of development. The value of such a pragmatic view is that such an approach provides a method and is useful if only for its simplification of the situation.

The Fifth Operational Problem: Survivorship Is Not Necessarily Recognizability

Since 1968, Binford has been working almost exclusively with faunal data, both archaeologically and ethnographically. In training students to observe and record faunal material, we have always taken the position that there *is no unidentifiable bone.* All bones, even the smallest fragments, may be identified with sufficient training in osteology. In our experience, we can identify the fragments of shaft that are adjacent to practically any articulator end. Since we are capable of this, should we record that indication of an articulator end as such? The reader may answer both yes and no. This identification indicates that such an end was probably present—information we would like to have. At the same time, the end is no longer present, which is also information we would like to have. In this example, the reader will agree that, given the aim of measuring survivorship of anatomical parts, no tabulation of an articulator end would be made. However, let us consider the problem of the distal humerus. This is an articulator end with a relatively high bone density in mature animals, but the analysis of X rays shows that it is also heterogeneous in density with very high values inside and around the olecronon fossa, but with decreasing densities on the actual articulator condyles. Since the olecronon fossa is quite distinctive, it is highly recognizable. If we encounter a fragment of long bone shaft with a small remnant of the olecronon fossa present, should we record it as the presence of an articulator end? If our aim is to estimate MNI of individuals or parts originally present at the site, the answer would be an unqualified yes; however, since we are interested in survivorship, the answer is not clear—something survives, but of course not everything does. Let us contrast this situation with a bone such as the distal tibia (its density in a mature sheep is 1.69, while the distal humerus is 1.72). X-ray analysis shows that this bone is both dense and importantly homogeneous as compared to the distal humerus. Let us suppose that we observe a section of long bone shaft with a telltale remnant of the articulator surface of the distal tibia remaining. We must ask the same question: Do we record an articulator end as present because it is recognizable? If we do so, does it mean the same thing as recording an analogous remnant of the distal humerous as present? The answer must be that it would not mean the same thing in these two cases as regards survivorship. In short, we are suggesting that we do not at present have an adequate instrument for measuring survivorship for bones. Tabulations of MNI (minimal numbers of individuals) represented by different anatomical parts are primarily reflecting "recognizability," with some sensitivity to the "grain" or detailed ostological knowledge needed to make an identification. For instance, if an articulator end is "essentially complete" and may be identified from its gross morphological features, it is probably recorded as present and, in turn, in such a study as this, as "surviving." This is certainly true for the data presented in this chapter. This is, however, almost certainly a biased measure of survivorship, given the fact that some bones are more recognizable than others. A good example is the differences between a distal humerus versus a distal femur. Both are highly "recognizable," while many people may have more difficulty identifying partially destroyed or unfused ends of the radio-cubitus versus the tibia. There is no solution to this problem at present; however, it must be remembered that MNI tabulated as "recognizable" may well be a poor measure of "survivorship" per se. This problem is almost certainly increased when comparisons are made between bone inventories produced by different observers. We may, therefore, anticipate some discrepancies between an anticipated "survivorship" curve and the data points in a comparison between expected and observed values; the latter are probably best taken as measures of "recognizability."

Evaluating the Utility of Our Arguments and Suggested Procedures

In order to assess the relationship between survivorship and bone density, we need a control population of bones that come from animals homogeneous in age composition. In addition, we need to know the bone densities for animals of that age, and, finally, we need this initial population of bones to be subjected to a constant agent of attrition. Clearly, we do not have such controlled data. For this reason, we have developed a technique that is designed to partition a population of faunal remains into sets corresponding to animals of different ages. Simply stated, we cannot measure directly the relationships between bone density and survivorship. Instead, we have decided to develop an analytical method and will apply the procedure to a series of faunal samples known to be heterogeneous in age composition. If we can fit an age structure to the population and thereby account for the survival population in terms of mixes of animals of different ages with their accompanying differences in bone density, these fitted mixes should correspond to the data available on both age and season of occupation for the samples. If this succeeds, we believe that a strong argument can be made that the variability has been explained, and that the determinant variable is bone density, in the context of an agent of attrition, acting on populations originally variable in age composition.

Case One: The Navajo Winter Site

An analysis of the data from the Navajo winter site (Table 3.5) was performed using MNI estimates, that is, actual numbers of individuals represented by each anatomical part. Regressions were run against these data using the BMD P3R nonlinear regression program for Equation VIII. Six separate regressions were performed using six separate organizations of Equation VIII. Each organization represented bone densities for animals of different age intervals. The actual organization of each regression is as follows:

$$F = P_1 (\operatorname{atan}(P_2) + \operatorname{atan}(P_3 X_1 - P_2))$$
$$+ P_4 (\operatorname{atan}(P_2) + \operatorname{atan}(P_3 X_2 - P_2))S$$
$$+ P_5 (\operatorname{atan}(P_2) + \operatorname{atan}(P_3 X_3 - P_2))$$
$$+ P_6 (\operatorname{atan}(P_2) + \operatorname{atan}(P_3 X_4 - P_2))$$
$$+ P_7 (\operatorname{atan}(P_2) + \operatorname{atan}(P_3 X_5 - P_2))$$
$$+ P_8 (\operatorname{atan}(P_2) + \operatorname{atan}(P_3 X_6 - P_2))$$

Where:
$F = part\ frequency$
$X_1 = $ density of part at age 1
$X_2 = $ density of part at age 2
$X_3 = $
$X_6 = $ density of part at age 6

The six age variables were changed according to the format indicated in Table 3.10.

Values for the variables were read for each faunal part, from the graph, as illustrated in Figure 3.14 (the aging curves). The resulting values are summarized in Table 3.11. Each variable is a column vector, of dimension 31×1, where each row represents a faunal part. Each row element was assigned the value obtained by averaging the values at the age limits of each interval listed in Table 3.10. For example, the expected density of the atlas vertebra at age 12 months is 1.20 and, at age 14 months, is 1.33. The value assigned was then $\dfrac{1.20 + 1.33}{2}$, or 1.27. Notice that this value is not very different from the value read from the graph for age 13 months, which is 1.28. In summary, the value of variable two, case four, regression one is 1.27. (See Table 3.11 and Figure 3.14.)

Each regression was performed, the residual sum of squares inspected, the significance range of each parameter evaluated, and the number of animals in each age class evaluated. The results are summarized in Table 3.12.

Table 3.10
Age Class (X) of Density Values Entered
in Months post Birth[a]

Regression or run number	1	2	3	4	5	6
1 (May)	0–2	12–14	24–26	36–38	48–50	60–62
2 (July)	2–4	14–16	26–28	38–40	50–52	(65)
3 (Sept.)	4–6	16–18	28–30	40–42	52–54	(65)
4 (Nov.)	6–8	18–20	30–32	42–44	54–56	(65)
5 (Jan.)	8–10	20–22	32–34	44–46	56–58	(65)
6 (March)	10–12	22–24	34–36	46–48	58–60	(65)

[a] Values for the 90-month sheep were entered for all equations of X_6 beyond run number two.

Table 3.11

Summary of Estimated Bone Densities for Sheep that Could Be in a Death Population during Six Separate Seasons of the Year

Regression number	One (1)						Two (2)					
Months of relevance	February–May						April–July					
Mean month	March–April						May–June					
Age in months	0–2	12–14	24–26	36–38	48–50	60–62	2–4	14–16	26–28	38–40	50–52	65
Antler	.56	.86	1.099	1.169	1.219	1.230	.630	.940	1.120	1.179	1.219	1.230
Skull	1.099	1.410	1.530	1.580	1.620	1.639	1.200	1.429	1.540	1.589	1.620	1.630
Mandible	1.099	1.419	1.559	1.629	1.719	1.759	1.200	1.450	1.570	1.650	1.719	1.759
Atlas	.850	1.200	1.450	1.469	1.490	1.500	.920	1.330	1.459	1.469	1.490	1.500
Axis	.880	1.200	1.370	1.379	1.379	1.389	.940	1.270	1.370	1.379	1.379	1.389
Cerv. V.	.820	1.139	1.259	1.270	1.280	1.290	.900	1.169	1.270	1.270	1.280	1.290
Thor. V.	.850	1.120	1.299	1.330	1.360	1.370	.920	1.179	1.299	1.339	1.360	1.370
Lumb. V.	.880	1.200	1.400	1.419	1.429	1.440	.940	1.270	1.410	1.429	1.429	1.440
Pelvis	.880	1.150	1.360	1.570	1.669	1.709	.940	1.219	1.410	1.480	1.669	1.709
Ribs	.820	1.099	1.139	1.139	1.150	1.150	.900	1.110	1.130	1.139	1.150	1.150
Sternum	.460	.590	.620	.640	.660	.670	.520	.600	.620	.640	.660	.670
Scapula	.910	1.070	1.240	1.429	1.639	1.690	.980	1.080	1.280	1.469	1.639	1.690
Humerus P.	.610	.740	0.800	.830	.860	.870	.650	.750	.810	.830	.860	.870
Humerus D.	.940	1.099	1.230	1.419	1.660	1.730	1.009	1.120	1.270	1.459	1.660	1.730
Radio-cub P.	.910	1.070	1.360	1.520	1.620	1.639	.980	1.160	1.400	1.540	1.620	1.639
Radio-cub D.	.730	.910	1.099	1.250	1.450	1.520	.790	.950	1.129	1.290	1.450	1.520
Carpals	.650	.900	1.110	1.259	1.440	1.509	.700	.980	1.129	1.280	1.450	1.520
Metacarpal P.	.650	.970	1.290	1.290	1.299	1.299	.740	1.099	1.290	1.290	1.299	1.299
Metacarpal D.	.800	.950	.960	1.110	1.290	1.349	.870	.950	.970	1.139	1.290	1.349
Femur P.	.730	1.00	1.169	1.330	1.480	1.520	.800	1.070	1.230	1.370	1.480	1.520
Femur D.	.900	1.030	1.080	1.129	1.190	1.209	.960	1.049	1.099	1.129	1.190	1.209
Tibia P.	.800	.950	1.070	1.240	1.459	1.540	.860	.980	1.099	1.280	1.459	1.540
Tibia D.	.730	1.030	1.200	1.379	1.639	1.690	.800	1.110	1.250	1.419	1.639	1.690
Tarsals	.700	.930	1.160	1.309	1.480	1.549	.770	1.020	1.190	1.339	1.480	1.549
Ast.	.700	.930	1.160	1.309	1.480	1.549	.770	1.020	1.190	1.339	1.480	1.549
Cal.	.700	.930	1.160	1.309	1.480	1.549	1.770	1.020	1.190	1.339	1.480	1.549
Metatarsal P.	.730	1.030	1.259	1.309	1.360	1.360	.800	1.110	1.259	1.330	1.360	1.360
Metatarsal D.	.730	.970	1.110	1.230	1.309	1.309	.800	1.020	1.139	1.250	1.309	1.309
Phalange 1	.600	.700	.730	.750	.780	.800	.640	.700	.730	.750	.780	.800
Phalange 2	.600	.700	.730	.750	.780	.800	.640	.700	.730	.750	.780	.800
Phalange 3	.590	.680	.710	.730	.760	.780	.620	.680	.710	.730	.760	.780

(Continued)

Table 3.11 *(continued)*

Regression number	Three (3)						Four (4)					
Months of relevance	June–September						August–November					
Mean month	July–August						September–October					
Age in months	4–6	16–18	28–30	40–42	52–54	65	6–8	18–20	30–32	42–44	54–56	65
Antler	.670	1.000	1.299	1.179	1.219	1.230	.780	1.080	1.160	1.209	1.219	1.230
Skull	1.270	1.459	1.549	1.589	1.620	1.639	1.379	1.520	1.580	1.599	1.620	1.639
Mandible	1.270	1.469	1.580	1.660	1.719	1.759	1.360	1.540	1.629	1.679	1.719	1.759
Atlas	.950	1.400	1.459	1.469	1.490	1.500	1.070	1.440	1.469	1.480	1.490	1.500
Axis	.990	1.330	1.370	1.379	1.379	1.389	1.110	1.370	1.379	1.379	1.379	1.389
Cerv. V.	.960	1.210	1.270	1.280	1.280	1.290	1.120	1.259	1.270	1.280	1.280	1.290
Thor. V.	.970	1.240	1.309	1.339	1.360	1.370	1.080	1.290	1.330	1.349	1.360	1.370
Lumb. V.	.990	1.330	1.410	1.429	1.429	1.440	1.110	1.389	1.419	1.429	1.429	1.440
Pelvis	.990	1.290	1.469	1.599	1.669	1.709	1.110	1.339	1.559	1.629	1.669	1.709
Ribs	.950	1.129	1.139	1.139	1.150	1.150	1.070	1.139	1.139	1.150	1.150	1.150
Sternum	.550	.600	.630	.640	.660	.670	.590	.620	.630	.650	.660	.670
Scapula	1.030	1.139	1.339	1.530	1.639	1.690	1.050	1.209	1.400	1.580	1.539	1.690
Humerus P.	.670	.760	0.810	.840	.860	.870	.730	.790	.830	.850	.860	.870
Humerus D.	1.050	1.139	1.330	1.530	1.660	1.730	1.080	1.200	1.389	1.589	1.660	1.730
Radio-cub P.	1.030	1.230	1.429	1.570	1.620	1.639	1.049	1.309	1.490	1.599	1.620	1.639
Radio-cub. D.	.830	1.000	1.169	1.330	1.450	1.520	.870	1.059	1.240	1.379	1.450	1.520
Carpals	.740	1.049	1.169	1.299	1.440	1.509	.820	1.099	1.250	1.370	1.440	1.509
Metacarpal P.	.780	1.190	1.290	1.290	1.290	1.290	.860	1.280	1.290	1.299	1.299	1.299
Metacarpal D.	.910	.950	1.009	1.179	1.290	1.349	.940	.950	1.089	1.230	1.290	1.349
Femur P.	.850	1.120	1.270	1.400	1.480	1.520	.930	1.139	1.309	1.440	1.480	1.520
Femur D.	.980	1.059	1.110	1.139	1.190	1.209	1.020	1.070	1.120	1.169	1.190	1.209
Tibia P.	.890	1.020	1.139	1.330	1.459	1.540	.930	1.040	1.209	1.379	1.459	1.540
Tibia D.	.850	1.129	1.299	1.459	1.639	1.690	.950	1.169	1.360	1.530	1.639	1.690
Tarsals	.820	1.070	1.240	1.370	1.480	1.549	.880	1.129	1.129	1.419	1.480	1.549
Ast.	.820	1.070	1.240	1.370	1.480	1.549	.880	1.129	1.129	1.419	1.480	1.549
Cal.	.820	1.070	1.240	1.370	1.480	1.549	.880	1.129	1.129	1.419	1.480	1.549
Metatarsal P.	.850	1.179	1.270	1.339	1.360	1.360	.950	1.250	1.299	1.349	1.360	1.360
Metatarsal D.	.850	1.049	1.169	1.270	1.309	1.309	.920	1.080	1.219	1.309	1.309	1.309
Phalange 1	.670	.710	.730	.750	.780	.800	.700	.720	.740	.770	.780	.800
Phalange 2	.670	.710	.730	.750	.780	.800	.700	.720	.740	.770	.780	.800
Phalange 3	.640	.690	.710	.730	.760	.780	.670	.700	.720	.750	.760	.780

(Continued)

Table 3.11 *(continued)*

Regression number	Five (5)						Six (6)					
Months of relevance	October–January						December–March					
Mean month	November–December						January–February					
Age in months	8–10	20–22	32–34	44–46	56–58	65	10–12	22–24	34–36	46–48	58–60	65
Antler	.710	1.040	1.139	1.200	1.219	1.230	.740	1.059	1.150	1.200	1.219	1.230
Skull	1.320	1.480	1.559	1.599	1.620	1.639	1.340	1.509	1.570	1.599	1.620	1.639
Mandible	1.320	1.500	1.599	1.669	1.719	1.759	1.339	1.530	1.620	1.669	1.719	1.759
Atlas	.970	1.419	1.469	1.469	1.490	1.500	1.000	1.429	1.469	1.480	1.490	1.500
Axis	1.020	1.370	1.370	1.379	1.379	1.389	1.049	1.370	1.379	1.379	1.379	1.389
Cerv. V.	1.020	1.259	1.270	1.280	1.280	1.290	1.070	1.259	1.270	1.280	1.280	1.290
Thor. V.	.990	1.270	1.320	1.339	1.360	1.370	1.020	1.280	1.330	1.349	1.360	1.370
Lumb. V.	1.020	1.370	1.419	1.429	1.429	1.440	1.149	1.379	1.419	1.429	1.429	1.440
Pelvis	1.020	1.320	1.520	1.610	1.669	1.709	1.049	1.330	1.549	1.620	1.669	1.709
Ribs	1.000	1.1399	1.139	1.139	1.150	1.150	1.030	1.139	1.139	1.139	1.150	1.150
Sternum	.570	.610	.630	.640	.660	.670	.580	.620	.630	.640	.660	.670
Scapula	1.049	1.179	1.370	1.559	1.639	1.690	1.049	1.190	1.379	1.580	1.639	1.690
Humerus P.	.700	.770	.820	.840	.860	.870	.720	.780	.820	.850	.860	.870
Humerus D.	1.080	1.179	1.360	1.559	1.660	1.730	1.080	1.179	1.370	1.580	1.660	1.730
Radio-cub P.	1.040	1.259	1.459	1.589	1.620	1.639	1.040	1.280	1.469	1.599	1.620	1.639
Radio-cub. D.	.850	1.040	1.219	1.360	1.450	1.520	.860	1.049	1.230	1.370	1.450	1.520
Carpals	.760	1.080	1.209	1.320	1.440	1.509	.780	1.089	1.230	1.349	1.440	1.509
Metacarpal P.	.790	1.250	1.290	1.290	1.299	1.299	.810	1.270	1.290	1.299	1.299	1.299
Metacarpal D.	.940	.950	1.049	1.209	1.290	1.349	.940	.950	1.080	1.230	1.290	1.349
Femur P.	.870	1.129	1.280	1.419	1.480	1.520	.890	1.129	1.299	1.429	1.480	1.520
Femur D.	1.000	1.070	1.110	1.150	1.190	1.209	1.009	1.070	1.120	1.160	1.190	1.209
Tibia P.	.910	1.030	1.169	1.349	1.459	1.540	.910	1.030	1.179	1.360	1.459	1.540
Tibia D.	.870	1.150	1.330	1.500	1.639	1.690	.890	1.160	1.349	1.520	1.639	1.690
Tarsals	.840	1.099	1.270	1.400	1.480	1.549	.850	1.110	1.280	1.410	1.480	1.549
Ast.	.840	1.099	1.270	1.400	1.480	1.549	.850	1.110	1.280	1.410	1.480	1.549
Cal.	.840	1.099	1.270	1.400	1.480	1.549	1.850	1.110	1.280	1.410	1.480	1.549
Metatarsal P.	.870	1.230	1.280	1.349	1.360	1.360	.890	1.240	1.290	1.349	1.360	1.360
Metatarsal D.	.870	1.059	1.190	1.299	1.309	1.309	.890	1.059	1.200	1.309	1.309	1.309
Phalange 1	.680	.710	.730	.760	.780	.800	.690	.720	.740	.760	.780	.800
Phalange 2	.680	.710	.730	.760	.780	.800	.690	.720	.740	.760	.780	.800
Phalange 3	.660	.690	.710	.740	.760	.780	.660	.700	.720	.740	.760	.780

It should be recalled that each regression corresponds to a given month of occupation. For example, regression number one corresponds to the months of February, March, April, and early May, since only during these months could sheep of zero or 1 month in age have been killed—given a potential span of 2 months over which births might be expected.

Inspecting Table 3.12, it is clear that the most important regressions are those yielding the highest correlations and hence the lowest residual sum of squares (regressions four, five, and six), representing the year from *August through March*. Referring to the ethnographic descriptions of the sample, we find that informants reported this site to have been occupied from early October through early March. The agreement is as close as can be obtained given at least a 2-month uncertainty in birth dates of lambs.

Table 3.12

Summary Information on Results from Six (Month-Specific)
Multiple-Curvilinear Regressions between Age-Specific Bone
Densities and Survivorship of Bones on the
Navajo Winter Site

Regression numbers	1	2	3	4	5	6
Residual sum of squares	66.9	63.0	54.7	16.17	15.25	15.04
Value of R	.944	.947	.954	.987	.987	.988
Value of P_2	24.43	30.19	22.42	45.37	40.91	41.48
Value of P_3	21.25	23.96	16.68	28.76	25.74	25.92
Density at inflection point	1.14	1.26	1.34	1.57	1.59	1.60
F at inflection	34.95	42.14	26.27	75.62	67.95	69.47
Age Class 1 (P_1)	96.45	96.34	94.96	(77.11)[a]	(77.3)	(79.7)
	22.86	27.43	23.76	48.83	43.98	44.95
Age Class 2 (P_4)	0.0	0.0	0.0	(14.41)	(14.6)	(11.6)
	0.00	0.00	0.00	9.13	8.30	6.57
Age Class 3 (P_5)	1.68	1.29	1.63	(6.28)	(5.6)	(6.11)
	.40	.37	.41	3.98	3.20	3.45
Age Class 4 (P_6)	1.86	1.89	3.07	0.0	(0.0)	(0.0)
	.44	.54	.77	0.00	0.00	0.00
Age Class 5 (P_7)	0.0	.45	.31	.02	(0.0)	(0.0)
	0.00	.13	.08	.01	0.00	0.00
Age Class 6 (P_8)	0.0	0.	0	(2.16)	(2.51)	(2.5)
	0.00	0	0	1.37	1.43	1.43
Modal month	Feb.– May	April– July	June– Sept.	Aug.– Nov.	Oct.– Jan.	Dec.– March
Total "P" values	23.70	28.47	25.02	63.32	56.91	56.40
Months of relevance	Feb.– May	April– July	June– Sept.	Aug.– Nov.	Oct.– Jan.	Dec.– March

[a] Upper values in each row are percentages of total "P" values.

The estimates of the age structure of the original population upon which an agent of attrition acted is in essential agreement with the known conditions. Informants reported that there were approximately 20 young animals (54.0%) that died mainly of freezing and starvation during the winter, 13 adults (35.0%) butchered, and 4 aged animals (pets) (10.8%) that died of natural causes. Our analysis indicated 79.7% young animals, 17.7% young adults, and 2.5% very aged animals. The age structure of the original population is clearly reflected in our analysis; however, we appear to be overestimating the young animals and underestimating the old animals. Whether this is a function of our methods or of the accuracy in informant information cannot be clearly evaluated. However, the reader is referred to the data reported in Table 3.3, in which we note mandibles from at least six individuals between the ages of 0 and 4 months in age. These would be animals born at the winter camp in early spring. Informants reported that the move from the winter camp was made prior to the birth of lambs, since the pregnant females could be moved easily while animals with young lambs were nearly impossible to move without the loss of many lambs. The data from the mandibles suggest that some lambs arrived before the move, and these deaths were not reported to the interviewer when we obtained the informant estimates of the original population. The data from the mandibles tend to support our analytical results, namely, that there were more very young individuals than reported by the informants.

In addition, there is another possibility concerning the manner in which dogs received food during the winter occupation. Our apparent overestimation of young animals could be due to an oversurvival of bones from young animals. It should be noted that the young animals that informants reported as having starved or frozen to death were exposed to the dogs as *whole, unbutchered* animals that had not been already exploited by man. This means that the dogs were free to feed on the meat, cartilage, and viscera of these animals. As was mentioned previously, only hungry dogs really destroy bones. Given such a pattern of feeding, it is not unreasonable to anticipate an oversurvival of bones from such animals. We are unable to determine at this time whether the numbers of young animals were underestimated by informants (however, given the mandibles present, this seems likely) or whether there was an "oversurvival" of the bones of young animals due to the manner in which the dogs were fed the animals during winter. Both conditions may have obtained.

Finally, we know that some parts of some adult animals were given away. We do not know which parts were circulated outside the winter camp nor how extensive such circulation was, but this fact would contribute to a reduction in the number of older animals estimated in our analysis.

Given the aforementioned uncertainties in the ethnographic controls, the estimates of age structure provided by the analysis may well be more accurate than the ethnographic approximations.

The most impressive result of the analysis is, of course, that variations in age structure and the related bone densities allowed us to estimate the survival levels of different anatomical parts in the actual population quite accurately.

Inspection of Table 3.13 demonstrates that one can completely account for the variability in anatomical part frequencies observed as a function of bone densities in a population of variable age structure. This means that the pattern of relative anatomical part frequencies as observed is a product of the action of an agent of attrition operative on an original population of complete skeletons. (Given the results of this analysis, we would be justified in asserting that the original popula-

Table 3.13

Observed and Predicted MNI for Regression Number Six, Table 3.12[a]

Case no.	Case name	Predicted MNI	Std. dev. of pred. value	Observed MNI	Residual
1	Horn core	1.689706	.12100	3.000000	1.310294
2	Skull	16.540085	.75972	16.500000	−.040085
3	Mandible	21.393005	.75618	21.500000	.106995
4	Atlas	4.979019	.56791	4.000000	−.979019
5	Axis	4.120665	.28743	4.500000	.379335
6	Cerv. V.	3.564968	.30900	3.700000	.135032
7	Thor. V.	3.573328	.24655	3.200000	−.373328
8	Lumb. V.	4.430057	.31875	4.500000	.069943
9	Pelvis	9.781210	.64810	9.500000	−.281210
10	Ribs	2.866385	.32131	1.900000	−.966386
11	Sternum	.811196	.10118	.300000	−.511196
12	Scapula	7.050658	.41143	6.000000	−1.050658
13	Humerus Prox.	1.192881	.13909	1.500000	.307119
14	Humerus Dist.	7.357991	.43463	7.000000	−.357991
15	Radio-C. Prox.	7.202631	.29212	7.500000	.297369
16	Radio-C. Dist.	2.490264	.17446	2.500000	.009736
17	Carpals	2.322991	.16410	2.700000	.377008
18	Metacarpal Prox.	2.378772	.23755	2.500000	.121228
19	Metacarpal Dist.	2.132796	.23678	2.500000	.367204
20	Femur Prox.	2.871366	.19680	1.500000	−1.371366
21	Femur Dist.	2.520117	.28661	2.500000	−.020117
22	Tibia Prox.	2.831281	.20116	4.500000	1.668719
23	Tibia Dist.	6.342210	.43645	7.500000	1.157790
24	Tarsals	2.961294	.21357	3.599999	.638705
25	Ast.	2.961294	.21357	3.000000	.038706
26	Cal.	2.961294	.21357	2.500000	−.461294
27	Metatarsal Prox.	2.694233	.18539	4.000000	1.305767
28	Metatarsal Dist.	2.211608	.18613	2.500000	.288392
29	Phalange 1	1.077114	.13601	.870000	−.207114
30	Phalange 2	1.077114	.13601	.620000	−.457114
31	Phalange 3	1.003502	.12442	.370000	−.633502

[a] Correlation coefficient = .988.

tion of bones present at the site was a population of bones from complete animal skeletons prior to the operation of an agent of attrition.) Of course, we knew this, and, therefore, it provides a very good test of the utility of the methods proposed.

In addition, we note that the values of bone density at the inflection points of the curves that best fit the data are 1.57, 1.59, and 1.60 for regressions four, five, and six. These values may be taken as estimates of the power of the agent of attrition operative, since bones of greater density exhibit a decreasing rate of attrition with increases in density.

Finally, the values of P_3 are taken as the best indicators of the slope of the curve at the inflection point (independently of the effect that sample size has on the actual values of slope). We note that these values are very similar (see Table 3.12) and indicate a curve of moderate slope. These values will prove useful in comparisons between populations of bone subjected to different agents of attrition.

The Navajo Summer Site

We performed an analysis using the same procedure as that outlined for the Navajo winter site. Table 3.14 summarizes the results obtained in a manner analogous to that used in Table 3.12 for the winter site.

Inspection of Table 3.14 shows that we are dealing with a very different situation than was the case with the results from the winter site. It is clear that the

Table 3.14

Summary Information on Results from Six (Month-Specific) Multiple-Curvilinear Regressions between Age-Specific Bone Densities and Survivorship on the Navajo Summer Site

Regression number	1	2	3	4	5	6
Residual sum of squares	109.66	115.49	116.26	115.12	115.49	116.11
Values of R	.916	.911	.911	.911	.911	.911
Value of P_2	11.77	8.94	8.60	9.36	9.22	9.07
Value of P_3	7.09	5.50	5.26	5.49	5.39	5.31
Density at inflection point	1.66	1.62	1.63	1.70	1.71	1.71
Age Class 1 (P_1)	23.3 (78.5%)	5.03 (39.14%)	2.74 (24.8%)	6.56 (43.0%)	5.32 (37.2%)	3.79 (28.87%)
Age Class 2 (P_4)	0.0	0.0	0.0	0.0	0.0	0.0
Age Class 3 (P_5)	0.0	0.0	0.0	0.0	0.0	0.0
Age Class 4 (P_6)	0.0	0.0	0.0	0.0	0.0	0.0
Age Class 5 (P_7)	0.0	7.82 (60.86%)	8.29 (75.16%)	0.93 (6.11%)	1.39 (9.72%)	2.29 (17.44%)
Age Class 6 (P_8)	6.41 (21.6)	0.0	0.0	7.74 (50.82%)	7.59 (53.08%)	7.05 (53.69%)
Months of relevance	Feb.–May	April–July	June–Sept.	Aug.–Nov.	Oct.–Jan.	Dec.–March

contrast in the residual sum of squares, which immediately identified the season of occupancy as the winter site, does not unambiguously identify the season in this sample. The lowest value (109.66) coincides with the months of known initial occupancy of the site; however, the difference between residual sums for the other months do not discriminate between summer and winter occupation. In addition, we note that no regression exhibits a fit so close to the data as we witnessed in the winter data. Since the agents of attrition are constant (the same dogs), the character of the ethnographic documentation is nearly identical, and the assumption that complete animals were introduced is supported in both cases, why are our methods neither as discriminating nor as accurate with these data as with the winter data? Several points are of interest; first, the lowest residual sum of squares is obtained for the regression that corresponds to the period of birth for lambs. That solution indicates an age structure of 78% of the animals dying at or near birth and 22% fully mature animals. All other solutions indicate a reverse structure with a bias between two-thirds and three-forths old and mature animals and only one-third to one-fourth young animals. Informants insisted that the move to the summer site was normally made prior to the birth of the lambs. This means that the site was, in fact, occupied during the period for which the lowest residual sum of squares is indicated. However, interviews regarding animals butchered at the location clearly document that only mature animals were killed. No mention was made by informants of lambs contributing to the faunal population. Anyone familiar with sheep herding knows that it is very rare and highly unlikely that some lambs will not be lost at birth or shortly thereafter, yet the informants made no mention of this. The questions, however, were put to them in terms of what animals they butchered. It appears that they answered these questions explicitly, never mentioning the lambs that died during the birth period. It would appear that we have a situation in which a number of lambs died during the lambing period. This rate of death did not continue beyond this period; therefore, the structure of the population contributing to the archaeological remains changed during the course of the occupation. This means that no single time-related regression would summarize the population. We would expect the latter only if the character of the inputs to the archaeological assemblage remained relatively unchanged throughout the duration of the occupation. Given such a shift, at least two separate regressions need be combined in order to account for the population as recovered from the summer site. This compound time-related structure probably accounts for the lower "r" values in this solution.

One might ask, given this argument, why the anticipated "other regression" (the additional one that must be combined with the "Feb.–May" regression) is not recognizable from the differences between the residual sums of squares, for regressions 2–6 are essentially the same. In order to understand this, we must refer back to the age–density graphs (Figure 3.14). Inspection shows that the rates of change in density for animals between zero and 20 months is quite high, change in density slows down between 20 and 40 months, and, for animals greater than 40 months in age, there is little change of density with age, relative to younger animals. This means that, for populations composed of high proportions of young animals, our techniques will be highly discriminating since there are major differences in density associated with relatively short lapses of time. For a population largely constituted of mature animals, however, we may expect greatly reduced variations in density associated with lapses in time. In short, the correlations between density profiles for mature animals of slightly different ages is relatively high, while such correlations decrease appreciably as the age of the population under study is reduced.

The results of our analysis demonstrate that we are dealing with a population whose age structure is about as extreme as may be imagined—numbers of lambs that died at or near birth and numbers of fully mature sheep that were killed over an extended period of time. This picture is complicated by the fact that the period of time over which mature animals were regularly introduced was much longer than the period of time over which the young animals were introduced. This means that the old animals will provide a poor basis for seasonal recognition and the young animals will be relevant only to a single time period. Nevertheless, a single regression is attempting to account for both young and old within a given time frame, and this is, of course, impossible. The best clue to this situation is given by the asymptotic standard deviations of the age related parameters $P_1, P_4,$ $P_5, P_6, P_7,$ and P_8. Table 3.15 summarizes these values for the regressions and age classes used in the analysis. Inspection of Table 3.15 indicates that in only four cases do the values of the parameter exceed the value of its asymptotic standard deviation; only those four terms in the equations are actually very closely fitted to the data. It is important that these are exclusively related to summer months— the known period of occupation—and they reflect the behavioral situation. All

Table 3.15

Parameter Values with Asymptotic Standard Deviations Displayed below Each Value

Age Class 1	23.3	5.03	2.74	6.56	5.32	3.79
(P_1)	16.9	9.1	7.4	9.6	8.7	8.2
Age Class 2	—	—	—	—	—	—
(P_4)						
Age Class 3	—	—	—	—	—	—
(P_5)						
Age Class 4	—	—	—	—	—	—
(P_6)						
Age Class 5	—	7.82	8.29	0.93	1.39	2.29
(P_7)		3.9	4.2	9.6	10.0	10.7
Age Class 6	6.41	—	—	7.74	7.59	7.05
(P_8)	2.6			8.0	8.2	8.47
Months of relevance	Feb.–May	April–July	June–Sept.	Aug.–Nov.	Oct.–Jan.	Dec.–March

values for mature animals during the summer contribute to the fit to the data, while only the youngest animals during the period of lambing are closely fitted to the data. Thus, despite the complications with the assemblage, the results monitor in an accurate and understandable manner the actual situation existing behind the accumulation of the faunal sample.

The Nunamiut Dog Yard

In the case of the Nunamiut dog yard, we obtained both the feeding record and the bones surviving after the dogs had finished feeding, thereby providing the opportunity to evaluate our methods in a different context. In the two Navajo cases, whole animals had been exposed to attrition by dogs; therefore, sample sizes were variable only at the level of numbers of animals contributing to the population. With the Nunamiut data, this is not the case, and sample sizes vary among the anatomical parts as a function of differential feeding of different parts. We may expect that this inability to "hold constant" the sample size among the anatomical parts may well complicate the analysis.

In addition, we have densities monitored by a single caribou, with no knowledge as to the patterns of bone density variation with changing age of the animal. Furthermore, we have no idea of the actual age structure of the animals from which the parts were removed for feeding to the dogs. In short, not only is sample size variable by anatomical part, but age structure may well also vary by anatomical part, since only parts were fed to the dogs, not whole animals. Therefore, we are limited in our comparison to parts of variable sample sizes (each with potentially independent or at least partially independent age structures). In addition, the density data available is from a single mature caribou. Our sole clue relative to age structure is the knowledge that the Nunamiut only store for summer consumption the anatomical parts of mature animals. Therefore, we may anticipate age-related variations in density to be of minimal relevance.

In this case, rather than entering raw MNI data, we are forced to run the density values for the single caribou against the percentage survival values, that is the value obtained by dividing the MNI's surviving by the MNI's known to have been fed to the dogs originally (Table 3.2, Column 10). Figure 3.16 summarizes in graphic form the relationship between density and survivorship of bones exposed to dog gnawing. In order to evaluate the obvious curvilinear relationship indicated in Figure 3.16, a least squares fit of the data was attempted, using first-, second-, third-, and fourth-order polynomial equations. All fitting was performed with the obviously deviant values for the metacarpal omitted. It was found that, with a first-order equation (linear fit), the value for the correlation coefficient (r^2) was .746. For a second-order equation, the value increased to .859, while with a third-order polynomial, the correlation coefficient reached a value of .879. When a fourth-order polynomial was attempted, the matrix was judged to be unstable. This means that the third-order polynomial provided the best estimate

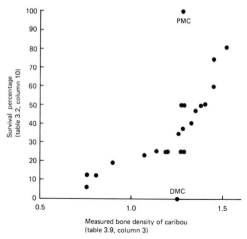

Figure 3.16 Relationship between bone density and survival percentages for caribou bones.

of the form of the relationship between bone density and survival percentage. The equation that best estimates the character of the relationship is expressed as follows:

$$\text{survival percentage } = -352.778 + 1050.4(\text{D}) - 1008.695(\text{D}^2) + 332.822(\text{D}^3)$$

where D = measured bone density of mature caribou. As mentioned earlier, the fit between expected survival percentages calculated with the above formula and the actual values observed from the Nunamiut dog yard is measured by a correlation coefficient (r^2) of .879.

Table 3.16 summarizes the observed and predicted values together with the residuals and original sample sizes in MNI's. We see in Table 3.17 that there is some tendency for the size of the residuals to be inversely proportional to the initial sample size. We reasoned that, in addition, one might expect such a relationship to be further conditioned by density. Dogs may not exercise an option on highly dense parts, but they are free to destroy soft parts a little, not at all, or completely. Under these conditions, if few parts are exposed to the dog, there may be an increase in variance as an inverse function of density. An example will clarify this point. Suppose the dog is fed two mandibles and two proximal humeri. The dog cannot destroy the mandibles since they are dense; however, he can eat none, one, or two of the humeri, which are quite spongy. These possibilities could result in survival percentages of 0.0%, 50.0% or 100.0%. Suppose the density of the humerus is such that, relative to other bones, we would expect the dog to destroy 87.5% of the proximal humeri fed to it. The dog would have to receive as input at least eight humeri before having any possibility of behaving as it "should." On the other hand, we may expect it to behave "appropriately" with respect to dense bones, even given small populations or small numbers of

Table 3.16

Observed and Predicted Frequencies of Anatomical Parts Expressed in Percentage Survival Values for Regression Solution to the Nunamiut Dog Yard Sample

	Survival percentages			Original sample size
	Predicted	Observed	Residuals	
Antler	—	—	—	—
Skull	73.91	—	—	—
Mandible	91.36	—	—	—
Atlas	64.20	75.0	+10.80	4.0
Axis	50.52	50.0	−0.52	4.0
Cerv. v.	37.10	37.5	+0.40	8.0
Thor. v.	35.12	35.0	−0.12	9.0
Lumb. v.	45.81	47.8	+1.99	14.0
Pelvis	82.18	81.8	−0.38	11.0
Ribs	24.04	22.7	−1.34	11.5
Sternum	9.02	12.5	+3.45	2.0
Scapula	54.04	50.0	−4.04	5.0
Humerus p.	16.77	—	—	—
Humerus d.	55.91	—	—	—
Radio-cub. p.	43.01	—	—	—
Radio-cub. d.	47.31	—	—	—
Carpals	29.67	—	—	—
Metacarpal p.	37.09	100.0	+62.91	0.5
Metacarpal d.	34.21	0.0	−34.21	0.5
Femur p.	38.16	50.0	+11.84	2.0
Femur d.	26.89	25.0	−1.89	2.0
Tibia p.	29.67	40.0	+10.33	2.5
Tibia d.	66.49	60.0	−6.49	2.5
Tarsals	38.16	25.0	−13.16	2.0
Ast.	37.09	50.0	+12.91	2.0
Cal.	37.09	25.0	−12.09	2.0
Metatarsal p.	43.01	40.0	−3.01	2.5
Metatarsal d.	30.32	25.0	−5.32	2.0
Phalange 1	18.18	18.5	+0.32	2.0
Phalange 2	13.13	12.5	−0.63	2.0
Phalange 3	9.02	6.0	−3.02	2.0

"chances" to perform in this manner. Archaeologists will recognize this as an instance of the "law of large numbers" which may be complicated somewhat by bone density itself.

Figure 3.17 illustrates the relationship between the residuals and sample sizes for the Nunamiut dog yard. It is clear that we have a steep poisson distribution indicated for the relationship between the two variables. This supports the argument that the "noise" in the relationship measured by the third-order polynomial fit to the data is primarily a function of variable sample sizes in the population which was subjected to attrition or destruction by the dogs. As in the earlier cases, we find that bone density is the best predictor of survivorship, and importantly

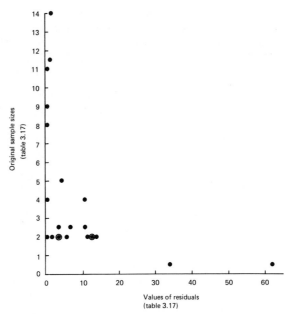

Figure 3.17   Relationship between residuals and sample size for Nunamuit dog yard sample.

that attritional processes act to not only reduce the number of bones remaining for observation but to modify the original form of the structure of the population.

The Case of the Hottentot Goat Sample

The analysis of this case is interesting and important for a number of reasons. This case provided the first body of data ever presented in support of the argument that bone density, in the context of an agent of attrition, could and would modify the proportions of parts surviving such that they no longer resembled the composition of the original population.

C. K. Brain (1969) collected samples of goat bones from a number of Hottentot sites along the Kuiseb River of the Namib Plain of Southwest Africa. The situation there was similar to that described for the Navajo; namely, whole goats were butchered on the sites, and the parts were consumed and eventually discarded around the living area where free-ranging dogs then had unrestricted access to all discarded bones and food remnants. Some minor differences were noted by Brain: The Hottentots systematically broke bones for marrow, which the Navajo no longer do; they even occasionally gnaw soft bones themselves, resulting in some reduction in survivorship before the dogs have access to the bones.

The collection to be analyzed was gathered in several places and grouped into a single population by Brain. The original collection consisted of 2373 goat bone elements. The MNI's for the standard list of anatomical parts used thus far is presented in Table 3.17. These data were taken directly from Brain (1969).

We have several interests in this sample. Initial studies of the bone density of animals as different as sheep and caribou showed that there was considerable correlation between animals of different species at roughly comparable ages. We wished to discover the degree to which an analysis that used, as a reference, dimension bone densities of a species different from that actually being analyzed would allow the reliable recognition of a density-related pattern of survivorship in anatomical parts. Second, since we have no hope of obtaining density measurements for bones as they existed in life for past or extinct species, we wished to gain some perspective on the degree to which we could analyze faunal remains

Table 3.17

Observed and Predicted MNI Values for Hottentot Goat Population,
Regression One of Table 3.18

	Predicted MNI	Std. dev. of pred. value	Observed MNI	Residual
Skull	24.470627	3.26724	28.500000	4.029373
Mandible	58.816055	6.47421	58.500000	−.316055
Atlas	14.359016	2.74548	12.000000	−2.359016
Axis	10.345500	2.33812	14.000000	3.654500
Cerv. V.	7.661307	1.71906	2.400000	−5.261308
Thor. V.	9.119071	1.75040	1.700000	−7.419071
Lumbar	11.795272	2.42852	3.900000	−7.895272
Pelvis	31.268372	3.48839	17.000000	−14.268372
Ribs	5.529793	1.29068	6.500000	.970207
Scapula	25.162888	2.93058	17.500000	−7.662888
Humerus prox.	2.740068	.58783	0.0	−2.740068
Humerus dist.	34.647049	5.90407	41.000000	6.352951
Radio-C. prox.	20.529556	3.80721	32.500000	11.970444
Radio-C. dist.	10.584417	1.55043	11.000000	.415583
Metacarpal prox.	8.108930	1.84498	16.000000	7.891070
Metacarpal dist.	6.397655	.95017	11.500000	5.102345
Femur prox.	11.248020	1.57541	9.000000	−2.248020
Femur dist.	5.588030	1.01901	4.500000	−1.088030
Tibia prox.	11.052730	1.76882	6.500000	−4.552730
Tibia dist.	24.832626	3.12614	36.000000	11.167374
Astral.	12.054209	1.73548	8.000000	−4.054209
Calcanium	12.054209	1.73548	7.000000	−5.054209
Metatarsal prox.	8.599144	1.47437	19.500000	10.900856
Metatarsal dist.	6.808325	1.07568	10.000000	3.191675
Phalange 1	2.332046	.52468	.870000	−1.462045
Phalange 2	2.332046	.52468	.870000	−1.462045
Phalange 3	2.227922	.50162	.870000	−1.357922

from animals or populations of animals slightly different from modern representatives. Clearly, *Capra* (goats) and *Ovis* (sheep) are very close phylogenetically—so close in fact that even the best faunal specialists have difficulty distinguishing bones from the two genera (see Hole *et al.* 1969: 266–293). If data from modern *Ovis* are adequate approximations of data from *Capra,* then we could argue that data from modern examples of species that existed in some variable form in the past should be adequate for the type of analysis advocated. For example, data from contemporary Alaskan caribou could be used as a reference dimension for studying survivorship of bones from European reindeer deposited during the late Pleistocene. Table 3.18 summarizes the results of our analysis of Brain's data using the same methods employed in the analysis of both Navajo camps. Several facts are of interest in this analysis. First, it is clear that density is a major determinant of the patterns of survivorship observed in the goat data. It is important, however, that the densities are taken from sheep, not goats. By using the aged data on sheep bone density, the standard error of the estimate is shown to be less than half the value of the standard deviation of the mean for the actual population of goat bones observed. That is, if all frequencies of bones were estimated

Table 3.18

Summary Information on Results from Six (Month-Specific) Multiple-Curvilinear Regressions between Age-Specific Bone Densities and Survivorship of Bones in Hottentot Villages

Regression number	1	2	3	4	5	6
Correlation coefficient	.894	.893	.892	.893	.893	.893
Standard error of the estimate	6.48	6.51	6.56	6.54	6.52	6.53
Standard deviation of observed mean	14.21	14.21	14.21	14.21	14.21	14.21
Residual sum of squares	1051.98	1060.27	1074.80	1068.81	1063.16	1064.97
Value of P_2	42.35	76.16	32.58	130.09	149.65	28.03
Value of P_3	23.54	42.10	18.32	71.95	82.62	15.79
Density at inflection point	1.80	1.80	1.78	1.81	1.81	1.78
Age Class 1 (P_1)	0.0	0.0	46.48 (36.5%)	91.66 (19.9%)	0.0	0.0
Age Class 2 (P_4)	0.0	0.0	28.42 (22.3%)	116.20 (25.2%)	191.69 (39.9%)	43.71 (51.4%)
Age Class 3 (P_5)	65.35 (48.8%)	107.03 (44.8%)	0.0	0.0	0.0	0.0
Age Class 4 (P_6)	0.0	0.0	0.0	0.0	0.0	0.0
Age Class 5 (P_7)	19.75 (14.7%)	43.31 (18.1%)	27.43 (21.6%)	134.70 (29.2%)	131.07 (27.3%)	13.53 (15.9%)
Age Class 6 (P_8)	48.79 (36.4%)	88.53 (37.1%)	24.85 (19.5%)	118.70 (25.7%)	157.92 (32.8%)	27.80 (32.7%)
Month of relevance	March	May	July	Sept.	Nov.	Jan.

using the mean frequency for the surviving bones, all parts should fall within ±14.21 MNI's of the mean. Using the density information, the survivorship of any given bone can be expected to vary in 95% of the cases between ±6.48 MNI's, using the first regression as an example.

Second, there are no marked discrepancies in the values of the standard error of the estimates between the six age-related regressions performed. This indicates that all time-related regressions account about equally for the observed population of bones. No major discrepancies were noted in the standard deviations of the parameters, as was the case in the Navajo summer camp sample; therefore, this analysis indicates that animals were being added to the faunal population throughout the year—a condition that Brain (1969) reported to have been the case.

Our analysis clearly shows a bi-modal age structure with animals between 16 and 26 months of age making up a considerable proportion of the population (38.7%), while animals greater than 46 months of age account for the other primary age group represented (51.7%). A few animals between 4 and 6 months are indicated (9.4%). Brain's analysis of the age structure of the goat population based on a classification of mandibles also indicates a strongly bi-modal age structure; however, the ages indicated by the two methods are different. Brain estimates that .85% of the mandibles surviving are from animals between 0 and 6 months of age, 34.2% of surviving mandibles are from animals between 6 and 12 months of age, 11.1% are from animals between 12 and 20 months in age, and 53.8% from animals older than 20 months. The modal age indicated by Brian's methods is approximately 10 months, while our methods indicate about 21 months of age for the young animals present. Except for this discrepancy of about 11 months for the modal age of the young animal segment of the population, the age structure indicated by Brain's analysis of mandibles and our analysis is remarkably similar. Part of the difference may be accounted for by Brain's use of Cornwall's (1956) tables of tooth eruption for sheep as the basis for his aging of goat mandibles. Comparison of eruption tables presented by Silver (1963) for modern breeds of sheep and goats does not reveal major differences in anticipated eruption times; however, these tables are for "modern" commercial breeds of domesticated animals. Silver (1963:263–265) notes repeatedly that eighteenth-century authors consistently cite later eruption dates for sheep, goats, and pigs. Similarly, a comparison between the eruption dates given by Giles (1969) for wild North American bighorn sheep (*Ovis canadensis*) compared with the eruption times given by Silver (1963:263–264) for "improved breeds" of domestic sheep and goats is instructive (see Table 3.19). It is clear that modern "improved breeds" of sheep and goats have similar eruption times, while goats show later first molar eruption times. Comparison with the wild sheep tends to confirm Silver's suspicion that modern domestic forms mature more rapidly than wild "hill or rough goats and sheep." If the goats of the Hottentot do not qualify as "improved or modern commercial" breeds, we may expect Brain's estimates of age to be somewhat too young for the younger animals; nevertheless, differences

Table 3.19

Comparative Data on Tooth Eruption Ages for Sheep and Goats

Tooth	Domestic sheep	*Ovis canadensis*	Modern goats
First molar	3 months	12 months	5–6 months
Second molar	9–12 months	12–16 months	8–10 months
Third molar	18–24 months	36–42 months	18–24 months

between eruption times for the second molar are not sufficient to account for the approximate 11-month discrepancy between estimates of age based on tooth eruption and those based on bone density. It is possible, given Brain's description of the environment of the Hottentot villages, that nutrition may well have been a problem in the goat population.

> Stretching across the Namib Plain from the escarpment in the east to Walvis Bay in the west is the Kuiseb River, dry throughout the year, except after sporadic rain. . . .
>
> The Namib Plain, where it is traversed by the Kuiseb River, is extremely inhospitable. To the south is an immense area of high dunes while northwards featureless gravel plains extend for many miles. . . . The economy of the Hottentots is built around their goat herds and these, in turn, are dependent upon the Kuiseb River for survival. They subsist very largely on the dry seed pods of Acacia albida. . . .
>
> The aridity of the environment results in a general absence of vegetation around the villages. . . .
>
> The average rainfall in the Kuiseb study area is less than 1 inch per year . . . [Brain 1969:14,16].

Searching for some clue to the effects of sustained nutritional deprivation, the work of Lewall and Cowan (1963) was noted. These researchers studied patterning in the rates of epiphysial closure for the black tailed mule deer *(Odocoileus hemionus),* showing that animals on poor range might be expected to exhibit delayed closure of epiphysis by as much as 2–3 months at age 1.5 years and, if continually exposed to drought and poor nutrition, may show delayed patterns of epiphysial closure as great as 12–16 months at age 5. Since epiphysial closure is one aspect of ossification, we may well expect to observe a slower rate of bone densification among populations suffering from chronic nutritional problems. This would have the effect of biasing our age estimates, based on bone density, in favor of younger animals. This bias is, of course, in the opposite direction and appears to be of no aid in understanding the discrepancies in age between the tooth eruption and bone density methods. Of course, the difference may relate directly to differences between sheep and goats in the patterns of non-allometric bone densification with increasing age.

Makapansgat Fauna

Raymond Dart investigated over 7000 bones that were found in association with Australopithecine remains at Makapansgat. He found serious disproportions in the skeletal parts preserved at the location. He noted that parts of the skull were common, accounting for 34.5% of all identifiable fragments. On the other hand, vertebrae were rare, representing only 1.4% of the expected numbers, given his estimates of the numbers of individuals originally present.

Dart interpreted his findings as evidence remaining from the hunting and tool using behavior of the Australopithecines. For instance, he states:

> The disappearance of tails were probably due to their use as signals and whips in hunting outside the cavern. Caudal and other vertebrae may also have disappeared because of the potential value of their bodies as projectiles and their processes as leavers and points . . . femora and tibia would be the heaviest clubs to use outside the cavern, that is probably why these bones are the least common. Humeri are the commonest of the long bones; probably because they would be the most convenient clubs for the women-folk and children to use at home [Dart 1957b:85].

Subsequently, many writers have cited both Dart's findings and his convictions as evidence for the developed hunting skills and basic predatory behavior of our earliest Pleistocene ancestors. Others have been skeptical since Dart's arguments seemed inconsistent with the findings of food remains on living floor excavated in Olduvai Gorge where there seemed little evidence to suggest the behavior of a skilled hunter (Leakey 1971). Regardless of the skepticism, arguments that cite seemingly different or incompatible types of data do not prove that the Australopithicines were not capable of a diversity of behavioral modes or strategies. In this situation, we need a strong *explanation* for the data upon which Dart based his behavioral interpretations. C. K. Brain (1969) attacked this problem by collecting the fauna from the Hottentot villages just analyzed, arguing that the survivorship of bones was related to the action of an agent of attrition—dogs—differentially destroying bones as a function of their densities. The pattern of survivorship in the Hottentot case was then compared to the pattern in the bovid remains from Makapansgat. The results were tantalizingly similar but by no means identical. Brian concluded that the differences were related to the heterogeneous species composition of the Makapansgat population and that the similar pattern was strong support for the argument that the Makapansgat population represented bones surviving from complete skeletons that were acted upon by an agent of attrition. Despite Brain's pioneering work, skeptics could still dismiss his results (Read-Martin and Read 1975) by pointing to the fact that he had not explained, only interpreted, the observed differences between his Hottentot goat population and the Makapansgat fauna.

This objection led Read-Martin and Read (1975) to try "again" at a behavioral interpretation of the Makapansgat fauna. They offer a number of generalizations: "propositions for faunal analysis" that summarize their expectations for differential treatment of anatomical parts and animals of different sizes as far as their introduction to habitation sites are concerned. The authors then present data from three German archaeological sites, presumably cited as examples of "typical human behavior" as regards the introduction of anatomical parts into living sites. Then a statistical comparison is made between the German sites and the fauna from Makapansgat. They present a convincing argument for structural differences between the Makapansgat fauna and the three German sites. Makapansgat had far too many cranial fragments, large animals were better represented than small animals, and so on. Having read all this, we were prepared for the logical conclusion—Makapansgat was a kill site, not a residential site. Unfortunately, we were disappointed; the conclusion was that *(a)* it was a habitation sites, and *(b)* Australopithecines did not behave according to the "propositions for faunal analysis." Australopithecus was scavenging the kills of other predators for food. Thus the arguments rage on: opinions with no attempt to understand through evaluated explanatory argument. This chapter is such an attempt, and its utility is probably tested on a no more provocative and important assemblage of fauna than that of Makapansgat.

Several changes had to be made in the basic data reported before the Makapansgat statics could be analyzed. As originally reported, MNI's were based on the maximum number of individuals represented by analogous bones. That is, if there were five right half-mandibles and nine left, a value of nine would be reported. Since we are interested in survivorship, such reporting is misleading, and we need the data in the form of a standardized value of numbers surviving that is simply the sum of parts remaining divided by the number present in a complete skeleton. In the aforementioned example, we could divide the total number of half-mandibles (14) by the number in the body (2) and obtain a survivorship MNI of 7. These changes were made in the data reported from Makapansgat (as we have done in all cases reported and analyzed thus far), and an initial analysis was performed to determine whether, given a suspected heterogeneity of species in the Makapansgat population, our data from sheep or perhaps the data from the caribou might be more appropriate, or whether both might account for some of the variation in the sample. It should be pointed out that the data used here are only those summarized by Dart as representing a variety of antelope species of which at least 39 individuals were large forms like kudu, 126 were medium-sized animals like wildebeest, 100 were small forms like gazelle, and 28 were very small like duiker.

Our initial analysis was concerned simply with determining whether or not inclusion of the density data from the caribou might be helpful when analyzing a population of animals including both large and small forms. The function used was as follows:

$$F = P_1(\text{atan}(P_2) + \text{atan }(P_3 X_a - P_2))$$
$$+ P_4(\text{atan}(P_2) + \text{atan }(P_3 X_b - P_2))$$
$$+ P_5(\text{atan}(P_2) + \text{atan }(P_3 X_c - P_2))$$
$$+ P_6(\text{atan}(P_2) + \text{atan }(P_3 X_d - P_2))$$

where

X_a = the measured densities of the 6-month sheep
X_b = the measured densities of the 19-month sheep
X_c = the measured densities of the 90-month sheep
X_d = the measured densities of the mature caribou.

The results of this analysis are summarized in Table 3.20. Several conclusions seem clearly warranted by this analysis:

1. *Inclusion of the data from the caribou is of no utility in accounting for the faunal frequencies observed at Makapansgat.* In our analysis, no variance was pivoted on the caribou data.
2. *The relationship between bone density and proportions of anatomical parts recovered at Makapansgat is very high* (correlation coefficient = .799).
3. *The population of animals at Makapansgat appears to be constituted of at least two major age classes, young animals and very old animals.* In this analysis, no variance was pivoted on the density data of the 19-month sheep.

Given these conclusions, we decided to run the Makapansgat data again, using the same strategy employed in the analysis of the Navajo and Hottentot data, that is, a suite of regressions each corresponding to the densities of animals at various months post birth.

The data summarized in Table 3.21 demonstrates nicely that *(a)* the Makapansgat fauna is composed essentially of young and extremely old animals, with a bias in favor of young; *(b)* this fauna was accumulated primarily during the summer months of the southern hemisphere coinciding with the period of rains under modern conditions; *(c)* finally, the low standard errors for the estimate and the high correlation coefficients strongly support the argument that *all the variability in anatomical parts observed at Makapansgat may be understood as the result of a population of predominately young (85.5%) and some very old animals (14.5%) that were originally present as complete skeletons and were acted upon by an agent of attrition.* This analysis provides no support whatsoever for the argument that the differential frequencies of anatomical parts observed at Makapansgat are a function of selection by hominids, other animals, or introduction to the location of selected parts of the skeleton from other places. Complete animals were originally present. The age structure indicated is a near classic example of the death population expected at the hands of a predator. For instance, Buechner (1960),

Table 3.20

Summary Data for a Single Multiple-Curvilinear Regression of Bone Densities from Four Animals against the MNI's Surviving for Twenty-Six Anatomical Parts at Makapansgat

Summary statistics	Value of parameters
Correlation coefficient for observed and expected = .799	$P_2 = 24.44$
Standard error of the estimate = 30.31	$P_3 = 13.68$
Standard deviation for the mean of observed MNI's = 49.71	$P_1 = 297.53$ (6-month sheep)
Residual sum of squares = 22,052.6	$P_4 = 0.0$ (19-month sheep)
Density at inflection point = 1.79	$P_5 = 119.12$ (90-month sheep)
	$P_6 = 0.0$ (mature caribou)

Table 3.21

Summary of the Results[a]

	1	2	3	4	5	6
Correlation coefficient	.61	.87	.87	.89	.51	.66
Standard error of the estimate	40.28	24.72	26.14	24.05	69.7	38.1
Residual sum of squares	38,968.0	14,672	16,405	13,880	116,638	34,936
Value of P_2	13.41	89.9	89.91	89.9	4.88	6.98
Value of P_3	8.89	98.5	91.6	87.2	20.6	5.06
Density at inflection point	1.51	.91	1.01	1.03	.23	1.38
Age Class 1 (P_1)	309.27	49.19	49.87	50.9	0.14	149.87
Age Class 2 (P_4)	0.0	0.0	0.0	0.0	0.0	0.0
Age Class 3 (P_5)	0.0	0.0	0.0	0.0	0.0	0.0
Age Class 4 (P_6)	0.0	0.0	0.0	0.0	0.0	0.0
Age Class 5 (P_7)	0.0	0.0	0.0	0.0	0.0	0.0
Age Class 6 (P_8)	0.0	9.8	9.4	8.6	0.0	0.0
Month of relevance[b]	March (Sept.)	May (Nov.)	July (Jan.)	Sept. (March)	Nov. (May)	Jan. (July)

[a] Standard deviation of the mean for the sample $= 49.71$.
[b] Months in parentheses are southern hemisphere equivalents.

in a reanalysis of basic data reported by Murie (1944) regarding the effects of predation by wolves on a wild population of Alaskan mountain sheep (*Ovis dalli*), summarizes the death structure as follows: ". . . very high mortality among lambs, extremely low mortality in the age groups between one and nine years of age and high mortality in the older age groups beyond approximately ten years" (p. 85).

This same pattern of maximum death in the youngest and oldest age classes is what our analysis indicated.

We conclude that, based on the survivorship of anatomical parts at Makapansgat, there is absolutely no basis for the assumption that the hominids present played a behavioral role in the accumulation of the deposit.

Comparative Summary

We observed that the relative frequencies of anatomical parts remaining for archaeological observation on two Navajo sites were different. Information obtained from informants and from observation showed that the only major differences between the two sites was in the season of occupation and in the correlated difference in the age structure of the death population of sheep at the two locations. Both sites were characterized by exposure of complete skeletons of animals killed or dying to free ranging dogs. We proposed that the difference between the observed frequencies of anatomical parts preserved for archaeological observation and the frequencies present in the complete skeleton of a sheep was a function of differential destruction of anatomical parts by the dogs. Furthermore, we suggested that the probabilities of survival for a given anatomical part would vary with the bone density and, second, that bone density varied with the age of the animals subjected to attrition. We also observed that there were vast differences between the patterns of survivorship at the Navajo sites and at Eskimo sites where dogs had been fed. We knew, through observation and information from informants, that the Eskimo dogs did not have access to complete skeletons of caribou; instead, they had been selectively fed parts of caribou, in contrast to the situation at the Navajo sites. We concluded from this comparison that, although any given agent of attrition would destroy bones in direct proportion to their relative densities, the structure of the population of bones upon which such an agent operated would condition the character of the surviving population.

To evaluate these arguments, we studied three sheep and one caribou in terms of the pattern of bone density exhibited by different bones. In the case of the sheep, we discovered that *(a)* bones differed in density, and *(b)* the pattern of bone densification with increasing age was not an allometric growth process—bones changed in their density at different rates and magnitudes with age.

These findings supported our opinion that the different patterns of survivorship at the Navajo sites could be accounted for solely as a function of an agent of attrition operating on an original population of different age structure.

We then argued for an analytical strategy in which multiple-curvilinear regressions were run using an arctangent function partitioned in terms of the ages of animals possibly present at different time intervals since birth—representing different months of the year (since we could assume that most births occurred at essentially the same time of the year). The justifications and arguments for this procedure were presented, and the procedures were applied to the Navajo data, one example of the Eskimo data, the Hottentot goat data collected by Brain, and the provocative data from the very early site of Makapansgat. Some of our findings are summarized in Table 3.22.

The summary in Table 3.22 emphasizes several points. First, age variable bone densities for populations of variable age structure acted upon by an agent of attrition account, at a very high degree of accuracy, for observed variability in anatomical parts. Second, we note that, using a sheep model of densification in the analysis of goats and an extraordinarily mixed population of at least 30 species of African antelope, the fit is highly respectable. We conclude from this that research aimed at increasing the documentation of species other than those studied here may be selective rather than exhaustive, and, importantly, the study of modern species representatives can provide adequate models for at least some past populations. Referring to the ability to isolate the seasons of occupancy for faunal accumulations, the results from this preliminary study are most encouraging. In all cases of documented occupancy, our analytical procedures resulted in proper identifications. However, it must be kept in mind that, for faunal populations dominated by old animals, one can expect such procedures to be less accurate or definitive. We may expect that, the younger the population under study,

Table 3.22

Comparative Summary of Analytical Results

	Navajo sites		Hottentot sites	Makapansgat
	Winter	Summer		
Documented season of site use	Sept.–early March	Mid-March–early Sept.	Year round	Unknown
Analytically indicated season of use	Sept.–March	March–Sept.	Year round	Rainy season Nov.–March
Age structure analytically indicated				
Age Class 1	77.3%	47.5%	9.4%	85.5%
Age Class 2	14.6%	—	38.7%	—
Age Class 3	5.6%	—	38.7%	—
Age Class 4	—	—	—	—
Age Class 5	—	—	—	—
Age Class 6	2.5%	52.5%	51.7%	14.5%
Correlation coefficient of fit	.988	.916	.894	.890

the more accurate will be the seasonal indicators and, hence, the results obtained using the procedures developed here.

The recovery of accurate information on age structure seems highly likely and provocative. As we noted, the basic structure seems to be correctly indicated in the analysis of goats, but the specifics appear somewhat biased. This may well be due to differences between sheep and goats or to inaccuracies in the basic bone density data used in this analysis. One must recall that we had only three animals of known age and all other data was extrapolated from these three reference points. In addition, the laboratory procedures used in measuring bone density were not considered optimal by any means. We would not be surprised to discover that there are inaccuracies in our density approximations. Despite these acknowledged difficulties with the basic density data, we felt that the procedures developed and the preliminary results obtained were sufficiently provocative to be reported in detail, perhaps prompting others to obtain better data control through the study of bone density in animals through an age series.

Finally, we should comment on the procedures used. A multiple-curvilinear regression is not a simple calculation. When used along with the function developed here, it is essentially a search technique with no discrete solution. One must estimate values for the parameters when a curve fitting program is initiated. Different estimates may lead to very different results. We employed a constant set of parameter estimates throughout the analysis of all data, $P_1 = 1$, $P_2 = 9$, $P_3 = 5$, and all others are set at a value of 1. We could almost certainly have obtained better fits to the data had we elected to "experiment" with estimating the initial parameters. We chose to obtain more control over the comparative results by using a constant set of estimates. Others may well develop more satisfactory approaches to this type of analysis.

We should add a word of caution at this point; we have not developed a generally useful analytical method. Thus far, one can expect the procedure to work only if the *assumption* that the original population of bones upon which an agent of attrition operated was composed of complete skeletons is justified. If one has good independent reasons to suspect the action of an agent of attrition, then a failure to obtain a good fit can be taken as evidence that this assumption is not met—namely, that the original population was not composed of complete skeletons. This in itself may be useful information; however, at this time, we are unable to specify with any accuracy what that original population actually looked like. Clearly this is desirable, and it is a problem that will receive considerable attention in future work.

When thought is given to the more general aspects of this work, one point stands out—namely, the character of the population, in terms of both age structure and anatomical composition, upon which a process operates conditioning the resulting formal patterning in various ways.

We saw that, in the case of the Nunamiut dog yards, an identical process was at work—attrition by dogs—but the formal composition of resulting assemblages was highly variable. Herein lies the lesson: Most static populations of archaeological remains are the vectorial result of multiple causal interactions. We must approach such static–structural information from an analytical point of view, envisioning dynamics and complicated multivariate interacting causation. One can appreciate how a taxonomic approach using techniques for grouping assemblages that were once similar would distort our perception of the processes operative in the past. We might end up with any number of "groupings" for the faunal assemblages reported here, depending upon how we weighted different anatomical attributes. Similarly, we might obtain still other "assemblage types" through equal weighting strategies. What would they mean? What would such procedures reveal about the past? In my opinion they would primarily reveal confusion. Those engaged in such activities, however, would be convinced that their groupings were "real," and because of the ease of "identification" of new cases, they would argue that the meanings attributed to these observed differences and similarities must be correct, since, after all, the data were accommodated neatly in static terms. All the dog-yard assemblages were essentially identical in that all were the remains of volitional dog feeding. All assemblages were the density dependent modified result of an original assemblage. Thus, in these terms, they were all identical. On the other hand, most were different in their original faunal composition, reflecting finely tuned human behavior conditioned by seasonally relevant contingencies. Because of the attrition, we can suspect the observable assemblages not to reflect accurately these prior conditions. There is no way that a unidimensional taxonomic approach, so widely advocated in archaeology, could recover relevant organizational information from such data. In our experience, most, if not all, archaeological data are at least as complicated in their dynamic genesis as these reported here.

Acknowledging the preliminary nature of this study, with all its shortcomings, we are most excited by its potential. It would appear that we have offered a concrete demonstration that *at least some archaeological assemblages with low and attenuated archaeological "visibility" may, in fact, carry more information than some better preserved assemblages.* Only when a faunal assemblage has been subjected to attrition can one use an understanding of that process to obtain ready information on season of occupancy and age structure of the original population.

This situation is offered as a concrete example to the empiricists in the field who continuously point to the "incompleteness" of the archaeological record as a limitation on what we may learn from the past. As was said earlier, "the practical limitations on our knowledge of the past are not inherent in the nature of the archaeological record; the limitations lie in our methodological naivete . . . in our lack of [understanding] regarding the processes and events of the past" (Binford 1968:23).

ACKNOWLEDGMENTS

Many students have participated in various phases of this work. Mr. Mark Wimberly, together with Mr. Martin Topper, participated in the Navajo work. Miss Patricia Marchiando, Mr. Dan Witter, Mrs. Allison Witter, and Mr. Jean-Philippe Rigaud actively collected some of the data reported on Nunamiut dog yards. Laboratory work was conducted with the cooperation of Dr. James Sphuler. Mr. Jack Bertram developed the analytical techniques and mathematical models, and perfected the operation of the computer programs. He described his procedures in a "rough draft" manuscript which the senior author incorporated into the chapter presented here.

REFERENCES

Binford, Lewis R.
   1968   Archaeological perspectives. In *New perspectives in archeology,* edited by Sally R. and Lewis R. Binford. Chicago: Aldine, Pp. 5–32.
Brain, C. K.
   1969   The contribution of Namib Desert Hottentots to an understanding of Australopithecine bone accumulations. *Scientific Papers of the Namib Desert Research Station* No. 39: 13–22. (Walvis Bay, South West Africa)
Buechner, Helmut K.
   1960   The Bighorn sheep in the United States: Its past, present, and future. *Wildlife Monographs* No. 4. (The Wildlife Society, Chestertown, Maryland)
Chaplin, R. E.
   1971   *The study of animal bones from archaeological sites.* New York: Seminar Press.
Cornwall, I. W.
   1956   *Bones for the archaeologist.* London: Phoenix House Ltd.
Dart, R. A.
   1957a The Makapansgat Australopithecine Osteodontokeratic culture. *Proceedings of the 3rd Pan-African Congress of Prehistory.* (Tervuren, Belgium) Pp. 161–171.
   1957b The Osteodontekeratic culture of Australopithecus Prometheus. *Transvaal Museum Memoir* No. 10.

Dixon, W. J.
   1975   *B. M. D. P.* Berkeley: University of California Press.
Giles, R. H.
   1969   *Wildlife Management Techniques.* Washington, D.C.: The Wildlife Society.
Hartley, H. O.
   1961   Modified Gauss–Newton Method for fitting on non-linear regression functions. *Technometrics* **3**:269–280.
Hole, Frank, Kent V. Flannery, and James A. Neeley
   1969   Prehistory and human ecology on the Deh Luran Plain, an early village sequence from Khuzistan, Iran. *Memoirs of the Museum of Anthropology, University of Michigan* No. 1. (Ann Arbor)
Jennrich, R. I., and P. F. Sampson
   1968   Application of stepwise regression to non-linear least squares estimation. *Technometrics* **10**:63–72.
Leakey, Mary D.
   1971   *Olduvai Gorge*. Vol. 3. *Excavations in Beds I and II, 1960–1963*. Cambridge: Cambridge University Press.
Lewall, E. F., and I. M. Cowan
   1963   Age determination in black-tail deer by degree of ossification of the epiphyseal plate in the long bones. *Canadian Journal of Zoology* **41**(3):13–37.
Murie, Adolph
   1944   *The wolves of Mount McKinley.* U.S. National Park Service, Fauna Series, No. 5. Washington, D.C.: U.S. Government Printing Office.
Read-Martin, Catherine E., and Dwight W. Read
   1975   Australopithecine scavenging and human evolution: An approach from faunal analysis. *Current Anthropology* **16**(3):359–368.
Schiffer, Michael B.
   1972   Archaeological context and systemic context. *American Antiquity* **37**:156–165.
Silver, I. A.
   1963   The aging of domestic animals. In *Science in archaeology,* edited by Don Brothwell and Eric Higgs. New York: Basic Books. Pp. 250–268.
Sissons, H. A.
   1971   The growth of bone. In *The biochemistry and physiology of bone,* edited by Geoffrey H. Bourne. Vol. III. New York: Academic Press. Pp. 145–180.
Yellen, John E.
   n.d.   Cultural patterning in faunal remains: evidence from the !Kung Bushmen. In *Experimental Archaeology,* edited by D. W. Ingersoll. New York: Columbia University Press.

PART

Aquatic Resources
and
Human Adaptations

4

Strandloopers, Mermaids, and Other Fairy Tales: Ecological Determinants of Marine Resource Utilization—The Peruvian Case

University of New Mexico, Albuquerque

In fish must be recognized the first kind of artificial food, because it was not fully available without cooking. Fire was first utilized, not unlikely, for this purpose. Fish were universal in distribution, unlimited in supply, and the only kind of food at all times attainable. The cereals in the primitive period were still unknown, if in fact they existed, and the hunt for game was too precarious ever to have formed an exclusive means of human support. Upon this species of food mankind became independent of climate and of locality; and by following the shores of the seas and lakes, and courses of the rivers could, while in the savage state, spread themselves over the greater portion of the earth's surface. Of the fact of these migrations there is abundant evidence in the remains of flint and stone implements of the Status of Savagery found upon all the continents. In reliance upon fruits and spontaneous subsistence a removal from the original habitat would have been impossible [Lewis Henry Morgan, Ancient Society, *1877; 1963 edition edited by E. B. Leacock (Cleveland: World Publishing)].*

Introduction

Lee and DeVore (1968:3) state, "Cultural Man has been on the earth for some 2,000,000 years; for over 99 percent of this period he has lived as a hunter–gatherer. Only during the last 10,000 years has man begun to domesticate plants and animals, to use metals, and to harness energy sources other than the human body." We might add, as Binford (1968) has pointed out, that hunter–gatherers did not intensively exploit aquatic resources, particularly marine resources, until the post-Pleistocene period. With reference to the utilization of aquatic resources in general, both Binford (n.d.) and Clark (1948) emphasize the "early" development of Upper Paleolithic fishing in Europe prior to ca. 40,000 B.C. A cursory review of the archaeological literature concerning initial utilization of marine resources points to the relatively late appearance of coastal occupations (Table 4.1). Many anthropologists have assumed that the oceans of the world are veritable "cornucopias" of protein-rich animal resources awaiting exploitation by man. This basic, and previously unquestioned, assumption has perhaps been best stated by Sauer (1961:262–264):

> It may be proposed that, wherever man came from, the discovery of the tidal sea was a major event. The seashores must have had the strongest attraction for primitive and artless folk. Here was abundant and diverse food, waiting to be picked up or dug twice daily, and less subject to seasonal fluctuation than were land supplies. Fish and sea mammals were stranded occasionally. . . . Primitive man could hardly find a better prospect than beachcombing, which also was conducive to social grouping and reduced mobility.

We can see that a paradox arises when this basic assumption is considered with respect to the empirical world. If marine resources were so abundant and diverse, why were marine ecosystems virtually ignored by human populations until late in prehistory? Perhaps, more importantly, why were marine resources ever exploited at all?

Anthropological literature dealing with maritime hunter–gatherers is limited. We also find few causal arguments explaining the reasons for man's use of the ocean's food resources. Basically, there are three general types of extant causal arguments. First, and perhaps foremost, is the argument that changes in the biophysical environment have forced human groups to exploit the oceans. In 1925, V. Gordon Childe suggested:

> The changed conditions due to the inrush of salt water (rise of sea level following the Pleistocene) naturally affected profoundly the manner of life of the inhabitants of Scandinavia. The famous shellheaps or kitchen middens of Denmark may be the monuments of the Maglemose people adapted to the new environment [1925:13].

Again, in 1935, Childe argued that the "Azilian" people were forced out of western Europe by encroaching heavy forests because they lacked the stone ax.

Fitzhugh (1972:160) believes that the isostatic rebound of Labrador led to early utilization of the ocean in this region.

> Summer occupations grew in size and shifted further seaward from Sandy Cove into the Rattlers Bight-Winter Cove area, the last outpost of the mainland. This settlement was made possible after 2000 B.C. by the geological emergence of an ideal site with sheltered harbors and excellent marine hunting and fishing grounds.

Finally, Dumond (1969:1113) proposes that, for southwestern Alaska,

> the cause of this shift toward maritime resources is not certain. It has been suggested that the general lowering of temperature during the first millennium B.C. forced a greater reliance upon ocean products.

Table 4.1

Archaeological Evidence for Early Use of Marine Resources

Location	Site name and/or cultural period	Date	Reference
Africa, south coast	Klasies River Mouth cave; Middle Stone Age	80,000–90,000 B.P.	Klein 1974:249–284
	Oakhurst complex	13,000–6000 B.C.	Sampson 1974:310
Ireland and Scotland	Obanian culture	3805–3065 B.C.	Mackie 1968:412
Scandinavia	Ertebølle culture	3800–3200 B.C.	Clark 1975:167, 192
Italy, south coast	Grotta Romanelli	10,000 B.C.	
	Grotta La Porta	6500 B.C.	Whitehouse 1968:345
Spain, Cantabria	La Lloseta; Magdalenian period	15,656 B.P.	Clark 1971:1255
	El Cierro; Azilian period	10,712 B.P.	Clark 1971:1255
Portugal	Tejo Valley; Mesolithic period	no date	Roche 1960, 1966
Eastern Russia	Amur Estuary; Maritime culture	3000–2000 B.C.	Watson 1971:142, 157
	Peschanyy Peninsula near Kirovskiy	2197 B.C.	Okladnikov 1965:166
Japan	Natsushima shell midden	7491 B.C.	Kidder 1959
Philippine Islands	Duyong cave	5050 B.C.	Reinman 1967:153
Taiwan	Coastal Hoabinhian	10,000–3000 B.C.	Gorman 1971
Borneo	Agop Atlas cave	9000 B.C.	Harrisson 1971:363
Australia	New South Wales	2360 B.C.	Campbell 1972:283–286
	Tropical north coast	5000 B.C.	Binford n.d.
Tasmania	Storm Bay	8700 B.P.	
	South cave, Rocky Cape	8120 B.P.	
	Sister's Creek Site	6050 B.P.	Jones 1968:198–199
North America, Coastal Maine	Damariscotta Site	50–1130 A.D.	Snow 1972:212, 215
New York	Croton Point, Lower Hudson Valley	3900 B.C.	
	Montrose Point	3700 B.C.	
	Bannerman Site	2530 B.C.	
		4200 B.C.	Newman 1974
Florida	St. Johns River	2000 B.C.	
	Stallings Island	2500 B.C.	Stoltman 1972:54
Alabama	Bryant's Landing	2139 B.C.	Holmes and Trickey 1974
California	San Francisco Bay	3150–2310 B.P.	
	Little Harbor Site Catalina Island	1900 B.C.	Willey 1966
	Glen Annie Canyon	5320–4430 B.C.	Owen *et al.* 1964:477
British Columbia	Bella Coola area Dodge Island Site	2840 B.C.	Fladmark 1974:237–238
	Prince Rupert area Namu Site	2550 B.C.	Fladmark 1974:236–237
Aleutian Islands	Chaluka Site	1500 B.C.	MacCartney 1971:97
	Kodiak Island	3500–1000 B.C.	Fladmark 1974:243
Central America Panama	Monagrillo Site	2140 B.C.	Willey 1971
Maya Lowlands	Isla Cancun	130 B.C.	Andrews 1965:295
South America Colombia	Puerto Hormiga	3090–2552 B.C.	
	Barlovento	1560–1030 B.C.	Willey 1971
Brazil	Sambaqui de Maratua	7803 B.P.	
	Sambaqui de Gomes	2540 B.C.	Hurt 1964:28–29

Second, several anthropologists have posited that man's initial use of the ocean was made possible only after technological change. For example, Snow (1972:214) states:

> Elsewhere along the coast, aboriginal preferences were shifting toward the common clam. Other shellfish were gathered where available, but the clam became nearly a staple in the summer diet. Rising sea level and contingent ecological changes might explain the shift in some specific instances, but the development of tools and techniques for exploitation of the more widely available clam is the more economical hypothesis. Rising water seems to have forced beds to relocate, but did not exterminate them.

Third, several anthropologists have proposed that ideological changes are responsible for the shift toward increased utilization of marine resources. Most of these types of "explanation" concern man's increased awareness of his biophysical environment. Ritchie (1969a:54) states:

> If the Lamoka culture was, as has been suggested, an offshoot of the southeastern Archaic Shell Mound culture, the relative neglect of the local shellfish is difficult to understand, unless such food became prohibited by taboo, or was unnecessary because of the sufficiency of other and superior foods. It seems more reasonable to suppose that, in common with certain other eastern Archaic folk, they had not learned the esculency of such food.

Likewise, Fitzhugh (1972:167) suggests:

> The reasons for increasing exploitation of marine fauna, apparently correlated partially with duration of occupancy, is a logical consequence of increased familiarity and adaptation. Those cultures without time on the coast did not proceed as far in this direction as others and merely transferred their interior adaptation to the coast without innovation or modification.

Finally, Moseley (1975b:58) proposes that the Late Preceramic inhabitants of coastal Peru began to use marine foods "perhaps [because] it was simply a desire for dietary variation that opened the door to reliance on marine resources. . . ."

Apart from these three major types of causal arguments for the initial exploitation of the sea there are arguments that combine several of them (see Braun 1974). J. G. D. Clark (1952:62) provides one of the most potentially provocative models for explaining man's first intensive use of the sea:

> Broadly speaking it seems to be true that the extent to which this vast reservoir of food (the ocean) and raw materials was drawn upon was related directly to the pressure of population on the resources of the dry land. So long as subsistence was based mainly on hunting and gathering and the population remained sparse, the sea was comparatively neglected except for what could be gathered on the shore. With the spread of farming a noticeable advance may be noted both in offshore fishing and in the hunting of sea mammals, whether among communities or among marginal hunter–fishers . . . .

A major argument that is central to this chapter is that marine food resources are inferior to terrestrial resources, especially mammals, both in terms of human labor investment and in terms of protein yield. If we examine the gross and yet very significant differences between marine and terrestrial ecosystems, two reasons for the less "optimal" character of marine foods become apparent. First, the oceans, in general, are less productive per unit area than terrestrial environments. Even though the ratio of land-to-ocean surface for the world is 1 : 2.2, the ratio of terrestrial-to-marine net primary productivity is 4.7 : 1 (see Pianka 1974:48, Table 3.1.) Isaacs (1969) explains this phenomenon as a result of the nature of marine plant life and the dilution of food sources in a fluid environment. Second, marine mammals of large body size are at higher trophic levels in the food chain than are terrestrial mammals of large body size. This means that, due to the tremendous loss of energy between trophic levels, human populations exploiting marine mammals are in the fifth or sixth trophic level, whereas human groups who depend upon terrestrial mammals are in the third trophic level. The ecological implications for human groups will be discussed later.

In addition, primary production in marine ecosystems is restricted to the upper 5–35 meters of the ocean. Nutrients and detritus that are not quickly utilized in this upper or euphotic zone are lost due to settling. Unless lower levels of the ocean are disrupted and mixed by physical forces, such as monsoons or upwelling currents, these sources of energy are not later made available to the primary producers.

The following two sections of this chapter will deal with these aspects of marine ecology as they pertain to Prehistoric use of littoral food resources. First, I will present a general explanatory model that accounts for the shift in Prehistoric subsistence strategies from terrestrial to marine foods. Like Clark (1952), I believe that such a change did not occur in most areas of the world until inland human populations increased to levels approaching carrying capacity *(K)* of the environment. It should be pointed out, however, that, in certain environments, such as in northern latitudes, early human colonizers might have been forced to exploit aquatic foods, for example, anadramous fish, if their availability coincided with seasonal lows in terrestrial productivity (Binford n.d.). Unlike Clark, however, I argue that high population densities can be reached in particular ecological situations among nonagricultural societies. The current model is couched in terms of density-dependent factors with specific reference to two forms of natural selection, *r*-selection and *K*-selection. This density-dependent model for the initial use of marine foods will then be applied to the archaeological record of Peru. Although its further extension is beyond the scope of this chapter, the model can be applied to many empirical cases involving marine resource exploitation in world prehistory. Herein lies the utility of such a general explanatory model.

The second section of this chapter deals with the determinant effects of an upwelling current system upon Late Preceramic cultural systems on the Peruvian coast. In this case, what are the effects of a coastal upwelling zone on cultural systems that exploit the ocean? What are the cultural ramifications of the exploitation of such an anomalous marine ecosystem where the relatively low productivity of the ocean is greatly increased? Although the particular environmental factors are specific to the Peruvian coast in this case, the broader implications of the general ecological relationships that obtain between coastal populations and the marine food web are relevant to other coastal settings and to various cultural–environmental interactions as well.

Density-Dependent Factors and the Explanatory Model

Initially, the concept of density-dependent factors was formulated by Howard and Fiske (1911) who were conducting entomological studies of moths and associated parasites. They proposed that balanced populations of hosts and parasites were maintained by "facultative" agents, for example, parasites and predators that reduced populations during periods of high density. A second set of controlling agents were classed as "catastrophic," for example, storms, mudslides, high temperatures, and so on; they acted to reduce population size regardless of density level.

Lotka (1925) and Volterra (1926, 1931) presented a series of competition equations that described the inhibitory effects of interacting predator–prey populations upon the population growth of the species involved. Pianka (1974:135) sums up the interactions described in the Lotka–Volterra equations in the following statement: "In the absence of the other species, populations of both species increase at any density below their own carrying capacity and decrease at any value above it."

Thompson (1929) suggested that animal populations were controlled by intrinsic limitations in the organisms themselves. Bodenheimer (1928) and Uvarov (1931) believed that weather was the critical factor in the control of animal population size. In 1933, Nicholson wrote a controversial paper attacking the Lotka–Volterra predator–prey model and arguing that competition for food and space in the environment, not climate, was responsible for limiting population size. In 1935, Smith suggested that an animal population has a characteristic density determined by biotic factors, such as disease, parasitism, and predation; Smith relabeled these facultative agents as density-dependent factors. The abiotic or catastrophic agents subsumed under climate and natural disasters were then designated as density-independent factors.

Andrewartha and Birch (1954) rejected the dichotomy between biotic and abiotic factors and proposed that all variables controlling the size of animal populations were density-dependent. Food shortages and inaccessibility of resources were considered to be two of the most important of these variables. Lack (1954) concluded that bird populations were limited by increased mortality rates that accompanied high population densities. He believed, like Andrewartha and Birch, that food scarcity and resulting starvation served as the primary limiting factor for vertebrate populations.

Chitty (1957) represents the "self-regulation" school of ecologists who argue that intraspecific competition and genetic deterioration within animal populations prevent infinite multiplication. Finally, Wynne-Edwards (1962) proposes that ornithological studies suggest that populations utilize social behavior, for example, social displays, aggregations, territoriality, and social hierarchies, to readjust population size to existing food supplies.

Early researchers characterized the growth of animal populations by a sigmoid growth curve. This curve has been used to model the cummulative growth of yeast cells, *Paramecium,* flour beetles, fruit flies, and man. Kendeigh (1974:211) provides a brief summary of the cummulative curve:

> The sigmoid curve shows that a finite population grows slowly at first, then at an accelerating rate which is at maximum at the point of inflection, after which the population continues to increase but at a decelerating rate, finally becoming stabilized at the upper asymptote. The lower concave part of the curve is called the accelerating phase of growth and the upper convex part of the curve, the inhibiting phase of growth.

The two forms of natural selection operate along two distinct portions of the sigmoid population growth curve. The portion called "r-selection" operates along that portion of the curve that is characterized only by the instantaneous growth rate (r) or the maximum growth rate that a population can achieve (MacArthur and Wilson 1967). "K-selection" occurs under conditions of the highest population densities achievable given a carrying capacity (K) of an environment (Gadgil and Solbrig 1972:16). Each form of selection calls for a different adaptive strategy. The r-strategist utilizes a greater portion of its energy for reproductive purposes since it is operating under conditions of high density-independent mortality attributable to abiotic factors, for example, floods, droughts, storms, and ecosystemic perturbations. Margalef (1963, 1968), in referring to the r-strategist, points out that, in immature ecosystems, natural selection favors prolific species to insure survival in a fluctuating environment with highly unpredictable future system states. As Gadgil and Solbrig (1972:18) emphasize:

> Therefore, in a statistical sense, the causes of D.I. (density-independent) mortality are less predictable and, consequently, organisms divert energy to reduce their detrimental effects than when under D.D. (density-dependent) regulation (all other things being equal).

In addition, Pianka (1974:90) states that, under conditions of r-selection, organisms tend to maximize production (see also MacArthur and Wilson 1967).

The K-strategist, on the other hand, utilizes more energy for nonreproductive behavior—either for competition (both interspecific and intraspecific) for essential resources or in predator–prey relationships (Gadgil and Solbrig 1972: 18–19). The K-strategy involves increasing the survival potential of the individual and/or increasing the ability of the organism to secure essential resources (Gadgil and Solbrig 1972:19). The K-strategy also involves a trend toward increased efficiency in both activities (Pianka 1974:90).

We can see that human populations in high density contexts accomplish both aspects of the K-strategy, that is, increasing the survival potential of the individual and increasing the resource-capturing ability of the individual vis-a-vis the group through extrasomatic or cultural means (White 1959). For human, as opposed to animal, populations operating under K-selection, we would not expect that the character of natural selection would be different per se, but rather that the nature of adaptive responses would be quantitatively different. Human populations operating under K-selection would devote considerable amounts of energy to competition for vital resources. However, unlike genetically controlled animal populations, human groups would have numerous extrasomatic options or alternative responses available, including several forms of population regulation, such as abortion, infanticide, post-partum abstinence, and so on. In addition, human groups could restructure the relationship between producers and consumers and alter feeding strategies by moving resources to consumers, intensifying labor, increasing reliance upon domesticated plants and animals, or by emigrating to unexploited areas. Intraspecific competition, for animal populations in general and human groups in particular, is very intense due to the reliance of species members upon the same kinds of natural resources. As Kendeigh (1974: 197) points out, "Once an area is well saturated with established individuals, it is often more economical of energy for new individuals to seek homes elsewhere, even in less favorable situations, than to intrude."

The explanatory model for the initial utilization of marine resources is based on the assumption that these resources are either low-return or high-investment energy sources. Subsistence strategies involving such food resources are, therefore, selected only in those contexts in which alternative low-investment, high-return foods are inadequate for human populations. Birdsell (1968) has posited that hunter–gatherer populations are maintained below the carrying capacity of their environments. Disruption of this equilibrium situation can occur through environmental change causing a decrease in exploitable biomass, immigration of neighboring human populations, or by intrinsic population growth caused by an increase in the live birth rate. Human populations living under density-dependent selection would be expected to make K-strategy responses, both long term (genetic) and short term (extrasomatic or cultural) in nature. Marine resource exploitation might then be expected to occur in areas that are marginal to inland high population density regions or in environments, such as extreme northern latitudes, where aquatic and/or marine resources are available when terrestrial production is extremely low. Inland regions with high population densities might donate splinter populations to adjacent areas, thereby disrupting equilibrium conditions similar to those described by Birdsell (1968) and Binford (1968). Similarly, the effects of inland overexploitation of optimal resources could be felt in marginal zones as a reduction in overall carrying capacity. Regardless of the cause, the effect—reduced carrying capacity in environments adjacent to the ocean—would require hunting and gathering groups to begin to substitute less "optimal" food resources, for example, marine shellfish, pelagic fish, and sea mammals, for low-investment, high-return terrestrial mammals (this will be discussed later). Let us turn now to the examination of the archaeological record in order to evaluate the utility of the density-dependent model in explaining the initial intensive utilization of marine food resources—particularly shellfish—along the Peruvian coast.

The Initial Utilization of Marine Resources: The Peruvian Case

During the Late Preceramic V Encanto phase, hunting and gathering groups in the coastal region of Peru shifted their emphasis of subsistence strategies from terrestrial to marine resources (Lanning 1967:26–27). Prior to this period, Lanning (1963:44, 1967:48–53) argues, the fog vegetation or *lomas* biome played a significant role in the subsistence strategies of Preceramic hunter–gatherers who practiced seasonal movements between river valley, *lomas,* and tundra, *puna-lomas.* Lanning sees climatic changes during the Altithermal as having been a causal factor responsible for increased reliance upon sea foods. More specifically, alterations in Pacific atmospheric circulation patterns during the Altithermal caused increased upwelling and/or shoreward movement of the Peru Current system. This change in the current system increased the desiccation of the adjacent shore, causing the *lomas* vegetation and animal populations to retreat or to disappear.

Lanning's environmental model explaining the shift in Late Preceramic subsistence strategies is not at all unlike those presented by Childe, Fitzhugh, or Dumond. Craig and Psuty (1968) and Parsons (1970) have challenged Lanning's ideas by presenting evidence for climatic stability and insufficient *lomas* resources during the Holocene for coastal Peru. Craig and Psuty (1968:147–148) argue that the coastal environment has remained virtually unchanged during the Holocene. They found vast deposits of *Pecten* or scallop shells at Otuma on the southern coast of Peru which represent Prehistoric shellfish populations that existed as filter feeders in plankton-rich waters, suggesting that:

> There has been a steady-state in the marine regime around the Paracas Peninsula for at least the past few thousand years. Plankton do not flourish in warm, tropical waters and we must conclude that any changes in the littoral ecosystem near Otuma have been minor.

With specific reference to Lanning's contention that the *lomas* was reduced considerably in areal extent by increased aridity of the coast, Craig and Psuty (1968:153–154) emphasize that:

> If we consider these environmental factors (the abundance of "fossil" *Pecten* at Otuma, specialized adaptations of *lomas* vegetation, etc.) systematically . . . no progressive drying up of the coastal vegetation can be satisfactorily demonstrated at this time. . . . the prevailing wind, oceanic gyre, coriolis force and upwelling cannot be considered ephemeral factors active only since the end of the Pleistocene.

More recent work by Fung, Cenzano, and Zavaleta (1972) cited by Lynch (1974:362) tends to provide strong support for climatic stability for the Late Preceramic periods discussed in this chapter. Fung re-excavated the Chivateros quarry site on the central Peruvian coast and found that "The shallow 'deposits' were formed *in situ* under relatively constant climatic conditions, like those of the present, marked by warm summers and cool, damp winters." This conclusion is not only important because it excludes Lanning's ideas concerning the cause for the initial utilization of the Peruvian intertidal zone, but also because it justifies my reliance upon present-day information dealing with existing characteristics of the Peru Current upwelling system for the Late Preceramic periods. Lynch (1974:362) adds:

> Fung's interpretation also reinforces our picture of rather stable Quaternary climate on the coast of Peru, a reconstruction favored by the geologists Peterson and Dollfus (Fung *et al.,* 1972, p. 68) as well as the geographers Craig and Psuty (1968, pp. 123,126,153–155). Craig (personal communication, 1974) believes that the substantial reduction of lomas vegetation should be attributed to postconquest animal husbandry practices rather than climatic change. As the Peru Current is the controlling variable for coastal climate, the present regime must date back at least to the establishment of the anchovetas and the earliest production of guano. Craig feels that the thick guano deposits are proof of hyperaridity for at least 45,000 yrs, calculating that the maximum thickness of 150 m built up at about the same rate as in the recent past.

Moseley (1975b:42) also takes issue with Lanning concerning the importance of the *lomas* for Preceramic hunter–gatherers and the lack of evidence for climatic change during this period. Moseley, however, does not offer a stronger explanation for the increased reliance upon marine foods. Instead, he argues that, once coastal populations expanded their subsistence activities to include marine foods, they were, in a sense, trapped (Moseley 1975b:56). The addition of marine foods to their diet allowed population growth that placed even greater stress on the *lomas* resource food supply. With continued population growth, the *lomas* was overexploited, and marine foods then became essential. As was pointed out earlier, however, the weak point of this argument is that Moseley fails to provide an adequate explanation of why marine products were initially incorporated into Late Preceramic subsistence at all. If, as Craig and Psuty (1968) and Fung *et al.* (1972) believe, the environment of coastal Peru was stable throughout the Holocene, why did man "hesitate" to exploit the rich resources of the Pacific littoral—alluded to by Rowe (1963:297), Lanning (1963:51), Parsons (1970), and Moseley (1972:40)—until the third millennium B.C.? One might first suggest that many marine resources are located beyond the littoral ecotone and, therefore, require rather significant investments in labor and/or procurement technology, for example, water craft, navigation hardware, nets, compound hunting–fishing gear, floats, and so on. Indeed, there is little or no evidence of such a technology from the Preceramic periods of Peru (see Moseley 1975b:53–54). From the available information on coastal Preceramic subsistence (Engel 1963a; Lanning 1963; Donnan 1964; Moseley 1968, 1972, 1975b; Bird 1948; Parsons 1970), the most important animal foods were shellfish and sea lion, while the primary plant foods consisted of cattails, sedges, edible fruits, seaweeds, and grass seeds. Shellfish collecting could have been carried out with relative ease in the intertidal zone by young and old, male and female members of Prehistoric societies. Procurement technology would be minimal, requiring only spatulate prying implements, mussels forks, and baskets or carrying bags (see Greengo 1952:71–76; Stuart 1972:56–58).

If the various models or ideas proposed by Lanning and Moseley do not account for changes in subsistence strategies during the Encanto, Playa Hermosa, and Conchas phases of the Late Preceramic period for Peru (see Lanning 1963, 1965, 1967; Moseley 1968, 1972, 1975b; Patterson 1971a,b; Patterson and Lanning 1964; Patterson and Moseley 1968), is there an adequate alternative explanatory model? I believe that the general density-dependent model discussed earlier better explains the initial utilization of marine resources on the Peruvian coast because it not only subsumes a whole series of Prehistoric cultural processes on both the sierra and the coast, but also because the model has general applicability to early use of marine resources throughout geographical space and archaeological time. Let us now turn briefly to the archaeological record of highland Peru, specifically the Ayacucho area, to look at the evidence that might support this model.

Recent archaeological investigations in the Ayacucho region of the south-central Peruvian highlands under the direction of Richard S. MacNeish (1969, 1970) provide an interesting perspective on Peruvian prehistory. A cursory review of information available thus far suggests that a number of cultural developments occurred initially in the highlands. First, the earliest date for human occupation in Peru is from Pikimachay cave near Ayacucho where sloth vertebrate associated with the Paccaicasa cultural complex produced a date of $19,600 \pm 3000$ radiocarbon years (MacNeish 1970:13). In contrast, the earliest date for early man in the coastal region is $12,795 \pm 350$ radiocarbon years (Ossa and Moseley 1972:15) from Quirihuac shelter in the Moche Valley. Following the initial occupation of the highlands, there were a number of cultural developments that provide evidence of various Prehistoric behavioral adaptations that appear in the Andes prior to the Pacific Coast. Several of these cultural developments are listed in Table 4.2. For the purpose of this chapter, the most significant of these developments are sedentism, the origins of agriculture, and animal domestication. I suggest that these developments were causally linked to ecological factors in the Peruvian highlands and represent adaptive responses to density-dependent K-selection.

I propose that the preeminence of the highlands can be attributed to an extremely high ecological diversity created by altitudinal variation. The nature of this diversity is discussed by Schwabe (1969):

> The Andean region of South America, stretching as it does over 70° latitude and being very strongly determined by the afore-mentioned geophysical processes, is one of the most uniquely varied ecological structures of the earth occupying a continuous substratum [p. 119].

Table 4.2

Temporal Comparison of Cultural Developments in Coastal and Highland Peru[a]

Cultural development	Coast	Highlands
Initial occupation	10,845 B.C. Quirihuac shelter Moche Valley	17,650 B.C. Pikimachay Cave Ayacucho Valley
Projectile points	10,000 B.C. Paijan, La Cumbre, north coast	15,000 B.C. Pikimachay Cave Ayacucho Valley
Ground stone tools *(Manos* and *Metates)*	7000–6000 B.C. (?) Arenal Complex, central coast	6600–5500 B.C. Jaywa Complex Puente and Jaywamachay shelters Ayacucho Valley
Sedentary communities	2500 B.C. north-central coast	4300–2800 B.C. Chihua Complex Ayacucho Valley
Ceramics	1700 B.C. Huaca La Florida, central coast	1800 B.C. Wari-Jirca phase Kotosh
Domesticated plants Gourd *(Lagenaria)*	3000 B.C. Chilca Site, central coast	5500–4300 B.C. Piki Complex Ayacucho Valley
Pepper *(Capsicum)*	2500 B.C. Huaca Prieta, north coast; Pampa, central coast	5500–4300 B.C. Piki Complex Ayacucho Valley
Squash *(Cucurbita moschata)*	2770 B.C. Huaca Prieta 3000 B.C. (?) Pampa Site	2800–1700 B.C. 5500–4300 B.C. (?) Ayacucho Valley
(Cucurbita ficifolia)	2500 B.C. Huaca Prieta, north coast	1000–400 B.C. 2800–1700 B.C. (?) Cachi Complex Ayacucho Valley
Corn *(Zea mays)*	1950 B.C. Huarmey Site, north-central coast	3000–2500 B.C. Rosamachay Cave Ayacucho Valley
Beans *(Phaseolus vulgaris)*	4700 B.C. Northern Chile	5600 B.C. Guitarrero Cave Callejon de Huaylas
Beans *(Phaseolus lunatus)*	2500 B.C. Huaca Prieta, north coast	5600 B.C. Guitarrero Cave Callejon de Huaylas

Table 4.2 *(continued)*

Cultural development	Coast	Highlands
Cotton		
(Gossypium)	3000 B.C. (?)	4300–2800 B.C. (?)
	Chilca Site,	Chihua Complex
	central coast	2800–1700 B.C.
	2500 B.C.	Ayacucho Valley
	Huaca Prieta,	
	north coast	
Lucuma		
(Lucuma)	2500 B.C.	3000 B.C. (?)
	Huaca Prieta,	Pikimachay Cave
	north coast	Ayacucho Valley
Domesticated Camelid		
(Llama glama)	Initial Period	4000–1000 B.C.
	ca. 1800–900 B.C.	Ayacucho Valley
Guinea Pig	Initial Period	4000–1000 B.C.
(Cavia)	ca. 1800–900 B.C.	Ayacucho Valley

[a] Data on domesticates are taken primarily from Flannery (1973:304–305).

> This area, especially in its southern half, is characterised by a complex, and, in many places, an exceedingly small-scale differentiation probably unique in the whole biosphere. . . . The Andean-Pacific area is thus characterised by an unusually small scale mosaic which leads to a sharp individualization of its landscape types [p. 122].
> Thus Andean South America, at least from the equator southwards, is characterised by a regional and microclimatic fine-scale mosaic which may be considered to be unique in the whole biosphere in its sharpness and detail. Which of the determining causes is to be considered decisive in each case for an ecological characterisation of the area will depend on the geographical latitude, height above sea level and the exposition of the area . . . [p. 123].

Apparently, early man in South America followed the Andean chain southward through the biome similar to the present-day *páramo-puna-altiplano*. These biomes supported low diversity–low equability communities of plants and animals. Here we would expect to find aggregates of large herbivorous mammals like the camelids. With long-term exploitation of existing ungulate populations, including the cervids, such as the whitetail deer, early hunters were forced to move into adjacent, more ecological diverse zones created by mountainous terrain. At this time, human populations found themselves in a situation analogous to that described by Glassow (1972:295) for the Basketmaker of the American Southwest. Preagricultural, sedentary communities or a bipolar wet-season–dry-season settlement pattern could have been established in areas where there was ready access to several adjacent ecosystems and their ecotonal boundaries. Populations living near several adjacent communities and their ecotones are in an optimal position to exploit the benefits of the *edge effect* as discussed by Odum (1971:157):

> The ecotonal community commonly contains many of the organisms of each of the overlapping communities and, in addition, organisms which are characteristic of and often restricted to the ecotone. Often, both the number of species and the population density of some of the species are greater in the ecotone than in the communities flanking it.

Preagricultural highland groups, like the Basketmaker of North America, would have had a centralized position from which to gain access to different biotic communities while remaining in one or two settlements throughout the year (for examples of these biotic communities, see MacNeish 1969: Fig. 2). If early hunters disrupted the population equilibria of cervid or camelid populations in the high Andes by overexploitation leading to reduced herd sizes and increased hunting time, we might expect to observe the situation described by Pianka (1974:208):

> Should food be scarce, foraging animals are unlikely to bypass potential prey, whereas during times of (or in areas with) abundant food, individuals may be more selective and restrict their diets to only the better food types. Thus a low expectation of finding prey, or a high mean search time per item, demands generalization, whereas a higher expectation of locating prey items (short mean search time per item) allows some degree of specialization.

In short, we might expect to observe a shift from mobile, specialized hunters to less mobile, generalized hunter–gatherers in the Peruvian highlands prior to the appearance of intensive utilization of marine resources along the Pacific Coast.

In a recent study by Binford and Chasko (n.d.), we find that, for the Nunamuit Eskimo of northern Alaska, a shift from mobile hunting to sedentism was followed by marked population growth. Rapid population increase for the Nunamuit is not attributable to a depressed death rate, but rather to an increased live birth rate. This change has been shown to be correlated significantly with increased stability in caloric intake, reduced male absentism, and increased consumption of carbohydrates, all of which are associated with sedentism. In addition, a reduction in the miscarriage rate among less mobile females also contributes to the multidimensional cause of an increased live birth rate. Binford proposes that, with sedentism, there is a reduction in the amount of effective resource space utilized by the population. With this reduction, there would be a tendency toward overexploitation of larger animals due to the nature of the pyramid of numbers (animals of larger body size are less numerous in an ecosystem; see Odum 1971:79–81). As the sedentary human population continued to exploit a particular area, there would be a shift toward a decreased reliance upon large mammals and an increased utilization of plant foods, for example, agriculture, with higher levels of consumed carbohydrates. Increased reliance on plant foods would probably be associated with labor organizational changes involving a decrease in specialized hunting activities and a consequent decrease in male absentism which would contribute to increased number of conceptions.

In summary, I propose that ecological diversity in the highlands of Peru created situations in which hunting and gathering societies could reduce their residential mobility, becoming less mobile and, in some cases, sedentary. Associated with sedentism or reduced mobility were dietary changes, alleviation of stress upon pregnant females, shifts in labor organization, and systemic changes between man and environment that cumulatively affected fertility and initiated marked population increases in the Peruvian highlands during the Late Preceramic periods. Conditions that allow hunting and gathering groups to reduce their mobility and/or become sedentary and the resultant increase in live birth rates then disrupt the equilibrium between human population size and available resources described by Birdsell (1968). Under conditions of high population density, ecologists argue that the K-strategist attempts to increase his ability to secure vital resources. Perhaps this strategy is reflected in the archaeological record of the highlands in the early appearance of domesticated plants and animals. Also, under conditions of K-selection, one of the options open to portions of a population is emigration into less densely occupied areas. For Prehistoric human groups in the Peruvian highlands, we might expect splinter groups to have moved into adjacent, more sparsely inhabited regions, including the western slopes of the Cordillera Occidental and the coast. Areal expansion and readjustments of population to available natural resources in the Peruvian Andes would have forced hunter–gatherers near the coast to shift the emphasis of their subsistence strategies toward increased reliance upon marine resources as a density-dependent response to conditions in the highlands.

Feeding Strategies and Second-Rate Marine Resources

Although a comprehensive discussion of feeding strategies (see Schoener 1971; Pianka 1974) is beyond the scope of this chapter, it is important to emphasize at this point that man's subsistence-related behavior is subject to selective pressures covered by the laws of thermodynamics (see Gallucci 1973:342). With reference to this matter, Emlen (1966:611) states: "natural selection will favor the development of feeding preferences that will, by their direction and intensity, and within the physical and nervous limit of the species, maximize the net caloric intake per individual of that species per unit time."

With respect to the initial utilization of marine foods by man on the coast of Peru, Pianka's (1974:143) comments are quite appropriate:

> Consider next the manner in which an expanding population makes use of a resource continuum or a habitat gradient. Again, the argument applies equally well to resource categories that are not continuous, but discrete. The first individual will no doubt select those resources and/or habitats that are optimal in the absence of competition. However, as the density of individuals increases, competition among them reduces the benefits to be gained from these optimal resources and/or habitats, and favors deviant individuals that use less "optimal," but also less hotly contested, resources and/or habitats. By these means, intraspecific competition can often act to increase the variety of resources and habitats utilized by a population.

Marine resources for Preceramic nonagricultural societies in Peru, and in many other areas of the world, were not only less hotly contested resources, but they also had a very low pay-off in terms of human nutrition except under intraspecific competition or subsistence-related stress conditions. Recent investigations conducted by Parmalee and Klippel (1974) have demonstrated that fresh-water shellfish are a relatively poor food source. If we examine the exploitation of marine shellfish in terms of protein yield per organism and per unit weight of organism, it becomes quite apparent why, in Sauer's words, the "abundant and diverse food, waiting to be picked up or dug twice daily" was not used by early hunter–gatherers in South America and around the world.

If we assume that the daily minimum protein requirement for adults is 40 grams (Abbott 1966:3), it would be necessary for an individual to collect 494 mussels per day if no other protein sources were utilized. One hundred grams of shellfish meat, in this case, yields 7.5 grams of protein, and one mussel provides 1.065 grams of meat (Cook 1946:51–52). If the equivalent values are then compared to the protein yield from one deer (*Odocoileus* sp.), we gain a rather interesting perspective on shellfish collecting versus terrestrial hunting.

The whitetail deer has an average live weight of 63.6 kilograms of which 50% or 31.8 kilograms is edible meat (not including bone marrow). The edible meat from one deer provides 21 grams of protein per 100 grams of meat or a total of 6.7 kilograms of protein. In order to obtain an equivalent amount of protein from shellfish, one would have to collect 83,422 mussels. The total wet weight of meat would equal 88.8 kilograms, and the total weight of the collected organisms including shell would be 297.4 kilograms. The same amount of animal protein is contained in 10,593 clams, which have a meat weight of 90.3 kilograms and a total weight of 408.1 kilograms including shells. If we use these weight values for animals processed and protein gained, the following ratios are obtained for clams, mussels, and deer, respectively: 61 : 1, 44 : 1, and 9.5 : 1. These calculations demonstrate, therefore, that hunter–gatherers, as opposed to shellfish collectors, would not only secure more animal protein per unit weight with large mammals, but they would also have less weight to transport if producers carried food to consumers. Incidently, there is evidence for the Peruvian coast that Prehistoric groups transported shellfish in their shells to sites located many kilometers inland. Engel (1973:272) states, for example, "Shellfish was their [preagricultural groups on the south coast] basic source of protein; they carried tons of marine shells as far as 60 mi. inland, even up to the high Andean caves." One can see, therefore, that shellfish collecting is a labor-intensive strategy in which not only does the food item contain less "optimal" amounts of protein, but also producers in the society would have to spend an inordinate amount of time each day or so collecting food for dependents.

Shellfish have been utilized by human populations throughout the world from extreme southern to extreme northern latitudes. If we examine the ethnographic literature, we find that many of these groups utilize shellfish only during periods of severe food shortage, such as intermittent famine or annual lows in environmental productivity, that is, late winter and early spring. Rau (1884:216) refers to one such case which demonstrates the secondary importance of shellfish in many aboriginal diets:

> Cabeza de Vaca was the first to allude to North American shell-deposits. He sojourned as a prisoner on an island (Isla del Malhado) in the Gulf of Mexico, watched by a number of Indians, who, on account of a famine on that island, were compelled to leave it. They proceeded to *terra firma*, visiting the neighboring bays, which abounded in oysters. "For three months," the Spanish author says, "they subsist on these shellfish, and drink very bad water. Wood is there very rare, and the country is full of mosquitoes. They construct their cabins of mats, and erect them on heaps of oyster-shells, upon which they sleep naked."

In similar ethnohistoric case, Jochelson (1933:11) cites an instance described by the merchant Tolstykh in his diary concerning the Aleuts of the Aleutian Islands:

> In the winter when the digging of roots is impossible and the stormy sea prevents hunting and supplies are wanting, they are threatened by famine. Then they go with their wives and children to the shore, gather seaweed and every kind of shells, and are glad when they find a stranded whale or some other sea-mammal. And under such poor conditions their lives are passed.

Many ethnographic accounts of aboriginal use of shellfish are quite similar to these. In fact, shellfish seem to be utilized as food only during periods of famine or low terrestrial productivity, that is, during late winter and early spring in the higher latitudes. Perhaps we should reevaluate our established assumptions concerning the role that shellfish play in the subsistence of hunter–gatherers, not only for coastal Peru, but also for coastal adaptations in general.

Investigations concerned with Peruvian Late Preceramic subsistence are greatly hampered by the lack of adequate theoretical and methodological approaches to midden analysis and subsistence activities. Theoretical groundwork is needed to generate expectations and empirical tests for those aspects of Prehistoric environment (see Binford and Bertram, and Schalk, this volume) and subsistence strategies that are not materially manifest in the archaeological record. Several of the necessary aspects related to archaeological theory involving Prehistoric plant, animal, and human ecology are discussed by Parsons (1970:301–302). In addition, Parsons (1970:303) emphasizes the need for appropriate recovery techniques for midden excavation. Assessing the relative importance of various food items in Prehistoric diet also requires that archaeologists develop appropriate *units of analysis* for dealing with different kinds of plant and animal foods represented in the midden. It is not possible to compare kernels of maize, fragments of animal bone, and kilograms of shells unless these remains are converted from *units of observation* into *units of analysis*. This process was accomplished earlier in the chapter for mussels, clams, and whitetail deer. For example, if one adult bull sea lion is represented in a particular midden stratum by one bone (assuming that the sea lion's total weight is 540 kilograms and that one-half of the animal is edible), the equivalent weight of shellfish (mussel) meat would be represented by some 413,144 single shell valves. In many instances, archaeologists might assign more importance to shellfish in the Prehistoric diet than to sea lion because they lack appropriate units of analysis.

I suggest at this point that this concern with units of analysis is lacking in the archaeological investigations on the Peruvian coast. To the best of my knowledge, there are no studies that deal with animal food resources in terms of anatomical parts, minimum number of individuals, or quantity of meat and protein represented in the various midden deposits along the Peruvian coast. Moseley's excavations in the Ancon-Chillon region of the central coast revealed extensive middens containing various marine fish, birds, and sea mammals in addition to different species of mussels, clams, scallops, and tunicates. Moseley (1968:262) states, however, that legumes and rhizomes, "certainly must have been of considerable importance, yet marine invertebrates were beyond question the food staple." Perhaps the importance of shellfish in the diet of the Cotton Preceramic period populations should be reassessed. A coastal village of 1500 persons, based on previously discussed daily protein requirements per individual, would require 741,000 mussels per day or 2.7×10^8 mussels per year. No doubt the shellfish beds along the rich Peruvian coast were reduced considerably during the Cotton Preceramic period, for the subsistence base was expanded to include sea birds, such as cormorants, gulls, and gannets, as well as pelagic fish. Sea mammals were also exploited to some degree. The Humboldt Current along the Peruvian coast contained tremendous herds of blue whales, sperm whales, killer whales, baleen whales, fur seals, sea lions, porpoises, and dolphins (Schweigger 1947). The north-trending cool waters of the Peru Current upwelling system support vast herds of these sea mammals almost up to the equator. Their extreme abundance is emphasized by studies showing that, during the early 1900s, over 75,000 South American sea lions were being killed annually on the offshore rookeries along Peru's coastline (Scheffer 1958:54). Why do we see relatively little evidence in the Peruvian archaeological record for the exploitation of sea mammals?

Sea lions were hunted, or at least eaten during the Late Preceramic periods, particularly at Otuma (Engel 1963b:79), in occupation Period 2 at Asia (Engel 1963b:78), at Chilca (Donnan 1964:142), and at Banco Verde, the Tank Site, and Pampa (Moseley 1968). These marine mammals inhabit portions of the littoral, offshore islands, and the open ocean that are not easily accessible to human groups without water craft. Except during the breeding season, sea lions remain at sea for a great part of the year on feeding expeditions (Nishiwaki 1972:151). Even if Prehistoric hunters were able to locate sea lion populations near the shore, stalking them may have been extremely dangerous and difficult. During the breeding season, when large herds aggregate at various stations along the coast, the bulls are extremely aggressive, and guards are posted around the herd to warn the others in case of danger (Nishiwaki 1972:143,145). Nishiwaki (p. 140) comments, "These sea lions are very cautious animals. They often haul out on land to rest but quickly escape into the water with the slightest alarm. When an individual is shot, the entire group disappears into the water."

An additional procurement problem associated with sea mammal hunting is that, once they are shot, they often sink immediately. Depending on seasonal fluctuations in body fat content and the salinity of the ocean, sea mammals may be lost unless a harpoon with an attached line is used or unless the animal is taken on land. For example, Kemp (1971:110) remarks that, for the Baffin Island Eskimo, "much of the potential harvest is lost because the animals sink when they are shot. In 1967 and 1968 the villagers lost five whales, five bearded seals and 47 common seals." As we are well aware, the coastal Eskimo, various Indian groups of the Northwest Coast, for example, Makah and the Nootka, and the Yahgan of Tierra del Fuego are examples of groups that have developed elaborate technologies for coping with the exigencies of sea mammal hunting. The Preceramic coastal groups of Peru apparently did not have such a technology.

Finally, I suggest that sea mammals were not utilized until early hunters and gatherers were experiencing density-dependent selection. The argument concerning the less than optimal subsistence status of shellfish is based primarily on the necessary shift to a labor intensive strategy that requires a considerable expenditure of search time and energy in relation to the time and energy returns. Sea mammals, on the other hand, occur in large food "packages" and, like terrestrial mammals, represent more resource for less time and energy expended. If we argue, however, that mammalian resources are exploited primarily for their protein value and, if we then devise a suitable *unit of analysis* to compare protein returns from terrestrial and marine mammals, a very provocative picture emerges. For such comparative purposes, I chose to calculate the ratio of protein to edible meat (excluding viscera) of various land and sea mammals (see Table 4.3). Examination of Table 4.3 demonstrates that there is a

Table 4.3

Ratio of Protein to Edible Meat for Terrestrial and Marine Animals

Food resource	Protein/Edible Meat
Caribou	.24
Moose	.25
Deer, whitetail	.21
Seal, fur	.10
Seal, hair	.10
Sea lion	.11
Porpoise	.09
Whale (including blubber)	.10
Fish, marine	.17
Birds, marine	.15
Clams	.13
Oysters	.10
Scallops	.15

marked difference in the relative amount of protein contained in those mammals that live in the sea as opposed to those mammals that live on land. Sea mammals contain approximately one-half as much protein as terrestrial mammals. Why does such a distinction occur? Perhaps one of the most significant reasons for the lower protein content of sea mammals is described by Bryden (1972:48–49):

> By far the greatest amount of dissectible adipose tissue in marine mammals is found in the hypodermis, that is the blubber layer. . . . The adaptations of the skin of mammals to the aquatic habitat . . . are pertinent to the present discussion. These adaptations prevent excessive cooling in water, which has a much higher heat conductivity than air. . . . (This loss of heat can be prevented in two ways—(1) in some semi-aquatic mammals dense hair covering with an underlying fur layer provides adequate thermal regulation for animals that do not remain in the water for long thermal regulation for animals that do not remain in the water for long periods; (2) for animals that are exposed to the water for long periods of time a thick layer of subcutaneous fat has developed for insulation.) Such an adaptation can be seen in the Cetacea, in the majority of Pinnipedia, and in Sirenia.

The ramifications of such an aquatic adaptation in terms of animal composition is shown in Table. 4.4. Note that sea mammals contain more fat or blubber, less bone, less viscera, and, in the cases of the baleen whales *(B. musculus, B. physalus,* and *B. borealis),* more muscle than the terrestrial mammal *Rangifer* spp. (caribou).

Sea mammals differ from terrestrial mammals not only in terms of a lower protein content, but also in terms of their relative positions in the trophic organization of particular ecosystems. Caribou, for example, feed primarily upon grasses, moss, and lichens; they are, therefore, primary consumers in the second trophic level of the tundra ecosystem. Sea mammals, on the other hand, feed on fish, cephalopods, shellfish, macroplankton, sea birds, and so on and are secondary or tertiary consumers in the fourth or fifth trophic levels of marine ecosystems (Scheffer 1958:115). What, therefore, are the implications for man as a hunter of terrestrial and marine mammals? If man exploits land mammals, he is

Table 4.4

Composition of Terrestrial and Marine Mammals Expressed as a Percentage of Total Body Weight

Mammal	Fat or blubber	Muscle	Bone	Viscera	Reference
Sperm whale	34	35	11	8	Omura 1950
Blue whale	27	40	16	11	Nishiwaki 1950
Fin whale	24	45	17	10	Nishiwaki 1950
Sei whale	22	62	15	9	Omura 1950
Right whale	40	30	14	13	Omura 1950
Elephant seal	30	28	7	9	Bryden 1972
Caribou	10	35	20	35	Hall 1971
Alpaca	2.1+	47	9	16	Based on Thomas 1973
Llama	2.0+	46	9	14	Based on Thomas 1973

a secondary consumer (if the mammals are herbivores) in the third trophic level; on the other hand, if man exploits sea mammals, he is a tertiary or quaternary consumer in the fourth or fifth trophic level. As we are well aware, no transfer of energy can be 100% efficient as described by the laws of thermodynamics. Therefore, as energy is passed "up" from producers to various levels of consumers in the trophic structure of an ecosystem, less and less energy is available to the next trophic level. Approximately 15–20% of the energy in one trophic level is passed on to the next level. Thus, the greater the number of intervening trophic levels between primary producers and human consumers, the less energy there is available to the human population. Not only do carnivores or hunters exploiting these higher trophic levels receive less energy, but they also have fewer animals to exploit. As Pianka (1974:225) states:

> A result of this rapid reduction in the availability of energy is that animals at higher trophic levels are generally much rarer than those at lower ones. Moreover, decreasing availability of energy places a distinct upper limit on the number of trophic levels possible, with about five or six being the normal maximum.

I would suggest at this point that human subsistence strategies, both past and present, do not include those that focus upon the exploitation of carnivores in general, such as bear, canids, cats, and so on (given alternative animal populations in lower trophic levels). Sea mammals are then a notable exception to this generalization. Finally, as was mentioned earlier, the oceans are generally much less productive than are the continental land masses. Most marine ecosystems are "second-rate" ecosystems as compared to terrestrial ecosystems.

In summary, I suggest that marine resources are low-return subsistence resources due to a need for labor intensification, in the case of shellfish and small food package-sized marine organisms, and due to their low protein content. A number of factors combine to create an evolutionary threshold that is too costly for human populations to cross unless they are experiencing density-dependent selection. This subsistence-related threshold is so costly to cross, in fact, that, given the option, we should expect to see human groups shift away from the exploitation of the sea, at least in nonindustrial societies, whenever possible.

An evaluation of the overall role played by marine resources in Late Preceramic subsistence will have to await analysis of existing collections and conduction of problem-oriented archaeological investigations that will not necessarily include excavation. There is already existing evidence for the extensive utilization of plant resources, both wild and domesticated, including junco, berries, tubers, fruits, seaweeds, peppers, cotton, gourds, and so on. None of these plants, however, were suitable as staples. Pickersgill (1969:57) states:

> The plants widespread in cultivation during the Preceramic stage did not include any crops fitted to serve as a staple. Beans, squash, achira, chili peppers, and guava constituted useful additions to, rather than basic items in, the diet; and, throughout the Preceramic, people relied on seafood rather than on agricultural products for their subsistence.

Ecological Determinants of Coastal Adaptations: The Peruvian Case

The early temples and ceremonial centers of the north-central region—Rio Seco, Chuquitanta, La Florida, the terraced structures at Ancon, Las Haldas, the Las Haldas temple at Culebras, Toril and Kotosh—represent the earliest monumental buildings of any kind known in the Americas. They were probably all built between 2000 and 1500 B.C. They give evidence of a well-developed pattern of public ritual, an economy of sufficient abundance to free a good deal of labor from subsistence activities, and a measure of social stratification and specialization. They show, too, that it was in the north-central region, both coast and highlands, that civilization first developed in Peru. They were built at a time of fairly light population densities and on the basis of a mixed economy in which, on the coast, littoral harvesting played a greater role than did farming. *They have no obvious ecological explanation,* and I am unwilling, at their point, to venture a guess as to why these great early centers were built [Lanning 1967:189; emphasis mine].

As Lanning has pointed out, the north-central Peruvian coast is a distinctive archaeological zone. As early as the third millenium B.C., the north-central coast and a portion of the central coast began to establish a preeminent position in Peruvian prehistory. In fact, the earliest evidence of human occupation of coastal Peru comes from the northern border of this region in the Moche Valley. Prehistoric hunter–gatherers were living in the western lowlands of Peru some 12,000 years ago (Ossa and Moseley 1972). Later, during the Preceramic V and VI periods, several large settlements appeared between the Chicama and the Omas Rivers. This same region was also characterized by sizeable Initial Period occupations and the establishment of major ceremonial centers at Cerro Sechin, Huaricanga, Culebras, Las Haldas, the Tank Site, and La Florida. During the Early Intermediate Period, the Chicama–Moche area was the center of the Moche state. Finally, prior to the emergence and expansion of the Inca in the highlands, the Chimu state or Chimor Kingdom developed and gained control of the Peruvian coast from Tumbes in the north to the Río Chillón in the south. The great city of Chan Chan in the Moche Valley covering more than 20 square kilometers and containing an estimated 25,000–30,000 inhabitants served as the capital of this immense state (Moseley 1975a:219–225). During the period that Lanning and Patterson (1967:26,71–72) have designated as Preceramic V and VI (4200–2500 B.C. and 2500–1800 B.C., respectively), the coastal region between the Chicama and the Omas Rivers is characterized by the appearance of sedentary communities with domestic and public architecture, large cemeteries with high-status burials, distinctive art styles expressed in textiles, domesticated plants and animals, and differentiated settlement patterns (Lanning 1967:57). As Lanning (1967:77) suggests, "The coastal region from Las Haldas to Asia stands out as a nucleus of innovation and cultural development during Period VI." Moseley (1972:30) and Patterson (1973:59–62) have proposed that the Late Preceramic periods, that is, those of the Cotton Preceramic, were characterized by considerable population growth for the central and the north-central Peruvian coast.

After reviewing the literature concerning the prehistory of coastal Peru (Bird 1948; Steward and Faron 1959; Engel 1957, 1958, 1960, 1963a,b, 1964, 1966a,b;

Rowe 1963; Lanning 1963, 1965, 1967; Moseley 1968, 1972, 1975b; Patterson 1971a,b; Patterson and Lanning 1964; Patterson and Moseley 1968), it is obvious that our understanding of the archaeological record has progressed considerably during the last 15 years. There are, however, many provocative problems awaiting the archaeologist. For example, beginning with the Preceramic V and VI periods, a marked contrast develops between the northern and southern coastal regions. Initially, this contrast is characterized by the south coast's lag in shifting from hunting and gathering to fishing and shellfish collecting. This contrast has been summarized by Willey (1971:102):

> Lanning is of the opinion that in the South and Far South the Pacific Littoral tradition was never firmly established and that the populations of these subareas remained in the old Andean Hunting–Collecting condition of seasonal transhumance between lomas and shore for a much longer time than those farther north.

As an outgrowth of this contrast we might ask, why, following man's initial use of the sea, was the north-central Peruvian coast one of the only areas along the entire western coastline of South America to support large, nonagriculturally based sedentary communities? Why were there no large Initial Period ceremonial sites analogous to Cerro Sechin, the Tank Site, Las Haldas, Huaricanga, or Culebras on the southern coast of Peru? Why does the earliest evidence for complex coastal sociocultural systems appear on the northern coast? Carneiro (1970:734–736) does offer an "environmental circumscription model" to explain the formation of the state on the Peruvian coast, but he does not explain why states developed first and foremost along the northern coast.

In the following portion of this chapter, I will offer an ecological explanation that suggests that particular ecological characteristics of the Peru Current system determined the distribution of certain Late Preceramic settlements along a restricted area of the Peruvian coast. Once the shift toward increased reliance upon marine resources was made, coastal populations began to distribute themselves along those areas of the coast that provided the most optimal food resources—specifically in the area between 7° and 12° south latitude. Sedentism resulted in marked human population growth. Once again, density-dependent selection (combined with ecological instability) provided the impetus for the development of complex sociopolitical organizations, for a shift toward increased reliance upon domesticated plants, and for the establishment of settlements away from the coast near arable land and stream waters for irrigation.

Cultural systems, like all living systems, require a flow of energy, matter, and information for maintenance of their integrity and their very existence. Prehistoric cultural systems along the coast of Peru "mapped" the distribution of marine resources into their organization in order to obtain energy and matter from the sea. Buckley (1968:491) discusses this mapping process for complex adaptive systems as one in which "an adaptive system acquires features that permit it to discriminate, act upon, and respond to aspects of the environmental variety and its constraints." The result of this particular mapping process was the juxtaposition of settlements and concentrations of marine resources. The restricted distribution of Late Preceramic sites and associated cultural developments can then be explained with reference to an argument that logically connects or systematically unifies human behavior and particular ecological parameters.

Late Preceramic Archaeology

For the purposes of this discussion, I have chosen 10 Late Preceramic archaeological sites (see Figure 4.1) from the north, north-central and south-central coasts of Peru as examples of early sedentary coastal communities. These sites are assumed to represent sedentary human populations based on their size, extensive middens, "permanent" domestic structures, public structures, and large cemeteries. We should not forget, however, that yearround occupation has not been confirmed.

In the northern coastal Chicama River valley lies Huaca Prieta de Chicama, where Junius B. Bird conducted excavations in the 1940s as part of the Viru Valley Project. This site was one of the first to yield conclusive evidence of Preceramic occupation of the Peruvian coast. Huaca Prieta covers approximately 6000 square meters or .6 hectares, forming a truncated mound 12 meters thick. Three radiocarbon dates from the Preceramic levels are 4257 ± 250 radiocarbon years: 2307 ± 250 B.C.; 4044 ± 300 radiocarbon years: 2094 ± 300 B.C.; and 3572 ± 220 radiocarbon years: 1622 ± 220 B.C. (Bird 1951). Bird estimates that several hundred persons lived at this site around 2550 B.C. Architectural features associated with the Preceramic deposits are simple, well-constructed subterranean one- and two-room domestic structures made of large beach cobbles and mud mortar. Surrounding midden contained abundant marine faunal remains, such as sea urchins, shellfish, sea lion, and porpoise, as well as domesticated and wild plants, such as squash, peppers, lima and jack beans, gourds, cotton, cat-tail tubers and roots (Bird 1948:21–28).

To the south of Huaca Prieta de Chicama, there is a similar large mound, Huaca Prieta de Guañape or Huaca Negra (Strong and Evans 1952:7), which is located in the Virú River valley. The mound of *huaca* covers an area roughly 300 meters in diameter or 6.78 hectares. Preceramic domestic structures are constructed of clay "lumps" cemented together with mud mortar. One of the rooms measured 5.75 by 3.0 meters. Walls were plastered with mud, and floors were of hard clay. Fourteen wooden roof beams were revealed during excavation. The remains of large deep-water mussels, marine snails, sea urchins, rock crabs, sand sharks, and rays were recovered from the midden (Strong and Evans 1952:7).

Mongoncillo, near the plain of Haldas 330 kilometers north of Lima, is a Preceramic site consisting of several "high mounds containing shells of snails . . . together with a mixture of ashes and refuse . . . also marine shellfish, fish and

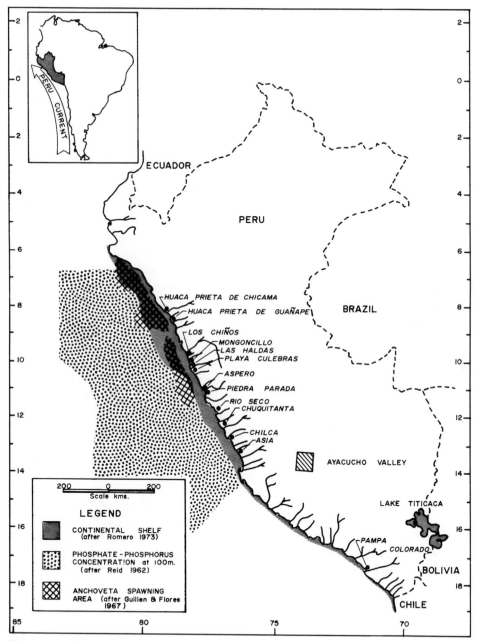

Figure 4.1 Distribution of Late Preceramic sedentary communities and select aspects of the Peru Current system.

181

other seafood. The presence of wood, canes, huts, food remains, and human skeletons speaks in favor of a settled life" (Engel 1973:275).

In the Nepeña Valley near the coast is the Los Chinos 1 Site which has also been assigned to the Late Preceramic period (Lumbreras 1969:43). The architecture at this site consists of a number of houses constructed out of irregular cobbles and mud mortar. These domestic structures are, in many cases, subterranean, measuring 1.5 by 1.8 meters on a side and 1.5 meters deep. Houses are scattered randomly along the slopes of several hills adjacent to the Nepeña Valley (Lumbreras 1969, 1974:43).

Las Haldas is one of the largest Preceramic sedentary communities at present on the Peruvian coast. The area of the site is approximately 200 hectares. Las Haldas is located between the Casma and the Sechin Rivers. A radiocarbon dating of 3580 ± 130 radiocarbon years: 1631 ± 130 B.C. was obtained from fragments of preserved cane near the temple floor (Ishida, Izumi, and Terada 1958). Numerous nonagglutinated stone and mud mortar houses were perhaps occupied by 500–1000 persons (Lanning 1967:64); on the other hand, Rowe (1963:297) believes that Las Haldas supported a population of 10,000. Lower levels of the half meter deposit contained some of the earliest maize yet found on the Peruvian coast in association with gourds, cotton, and beans. The maize has been dated at 3792 ± 100 radiocarbon years: 1842 ± 100 B.C. (Willey 1971:109; Engel, 1963a:11). In addition, a considerable portion of the midden contains marine shellfish from both the rocky and the sandy littoral zone. At least one pyramid at Las Haldas has been assigned to the Late Preceramic period; it is composed of 7 platforms that combine to form an elongated structure 465 meters long and approximately 60 meters wide (see Engel 1957:Fig. 4).

The Culebras Site of approximately 1–2 hectares is situated near the mouth of the Culebras River. Two- and three-room basalt block and mud mortar domestic structures occupy several stone-faced terraces on a hillslope. Some of the houses have a number of superimposed clay floors which probably indicate a long-term occupation. In addition to the domestic dwellings, there are a number of larger structures with rectangular wall niches, buildings of various shapes and sizes, and a wide stone stairway that cross-cuts the terraced slope (Engel 1957:66–68; Lumbreras 1969, 1974:43). A number of human burials were found in tombs, in wall niches outside the houses, and in a hilltop cemetery. Individuals were tightly flexed, wrapped in woven vegetal fiber mats, and interred with various forms of grave goods, such as personal ornaments, stone tools, gourd vessels, and baskets (Engel 1957:66–68). The estimated population of Culebras is 500–1000 persons (Moseley and Willey 1973:463; Lanning 1967:63).

Aspero, a Cotton Preceramic period site, covers 13.2 hectares of a hilly flank of the Supe River valley. Moseley and Willey (1973) have recently revisited this site and have reevaluated its significance as a Preceramic manifestation. The site is considered to date from between 2275 B.C. and 1850 B.C. based upon a textile chronology developed for the Ancon–Chillon area (Moseley and Willey 1973:461–462). They have also confirmed the presence of six large platform mounds that are considered to be corporate labor structures dating to the Late Preceramic periods. Several of these mounds appear to be over 50 meters long (Moseley and Willey 1973:454, Fig. 1). The accumulated midden on the site is quite deep (in excess of 2 meters) and contains marine shellfish (predominantly *Mesodesma* clams), fish, birds, and sea lion bones, as well as gourds, maize, and seaweed. Like Culebras, domestic structures were placed on artificial terraces cut into the midden slopes (Moseley and Willey 1973:463).

Río Seco de Leon is located near Chancay Valley in a dry canyon. The site consists of small domestic wattle and daub, semi-subterranean houses, and several large platform mounds covering large interconnected subterranean rooms.

> Some rooms have doors with lintels made of the trunk of some cactus. The rooms do not seem to have been inhabited; no refuse was found on the clay floors; the walls are finely faced and possess patterns made with cobbles and alternating rows of slabs and crude clay bricks. These rooms were later filled in with large blocks similar to the ones used for the construction [Engel 1963b:12].

These mounds vary from 1 to 3 meters in height. The largest structure, Mound 6, contains rooms built of large stones, coral blocks, and whale bone. Mound 7 also contains rooms in which the walls have rubble-clay cores and are plastered with clay. Some of the walls at Rio Seco are 3 meters high (Engel 1958:24). Río Seco covers 11.8 hectares and is situated at a distance of more than 20 kilometers from arable land and known sources of potable water. Midden deposits reach a depth of 1.5 meters and contain predominantly marine shellfish from an open, sandy beach environment (Wendt 1964:237). Domesticated plants apparently were of minimal importance. Relatively recent investigations by Wendt (1964:243) indicate that there are an estimated 2400–3000 human burials at the site. Two radiocarbon dates from Río Seco are 3800 ± 100 radiocarbon years: 1850 ± 100 B.C. and 3740 ± 100 radiocarbon years: 1790 ± 100 B.C. (Engel 1957).

Chuquitanta, or El Paraiso, occupies approximately 50 hectares on the southern alluvial flood plains of the Chillon River about 3 kilometers from the coast. Remains of 9 platform mounds cover a core area of 6.3 hectares. Three of these mounds form a U-shaped structure with parallel "wings" over 450 meters long which enclose a large plaza measuring 200 by 400 meters (Lanning 1967:70–71). Several archaeologists, contrary to Lanning (1967:71), believe that there are no structures at Chuquitanta that were specifically "ceremonial" in nature (Engel 1967; Patterson and Moseley 1968; Moseley and Willey 1973). Many of the constructions are composed of small, contiguous rooms joined by passageways. One building, Unit 1, however, which was reconstructed by Engel (1966a) contrasts with the others. It is 50 meters square with walls over 1 meter thick. Willey (1971:99) suggests that Unit 1 may have been a temple or "palace." Subsistence was based primarily upon marine resources such as rock-dwelling shellfish, sand-dwelling shellfish, fish, and sea lion; however, deer bones were also present in the midden, as well as several forms of domesticated plants, such as lima beans, squash, pacae, and lucuma (Patterson and Moseley 1968:118). Engel conservatively estimates the population of Chuquitanta at 1500 persons. One radiocarbon dating of 3570 ± 150 radiocarbon years—1680 ± 150 B.C. (Engel 1967)—falls well within the estimated terminal building stage (1800–1500 B.C.) at the site. This site was abandoned, never to be reoccupied after 1750 B.C., and Patterson (1971b:198) suggests that most of the inhabitants resettled at nearby Huaca La Florida.

The Chilca 1 Monument Site lies 67 kilometers south of present-day Lima near the Chilca *quebrada*. Chilca was a village of conical cane and grass huts located about 3–4 kilometers from the coast. Donnan (1964:142) excavated a collapsed semi-subterranean house structure of cane, whalebone, and grass from which he obtained a radiocarbon date of 3420 B.C. The remains of 7 individuals ranging in age from 18 to 40 years (2 females and 5 males) were found on the house floor. The bodies, like other Preceramic interments on the Peruvian coast, were wrapped in woven vegetal fiber mats (Engel 1963b; Donnan 1964). Engel believes that approximately 100 families, or 500 persons, lived at Chilca at one time. Subsistence resources were primarily marine shellfish with secondary reliance on fish and sea lion. In addition, two species of domesticated beans were recovered from the midden (Engel 1967).

The southernmost Late Preceramic site with "permanent" architecture is Asia: a group of scattered shell mounds with an area of 3 hectares, situated on the Omas River. Engel (1963b) excavated one of these mounds, Unit 1, in its entirety revealing a multiroomed *"pueblito"* of adobe and stone measuring 12 meters on a side. Forty-nine individuals were interred beneath the floor and in the surrounding midden of Unit 1. The burials were generally flexed, wrapped in woven vegetal mats, and accompanied by various forms of grave "offerings" (Osborn n.d.). Food resources utilized were shellfish, sea lion, fish, for example, corvina, robalo, guitarfish, shark, and ray; marine birds, for example, cormorants and pelicans; plants, for example, red peppers, beans, guava, berries, fruits, tubers, grass seeds, and seaweed (Parsons 1970:299). One radiocarbon date from Asia is 3264 ± 100 radiocarbon years: 1314 ± 100 B.C. It is one of the latest Preceramic occupations on the coast of Peru (Engel 1963a:85).

The southern range of Preceramic coastal villages can be extended to the site of Pampa Colorado near Ocona and Camana on the far southern coast. Actually, Pampa Colorado is a number of "settlements" stretching for about 3 kilometers along the inland side of an extensive hilly *lomas* area. No ceramic materials are associated with these shell middens, and Engel (1973:273) uses lithic artifacts similar to Playa Chira and Quiqche "types" to assign a date for Pampa Colorado of pre-5000 B.C. Farther north is the Paloma Site, a series of shell mounds that cover a vast plain "for over a mile." These mounds are situated in the *lomas*, which is a considerable distance from the coast. Engel (1973:274) suggests that:

> The Paloma settlers were already living, at least during part of the year, a settled village life; I have counted up to 100 round reed huts, the remains of their posts found in holes dug inside a

slightly depressed circle some 2.5 meters in diameter, on a plain now covered with refuse and shells. . . . Carbon-14 dates are in the 7,000–6,000 B.P. range.

It should be pointed out that Asia is the southernmost Preceramic settlement on the Peruvian coast with "permanent" architecture. Pampa Colorado, Paloma, Village 304 near Chilca Canyon (Engel 1973:57), and several other early communities do not, as far as we know, have stone and mud mortar houses, large terraced residential areas, corporate cemeteries, or enormous public structures or platform mounds. There is no evidence of similar archaeological manifestations on the Pacific Coast of Chile although there are sizable shell middens (see Bird 1943).

In the model presented earlier as an explanation for initial exploitation of marine resources, we saw that mobile hunting and gathering strategies were terminated and groups became sedentary. One might then ask why sedentary communities were established on such a large and complex scale between the Chicama and the Omas Rivers? A portion of South America's Pacific Coast is unfavorable for yearround exploitation of marine resources due to inclement weather, that is, winter storms that create rough surf. The effects of inclement weather upon the Yahgan of Tierra del Fuego, for example, are described by Stuart (1972:62): "Although sources agree that food is regularly available throughout the year, there are often short periods of hunger due largely to bad weather." The effects of storms upon exploitation of littoral resources must be ruled out, for the most part, as we move northward from Tierra del Fuego and southern Chile into the more equatorial latitudes where climatic variability throughout the year becomes less marked. Craig and Psuty (1968:8) do state that wind storms, referred to as *paracas,* create a crashing surf that makes fishing impossible, but apparently these occur only during the afternoon.

Certain sections of the desert coast of western South America lack adequate supplies of fuel and potable water. Even in the most barren stretches of the Atacama Desert, however, there are supplies of "unearned" fuel in the form of various seaweeds that wash ashore, for example, thick-stemmed *huiro* kelp that breaks free from the sea bottom and drifts to shore in northern Chile (Bird 1943:186). Other sources of fuel from the sites along the desert coast of Peru are discussed by Engel (1963a:77).

No debris of large trunks or branches was found in the ashes at Asia, for example: "The scarcity of big trees is evidenced by the use of tiny twiglets. On the other hand, the rarity of *Tillandsias (lomas* grass), which constitute the fuel of poor sites on the north coast, could be an indication of abundant brush and bushes (near Asia) (Engel 1963a:77)."

Even in one of the driest deserts of the world, Prehistoric populations were able to locate potable water sources in the *lomas,* in the barren sandy desert, and along the shoreline itself. In the *lomas* and in portions of the desert, wells were dug to trap subterranean water from perched water tables (Engel 1963a:271). All of this water, one might add, is an "unearned" resource (Birdsell 1968:231) that originates in the highlands. As Engel (1963a:6) points out, "After very rainy seasons in the sierra, the freshwater level rises above the ground surface and, if undisturbed for long enough, a lagoon forms." Near the ocean, it is possible to find fresh water, as Engel (1963a:6) has observed near Asia:

> From personal observation we can add that when approaching the sea, the fresh water forms a sheet, or level, which, if undisturbed, remains on top of the salt water. This fresh water becomes slightly brackish from contact with the salty ground, but one can drink it, and though it is not ideal for agriculture it gives life to certain plants.

As summarized by Day (1974:183), much of the coast consists of an extremely porous stratum of "quaternary sands and gravels that act as a natural aquifer."

In addition to these sources, there are perennial streams that descend the western slopes of the Andes carrying glacial melt and run-off from the intermontane valleys and the Cordillera Occidental. Craig and Psuty (1968:98) suggest, also, that Prehistoric groups may have constructed dew traps consisting of smooth, rounded stones piled over a hole dug in the desert floor, to condense and collect moisture from the winter fog or *garuá*.

Admittedly, the distribution and quantity of fuel and water would play some role in determining the location of sedentary communities. There is no reason, however, to believe that fuel would have been vital resource, since heating of habitation areas is unnecessary along the Peruvian coast and marine foods, particularly shellfish, can be cooked in heat-retaining, low-cost fuel facilities perhaps similar to the features described by Moseley (1973:458–459) or can be eaten raw (see Greengo 1952:76–82). Water sources do not seem to be scarce, nor do they appear to be clustered in any regional pattern. Let us now turn to an examination of the Peruvian Current system which provided marine resources for preagricultural groups.

Oceanography and Marine Ecology of the Peru Current System

Marine primary productivity is limited by two key factors: solar energy and nutrient salts (Russell-Hunter 1970:54). As the aquatic counterpart to terrestrial vegetation, phytoplankton, or microscopic green plants, capture available sunlight and nutrient salts to generate primary production for the marine ecosystem through the process of photosynthesis. In tropical oceans, primary production is quite low, even though equatorial waters receive adequate amounts of solar energy yearround. Dissolved nutrient salts are not present in sufficient quantities to boost production. Their scarcity in the upper layers, or the euphotic zone, of the tropical oceans can be attributed to the presence of a thermocline or a density stratification of sea water that traps dissolved nutrients in a lower zone of dense, cool water beyond the "reach" of phytoplankton (Russell-Hunter 1970:97). Unless this thermoclinal situation is disrupted by physical mixing forces, for example, monsoons and upwelling, tropical oceans are more or less aquatic "deserts." Russell-Hunter (1970:97), for example, states:

The total nitrate concentration in the surface waters for 20° of latitude on either side of the equator is usually about 1/100 of the winter concentrations in the least fertile temperate seas. Phosphate levels in the same region often lie below the limit of detection (less than 1/100 the winter levels in temperate seas), and the only phosphate-rich waters within the tropics lie at depths below 150 meters, the richest concentrations being found in dense, cold water at depths between 600 and 1000 meters.

As previously mentioned, upwelling currents carry cold, dense water from lower strata toward the surface, disrupting the thermocline. There are several major areas of upwelling around the world, and some, if not the vast majority of them, occur in tropical oceans. The oceanographic phenomenon of upwelling has been treated comprehensively in various works (Sverdrup 1938; Hidaka 1954; Yoshida 1955, 1967; Wooster and Reid 1963; Smith 1969; Cushing 1971). Major areas of intense upwelling are located off the coasts of Washington and Oregon, southern California, the Gulf of Panama, the Canary Islands and Portugal, western South Africa, southwest Arabia, Malabar in India, and western Chile–Peru (Cushing 1971:284–293). For the purpose of this chapter, we are concerned with the last of these upwelling regions. Although it was not realized until quite recently that the Peru Current was an area of upwelling, the unusual characteristics of this region of the Pacific Ocean have been recognized for several hundred years.

One of the earliest recorded references to the Peru Current was made by Zarate, in 1543, during his travels in Peru for the King of Spain;

This wind (the South-Easter) is also the cause of the predominant northward flow in those seas. Some however ascribe it to another cause: that since the waters discharge themselves into the Magellan straits, which are so narrow as to be barely two leagues across, they are far too great to go through. Moreover they meet there the waters of the Northern Sea, which force them back. Unable to enter the straits, they consequently surge backwards; which is why the current runs north. This makes an additional difficulty for ships on the voyage from Panama to Peru. Not only are the winds always against them, but for a large part of the year the currents too. Therefore, unless they sail close to the wind or in its teeth, they cannot make the voyage.

All along the coast of Peru there are great fisheries, which yield all kinds of fish and many seal [Cohen 1968:39].

Prior to Zarate's travels, the Spanish *conquistadores* had discovered the abnormally cool waters of the Peru Current and had used the current to cool their drinking flasks (Acosta 1964, as quoted in Gunther 1936:39). In 1802, A. von Humboldt observed that the Peru Current was cooler than the surrounding air and ocean; and, in 1911, he proposed that the cool waters of the current originated in the Antarctic region (Gunther 1936:110,112). The Peru Current was named after A. von Humboldt in a study by Berghaus in 1837 (Gunther 1936:113).

This current system runs parallel to the coast of Chile and Peru between 40° and 4° 40′ S. latitude—a distance of 2240 kilometers (Morrow 1957:145). Paradoxically, this current system, like several other upwelling areas, simultaneously creates one of the earth's driest terrestrial environments and one of the ocean's most productive ecosystems. The maximum width of the system is 660 kilometers, and its maximum surface area is 1,436,000 square kilometers, with a total upwelling area of 21,000 square kilometers (Morrow 1957:147). This vast expanse of cool tropical ocean has a significant effect upon the climate and the physiography of Chile and Peru.

> The effect of a relatively cold water surface is to stabilize the warmer tropical air above. An inversion which lasts throughout the year is maintained by the cool Humboldt Current and the dynamically warmed upper air. The combined result of these mechanisms is that rain is almost eliminated.
>
> An important climatic phenomenon caused by the cooling of the air above the Humboldt Current is the formation of stratus clouds at or near the surface.
>
> Except for a brief midsummer period they prevent extreme heating at the surface . . . [Eidt 1969:60–61].

Thus, we see that the Peru Current system plays a primary role in the creation of the coastal Peruvian–Atacama Desert. This relatively narrow band of desert, ranging in width from 30 to 40 kilometers parallels the entire coastline of present-day Peru and northern Chile (Parsons 1970:292; Moseley 1972:26). Enormous barchans, or crescent-shaped sand dunes, accentuate broad expanses of barren desert floor that is almost totally devoid of vegetation and animal life. As Parsons (1970:292) points out, "Weberbauer (1923:305) tells us that it is not unusual to pass 50 kilometers without seeing a single plant." Unlike the classic "scorching sand, blistering heat" deserts that come to mind for many of us, the Peruvian desert is almost continually blanketed with dense stratus clouds, and temperatures are mild. The average annual temperature in Lima (12° S. latitude), for example, is 19°C with a high of 23°C in February and a low of 15.9°C in August (Eidt 1969:77). The desert coast is completely "socked-in" by a dense layer of low-lying stratus clouds, or the *garuá,* between June and December (Eidt 1969:77). The *garuá* creates a plant community comprised of lichen, moss, rhyzomes, xerophytic bushes, and drought resistant trees, for example, *Mimosa* and *mito* (Engel 1973:271). These plants depend primarily upon water that condenses from the fog; however, Engel (1973:271) argues that many plants of the *lomas* utilize hidden subterranean water. Effective moisture in the form of fog and dew for the coast near Lima (at 140 meters above sea level) is usually no more than 4.8 millimeters per year (Eidt 1969:77). Rainfall in the coastal desert is negligible and occurs only if there is a particularly severe El Niño countercurrent that causes collapse of the marine ecosystem and climatic deterioration. The ecological effects of El Niño on the Peru Current system will be discussed later.

A series of 40 rivers descend the western slopes of the Cordillera Occidental from altitudes in excess of 5000 meters. Many of these drainages are dry for most of the year, and only 10 rivers reach the coast as perennial streams. Below 500 meters, the river gradients flatten out, and immense deposits of alluvium settle near the river mouths. These perennial streams cross-cut the coastal desert forming linear zones of hydrophytic vegetation (Parsons 1970:295). In addition, there are subterranean water sources in the *lomas* adjacent to the desert that were tapped by Prehistoric inhabitants (Engel 1973).

The oceanographic aspects of the Peru Current system have been discussed in an excellent overview by Wyrtki (1966:33–68). This system is one of the major regions of upwelling in the Pacific Ocean. The upwelling is powered by a cyclonic circulation pattern in the atmosphere above the Pacific Ocean that moves water northward along the western coast of the South American continent toward the equator. The upwelling of submarine water is caused by horizontal divergence (the Ekmann effect) in which trade winds driven by the cyclone gyre force sur-face water northward along the coast and the Coriolis effect pushes water away from the coast. The Coriolis effect is caused by the rotation of the earth. Air and water currents are acted upon by the generated centripetal forces that deflect currents into a counterclockwise direction in the southern hemisphere. Surface ocean water is pushed aside, and submarine layers rise to the surface (Smith 1969:12; Cushing 1971:257–258).

As Yoshida (1967) has shown, the western boundaries of large land masses are prime areas for upwelling: "The most intense upwelling is in the coastal regions off the west coasts of continents where a one-sided divergence of the surface layer is induced by a wind stress parallel to the coastal boundary" (in Smith 1969:27).

The Pacific cyclone gyre, coupled with a northward trending coastline, pro-duces an especially intense region of upwelling off the coast of Peru.

> The amount of upwelling varies with the relationship between the shape of the coast and the open-ocean circulation, both in general and in the local projections of the coastline. For instance, the temperature of the water off Callao, Peru, where the coast trends NW and where the upwelling is great, is 3 degrees cooler than near Antofagasta, Chile, 2,400 kilometers farther south. The effect of the current along the coast is lengthened in South America because the land bends northwestward parallel to the Humboldt Current approximately at the border between Chile and Peru [Eidt 1969:60].

The Humboldt Current is, in fact, a system of parallel currents. First, the Peru Coastal Current flows northward along the shoreline of Chile and Peru between 24° S. latitude and 15° S. latitude where a considerable portion of these waters is deflected away from the coast. The remainder of this current diverges from the coast at 5° S. latitude (Wyrtki 1966:59). Second, the Peru Oceanic Current also moves northward at a considerable distance offshore, but it plays a rather insig-nificant role in the system. Third, a submarine current carries warm equatorial waters southward. Wyrtki (1966:60) comments, "This current carries equatorial subsurface water of high salinity and low oxygen content and supplies most of the water engaged in the upwelling processes along the coast north of 15° south latitude."

Temperatures for the Peru Current system range from 14.44°C to 17.78°C (Murphy 1923:76). Net transport of water in the upwelling region increases along a north–south gradient, for example, at 22° S. latitude, net transport *(NT)* is 2.0×10^{12} cubic centimeters; at 15° S. latitude, $NT = 6.0 \times 10^{12}$ cubic centimeters; at 5° S. latitude, $NT = 1.0 \times 10^{13}$ cubic centimeters (Wyrtki 1966:59). The oxygen minimum layer, measured by the amount of dissolved oxygen in concentrations less than 1 millimeter per liter of water, is only 800 meters deep. This is relatively shallow when compared to other areas of coastline; for example, Mexico's west coast oxygen minimum layer is 1200 meters deep. A map of this layer for the western shore of South America (Wyrtki 1966:51) illustrates that this thin layer is restricted to the region between 12° S. latitude and 7° S. latitude. The significance of this region will be discussed later in more detail.

The Peruvian Current system, as an upwelling area, establishes an anomalous marine ecosystem that is less "mature" than the surrounding ocean. The concept of maturity was developed by Margalef (1963; 1968) in an attempt to unify ecologists' ideas about succession in ecosystems. Margalef's maturity measure is based on a continuum of structural complexity and energy relations in ecosystems as governed by the Second Law of Thermodynamics (Margalef 1963, 1968; Patten 1959; Gallucci 1973). As mentioned earlier, all living systems require energy flow to maintain their integrity.

> If energy flow through a biological system does not continue (to some extent), then the system is no longer a living one, and its components will pass almost immediately to dissolution, both by autolysis (self-digestion) and decay. Living systems are maintained by the continuous flow of energy through them [Russell-Hunter 1970:16].

With increased maturity, there is a reduction in energy flow per unit of biomass, because more mature ecosystems are more efficient than less mature ecosystems. Immature ecosystems, such as arctic tundra and marine upwellings, are characterized by short food webs, low species diversity and equability, high production-to-biomass ratio, excess energy, and so on. Upwelling disrupts the thermodynamic trend toward increased maturity in the ocean by mixing nutrients and life forms that would otherwise be found in a complex, stratified marine ecosystem. Strickland (1972:352) states that "productivity and standing phytoplankton crops can be, and often are, extremely high and we have reason to believe that the trophodynamics of the whole food web is profoundly affected." With regard to this immature ecosystem, Krebs (1972:497) comments:

> In areas of upwelling, food chains are the shortest. This is primarily because of the size of the phytoplankton, many of which form colonies several millimeters in diameter. These large colonies of green plants can be eaten by large fish. Many of the fish that are abundant in areas of upwelling, like the sardines and anchovies, are herbivores.

The importance of plankton to marine ecosystems has been emphasized by Reid (1962:291), who proposes that the amount of these microscopic organisms in the world's ocean is greater than the total volume of all fishes, invertebrates, and sea mammals. Upwelling currents carry detritus and nutrients upward into the euphotic zone where phytoplankton, as primary producers, fix energy photosynthethically (Odum 1971:325). Thus, the implications of upwelling for the

Peruvian Current system are considerable. As Margalef (1963:372) observes, "Very productive fisheries belong to ecosystems of low maturity, with fluctuating supplies of inorganic nutrients and with notable pulses in plankton production. The less the maturity, the more important the 'abiotic' control of population."

Production in the Peru Current system is not constant throughout the year. Seasonal variation of phytoplankton is directly related to annual fluctuations in available sunlight and nutrients. According to Guillén, Mendiola, and Rondán (1971:158), the assemblage of plankton varies quantitatively and qualitively from season to season. During the winter, a reduction in solar energy reaching the ocean's surface (screened by fog, or the *garuá*) and an increase in vertical displacement of water tend to hold productoion down (Guillén, Mendiola, and Rondán 1971:175–176). In response to this variation in plankton, anchoveta aggregate and spawn during the late winter–early summer between 6° and 15° S. latitude along the coast of Peru (Cushing 1971:316–317). Upwelling is very intense during this period of the year.

The ecological implications of an upwelling region with an extremely short food web based on plankton populations go far beyond the creation of productive fisheries. Many of the primary consumers are, indeed, fish or planktivores, such as anchoveta, sardines, and some species of shark; but there are also baleen whales that have shortened their food chain by feeding directly upon plankton (Russell-Hunter 1970:92–93) and tremendous populations of shellfish, for example, mussels, clams, sea urchins, and crabs that remain relatively immobile while pumping plankton-rich waters through their bodies. Secondary consumers in the third trophic level of the Peruvian Current system consist of numerous fish species (for example, bonito, mackerel, corvina, and shark), enormous flocks of sea birds (for example, cormorants, pelicans, gannets, and penguins), and herds of sea mammals (for example, seals, sea elephants, and sea lions) (Parsons 1970:293–294).

Since this particular region of the Pacific Ocean possesses such a short food web, one can argue at this point that the distribution and abundance of plankton is directly correlated with the distribution and abundance of primary consumers. Therefore, we should expect to find large populations of shellfish along the coastline of Peru adjacent to portions of the upwelling system where there are high concentrations of plankton. Also, since plankton is dependent upon ocean currents for transport, we would expect high concentrations to survive only in areas of concentrated nutrient salts. Finally, as a result of these ecological interrelationships, we would then expect to find large populations of shellfish adjacent to areas of high nutrient concentration in the Peru Current system.

Recent studies by Reid (1962) have demonstrated that there is an isomorphic distribution of phosphate-phosphorus and zooplankton. Phosphate-phosphorus concentrations are low in oceanic currents associated with anticyclones and high in cyclones in the atmospheric circulation patterns (Reid 1962:290). This isomorphism, however, does not necessarily imply that zooplankton require high concentrations of these nutrients as had been previously thought: "Variations of

PO$_4$-P may or may not be important in themselves. They may be important as indicators of variations of other nutrients, such as nitrate, that are affected by the same processes, but are not present in excess" (Reid 1962:291).

Cushing (1971:267) argues that "the persistence of production in an upwelling area is due not to the presence of excess nutrients, but to the persistent addition of living material from a continuous band of temporary production cycles in the upwelling areas." In summary, Cushing (1971:271) proposes that "the implication is that the long-established correlation between production and nutrients is a consequence of the dependence of nutrient quantity on production and not the other way around."

For the west coast of South America, phosphate-phosphorus concentrations and zooplankton are extremely high between 15° S. latitude and 8° S. latitude. An unusually rich region of these nutrients and zooplankton is located off the north coast of Peru (see Reid 1962: Figs. 2a, b). As Reid suggested earlier, these concentrations of phosphate-phosphorus do not necessarily mean that plankton production depends upon these nutrients, for plankton may, in fact, produce them; but other vital nutrients may be concentrated in the area. These nutrients may be quite similar to trace elements that are so vital for terrestrial production.

In addition, marine productivity is related to salinity conditions in which the nutrient salt is sodium chloride. Guillén, Mendiola, and Rondán (1971:182) state that "the most abundant species and the higher productivity values are found in waters of the Peruvian coastal current with salinities between 35.1–34.8%." Their investigations (1971:165) revealed that

> the surface subtropical waters, identified by salinities greater than 35.1%, were present north of 13° S. (latitude) during all the year but were more pronounced during the summer and autumn. The major seasonal changes in salinity occured north of Punta Falsa (6° S. lat.) where waters from the equatorial zone (34.8–33.8%) are normally observed.

Another factor contributing to the extremely high marine productivity that characterizes the Peru Current system between the Chicama and the Omas Rivers is the nature of the continental shelf. This submarine shelf creates a broad expanse of shallow coastal water that is transitional between land and the bathyal zone (Odum 1971:330). Sunlight is able to penetrate effectively to depths of 30 meters along the continental shelf which supports abundant euphotic life. Wyrtki (1966:35) points out that "the continental shelf exceeds 50 kilometers width only along the coast of Central America between the Gulf of Tehuantepec and Nicaragua, in the Gulf of Panama, and along the coast of Peru between 7° and 11° S. (Latitude)." Schweigger (1947:22) emphasizes the importance of the continental shelf,

> De gran influencia sobre la vida que se manifiesta en o sobre el mar ha sido el hundimiento del antiguo litoral de la zona C [north and north-central Peruvian coast], por haberse formado asi frente a la costa actual un "shelf" sobre el que levantan las islas guaneras.

Periodically, the Peru Current ecosystem collapses dramatically. This phenomenon occurs cyclically every 25–40 years as a result of a severe fluctuation in equatorial wind currents that shift southward. Warmer surface waters are then forced southward over the cooler Peru Current system causing surface water temperatures to rise approximately 5° F. Immediately, plankton is killed, profoundly affecting consumer populations. As the dead plankton are exposed to sunlight, they decompose, giving off toxic gases, particularly hydrogen sulphide (Parsons 1970:294). The warm equatorial waters or El Niño countercurrent occasionally cause the *aguaje* effect (*agua enferma*—sick water or the Callao Painter) when the current is unusually strong:

> Friedler (1944:101) describes an occurence of the *aguaje* effect that he witnessed in 1941: ". . . millions of dead fish were floating in the bay and had been cast up on the beach—mostly anchovies, though large numbers of sharks, flounders, eels, blennies, rock fish, drum fish, sea bass, herring, guitar fish, crabs, clams, and octopuses were identified" [Parsons 1970:294].

According to Murphy (1923:70), the most severe effects of the El Niño, which occurs every 25–40 years, are restricted primarily to the zone between Paita (5°5′ S. latitude) and Pisco (13°43′ S. latitude). This, in fact, is the same zone of the Peruvian coast where the previously discussed Late Preceramic sedentary communities are located. This isomorphic distribution was the first clue that, given the maturity arguments of Margalef, led me to examine the physiographical and the ecological aspects of this coastal zone. It should be pointed out that the El Niño is a cyclical phenomenon that occurs to a minor degree each year in December (the El Niño refers metaphorically to the Christ Child) and to a major degree every 25–40 years. For example, records of abnormally high rainfall have been used to reconstruct the cycle of the severe El Niño indicating that the following years were marked by ecosystem collapse: 1728, 1770, 1791, 1828, 1864, 1871, 1877–1878, 1884, 1891, 1925, 1941, 1953, 1957–1958, ?, 1965–1966 (Wyrtki 1966; Bjerknes 1966). Although I have not explored the implications of this cyclical ecological phenomenon for the evolution of Late Preceramic sociocultural systems on the Peruvian coast, I suggest that such a cyclical input would probably be a significant factor in the evolution of cultural responses to restore equilibrium to subsistence-related subsystems. We might expect to see the evolution of sociopolitical subsystems that are suitable for managing the accumulation and redistribution of subsistence resources prior to and during periods of ecosystemic collapse. We might also begin to see evidence of calendrical systems that could be utilized to store information concerning these food crises and that could be used to predict future catastrophes. Perhaps the "public" structures at such sites as Culebras, Aspero, Rio Seco, and Chuquitanta were used to store food and related resources for just such periods of shortage. If, indeed, there has been little environmental change on the coast of Peru during the Holocene, then perhaps it is not surprising to see these large communities (with "ceremonial" components) appear along the richest and yet the most drastically affected zone of the coast between 7° and 12° S. latitude.

In summary, we find that the Peru Current system, as an upwelling system, creates a rather unique and unusually productive marine ecosystem along the western coast of South America from southern Chile to northern Peru. As might be expected in such a vast region, there are areas of differing productivity caused by variations in the width of the continental shelf, atmospheric circulation pattern, intensity of upwelling, available nutrient salts and detritus, and so on. The Peruvian coast between 7° and 12° S. latitude lies in juxtaposition to one of the most productive areas of the entire Humboldt Current. It is in this area that the usual low productivity of the oceans is increased markedly. There are six major reasons for this anomalous situation. First, the net transport of submarine water to the surface increases along a north–south gradient as the current approaches the equator. Second, the oxygen minimum layer is shallow along this particular zone where upwelling probably adds oxygen to the mixed waters. Third, Cushing (1971:316–317, Figs. 18a, b) demonstrates that there is a negative correlation between the distribution of anchovetas and zooplankton for the area between Punta Aquaje (6° S. latitude) and San Juan (15° S. latitude) during the period of aggregation and spawning. The significance of this negative correlation implies that this zone has extremely high primary productivity and also a high turnover rate which, in aquatic ecosystems, can lead to an inverted pyramid of numbers (Pianka 1974:226). Perhaps another significant factor is that animal organisms often migrate to more immature ecosystems to spawn so that their offspring can utilize the readily available, excess energy during their formative growth stage. Fourth, for the west coast of South America, phosphate-phosphorus concentrations and zooplankton are extremely high between 8° and 15° S. latitude. Regardless of whether zooplankton utilize or produce this extremely high concentration of PO_4-P, this zone is one of high primary productivity. Fifth, additional dissolved nutrient salts are necessary for optimal production in the marine environment. According to Guillen, Mendiola, and Rondan (1971), optimal salinity conditions for many marine organisms exist along the Peruvian coast between 7° and 11° S. latitude. Finally, the most severe effects of the El Niño countercurrent occur between 5°5' and 13°43' S. latitude.

Conclusions

If archaeologists, as anthropologists and scientists, are to attain their goal—the explanation of human behavior—they must do so with reference to a body of explicit, deductively derived theory. As scientists, anthropologists, in general, should seek to discover the underlying regularities of seemingly diverse and extremely complex human behavior, both past and present. In this regard, theory, as Hempel (1966:75–76) points out, "offers [a] systematically unified account of quite diverse phenomena. It traces all of them back to the same underlying processes and presents the various empirical uniformities they exhibit as manifestations of one common set of laws." In addition, a body of theory has predictive value; as Hempel (1966:77) suggests, "a good theory will also broaden our knowledge and understanding by predicting and explaining phenomena that were not known when the theory was formulated."

Although a large portion of this chapter deals with empirical observations concerning the Late Preceramic periods of coastal Peru, the primary purpose has been to present more general arguments concerning the initial intensive incorporation of marine food resources into hunter–gatherer subsistence strategies regardless of time and space. Three arguments for the low subsistence "pay-off" (see Binford n.d. for a discussion of this concept) of marine food resources were advanced: First, marine ecosystems, in general, are less productive (lower primary productivity values) than terrestrial ecosystems. Second, many marine foods of the easily accessible intertidal zone require the adoption of labor-intensive subsistence strategies related to small food-package sizes and low nutritional values, for example, shellfish, sea urchins, birds, and so on. Third, sea mammals are not only inaccessible throughout much of the year, but they are also high in the food chain where energy flow is greatly reduced and the ratio of protein to edible meat is about half that for terrestrial mammals.

I referred to the general theory of natural selection in order to generate a model or abstract simplification of those conditions under which we might expect human groups to experience selection pressures that would lead to the exploitation of low-return marine food resources. Application of the theory of natural selection, specifically, "r-selection" and "K-selection," which was originally formulated to deal with biological evolution, to an explanatory model for human behavior rests on the assumption that culture is an additional form of adaptation to selective pressures operating on human populations. Density-dependent natural selection developed as a concept as a result of the studies of MacArthur and Wilson (1967) in which they differentiated between adaptive advantage defined under conditions of an expanding, uncrowded population versus adaptive advantage determined under high population densities approaching carrying capacity. I argued that, under high human population density conditions in which considerable stress was placed on existing food resources, we might expect to observe human groups begin to exploit less than optimal food resources, such as marine shellfish, fish, and sea mammals—if these were present.

The secondary purpose of this chapter was to examine a specific empirical case in some detail. The Peruvian example was chosen for several reasons: *(1)* I have some familiarity with the data: *(2)* there is a growing body of reliable archaeological data for both the coast and the interior: *(3)* the coast lies juxtaposed with a relatively well-studied anomalous region of upwelling currents that serve to disrupt the usual low productivity of the marine ecosystem (of the oceans in general). Specifically, I am interested in the possible cultural ramifications of these unusual ecological conditions for Late Preceramic cultural systems of coastal Peru. The Peru Current system is quite unique, not only because it produces an extremely productive marine ecosystem, but also because this ecosystem, due to decreased maturity, is highly unstable and is subject to severe cyclical collapse. I advanced an argument linking various aspects of the Peru Current system's oceanographic and ecological character with settlement size and distribution, subsistence strategies, and sociocultural evolution along the coast between 7° and 12° S. latitude.

Recent attempts to explain the shifts in Prehistoric hunter–gatherer subsistence toward an increased reliance upon marine foods are quite similar to the attempts to account for the origins of agriculture. Models for explaining an increased reliance upon sea foods in western Europe, the east coast of North America, the Near East, Peru, and so forth, were developed to deal with specific archaeological data. No attempt has been made to formulate general theories that systematically unify seemingly diverse phenomena, nor have any attempts been made to develop empirical tests that would allow investigators to evaluate their ideas and assumptions about how the world operates. Ideas concerning man's use of the seas have been produced inductively from empirical observations. Hempel (1966:15) cautions us in this regard: "Scientific hypotheses and theories are not *derived* from observed facts, but are *invented* in order to account for them." Induction, in this case, allows the investigator to introduce his own biases into the explanation without subjecting them to empirical test. Sauer's (1961) presuppositions concerning the optimal seashore habitat for early man and the "obvious ease" of strandlooping are a classic example of how our subjective thoughts about the empirical world can be unquestioningly incorporated into anthropological interpretation.

The origins of coastal adaptations, that is, the utilization of marine resources, like the origins of agriculture, have been approached, for the most part, in an atheoretical manner. Flannery's (1973) recent review of the status of investigations concerning the initial domestication of plants might just as easily be applied to the studies of marine resource utilization. The general tone of his review article is one of pessimism tempered with skepticism. Concerning our understanding of agricultural origins in the Near East, Flannery (1973:283) states, "We may never know why agriculture began in the Near East." As for China and the Far East, the origins of agriculture are an "enigma" (p. 284). In Mesoamerica, "We still do not know *why* they [plants] were domesticated, and it will certainly be a long time before we do " (p. 287). Finally, concerning the Andes, Flannery (p. 302–303) states that he is unable to present an explanatory model because he is unfamiliar with the data base and he concludes that, for Peru, "What this all means in terms of process or developmental models is far from clear." Flannery (p. 307) ends his discussion by reiterating, "I did (do) not believe one model could (can) explain the origins of agriculture in all four regions discussed." He (p. 308) emphasizes that the agricultural revolution was a process and not an event:

> To search for "the first domestic plant" is to search for an event; it is poor strategy, it encourages bitter rivalry rather than cooperation, and it is probably fruitless. We should search instead for the processes by which agriculture began. To do that we need settlement pattern data; well-excavated living floors with plants left *in situ;* and samples of 100 specimens with a mean, standard deviation, and range of variation.

I feel that Flannery's review of the status of the archaeological investigation of the origins of agriculture points out quite well the theoretical vacuum that Binford refers to in the introduction of this volume that now exists for all archaeologists who have rejected the traditionalists' paradigm. Are we to believe that recent failures to generate general explanations about the origins of agriculture or the initial utilization of aquatic resources will be rectified by more meticulous excavation of cave floors and shell middens, by the collection of more adequate samples of well-preserved plants or mollusk shells, and by the completion of more detailed settlement pattern studies? The archaeological record, like the empirical world in general, possesses no intrinsic meaning that is awaiting discovery; it has no meaning until archaeologists, as cultural participants in the present, assign significance to their observations. Cave floors, shell middens, settlement distributions, and domesticated plants, in and of themselves, have nothing to "say" to the archaeologist. Flannery is correct in emphasizing a pessimistic outlook for archaeology given the present status of the field; he is also correct to point out that agricultural origins involve a process, not an event. We must remember, however, that the archaeological record does not contain meaning or process. Archaeologists cannot go initially to the archaeological record to discover why plants and animals were domesticated, why early hunter–gatherers began to exploit the food resources of the oceans differentially throughout time and space, or why early sedentary communities in coastal Peru appeared along a restricted portion of the coast. Archaeologists must formulate middle-range and general theory that will enable them, as anthropologists and scientists, to utilize the empirical world—the archaeological record—to test their ideas about why the world operates as it does.

ACKNOWLEDGMENTS

I would like to thank Gary S. Vescelius and Dr. Richard S. MacNeish for both directly and indirectly introducing me to Peruvian archaeology. My interest in the Peru Current system and in coastal archaeology in general was initiated in part by a 1970 article written by Mary Hrones Parsons (*American Antiquity* **35:** 292–304). I am greatly indebted to all the archaeologists who have worked on the coast of Peru, particularly those with whom I have taken issue in this paper.

The aspects of this chapter that prove to be enlightening to others are largely attributable to Lewis R. Binford—who is for many of us a rare combination of scientist, teacher, and friend. Randall Schalk also provided invaluable interest, comments, and criticisms throughout the course of my writing. Empirical errors and theoretical failures expressed in this chapter are solely my own.

Finally, I would like to express my deepest appreciation to Dr. and Mrs. Jack Gunn for their encouragement and assistance, which enabled me to first visit and work in South America.

REFERENCES

Abbott, J. C.
   1966   Protein supplies and prospects: The problem. In *World protein resources,* edited by R. F.
           Gould. *Advances in chemistry series* 57. Washington, D.C.: American Chemical Society.
Andrewartha, H. C., and L. C. Birch
   1954   *The distribution and abundance of animals.* Chicago: University of Chicago Press.

Andrews, E. W.
    1965   Archaeology and prehistory of the northern Maya lowlands: An introduction. In *Handbook of Middle American Indians,* edited by Gordon R. Willey. Vol. 2, pt. 1. Austin: University of Texas Press.
Bertalanffy, Ludwig von
    1968   General systems theory—A critical review. In *Modern systems research,* edited by Walter Buckley. Chicago: Aldine.
Binford, Lewis R.
    1964   Archaeological and ethnohistorical investigation of cultural diversity and progressive development among aboriginal cultures of coastal Virginia and North Carolina. Unpublished doctoral dissertation, University of Michigan.
    1968   Post-Pleistocene adaptations. In *New perspectives in archaeology,* edited by S. R. Binford and L. R. Binford. Chicago: Aldine.
    n.d.   The ecology of hunters and gatherers. Unpublished manuscript.
Binford, Lewis R., and William Chasko, Jr.
    1976   Nunamuit demographic history: A provocative case. In *Demographic anthropology,* edited by Ezra Zubrow. Albuquerque: Univ. of New Mexico Press. Pp. 63–143.
Bird, Junius B.
    1943   Excavations in northern Chile. *Anthropological Papers of the American Museum of Natural History* **38:**173–317.
    1948   Preceramic cultures in Chicama and Viru. *Memoirs of the Society for American Archaeology* **25:**6–29.
    1951   South American radio-carbon dates. In *Radio-carbon dating,* edited by F. Johnson. Society for American Archaeology *Memoir* No. 8. Pp. 37–49.
Birdsell, Joseph B.
    1968   Some predictions for the Pleistocene based on equilibrium systems among recent hunters–gatherers. In *Man the hunter,* edited by R. B. Lee and I. DeVore. Chicago: Aldine.
Bjerknes, J. (1966) El Niño. *Bulletin Inter-American Tropical Tuna Commission* **12:**25–86.
Bodenheimer, S. F.
    1928   Welche Faktoren regulieren die Individuenzahl einer Insektenart in der Natur? *Biol. Zentralbl.* **48:**714–739.
Braun, David P.
    1974   Explanatory models for the evolution of coastal adaptations in Prehistoric eastern New England. *American Antiquity* **39**(4):582–596.
Bryden, M. M.
    1972   Growth and development of marine mammals. In *Functional anatomy of marine mammals,* edited by R. J. Harrison. New York: Academic Press.
Buckley, Walter
    1968   Society as a complex adaptive system. In *Modern systems research,* edited by Walter Buckley. Chicago: Aldine.
Campbell, U.
    1972   Some radiocarbon dates for aboriginal shell middens in the lower Macleay River, New South Wales. *Mankind* **8:**283–286.
Carneiro, Robert L.
    1970   A theory of the origin of the state. *Science* **169:**733–738.
Chang, Kwang-Chih
    1970   Archaeology of Taiwan. *Asian Perspectives* XII: 57–73.
Childe, V. Gordon
    1925   *Dawn of European civilization.* New York: Alfred A. Knopf.
    1935   *Prehistory of Scotland.* London: Kegan Paul.
Chitty, Dennis
    1957   Self-regulation in numbers through changes in viability. *Symposia of Qualitative Biology* **22:**277–280; 112,113.

Clark, Grahame
  1969   *World prehistory: A new outline.* Cambridge: Cambridge University Press.
Clark, G. A.
  1971   The Asturian of Cantabria: Subsistence base and the evidence for post Pleistocene clima-
         tic shifts. *American Anthropologist* **73:**1244–1257.
Clark, J. G. D.
  1948   The development of fishing in Prehistoric Europe. *Antiquity* **28:**45–85.
  1952   *Prehistoric Europe: The economic basis.* New York: Philosophical Library.
  1975   *The earlier Stone Age settlement of Scandinavia.* London: Cambridge University Press.
Cohen, J. M.
  1968   *The discovery and conquest of Peru: A translation of Books I and II of Augustin de Zarate 1556.*
         Middlesex, Eng.: Penguin Books.
Cook, S. F.
  1946   A reconstruction of shell mounds with respect to population and nutrition. *American
         Antiquity* **12:**50–53.
Craig, A. K., and N. P. Psuty
  1968   The Paracas papers—Studies in marine desert ecology I. *Occasional Papers.* Department of
         Geography, Florida Atlantic University.
Cushing, D. H.
  1971   Upwelling and the production of fish. *Advanced Marine Biology* **9:**255–334.
Day, Kent C.
  1974   Walk-in wells and water management at Chanchan, Peru. In *The rise and fall of civilizations:
         Modern archaeological approaches to ancient cultures,* edited by J. A. Sabloff and C. C.
         Lamberg-Karlovsky. Menlo Park, California: Cummings.
Donnan, Christopher
  1964   An early house from Chilca, Peru. *American Antiquity* **30:**137–144.
Dumond, Don E.
  1969   Prehistoric cultural contacts in southwestern Alaska. *Science* **166:**1108–1115.
Eidt, R. C.
  1969   The climatology of South America. In *Biogeography and ecology in South America.* Vol. 1.
         The Hague: Junk N. V.
Emlen, J. M.
  1966   The role of time and energy in food preference. *American Naturalist* **100:**611–617.
Engel, Frederic
  1957   Early sites on the Peruvian coast. *Southwestern Journal of Anthropology* **13:**54–68.
  1958   Algunos datos con referencia a los sitios Preceramicos de la costa Peruana. *Arqueologicas
         Publicaciones del Instituto de Investigaciones Antropologicas* **3.** (Lima)
  1960   Datos con referencia al estudio de sitios Prehistoricos en su concepto morflogico y
         climatologico, antiguo Peru. (Lima)
  1963a A preceramic settlement on the central coast of Peru, Asia I. *Transactions of the American
         Philosophical Society* **53**(3):1–139.
  1963b Notes relatives à des explorations archeologiques à Paracas et sur la cote sud du Perou.
         Travaux de l'Institut Francais d'Etudes Andines **9:**1–72.
  1964   El Preceramico sin algodon en la costa del Peru. *35 Congreso Internacional de Americanistas,
         Actas y Memorias* **3:**141–152.
  1966   *Geografia humana Prehistorica y agricultura Precolombina de la Quebrada de Chilca.* Lima:
         Universidad Agraria.
  1967   Le complexe Preceramique d'El Paraiso (Perou). *Journal de la Societé des Americanistas*
         55(1):43–96.
  1970   Explorations of the Chilca Canyon, Peru. *Current Anthropology* **11**(1):55–58.
  1973   New facts about pre-Columbian life in the Andean *Lomas.* Current Anthropology
         14(3):271–280.

Evans, J. D.
   1969   The exploitation of mollusks. In *The domestication and exploitation of plants and animals,* edited by P. J. Ucko and G. W. Dimbleby. London: Duckworth. Pp. 479–484.
Fitzhugh, William
   1972   Environmental archaeology and cultural systems in Hamilton Inlet, Labrador. *Smithsonian Contributions to Anthropology* **16.** Washington D.C.: Smithsonian Institution Press.
Flannery, Kent V.
   1973   The origins of agriculture. *Annual Review of Anthropology* **2:**271–309.
Fladmark, Knut R.
   1974   A paleoecological model for Northwest Coast prehistory. Unpublished doctoral dissertation, University of Calgary, Alberta, Canada.
Freeman, L. C.
   1973   The significance of mammalian fauna from paleolithic occupations in Cantabrian Spain. *American Antiquity* **38**(1):3–44.
Fung Pineda, Rosa, A. Cenzano, and P. Zavaleta
   1972   El taller litico de Chivateros, valle de Chillon. *Revista del Museo Nacional* **38:**61–72.
Gadgil, M., and O. T. Solbrig
   1972   The concept of r- and K-selection: Evidence from wildflowers and some theoretical considerations. *American Naturalist* **106:**14–31.
Gallucci, Vincent F.
   1973   On the principles of thermodynamics in ecology. *Annual Review of Ecology and Systematics* **4:**329–357.
Glassow, Michael A.
   1972   Changes in the adaptations of southwestern basketmakers: A systems perspective. In *Contemporary archaeology: A guide to theory and contributions,* edited by Mark Leone. Carbondale, Ill. Southern Illinois University Press.
Gorman, Chester
   1971   The Hoabinhian and after: Subsistence patterns in southeast Asia during the Late Pleistocene and early recent periods. *World Archaeology* **2**(3):300–320.
Greengo, Robert E.
   1952   Shellfish foods of the California Indians. *Kroeber Anthropological Society Papers* **7:**63–114.
Guillen, Oscar, Blanca Rotas de Mendiola, and Raquel Izaguirre de Rondan
   1971   Primary production and phytoplankton in the coastal Peruvian waters. In *Fertility of the sea,* edited by J. D. Costlow. Vol. 1. New York: Gordon and Breach.
Gunther, E. R.
   1936   A report on oceanographical investigations in the Peru coastal current. *Discovery Report* **13:**109–276.
Hall, Edwin S.
   1971   Kangiguksuk: A cultural reconstruction of a 16th century Eskimo site in northern Alaska. *Arctic Anthropology* **8**(1):1–78.
Harrisson, Tom
   1971   Radio-carbon dates for Sabah and Brunei (related to Sarawak). *The Sarawak Museum Journal* **XIX** (38–39):363–366.
Hempel, Carl G.
   1966   *Philosophy of natural science.* Foundations of philosophy series. Englewood Cliffs, N.J.: Prentice-Hall.
Hidaka, K.
   1954   A contribution to the theory of upwelling and coastal currents. *Transactions of the American Geophysical Union* **35**(3):431–444.
Holmes, Nicholas H., and E. Bruce Trickey
   1974   Late Holocene sea-level oscillations in Mobile Bay. *American Antiquity* **39**(1):122–124.

Howard, L. O., and W. F. Fiske
    1911   The importation into the United States of the parasites of the gypsy moth and the
           brown-tail moth. *Bulletin U.S. Bureau of Entomology* No. 91: 169–183.
Hurt, Wesley R.
    1964   Recent radiocarbon dates for central and southern Brazil. *American Antiquity* **30**(1):25–33.
Isaacs, John D.
    1969   The nature of ocean life. *Scientific American* **221**(3):146–162.
Ishida, Izumi, and Terada
    1960   Andes, Report of University of Tokyo Scientific Expedition to the Andes 1958. Andean
           Institute, University of Tokyo, Tokyo.
Jochelson, Waldemar
    1933   History, ethnology and anthropology of the Aleut. *Carnegie Institute of Washinton Publica-
           tion* No. 432. Washington, D.C.: W. F. Roberts.
Jones, Rhys
    1968   The geographical background to the arrival of man in Australia and Tasmania. *Archaeol-
           ogy and Physical Anthropology of Oceania* **3**:186–215.
Kemp, William B.
    1971   The flow of energy in a hunting society. *Scientific American* **224**:104–115.
Kendeigh, Charles S.
    1974   *Ecology: With special reference to animals and man.* Englewood Cliffs, N.J.: Prentice-Hall.
Kidder, H. E., Jr.
    1959   *Japan before Buddhism.* New York: Praeger.
Klein, Richard G.
    1974   Environment and subsistence of Prehistoric man in the Southern Cape Province, Africa.
           World Archaeology **5**(3):249–284.
Krebs, Charles J.
    1972   *Ecology: Experimental analysis of distribution and abundance.* New York: Harper and Row.
Lack, David L.
    1954   *The natural regulation of animal numbers.* New York: Oxford University Press.
Lanning, Edward P.
    1963   A pre-agricultural occupation on the central coast of Peru. *American Antiquity*
           28(3):360–371.
    1965   Early man in Peru. *Scientific American* **213**(4):68–76.
    1967   *Peru before the Incas.* Englewood Cliffs, N.J.: Prentice-Hall.
Lanning, Edward P., and Thomas C. Patterson
    1967   Early man in South America. *Scientific American* **217**(5):44–50.
Lee, Richard B.
    1968   What hunters and gatherers do for a living, or, how to make out on scarce resources. In
           Man the hunter, edited by R. B. Lee and I. Devore. Chicago: Aldine.
Lee, R. B., and I. DeVore (Editors)
    1968   *Man the hunter* Chicago: Aldine.
Lotka, A. J.
    1925   *Elements of physical biology.* Baltimore: Williams and Wilkins.
Lumbreras, Luis G.
    1969   *Antiguo Peru: de los pueblos, las culturas y las artes.* Lima: Francisco Mencloa Editores.
    1974   *The peoples and cultures of ancient Peru.* Translated by Betty J. Meggers. Washington, D.C.:
           Smithsonian Institution Press.
Lynch, Thomas F.
    1967   The nature of the central Andean Preceramic. *Occasional Papers of the Idaho State Museum*
           No. 21. (Pocatello, Idaho)
    1974   The antiquity of man in South America. *Quaternary Research* **4**:356–377.
MacArthur, R., and E. O. Wilson
    1967   *The theory of island biogeography.* Princeton, N.J.: Princeton University Press.

MacCartney, A. P.
    1971   A proposed western Aleutian phase in the Near Islands, Alaska. *Arctic Anthropology*
           8:92–142.
MacNeish, Richard S.
    1969   *First annual report of the Ayacucho archaeological–botanical project.* Andover, Mass.: Peabody
           Foundation.
    1970   *Second annual report of the Ayacucho archaeological–botanical project.* Andover, Mass.: Peabody
           Foundation.
Mackie, Evan W.
    1968   Radiocarbon dates for two Mesolithic shell heaps. *Proceedings of the Prehistoric Society*
           38:412–416.
Margalef, Ramon
    1963   Certain unifying principles in ecology. *American Naturalist* **97**:357–374.
    1968   *Perspectives in ecological theory.* Chicago: University of Chicago Press.
Meggers, Betty J., Clifford Evans, and Emilio Estrada
    1965   Early formative period of coastal Ecuador. *Smithsonian Contributions to Anthropology* Vol. 1.
           Washington, D.C.: Smithsonian Institution Press.
Morrow, James E.
    1957   Shore and pelagic fishes of Peru. *Bulletin of the Bingham Oceanographic Collection, Peabody
           Museum of Natural History* No. 16.
Moseley, Michael E.
    1968   *Changing subsistence patterns: Late Preceramic archaeology of the central Peruvian coast.* Unpub-
           lished doctoral dissertation, Department of Anthropology, Harvard University.
    1972   Subsistence and demography: An example of interaction from Prehistoric Peru. *South-
           western Journal of Anthropology* **28**:25–49.
    1975a Chan Chan: Andean alternative of the preindustrial city. *Science* **187**:219–225.
    1975b *The maritime foundations of Andean civilization.* Menlo Park, California: Cummings.
Moseley, Michael E., and G. R. Willey
    1973   Aspero, Peru: A re-examination of the site and its implications. *American Antiquity*
           38(4):425–467.
Murphy, R. C.
    1923   Oceanography of the Peruvian littoral with reference to the abundance and distribution
           of marine life. *Geographical Review* **13**:64–85.
Newman, Walter S.
    1974   A comment on Snow's "Rising sea level and Prehistoric ecology in northern New En-
           gland." *American Antiquity* **39**(1):135–136.
Nicholson, G.
    1933   The balance of animal populations. *Journal of Animal Ecology* **2**:132–178.
Nishiwaki, M.
    1950   *Scientific report of the Whale Resource Institute* **4**:184–209.
    1972   General biology of sea mammals. In *Mammals of the sea: Biology and medicine,* edited by
           S. H. Ridgeway. Springfield, Ill.: Charles C. Thomas. Chap. 1.
Odum, Eugene P.
    1971   *Fundamentals of ecology.* 3d ed. Philadelphia: W. B. Sanders.
Okladnikov, A. P.
    1965   The Soviet Far East in antiquity: An archaeological and historical study of the maritime
           region of the U.S.S.R.. *Arctic Institute of North America Anthropology of the North: Translation
           from Russian Sources* No. 6. Toronto: University of Toronto Press.
Omura, H.
    1950   *Scientific report of the Whale Resource Institute* **4**:1–13.
Osborn, Alan J.
    n.d.   Non-agricultural sedentary communities and their sociopolitical implications for coastal
           Peru. Unpublished manuscript.

Ossa, Paul, and Michael E. Moseley
    1972   La Cumbre: A preliminary report on research into the early lithic occupation of the
           Moche Valley, Peru. *Ñawpa Pacha* **9**:1–16.

Owen, Roger C., *et al.*
    1964   The Glen Annie Canyon Site, SB-142: An Early Horizon coastal site of Santa Barbara
           County. *Archaeological Survey Annual Report 1963–1964.* Los Angeles: University of
           California Press.

Parmalee, Paul W., and Walter E. Klippel
    1974   Freshwater mussels as a Prehistoric food resource. *American Antiquity* **39**(3):421–434.

Parsons, Mary Hrones
    1970   Preceramic subsistence on the Peruvian coast. *American Antiquity* **35**:292–304.

Patten, Bernard C.
    1959   An introduction to the cybernetics of the ecosystem: The trophic–dynamic aspect. *Ecology*
           40(2):221–231.

Patterson, Thomas C.
    1971a The emergence of food production in central Peru. In *Prehistoric agriculture,* edited by
           Stuart Struever. Garden City, N.Y.: Natural History Press. Pp. 181–207.
    1971b Central Peru: Its population and economy. *Archeology* **24**:316–321.
    1973   *America's past: A New World archaeology.* Glenview, Ill.: Scott, Foresman.

Patterson, Thomas C., and Edward P. Lanning
    1964   Changing settlement patterns on the central Peruvian coast. *Ñawpa Pacha* **2**:113–123.

Patterson, Thomas C., and Michael E. Moseley
    1968   Late Preceramic and Early Ceramic cultures of the central coast of Peru. *Ñawpa Pacha*
           6:115–133.

Pianka, Eric R.
    1974   *Evolutionary ecology.* New York: Harper and Row.

Pickersgill, Barbara
    1969   The archaeological record of chili peppers (*Capsicum* Spp.) and the sequence of plant
           domestication in Peru. *American Antiquity* **34**(1):54–61.

Rau, Charles
    1884   Prehistoric fishing in Europe and North America. *Smithsonian Contributions to Knowledge*
           25.

Reid, J. L., Jr.
    1962   On circulation, phosphate-phosphorus content, and zooplankton volumes in the upper
           part of the Pacific Ocean. *Limnology and Oceanography* **7**(3):287–306.

Reinman, Fred M.
    1967   Fishing: An aspect of oceanic economy—an archaeological approach. *Fieldiana* **56**(2).

Ritchie, William A.
    1969a *The archaeology of New York State.* New York: Natural History Press.
    1969b *The archaeology of Martha's Vineyard.* New York: Natural History Press.

Roche, Jean
    1960   Le Gisement Mesolithique do Moita do Sebastao (Muge, Portugal). *Instituto de Alta Cultura*
           Vol. 1. (Lisboa)
    1966   Balance de un siglo de excavaciones nen los concheros mesoliticos de muge. *Ampurias*
           28:13–48. (Barsalona)

Rowe, John H.
    1963   Urban settlements in ancient Peru. *Ñawpa Pacha* **1**:1–27.

Russell-Hunter, W. D.
    1970   *Aquatic productivity: An introduction to some basic aspects of biological oceanography and limnol-
           ogy.* New York: MacMillan.

Sampson, C. G.
    1974   *The Stone Age of southern Africa.* New York: Academic Press.

Sauer, Carl O.
    1961   Sedentary and mobile bents in early societies. In *Social life of early man,* edited by S. L. Washburn. Chicago: Aldine.

Scheffer, Victor B.
    1958   *Seals, sea lions and walruses: A review of the pinnipedia.* Stanford, Calif.: Stanford University Press.

Schoener, Thomas W.
    1971   Theory of feeding strategies. *Annual Review of Ecology and Systematics* **2**:369–404.

Schwabe, G. H.
    1969   Towards an ecological characterization of the South American continent. In *Biogeography and ecology of South America* Vol. I. edited by E. J. Fittkau, *et al..* The Hague: Junk N. V..

Schweigger, Erwin
    1947   *El littoral Peruano.* Compañia Administradora del Guano. (Lima)

Smith, A. S.
    1935   The role of biotic factors in determining population densities. *Journal of Economic Entomology* **28**:873–898.

Smith, R. L.
    1969   Upwelling. *Oceanography and Marine Biology Annual Review* **6**:11–46.

Snow, Dean R.
    1972   Rising sea level and Prehistoric cultural ecology in northern New England. *American Antiquity* **37**(2):211–221.

Solomon, M. E.
    1958   Meaning of density-dependence and related terms in population dynamics. *Nature* **181**:1778–1781.

Spooner, Brian (Editor)
    1972   *Population growth: Anthropological implications.* Cambridge, Mass.: MIT Press.

Steward, Julian H., and L. C. Faron
    1959   *Native peoples of South America.* New York: McGraw-Hill.

Stoltman, James B.
    1972   The Late Archaic in the Savannah river region. *Florida Anthropological Society Publication* No. 6, Vol. 25 (2, Pt. 2):37–72.

Strickland, John D. H.
    1972   The marine planktonic food web. *Oceanography and Marine Biology Annual Review* **10**:349–414.

Strong, William Duncan, and Clifford Evans
    1952   Cultural stratigraphy in the Viru Valley, northern Peru. *Columbia Studies in Archaeology and Ethnology* **4.**

Stuart, David E.
    1972   *Band structure and ecological variability: The Ona and Yahgan.* Unpublished doctoral dissertation, University Of New Mexico.

Sverdrup, H. U.
    1938   On the process of upwelling. *Journal of Marine Resources* **1**:155–164.

Thomas, R. B.
    1973   Human adaptation to a high Andean energy flow system. *Occasional Papers in Anthropology* No. 7. Pennsylvania State University, University Park, Pennsylvania.

Thompson, W. R.
    1929   On the relative value of parasites and predators in the biological control of insect pests. *Bulletin of Entomological Research* **19**:343–350.

Uravov, B. P.
    1931   Insects and climate. *Transactions of the Entomological Society of London* **79**:1–247.

Volterra, V.
    1926   Fluctuations in the abundance of a species considered mathematically, *Nature* **118**:558–560.

1931   Variation and fluctuations of the number of individuals in animal species living together. In R. N. Chapman (1939), *Animal ecology*. New York: McGraw-Hill. Appendix (pp. 409–448).

Watson, William
1971   *Cultural frontiers in ancient East Asia*. Edinburgh: Edinburgh University Press.

Wendt, W. E.
1964   Die prakeramische Sielung der Rio Seco, Peru. *Baessler Archiv, Neve Folge,* Band II (2):225–275.

White, Leslie A.
1947   The expansion of the scope of science. *Journal of the Washington Academy of Sciences* **37**:181–210.
1959   *The evolution of culture*. New York: McGraw-Hill.

Whitehouse, Ruth D.
1968   Settlement and economy in southern Italy in the Neothermal period. *Proceedings of the Prehistoric Society* **38**:332–367.

Willey, Gordon R.
1966   *Introduction to American archaeology: North and Middle America*. Vol. I. Englewood Cliffs, N.J.: Prentice-Hall.
1971   *Introduction to American archaeology: South America*. Vol. II. Englewood Cliffs, N.J.: Prentice-Hall.

Wooster, W. S., and J. L. Reid, Jr.
1963   Eastern boundary currents. In *The sea* edited by M. N. Hill. New York: Wiley Interscience.

Wynne-Edwards, V. C.
1962   *Animal dispersal in relation to social behavior*. Edinburgh: Oliver and Boyd.

Wyrtki, Klaus
1966   Oceanography of the eastern Pacific Ocean. *Oceanography and Marine Biology* **4**:33–68.

Yoshida, K.
1955   Coastal upwelling off the California coast. *Record of Oceanographic Works, Japan* **2**(2):8–20.
1967   Circulation in the eastern tropical oceans with special reference to upwelling and undercurrents. *Japan Journal of Geophysics* **4**(2):1–75.

5

The Structure of an Anadromous Fish Resource

RANDALL F. SCHALK
University of New Mexico

Introduction

Societies that are dependent upon anadromous fish are frequently cited as exceptions to generalizations about hunters and gatherers (cf. Murdock 1968:15; Suttles 1968:56). Reference is commonly made to high population density, large residential groups, sedentism, social stratification, warfare, and material wealth, as examples of some of the ways in which they are exceptional. Although such characteristics may seem unusual among the hunter–gatherers of the ethnographic horizon, high density foragers dependent upon anadromous fish are undoubtedly far more widely represented in the archaeological record. Since large areas of northeast Asia, western Europe, eastern North America, and regions around the Black Sea once supported an anadromous fish resource, fishing adaptations are perhaps far less distinctive of the margins of the North Pacific than is frequently assumed. What seems most distinctive about such adaptations is that the variability they exhibit has not been related to variations in the structure of the resource base.

Any attempt to offer ecological explanations for differences in cultural systems is dependent upon the capacity to compare the structural variations of environments. In other words, understanding of cultural evolution can be no better than the ability to compare and contrast different evolutionary contexts (i.e., ecosystems). It follows that the generation and testing of arguments concerning how and why cultural evolution occurs are facilitated neither by environmental descriptions, no matter how elaborate, nor by efforts to label environments with a word or phrase. It is the case, however, that much of the anthropological literature dealing with subsistence systems based on anadromous fish involves one of these two approaches and, as a result, perpetuates some enormous oversimplifications.

A brief examination of certain notions about the environment of the Northwest coast of North America best illustrates the nature of these oversimplifications. Although the potlatch is not of immediate concern here, discussions about that institution seem to contain some of the most explicit statements about the relationship between environment and culture to which this chapter is addressed.

Earlier writings on Northwest coast cultural systems placed little emphasis upon environment (Benedict 1934; Murdock 1936; Codere 1950). Mention of resources involved characterizations such as "fantastically abundant" (Codere 1950), "extremely productive" (Barnett 1968:76), "inexhaustible" (Benedict 1934), and what was implicit in these discussions was that a "rich" environment was a permissive one. This viewpoint has been restated in a slightly different form more recently:

> The development of Indian culture in this region argues strongly against a theory of environmental determinism. The limits of North Pacific culture can be defined with considerable precision. On the northwest, Yakutat Bay represented the last outpost of the culture pattern. . . . Yet in terms of physical environment there is no abrupt change in landscape, climate, flora, or fauna west of Yakutat Bay. Similarly, at the southern extreme, Cape Mendocino on the California coast can be marked as the border of the culture area, although the general environmental pattern extends with little variation to the San Francisco Bay region or a little further south. Nonetheless, the Indians inhabiting the coast south of Cape Mendocino had a basically California culture, not a North Pacific Coast one. These different cultures, thus occuring in the one evironment, cannot plausibly be deemed environmentally determined [Drucker 1965:7–8].

Challenging these more traditional ideas about the relationship between culture and environment, Suttles (1962) suggested that there were environmental constraints operating upon these cultural systems and that cultural variability might be viewed more profitably as a result of variations in environment:

> So it is with much of the writing on the Northwest Coast; if spatial and temporal variation in resources get any consideration, it is in relation to technology and seasonal movements. The extent of these variations and their implications for social organization, however, are rarely considered. It is my position that the social organization and ceremonialism of the Coast Salish of the area I have studied is intelligible only in light of these variations [1962:101].

Placing considerable emphasis on "spatial and temporal variation in resources," Suttles contended that the potlatch itself might be viewed as "part of a larger socio-economic system that enables the whole social network consisting of a number of communities, to maintain a high level of food production and to equalize its food consumption both within and among communities" (1962:304). These arguments provided the basis for a continuing debate over the relationship between the potlatch and environment.

Others extended Suttles argument (Vayda 1961; Piddocke 1965; Weinberg 1965; Harris 1968:306–314), and essentially all made the following three points: *(1)* that there were variations in resources from season to season, year to year, and place to place, *(2)* that there were periods of scarcity and even occasional starvation, and *(3)* that, as a result, particular institutions, such as the potlatch, served to adjust human populations to these conditions and, thus, were adaptive. Vayda (1961) summarizes this argument quite clearly:

> As the effectiveness of food production was varying from time to time and place to place, there were movements and counter-movements of food, wealth, and prestige from person to person and from group to group in such a way as to minimize the adverse effects (starvation, hostilities against neighbors, and death) of any local and temporary lack of success in food production. *In more general terms, the hypothesis is that the self-regulating economic systems served to distribute goods in a way that contributed to the survival and well-being of the people* [p. 623; emphasis mine].

This last sentence is a candid expression of the assumption, hardly an hypothesis, upon which "ecological" interpretations of the potlatch have been founded. The logical difficulties in the functional paradigm have been elegantly criticized elsewhere (Orans 1975), but of interest to the present discussion is the treatment of the environment by these authors (Vayda 1961; Piddocke 1965; Weinberg 1965; Harris 1968). Although these functionalist interpretations of the potlatch have been applauded for being "in conformity with nomothetic ecological principles" (Harris 1968:311), what we are really witnessing is the door being slammed in the face of an ecological inquiry. The simple documentation of fluctuations in resources, either by reference to commercial fishery catch statistics or other evidence, is the documentation of a meaningless truism. Instead of a characterization of the spatial and temporal structure of the resource base, these writers have provided a description of such a "nomothetic" character that it would seem to apply equally well to piñon nuts, bison and caribou populations, wheat crops in the American Midwest, and nearly *any* conceivable human resource. Since one might safely assume that no food resource is available with equal abundance everywhere and all the time, these "cultural ecologists" seem to have advanced little more than a *faith* that all cultural phenomena serve some adaptive purpose.

These functional interpretations have failed to increase our understanding of the structure of these particular environments and, at the same time, our understanding of the cultural systems involved. At most, they have only proposed yet another plausible interpretation of the potlatch couched in the jargon of ecology. It is not surprising that those of the environmental "permissiveness" persuasion have reasserted themselves.

> Now it is to be doubted that anyone who is reasonably familiar with the Northwest Coast and its native culture patterns would deny that there was considerable local diversity in natural resources. . . . What are the generalizations on uniformity of resources really mean is that through-

out the area there was one important food resource, salmon, which though seasonal lent itself to preservation for storage by use of a fairly simple storage technique [Drucker and Heizer 1967:149].

Rejecting what they call "economic determinism," Drucker and Heizer also reject the functionalist view of the potlatch as a redistributive system:

The classical anthropological picture of the Northwest Coast as a region prodigal in foodstuffs for its primitive inhabitants must stand as essentially correct. The idea of the potlatch as a sort of intertribal AID program to combat starvation does not fit the ecological facts [1967:149].

It would appear that both sides in this exchange have found it expedient to select a view of the environment consistent with their particular cultural interpretation. Since the "ecological facts" presented by Drucker and Heizer are the same ones cited by their opponents—mainly catch statistics of the commercial fishery—it is evident that the same "facts" mean different things to different people. Given these sorts of notions about ecology, it would appear that "ecological facts" could be marshalled in support of nearly any interpretation concocted by an imaginative anthropologist. Far from putting an end to the "lawlessness of culture" (Harris 1968:306), this is an invitation to more lawlessness.

The debate over whether the environment should be termed "abundant" or "fluctuating in abundance" seems to be misdirected. There is not much difference between the way in which these terms are being used and the way in which terms such as "Dionysian" or "megalomaniac" (Benedict 1934) were used in the past. The notion that ecosystems or even specific resources can be characterized with a word or phrase must be recognized as unrealistic. If such labeling constitutes "cultural ecology," then nearly all anthropologists have always been adherents to that approach. Clearly, any ecological investigation cannot treat the environment as a constant, regardless of what value is assigned to that constant.

In western North America alone, anadromous fish served as a major food resource for aboriginal groups from central California to western Alaska—a latitudinal gradient of more than 25 degrees. The terrestrial environments through which such fish migrated include redwood forests, semi-arid upland plateaus, temperate rainforests, and arctic tundras. Few, if any, kinds of human resources were ever of such great importance in such a variety of terrestrial ecosystems. It is a premise of this chapter that differences in the character of the fish resource within and between regions are central to an understanding of both archaeological and ethnographic variability throughout a very substantial portion of the earth's northern hemisphere.

The previous discussions strongly suggest the need for a reversal in research strategy and a systematic effort to model the structural variations of different environments that condition cultural systems. The remainder of this chapter attempts to outline what might be a more fruitful approach to understanding the dynamics of an important class of human food resources.

In the following section, a model for the structure of an anadromous fish resource is presented. This type of model is a prerequisite to the measurement of the resource as an independent variable in the environment of a multitude of extinct cultural systems. Unlike other efforts to characterize the resource for specific regions (Rostlund 1952; Baumhoff 1963; Sneed 1972), it is intended that this model might *(1)* facilitate the specification of selective pressures exerted upon cultural systems exploiting the resource in different regions, *(2)* provide a base line for comparing the nature of the resource for different cultural systems, *(3)* allow an increased capacity to retrodict the character of the resource for particular areas, and *(4)* provide a framework for the generation of analogies for approaching regions of the world where there is little historical information available about anadromous fish or the human populations that once exploited them.

The Structure of an Anadromous Fish Resource

Anadromous fish, as opposed to other migratory fish, are those that spend a protion of their lives in the sea and migrate into fresh water to spawn (Myers 1949). Beyond this general definition, however, there is considerable variation in the life cycles of different species. After spawning occurs, egg development may take from 1 to 4 months, and the small fish that emerge may either migrate immediately to sea or remain in fresh water for a few months or as long as 6 years. The length of ocean residence is also quite variable, ranging from less than a year to 5 years for most species. These kinds of variations are not only interspecific but, to a lesser extent, characteristic of the *same* species in different environments.

Anadromy, like many forms of animal migration (e.g., caribou, waterfowl), is an evolutionary response for coping with highly seasonal environments. It occurs primarily in and north of the temperate zone, and the differences between marine and riverine environments at these latitudes require some attention for insight into fish migration and the evolutionary pay-off achieved by participation in such dissimilar ecosystems.

Riparian environments of the temperate and more northerly latitudes are typically cold waters with relatively low primary productivity during the cooler portions of the year. Although cold water supports large concentrations of oxygen essential to fish respiration, the reduction of temperature during the winter means that such environments are food-scarce for substantial portions of an annual cycle. The result of a limited food supply is that such waters are incapable of supporting large secondary biomasses (i.e., fish) on a yearround basis. At the same time, however, these very conditions may be quite favorable for fish reproduction. The lack of a large standing secondary biomass means a reduction in potential predators upon eggs and young fish, and the presence of abundant oxygen is conducive to their development. The utilization of the riverine environment by most anadromous fish then is almost exclusively related to reproduction to the extent that many species (nearly all salmonids) cease feeding entirely upon entry into fresh water and die soon after spawning.

Riverine environments, unlike marine ones, are strongly influenced by the terrestrial ecosystems that surround them (Odum 1971:317; Krebs 1972:463). An obvious result of this basic difference is that there is much less seasonality in marine environments in terms of primary productivity (i.e., plankton production) and water temperature than in riverine environments at comparable latitudes. Primary productivity in the oceans may remain quite high throughout the year as far north as 60° N. latitude (Rhyther 1963). The presence of thermal inversions at these latitudes, in general, and, more locally, the presence of "upwelling" and continental shelves may substantially increase the evenness of productivity during an annual cycle (Rhyther 1963; Osborn, this volume). Recognizing these broad differences between marine and riverine environments of these latitudes, it is apparent why anadromous fish may be, in energetic terms, more than 95% the product of the marine stage of life (Davidson and Hutchinson 1938). It should also be evident, having pointed out the reproductive advantages of freshwater environments and the feeding advantages of the marine environments, that anadromy makes the best of both worlds. We now turn to the movement between these two environments.

Until quite recently, the exploitation of anadromous fish has been almost entirely focused upon that phase of the life cycle of approach and entry into rivers for spawning. It follows from this observation that variations in human exploitive systems must be most directly related to patterns in spawning migrations. It will be argued here that the determinants of patterns in spawning migrations are primarily those conditions that exist in riverine environments. The marine phase will, therefore, receive only passing attention, for it is of least interest in explaining cultural variability. It is asserted that those variables that influence the structure of spawning migrations are critical in any attempt to understand the structure of human extractive systems.

It has already been suggested that riverine environments are the product of the terrestrial environments from which they exact tribute. Both the discharge and temperature regimes of rivers depend upon conditions of terrestrial environments, and these two variables are undoubtedly of foremost importance in influencing the success of spawning and, thereby, the viability of fish populations. Nearly all the conditions that are known to damage eggs or destroy young fish may be traced to either variations in discharge or water temperature (Davidson and Hutchinson 1938:673; Saunders 1967; Smoker 1953; Mundie 1974; Hynes 1969; Hanamura 1966). Some of the obvious effects of variations in either of these variables would include flooding, drought, erosion of stream gravels, silting, overcrowding due to insufficient stream flow, freezing, and overheating. The success or even the possibility of spawning is clearly determined by these kinds of conditions.

The precision in the timing of arrival of spawners as well as their accurate homing abilities are both measures of the importance of fluvial environments in constraining the structure of fish migrations (Straty 1966:461). If successful spawning had the same probability of occuring at any time of year, and in any locality, then there would be not structure in fish migrations, and precision in timing and in homing would be unnecessary. The fact that these characteristics are well developed in all anadromous fish rules out all interpretations other than that these are fine-tuned adjustments to the rhythms and rigors of fluvial environments.

The marked tendency of anadromous fish to return with great accuracy even to the same vicinity of a tributary in which they originally hatched is frequently referred to as the "homestream theory" of fish migration (Banks 1968). Besides returning to their native streams after life cycles that may take them several thousand kilometers, runs generally occur within a few days of the same time each year (Atkinson *et al.* 1967:45; Jackson 1963:2). The concomitant of these uncanny behavioral capacities is that groups of fish from the same stream constitute "races" that are genetically distinctive breeding populations (Payne *et al.* 1971; Hanamura 1966). A "run" of fish into a large river system may be composed of several of these races, each bound for the particular tributary from which it originated and, in turn, where it spawns. The timing of arrival and entrance into fresh water and the capacity to migrate the necessary distance upstream to their respective spawning areas appear to be largely genetically programmed capacities that enable each race to cope with the unique set of conditions present in its particular spawning location (Zook, personal communication; Ishida 1966:24; Saunders 1967:23; Ricker 1960, 1966; Neave *et al.* 1967; Margolis *et al.* 1966:8). The spawning migration, then, is a process of progressive segragation of fish populations from the sea to the spawning grounds.

In summary, it has been pointed out that spawning migrations are quite precisely timed and that breeding populations return with remarkable accuracy to their native streams. These characteristics of migratory behavior may be adaptations to conditions present in specific rivers (particularly discharge and temperature regimes) and are necessary for successful spawning in such highly seasonal ecosystems. Since the focus of preindustrial human exploitation of anadromous fish is the spawning migration variability in human extractive systems should be most directly the result of differences in spawning environments. Throughout the discussion to follow then, the focus will be on differences in riverine environments.

Understanding the factors that determine the distribution and abundance of organisms is a central concern of ecology (MacArthur 1972; Pianka 1974; Krebs 1972), and, from the viewpoint of human predation upon anadromous fish, it has been argued that these variables may be considered independently of the marine phase of fish life-cycles. For the purpose of this discussion, distribution and abundance (productivity) are the two major areas to be discussed more specifically. In terms of distribution, the spatial and temporal structure of an anadromous fish resource are discussed. In terms of productivity, both the determinants of gross productivity and of fluctuations are examined.

Distribution: The Spatial Component

Although it is neither desirable nor possible to describe here the distribution of individual fish species, it would be useful to consider the general patterns of species distribution. Species diversity of all organisms is correlated with environmental stability (Levins 1968:60; MacArthur 1972), and the emphasis in this discussion is on the relationship between diversity of anadromous fish species and stability of riparian environments. Stability and species diversity are examined in terms of *(1)* differences in stability of riparian environments associated with latitude, and *(2)* differences in stability resulting from conditions independent of latitude.

Differences in Stability Associated with Latitude

The more common species of anadromous fish occur over very broad and overlapping latitudinal ranges in both the Atlantic and the Pacific Oceans. An examination of Figure 5.1 showing the northern and southern limits of spawning areas of the six species of Pacific salmon indicates that a large intermediate zone (approximately 45 to 60° N. latitude) is potentially the spawning habitat for all of these forms as well as a number of other anadromous species. It is also apparent that species diversity decreases both to the north and south of this central zone. Having acknowledged the correlation between species diversity and environmental stability, it is necessary to examine what variables associated with latitude produce such patterns in species distributions.

Two critical determinants of stability in riparian ecosystems are *runoff* (discharge) and *water temperature* (Baxter 1961; Chapman 1966:354; Hoar 1953:448–449), and it is obvious that both are directly dependent upon the periodicity of solar radiation as well as the climatic conditions prevailing in the terrestrial ecosystems in which rivers originate. Anadromous fish, like all poikilotherms, are quite sensitive to minor variations in water temperature (Krebs 1972:59–61; Odum 1971), and the immature stages of these species are particularly sensitive (Davidson and Hutchinson 1938:675). While there are variations between species in the temperatures at which spawning occurs, it is likely that there are latitudinal thresholds in the temperature of riparian environments beyond which individual species can not reproduce and which, therefore are limiting factors of species distributions (Davidson and Hutchinson 1938).

Toward the more northerly latitudes, increasing seasonality in solar radiation means that temperature variations are also greater and, therefore, cold stress or freezing may restrict the portion of the year when fish can spawn. Thus, it is not surprising that the degree of anadromy increases to north (Rounsefell 1958); those species (e.g., *Oncorhynchus gorbuscha, O. keta*)[1] whose young migrate imme-

---

[1] Latin names for the six species of Pacific salmon are given in Figure 5.1. Other anadromous species that will be referred to hereafter by their common names include steelhead trout *(Salmo*

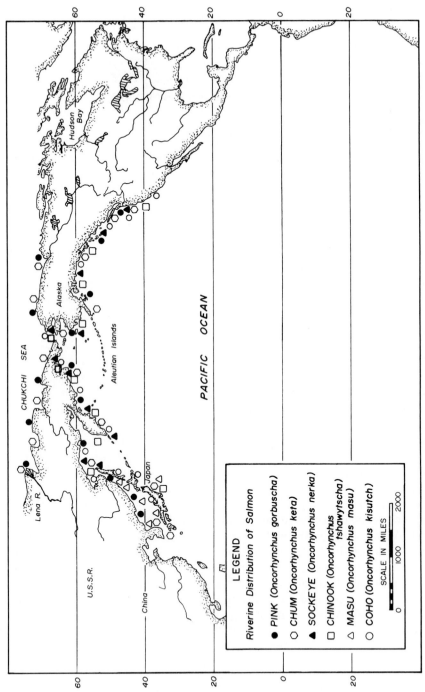

Figure 5.1 Spawning ranges of the six species of salmon native to the northern Pacific.

diately to sea upon hatching become increasingly predominate toward the north, and, at the northern extremes of fish distributions (e.g., northwest Alaska), they are the only anadromous species capable of spawning successfully. The scarcity of food and severe freezing in the rivers of the north exclude those species dependent upon longer periods of fresh water residency.

Moving southward, yearly water temperature regimes become more equable and spawning can occur for longer periods of the year. However, as the southern margins of anadromous fish distributions are approached, there are shorter periods of the year during which water temperatures are cool enough for spawning. Anadromy becomes a less profitable strategy toward the southern margin (e.g., southern California) due to increased productivity of freshwater environments and the increasing presence of freshwater species. Anadromous species predominating in this zone are those that spend long periods in fresh water (those that are less anadromous).

In the intermediate latitudes (i.e., about 45–60° N. latitude in western North America), variations in water temperature are small enough such that virtually all species may maintain viable spawning populations. In this sense, the Pacific salmon might be divided into two groups in terms of their capacities for coping with temperature regimes in riparian environments—a northern group (pink, chum, sockeye) and a southern group (chinook, coho). The life cycles of the former are better suited to the increased severity of temperature regimes to the north, and the latter to the more equable conditions to the south. Variations in water temperature provide but one source of instability in freshwater environments, however, and a more complete understanding of the distribution of species also requires consideration of variations in runoff along a latitudinal gradient.

Runoff is the water that falls as precipitation upon a catchment area and is not returned to the atmosphere through evapotranspiration (Morisawa 1968:12). The discharge regime of a river is the regular pattern of runoff during an annual cycle and is generally measured in volume of water per unit time (e.g., cubic feet per second). "Seasonality" in discharge may, therefore, be viewed as a measure of stability in riparian environments, and the evenness with which precipitation occurs through an annual cycle is a major determinant of the degree of stability in discharge. Thus, if precipitation occurs primarily in the form of winter rain (e.g., central California), watersheds tend to have high levels of runoff during the winter and reduced discharges during the summer. In contrast, rivers that run through coastal rainforests (e.g., western British Columbia) may receive precipitation quite continously throughout the year, and we would anticipate the presence of fewer species of anadomous fish in the former than in the latter, all other things being equal. Along a latitudinal gradient, however, those factors that cannot be held equal and that intervene between precipitation and runoff are evapotranspiration and temperature.

---

gairdnerii), white sturgeon (Acipenser transmontanus), Atlantic salmon *(Salmo salar)*, American shad *(Alosa sapidissima)*, and eulachon *(Thaleichthys pacificus)*.

Evapotranspiration is greatest in equatorial regions and decreases toward the higher latitudes. We would expect that, within the zone in which anadromous fish occur, it would be greatest toward the south. Most precipitation becomes runoff in the north because very little water is reclaimed by the atmosphere through evapotranspiration. In the more southerly areas on the other hand (e.g., California), evapotranspiration may tend to exaggerate periods of low runoff during seasons of reduced precipitation and during the warmer portions of the year. Although high evapotranspiration would reduce peak periods of discharge, it would also tend to amplify the lows in runoff, especially where precipitation is low during warm periods of the year (e.g., central California).

Temperature variations in an annual cycle increase in amplitude toward higher latitudes, and, due particularly to the effects of freezing and thawing of water, discharge regimes of rivers become increasingly less stable to the north. During periods of the year when terrestrial temperatures are below freezing, discharges may either be tremendously reduced or stopped altogether, and any precipitation that falls during these periods is stored until the spring thaw. The rather sudden release of water stored as snow and ice with the spring thaw results in peak periods of discharge. With increased cold stress toward the north, then, runoff regimes tend to exhibit greater seasonality, even with precipitation held constant.

Having considered some broad patterns in temperature, evapotranspiration, and precipitation, it is possible to anticipate their interaction. Starting at the southern extremes of anadromous fish distributions (e.g., central and southern California), precipitation is generally low, evapotranspiration high, and temperatures relatively high and equable. The obvious kind of instability most common in riparian environments of such areas is low discharge—periods when spawning is difficult or impossible due to insufficient stream flow. Excessive temperatures may also preclude spawning during the warmer portions of the year even if stream flow were sufficient. Moving northward to more central areas of anadromous fish distributions (e.g., Oregon to southeast Alaska), increased precipitation and decreased temperature and evapotranspiration probably produce the most equable riparian conditions throughout the yearly cycle. To the north of this central zone, evapotranspiration, temperature, and precipitation all decrease, but possibly the most important point is that runoff is minimal due to freezing for increasingly longer periods of the year. In terms of the conditions that anadromous fish respond to, it appears that stability in discharge of rivers diminishes both to the north and to the south of a broad intermediate zone where stability is highest. We have already seen that this pattern is approximately coincident with patterns of species diversity in anadromous fishes.

Thus far, attention has been focused on latitudinal variations in stability of riparian environments and on how these influence species diversity, but species diversity varies as a function of factors independent of latitude as well. It must be emphasized that, within the latitudinal zone in which individual species potentially occur (see Figure 5.1), they are not necessarily present in each river within that range. Although some species are known to spawn in many, if not most, rivers within their ranges (e.g., coho salmon, steelhead trout), others are not so ubiquitous. The salmon and white sturgeon, for example, are species that spawn only in larger watersheds and are scarce or absent in smaller streams. Similarly, the sockeye salmon generally requires lacustrine habitats for spawning and/or rearing and is rarely present in drainages with lakes. Such differences suggest that variations in the nature of rivers themselves determine whether or not a particular species will be present in any specific drainage within its potential latitudinal zone.

Differences in Species Diversity within and between Rivers

Species diversity varies directly with drainage size and inversely with distance upstream (Bohn, personal communication; Fulton 1968). Again, it is maintained that diversity is largely a function of stability, and the concern here is with how the structure of watersheds influences the stability of discharge. Two major differences *between* rivers in terms of watershed structure are size and storage capacity, but there are also differences in stability *within* rivers in terms of variations in temperature and discharge regime at different localities.

Variations in drainage size are directly related to differences in the runoff regime. In general, larger rivers have greater inherent stability in their discharge than do smaller rivers. Because larger rivers tend to drain a greater variety of terrestrial environments each of which has different climatic conditions, their discharge regimes are subject to far less fluctuation from localized climatic events in various districts within the drainage. Thus, larger rivers are capable of absorbing small fluctuations from individual tributaries whose cumulative effects may be considerably dampened in the lower stretches of the drainage. Similarly, larger rivers have less drastic responses to proportionate variations in runoff. Because the ratio of discharge to channel width tends to be lower for smaller streams than for larger ones, a decrease in discharge in a larger stream may amount to only a few inches reduction in stream *depth,* whereas a similar decrease in the discharge of a small stream may result in a very significant reduction in the *width* of the channel occupied by the stream (Baxter 1961; Margalef 1960). Such reduction can cause massive exposure of spawning gravels, and disturbance of spawning is one obvious consequence. This difference may also be related to the fact that larger rivers are capable of supporting runs of fish during periods of low runoff while small streams cannot.

Increased stability in discharge is also associated with increased water storage capacity within a watershed (Baxter 1961). The presence of lakes, bogs, swamps, and glaciers tend to increase the evenness of runoff by absorbing water during peak periods of precipitation. Similarly, the amount of vegetational cover and topographic relief are both factors effecting stability in that they influence the rate at which precipitation is translated into runoff. Areas with minimal surface vegetation and maximal topographic relief tend to translate precipitation into runoff quite rapidly and, therefore, have less stable discharge regimes.

Considered along a gradient from the mouth to the source of a river, many of the same generalizations apply such that decreases in stability (Margalef 1960; Odum 1971:320–321) and in species diversity (Fulton 1968) occur in that direction. For the same reasons that larger rivers are more stable in their discharge than smaller rivers, it is apparent that stability in discharge decreases upstream. Increases in stream gradient and topographic relief are generally associated with distance upstream, and decreased stability would, therefore, result from more rapid overland movement of precipitation in such areas.

Temperature gradients along the same transect of a river decrease upstream (Odum 1971:320). In most areas, this probably means that the upper areas of the watershed are suitable for spawning for shorter periods of the year or at least earlier in the year than areas downstream. In addition to such differences in temperature, fish bound for spawning areas further inland have greater distances to travel and must begin their journeys sooner (Straty 1966:562). Taken together, these conditions seem to account for the widely observed pattern that those fish that enter a river earliest migrate the farthest upstream to spawn (Foerster 1968:7; Baxter 1961:232; Straty 1966:462; Watanabe 1973:124), and spawning throughout the season tends to take place at locations progressively closer to the sea.

Differences in the distances that various species are capable of migrating might be seen as adaptations to various spawning niches within river systems. Some species migrate to the headwaters of the largest rivers (e.g., *Oncorhynchus tshawytscha, Salmo salar*) and may travel more than 2000 miles upstream to their spawning areas. The American shad *(Alosa sapidissima)* of the Atlantic, for example, is known to have migrated to the headwaters of the longest rivers in eastern North America (Walburg and Nichols 1967). On the other hand, many species have far more limited capacities of migration and tend to travel relatively short distances in fresh water. The chum salmon *(O. keta)*, the pink salmon *(O. gorbuscha)*, and the eulachon *(Thaleichthys pacificus)* of the Pacific all tend to spawn distances of less than a hundred miles from the ocean in the rivers of western North America. Although the chum salmon tends to migrate much further upstream in the rivers of northeast Asia, nevertheless, fewer species spawn in riparian environments as the distance from the ocean increases.

To summarize this discussion of spatial structure in the resource, it appears that there are three levels at which patterns may be discerned. The first is latitudinal, and it is suggested that species diversity is greatest in a wide central zone and, moving in either direction away from this zone, diversity decreases. Stability in the riparian habitat is correlated with species diversity, and latitudinal variations in discharge and temperature regimes are the primary determinants of stability in riparian environments. The second level at which patterns are observed is that of differences in rivers. It is suggested that larger rivers tend to be more stable than smaller rivers and, thus, capable of supporting more species. The third level recognizes differences within rivers in stability and temperature; stability decreases in an upstream direction and is accompanied by decreased species diversity.

Distribution: The Temporal Component

The time of year at which a particular run of anadromous fish enters a river and the time at which races arrive on their spawning grounds are remarkably consistent from year to year (Atkinson *et al.* 1967:45; Jackson 1963:2). This is a predictable result of the rather narrow temperature ranges at which eggs and young fish will successfully develop (Davidson and Hutchinson 1938) as well as the constraints imposed upon fish migration by discharge regimes (Hoar 1953:448–449). Recognizing the importance of temperature fluctuations for spawning and development, it is clear that shorter periods of spawning would result from increasing seasonality. There is, therefore, increasing temporal compression of fish runs towards higher latitudes. This is evident in Table 5.1 and Figure 5.2. In Figure 5.2, shad migrations into three rivers of eastern North America are reflected in the catches of the commercial fishery. In Table 5.1, the season of chinook salmon runs in several large rivers at various latitudes in western North America are shown. Several important characteristics of temporal structure in fish migrations at different latitudes are suggested.

Firstly, the period during which any particular species is available decreases to the north, and, in the Yukon River, for example, chinook salmon run for a little more than a month. Chinook migrations into the Sacramento River, on the other hand, might be separated into three distinct runs, but there are at least small numbers of fish entering the drainage throughout the year.

Table 5.1

Approximate Time of Chinook Salmon Runs and Growing Season for Four Major Drainages at Different Latitudes in Western North America[a]

River	North latitude	Average growing season	Time of chinook runs
Yukon	63	June 1 to Sept. 1 (3 months)	mid-June through late July (1+ months)
Fraser	49	May 1 to Nov. 1 (6 months)	May through September (5 months)
Columbia	46	April 1 to Nov. 1 (7 months)	April through October (7 months)
Sacramento	38	March 1 to Dec. 1 (9 months)	late August through June (10 months)

[a]Information from U.S. Weather Service 1966, Fry 1961, Galbreath 1966, Aro and Shepard 1967, and Atkinson *et al.* 1967.

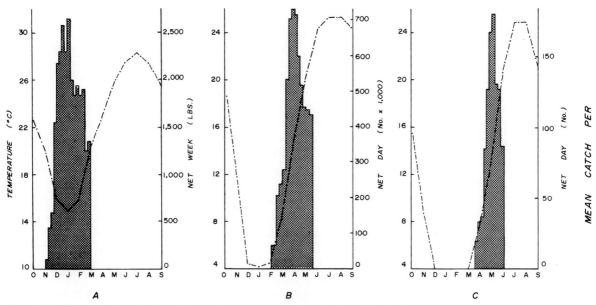

Figure 5.2 Shad catches at various times and water temperatures in three Atlantic Coast rivers.

Secondly, fish migrations become more temporally congruent with the terrestrial growing season to the north. Thus, while runs of fish into the rivers such as the Yukon occur during the midsummer, runs into the more southerly rivers, such as the Sacramento, occur during the spring, winter, and fall primarily. Again, this pattern must be understood in terms of the differences in temperature regimes at different latitudes. This increased congruency of fish runs with the warmer season of the year toward the north means that freezing fish as a storage technique is rarely a possibility. This, as will be seen shortly, is a significant constraint upon the way in which humans exploit anadromous fish.

A third observation is that the shorter duration of fish migrations at higher latitudes means that more fish migrate per unit time to the north. Commerical fishermen who have fished different areas along the coast are well aware of the drastic effects of these temporal patterns on fishing strategy.

In the Columbia River, commerical fishing takes place over a period of approximately 4 months. In Bristol Bay, Alaska, however, the bulk of the annual catch by a fishing boat may be taken in as little as two 24-hour periods of fishing (Bernard Howe, personal communication). An account by I. F. Pravdin of pink salmon entering the Bol'shaya River on the eastern coast of Kamchatka in 1926 gives a similar impression of the rate at which fish migrate through more northerly fisheries:

Although the weather was calm and sunny, an extraordinary noise could be heard coming from the middle of the river between its two main channels. The noise was somewhat similar to the noise of boiling water splashing in a gigantic cauldron. The population of the fishing camps rushed out to the bank. Standing there the fishermen feasted their eyes upon a tremendous school of fish which went up the river, making a very loud noise, as if a new river had burst into the Bol'shaya; the fish jumped out of the water continually. The noisy stretch of fish was at least one verst (1067m.) long and not less than 100m. wide, so that the size of the school could be estimated at several million specimens which all got to the spawning grounds upstream having passed the fishing camps completely unimpeded [Pravdin 1926, quoted in Berg 1962:194–195].

Although this is obviously an unusual occurence even in Kamchatka, it does indicate the importance of temporal structure in fish migrations even for modern fishing technologies. It is apparent that catching fish requires different methods when the migrations are temporally compressed, and, as will be seen later, temporal compression of the resource also implies increasingly formidable conditions for processing and storing fish.

Finally, temporal patterning in the fish resource is also related to species diversity. In rivers that have more species, the period during which fish may be taken is lengthened. Different species characteristically enter a river in a regular order from year to year, and, although these migrations may overlap considerably in time, there is undoubtedly a longer period during which fish may be taken in rivers with more species.

To summarize temporal patterns, it is evident that there are two major dimensions of variability. Ignoring species diversity and river size, fish migrations are more temporally compressed moving from south to north. In addition, the season during which fish move into rivers changes from all year round or throughout the winter at the southern extreme to midsummer at the northern extreme. Thus, congruency of fish migrations with the terrestrial growing season increases to the north. Ignoring latitude, the period of availability is obviously a direct function of species diversity. Thus, larger rivers, more stable rivers, and particularly the lower trunks of large and stable drainages offer longer periods of resource availability. Smaller rivers with few species or the upper tributaries of any drainage offer much shorter periods during which fish may be taken. The extreme temporal compression of resource availability would occur in small rivers of the far north.

Productivity

Fisheries biologists generally believe that the freshwater environment sets the limits for productivity of anadromous fish:

> In the ocean the pastures are thought to be vast, both in extent and quantity of food. No limits to the productive capacity, so far as salmon are concerned, have been discovered. Thus, so far as we know, the greater the recruitment of smolts [seaward migrating young fish] the greater the numbers of adult fish returning from the sea [Foerster 1968:372; reproduced by permission of Minister of Supply and Services Canada].

A stream's potential to produce fish, then, would seem to be a function of the amount of accessible spawning habitat and rearing area in the drainage (Bohn, personal communication; Chapman 1966; Egglishaw 1970). It follows that the productive capacity of a stream is associated with the size of the stream, and large rivers generally produce more fish than smaller ones. Similarly, the potential productive capacity of any locality along a river is a function of the quantity of utilizable spawning ground upstream from that locality (Baumhoff 1963).[2] "Potential" is used as a qualifier here because there are many conditions that determine how much of a stream's capacity is actually realized in a particular year and these will be ignored momentarily while differences in potential are considered.

While recognizing these regularities in productivity, then, it is not difficult to design measures for ranking different locations in terms of their relative productive potentials as Baumhoff (1963) has done for specific districts in California (see also Sneed 1972 for a similar study). Baumhoff's measure of the fish resource for a number of aboriginal groups in central and northern California indicates how relative indices of productivity can be derived from the observation that fish migration is a process of dispersing in a reticulate manner within a drainage system, and, therefore, potential productivity decreases upstream. Because such an index is relative, it is probably most useful within single drainages. It is less obvious how this sort of measure could be used along a latitudinal gradient. Some absolute measure of differences in productivity, possibly expressed as the ratio of fish biomass per unit area of spawning habitat, would be useful in comparing rivers in different environments. Unfortunately, the necessary quantitative data is presently unavailable.

Although catch records of the commercial fisheries are frequently cited by anthropologists in support of arguments about productivity (cf. Piddocke 1965; Drucker and Heizer 1967) and are employed in the following section of this chapter as well, writers often do not consider the limitations inherent in these statistics as measures of productivity. It cannot be assumed, for instance, that the cumulative productivity of many different tributaries of a large river, or even many different river systems, represented in catch records bears any direct relationship to the productivity of individual streams. The dynamics of individual fish populations are probably somewhat obscured in catches that are commonly taken from many different fish populations in widely separated areas.

Another difficulty with catch records is that they are in many ways an artifact of modern man rather than dependable measures of the distribution of productivity in the past. Thus, while rivers to the south of British Columbia contribute a relatively small percentage of the total yearly catch of salmon along the entire western coast, it is apparent that these rivers have suffered far greater damage at the hands of modern man. The more pristine rivers to the north of the areas of highest modern human population density seem to have sustained higher levels of productivity in all regions of the world's major fisheries for anadromous species (i.e., the Maritime provinces of eastern Canada, Scandinavia in western Europe, and Siberia in northeast Asia).

[2] The quantity of fish available to a group is also a function of the degree to which other groups, located downstream, exploit the resource.

There are two patterns in productivity along a latitudinal gradient that can be pointed to with somewhat greater confidence. Firstly, there are areas at the northern and southern margins of anadromous fish distributions where fish populations are present in considerably reduced quantities. Thus, while anadromous species spawn from Baha to the MacKenzie River in western North America, quantities great enough to support a commercial fishery are present only between Monterey Bay, California, and Kotzebue Sound, Alaska.

A second difference in productivity associated with latitude is related to differences in evapotranspiration. It was pointed out earlier that evapotranspiration decreased northward, holding precipitation constant, and we might expect the ratio of spawning habitat per unit area of land to increase to the north. Thus, a river in Alaska might not be more productive than one of the same size in California, but there is simply more riparian habitat per square mile of land in the former.

Before moving on to a discussion of variations in productivity, it would be helpful to encapsulate what has been said about productivity in general. First, the productivity of a river depends largely upon the amount of spawning habitat and rearing area present within the drainage, and, consequently, productivity is directly correlated with river size and inversely with distance upstream. Variations in productivity along a latitudinal gradient are less easily characterized. This is partially due to the lack of dependable quantitative data upon which any comparison might be based. Although differences in productivity associated with latitude remain largely unexplored here, the differences that may be found to exist may well be far less significant than other variations in the resource associated with latitude (e.g., temporal patterns) that are commonly ignored in anthropological literature.

Fluctuations in Productivity

Fluctuations in anadromous fish populations are undoubtedly induced by a multitude of factors impinging on all stages of the life cycle. However, a strong case could be made in support of the position that *most* of the year-to-year variance in production is a function of conditions in riparian environments and that the marine phase of life is far less important as a source of variance. Since fluctuations in abundance are a function of differences in either the success of reproduction or differences in rates of mortality, it appears that the freshwater stage of the life cycle is the major determinant of differences in both. There are, for instance, studies that indicate a strong relationship between the number of young fish migrating to sea and the number of mature fish of that generation returning to spawn (Foerster 1968:66,312). Admittedly, mortality is high throughout the life cycle (more than 99% mortality from egg to adult in some cases; cf. Foerster 1968:371), but mortality is by far the highest during the immature stages of the life cycle, and these stages are particularly vulnerable to conditions in riparian environments (Bakkala 1970:51). It is, therefore, not unreasonable to expect that differences in the stability of riparian habitats are the primary determinants of the variance in production in anadromous fish.

The conditions that influence the stability of riparian environments were discussed earlier, and, from that discussion, it should be possible to anticipate certain geographic differences in the year-to-year variance of fish populations. Along a latitudinal gradient, fluctuations in abundance should increase in amplitude both to the north and south of the broad central zone (e.g., Oregon to southeast Alaska in western North America) where stream flow and temperature regimes are most stable in terms of spawning requirements. In the central zone, fluctuations in abundance should be of relatively low amplitude. As a rough measure of latitudinal differences in fluctuations in abundance, I have utilized the catch records of the commercial salmon fishery in western North America for a 40-year period (Kasahara 1963).[3] Although I alluded earlier to the difficulties in using these records as precise measures of actual abundance, these records are, nevertheless, the best, if not the only, data presently available upon which a comparative measure of variance might be based.

In Figure 5.3, variance in catches during the 40-year period is plotted for six regions along the west coast.[4] It is evident that the computations support the general predictions about fluctuations in abundance based on differences in the stability of riparian environments. For each species, the greatest variance occurs either in the northern or southern areas of its distribution. The lowest variances for each species tend to occur in the intermediate areas. This same pattern is also evident for the combined biomass of all species in each region. Anomalously high variance for the state of Washington is probably the result of high variance in sockeye catches due largely to destruction of that species' spawning habitat in the Columbia river with construction of hydroelectric dams.

The graph of combined species suggests that the variances of the individual species are by no means synchronous and, in fact, may tend to cancel out one another somewhat in rivers with multiple species. This is understandable in view of the differences in life cycles between species. Because such differences involve variations in the time of year at which spawning occurs, in the kind of spawning habitat selected (e.g., current velocity, water depth, water temperature, location within the drainage, and so on), in the duration of freshwater residence, and in the duration of ocean residence, any source of instability in the riparian environment would have very different effects on each species. Even if different

[3] For all regions except British Columbia, yearly catches from 1922 to 1961 were considered; for British Columbia, the 40-year period was from 1920 to 1960. Because pink salmon have a marked 2-year cycle in abundance, only catches from every other year were computed so that variance for this species is based upon 20 catches rather than 40. Only 6 years of pink salmon catch records were available for Oregon so variance was based upon those six catches.

[4] To allow for comparability of variance between regions, catches were normalized by dividing each catch by the mean catch for that region during the 40-year interval. To minimize the effects of declining fish populations as one source of variance, the normalized catches were regressed against time. The variance, then, was calculated for the residuals of the regression.

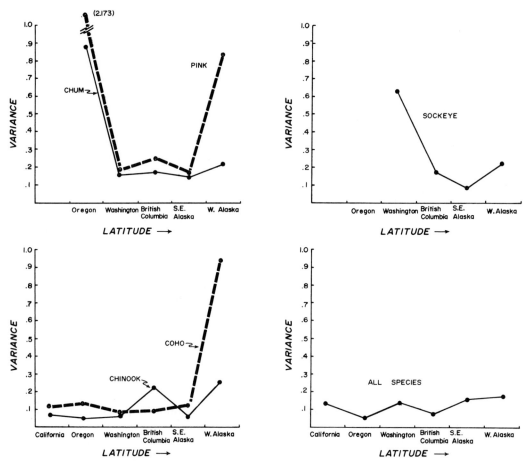

Figure 5.3 Variance in year-to-year commercial catches of five species of Pacific salmon for fishing regions along the west coast of North America.

species suffered heavy losses due to the same climatic event, the results in terms of reduced abundance would occur with different time lags. Thus, a very cold year that reduced spawning success of pink and sockeye salmon would result in a low return for pink salmon 2 years later and a low return for sockeye 4 or 5 years later due to the different rates of maturation in these two species.

For human populations situated in locations that offer access to increased numbers of fish species and/or increased numbers of distinct populations of the same species, we might anticipate an advantage in terms of security; increases in either would be associated with decreased amplitude of variance in year-to-year production of fish biomass. Fisheries biologists seem to be in accord on this point: "The available evidence indicates that when a number of spawning populations are combined, as in the case of a large watershed or a fishing area to which numerous streams contribute fish, the fluctuations are less extreme" (Neave 1966:77). Neave points out that fluctuations in population size in a single generation of pink salmon in small streams of British Columbia may involve five- to tenfold differences in abundance (p. 77). For large rivers, however, fluctuations in consecutive generations are rarely more than twofold. Thus, in terms of variance, it is again apparent that the size of a watershed is an important variable. Similarly, one might expect a gradient within a drainage, since the number of spawning populations potentially exploited decreases upstream.

Coincident with these differences in year-to-year variance of a fish resource is the aforementioned decrease in stability of riparian environments associated with stream size and distance upstream. Such differences in stability should cause abundance of fish populations that spawn further upstream in less stable environments to fluctuate far more than populations spawning in the lower parts of the same drainage. Similary, year-to-year fluctuations in abundance should increase as stream size decreases. These are, however, expectations for which there is presently little relevant quantitative data available for evaluation.

Generalized and Specialized Adaptations

Thus far, the model that has been presented can only be used to describe the structure of certain environments; taken alone, it does not imply much about what variations one might anticipate in human subsistence systems in these environments. Knowledge about available resources, and even information about their relative abundance for a particular environmental setting, allows little basis for predicting the extent to which or manner in which specific resources would be utilized. This is a point frequently unappreciated in proposed explanations for shifts in subsistence evidenced in the archaeological record (Braun 1974; Chard 1974; Fladmark 1974). Unless archaeologists are willing to argue that all cultural change is the result of environmental change and that there is only one kind of cultural system that can exist in a specific environment, explanation of the particular composition of a subsistence system must always be concerned with why certain resources are exploited and others are not. Also, archaeologists must consider what determines the *extent* to which different resources are exploited. The documentation of environmental change, then, can never in itself be an adequate explanation for observed changes in subsistence systems.

The difference between what resources are actually utilized as opposed to those available is commonly termed "niche breadth" by ecologists (Levins 1968; Colwell and Futuyma 1971; Pianka 1974). A species that utilizes few of the resources potentially available is said to have a "narrow niche" and might be called a "specialist"; one that utilizes many of the resources available to it is said to have a "wide niche" and might be called a "generalist." This same bipolar distinction provides a useful framework for considering variations in human adaptations as well (Binford n.d.; Hardesty 1975). The following discussion briefly considers what environmental conditions determine the degree of specialization. Subsequently, it is possible to anticipate certain variations in human subsistence systems.

Generalist adaptations are ones that tend to exploit resources in rough proportion to their actual abundance in the environment. They are indiscriminate consumers. Although generalization sacrifices efficiency in favor of flexibility (MacArthur 1972), it is apparent that this strategy is favored in certain environmental settings. Three major environmental characteristics that tend to favor generalized adaptations are (1) low stability, (2) low productivity, and (3) high seasonality (Levins 1968).

In environments with low stability, increased flexibility of a generalist offers more alternatives in the event of individual resource failures. Such failures are less likely to be critical to the generalist because there are other options available. Generalist strategies are also favored in environments with low productivity. Since expenditures in searching for food are greater where resources are scarce, the generalist compensates by being less discriminating about food items encountered. The third characteristic of environments that favors generalization is marked seasonality in productive cycles. As seasonality or temporal heterogeneity in productivity increases, it becomes more difficult to be discriminating about which resources are exploited.

Specialization, on the other hand, is favored in environments that are the opposite in these three respects. Specialization tends to be associated with highly stable environments, with high productivity, and with low seasonality. Although specialization implies less capacity of coping with instabilities, it also implies increased efficiency in the exploitation of fewer resources, and the major evolutionary advantage to specialization seems to be greater efficiency (Hutchinson 1957; Pianka 1974:199. This suggests one further characteristic of environments that conditions the degree of specialization.

Demographic pressure and competition tend to effect the width of the niche and, thus, the degree of specialization (Vandermeer 1972).[5] It is in this context, a competitive one, that increased efficiency in the exploitation of fewer resources is selected for (Hutchinson 1957; Colwell and Futuyma 1971; Pianka 1974:199). Osborn (this volume) discusses the importance of density-dependent selection favoring increased utilization of aquatic resources, and it is evident that density-dependent selection would tend to favor specialization.[6]

Specialization in environments of the temperate and higher latitudes involves certain difficulties, however, since, as was mentioned earlier, increasing seasonal-

[5] This change in niche is variously referred to as the difference between "fundamental" and "realized" niches (Hutchinson 1957), "virtual" and "actual" niches (Colwell and Futuyma 1971), or "pre-competitive" and "post-competitive" niches (Pianka 1974:192).

[6] It is interesting to note that the process of becoming more specialized as population density increases in directly analogous to the process of decreasing maturity of an ecosystem associated with population growth and agricultural intensification (see Athens, this volume). The important difference is that an adaptive system can become more specialized *without* any obvious impact on the ecosystem.

ity and decreasing stability are both conditions that oppose specialization. Population growth in these environments favoring specialization would be increasingly opposed to the north by greater seasonality and year-to-year instability in productivity. Storage of food is one evolutionary response that provides a compromise for these opposing forces. Food storage is a mechanism for *not* exploiting resources in proportion to their natural availability in the environment, and increased storage implies increased specialization. In fact, the degree of dependence upon stored foods might be utilized as one measure of specialization.

Thus far, the difference between generalized and specialized forms of subsistence have been discussed. The environmental characteristics that favor each were touched upon, and I suggested that demographic pressure (competition or density-dependent selection) is a force that tends to result in greater specialization. The importance of storage has been hinted at as one mechanism through which specialization occurs. Equipped with these arguments, it is now possible to examine some of their implications in light of the variations in an anadromous fish resource in different environments.

Implications and Discussion

Because all environments in which anadromous fish occur are environments with marked seasonality in productive cycles, it is reasonable to expect that hunter–gatherers not suffering from the effects of demographic pressure would tend toward generalized adaptations. Such adaptations would involve a wide variety of resources exploited during an annual cycle and little, if any, food storage. Under these conditions of relatively low population density, we could predict regional differences in the degree of dependence upon anadromous fish.

Toward the more southerly areas of anadromous fish distributions,[7] fish migrations occur during the late fall, winter, or early spring and, therefore, tend to be temporally congruent with periods of low terrestrial productivity. One might expect a significant advantage in exploiting the resource in these areas even at relatively low population densities. Because the duration of availability may be quite sustained in this zone, storage would not be necessary to exploit the resource for considerable portions of the year. These are the areas in which we anticipate the earliest archaeological evidence for systematic utilization of the resource by generalized foragers.

Moving northward, the decrease in temporal availability and the increasing congruence with other resources would suggest that anadromous fish would be of less importance to early generalist subsistence systems. In the absence of storage, these temporal aspects should make the resource less favorable toward the north and as a function of river size. Main stems of major drainages should be

---

[7] This zone corresponds broadly to the areas between southern California and Oregon in western North America, between Florida and Delaware in eastern North America, between Spain and southern France in western Europe, and between Korea and Japan south of Hokkaido in Asia.

somewhat more optimal in this regard; therefore, one might expect the earliest appearance of systematic utilization within this zone to occur in such contexts. Along a latitudinal gradient, these temporal qualities would diminish the utility of the resource to the extent that very little, if any, exploitation would be expected to the north of some latitudinal threshold. Exploitation would be limited to the actual duration of the run, and, where runs are brief, significant dependence upon fish would be precluded. To the north of this threshold, the shift to other aquatic resources with more advantageous temporal availability (e.g., sea mammals, shellfish, aquatic birds, and pelagic fish) should precede significant utilization of anadromous fish. The longer periods of availability of such resources and the fact that they may not be restricted to summer only at these latitudes[8] would favor incorporation of these resources into subsistence systems long before anadromous fish.

In addition to differences in the temporal availability, it was suggested that variance in productivity increased as drainage size decreased and also that the total quantity of fish potentially intercepted decreased with river size and distance upstream. These factors would allow less dependence upon anadromous fish for groups located on the upper parts of drainages or on smaller streams than for those located on the lower stretches of large drainages. Specialization in the use of anadromous fish should be greatest on the lower parts of a drainage system, and those groups located progressively further inland shoulsd tend toward more generalized forms of subsistence. Such a gradient is often noted by ethnographers (Smith 1940:24; Elmendorf 1960:256; Olson 1936:13–14; Drucker 1951:10).

Certain differences in rates of change evidenced in the archaeological record might be expected as well. In the more southerly areas, increasing dependence upon anadromous fish should involve a gradual process of decreasing mobility associated with population growth. Since these areas tend to have fish available during the winter and early spring, substantial increases in population could probably be sustained without storage. In these environments, anadromous fish would tend to increase the carrying capacity for human populations in the absence of storage, and populations might become relatively sedentary prior to seeing any necessity for storage. The archaeological sequences in these regions should evidence rather gradual and cumulative change. This is quite different from the way in which one might expect changes further north.

Utilization of anadromous fish toward the north becomes increasingly dependent upon the capacity to store. As a result, it is probable that the shift to systematic exploitation of the resource would be abrupt and coincident with the adoption of storage. Archaeological sequences should provide evidence of discontinuities, reflecting the significant organizational changes in cultural systems

---

[8] It is difficult to be more specific about the location of this threshold, but about 55° north latitude would be a reasonable guess.

associated with the implementation of a storage strategy. I am suggesting that exploitation of anadromous fish becomes more an all-or-nothing strategy toward the north and that the adoption of storage requires drastic changes in the entire cultural system. Because this may be less than obvious, the following section attempts to show how storage modifies the entire fabric of a subsistence system and, in turn, how the rest of the society is influenced by this change.

Implementation of a Storage Strategy

It is necessary to re-emphasize the logical bridge between specialization, storage, and the structure of the fish resource before proceeding, since this relationship is critical. Storage is one vehicle by means of which specialization occurs, and the degree of specialization upon anadromous fish is directly related to the ease with which fish can be stored in different environments.

Storage of any resource requires having enough of that resource so that quantities of it may be taken in excess of immediate consumption demands. Thus, resources that are aggregated spatially and temporally are generally favored as storage foods (Binford n.d.). But, as in so many things, moderation is the best strategy in the case of temporal aggregation. It is possible to have too many fish available in too short a time, and this can be a formidable barrier to the implementation of a storage strategy. Or, in terms of the generalist–specialist distinction drawn earlier, specialization of any resource tends to be opposed by increasing seasonality in productive cycles.

In several respects, the implementation of a storage strategy represents an evolutionary threshold. One of the more obvious changes associated with storage is that the carrying capacity of the environment is greater for storing adaptations as opposed to nonstoring ones. In the absence of storage, limits to population density are generally established by the abundance of the resource(s) exploited during the least productive part of an annual cycle. With storage, however, this is no longer the case. Stored food can be utilized to fill in these lows, and human subsistence systems thereby attain a new level of independence from natural environmental cycles in productivity. While exploitation of fish in the absence of storage may be minimal due to untimely occurrence or the short period of availability, once a storage strategy has been adopted, the same resource can be exploited either to the limits sustainable by the resource or to the limits of the cultural system to capture and process. With storage then, the locus of potential stress on a cultural system shifts from the point of lowest productivity in the yearly cycle to the period during which food is processed for storage.

Another change associated with storage is decreased mobility. Although it is often suggested that fishing and storage "allow" greater sedentism (Rostlund 1952:6; Murdock 1968:15), it is probably more accurate to say that decreasing mobility *requires* increasing dependence upon stored foods.

A third change associated with the adoption of storage of anadromous fish is related to settlement systems. The location for exploitation of the resource favored by a strategy that requires greater and more dependable quantities of fish tends to be larger water courses. Whereas access with minimal technological investment might take priority in the absence of storage, exploitation of locations where larger quantities of fish for storage could be dependably procured from year to year would tend to override considerations of easy access. In other words, exploitation at points on larger streams or further downstream would afford greater, more predictable quantities of fish at the possible expense of decreased spatial aggregation of fish.

This implies a fourth sort of change associated with storage—the technological innovations necessary to extract greater quantities of fish in less spatially constricted areas and in shorter periods of time (i.e., weirs, traps, seines, etc.). Other technological requirements concomitant with storage are all those facilities utilized in processing—drying racks, smokehouses, boxes, baskets, storage pits, and storage houses. It is apparent that storage requires a very substantial increase in technology, and one might argue that such an investment would not be feasible except for populations storing very large quantities of fish.

Lastly, all these changes would almost certainly be accompanied by reorganization of social systems. Although some of the possible social changes required will be treated later, it is important to recognize that the process of implementing a storage strategy, above all else, has far-reaching effects on labor organization and, in turn, upon social organization.

Although there are several processes of storing fish that have been described in ethnographic literature, drying and/or smoking seem to be the major processes employed almost everywhere. Concern here is not so much with a description of the process in any detail, but with an attempt to point out that it is more complex than is frequently thought and, depending upon the structural characteristics of the fish resource, may exert significant constraints upon the organization of labor.[9]

Unlike many storable plant foods, fish require immediate processing for storage since they spoil rapidly at normal air temperatures (McFarland 1925:61). Because of the timing of fish migrations at different latitudes, it is clear that freezing would rarely be a possible option with anadromous fish. Drying is a more demanding technique and generally takes between 10 days and 2 weeks (Laguna 1972:400); the exact time necessary varies with local conditions of humidity and air temperature. The process is not as simple as cleaning and hanging fish to dry; a good deal of preseason preparation is required, and daily attention is necessary during the entire interval of drying. To even begin the process, a whole series of construction and maintenance activities are necessary. Ignoring all the devices involved in the capture of fish, drying and/or smoking

---

[9] For an elaborate treatment of the details of this process, Laguna (1972:400–401) provides a good account received from a female Tlingit informant.

requires preparation of the facilities used in processing (smokhouses, drying racks, sun shades, etc.) as well as the facilities necessary for containing the finished product (storage pits, baskets, boxes, storage houses, etc.). These activities may be performed prior to the fishing season or even up to and during that season.

After the fish are cleaned and hung to dry, they require almost constant attention. They may be secondarily split and scored as the process proceeds, and they must be frequently moved about to insure even drying and proper distance from the heat or smoke source depending upon the stage of the individual fish in the process. Fuel must be provided for the fire, and those fish that have been completely dryed must be packed into containers or storage facilities. It is apparent that, in addition to the daily cleaning and hanging of fish just caught, there are a whole series of ongoing tasks related to all those fish taken on previous days. Furthermore, all this processing activity, commonly a female responsibility, must be done in addition to other daily subsistence requirements. To place these activities in perspective, two other variables must be considered.

The demands placed upon a group by the contingencies of storage would clearly be a function of *(1)* the quantity of stored fish required and *(2)* the structural characteristics of the resource itself in the local environment. The length of time that fish are available, in particular, would be a very important determinant of the demands associated with procuring and processing the necessary quantity. Estimates of the quantity of fish stored are scarce in ethnographic literature, but it is possible to estimate the quantity for specific aboriginal groups on the basis of some other factors that are better known.[10]

As an example of the severe demands placed upon a labor force by the implementation of a storage strategy in some environments, I have estimated the quantity of stored fish that a housegroup of Tlingit might require (the housegroup is the productive unit; Oberg 1973:79). Stored salmon provided the major food item for about 5 months during the winter (Oberg 1973:75). Given the number of people in a housegroup, the length of time during which stored fish was relied upon, and an estimate of the amount of fish consumed per day per capita, the total amount of fish stored by a housegroup is estimated to be 11,250 pounds of fish.[11] This may seem to be a tremendous amount of fish, but there is

[10] Hewes (1973) has estimated annual per capita consumption of salmon for a number of aboriginal groups in western North America.

[11] An average housegroup might include about 30 people in 5 or 6 families (Laguna 1972:401). If we assume a producer to dependent ratio of 1:1.7 (this ratio is based upon the average number of *potential* producers for a large sample of the world's hunter–gatherers; Binford, personal communication), then such a group would have about 11.2 producers of which about half might be procurers (males) and half processors (females). Since salmon have been estimated to be about 1000 calories per pound (Hewes 1973; Baumhoff 1963; Rostlund 1952:4), 2½ pounds (wet weight) per capital per day consumption during the winter seems to be a reasonable estimate. With these figures, it is possible to calculate the minimal amount of fish needed to meet group requirements: 30 people × 2.5 pounds dried fish/per person × 150 days = 11,250 pounds.

Table 5.2

Temporal Patterns of Pink Salmon Migrations into Sashin Creek, Southeast Alaska
for the last ten Escapements of More Than 1000 Fish[a]

Year of escapement	Number of adults in escapement	Date of entry of portions of escapement			Elapsed days between dates of entry	
		10%	50%	90%	10 and 50%	10 and 90%
1947	1486	Sept. 7	Spet. 14	Sept. 22	7	15
1949	4902	Sept. 2	Sept. 12	Sept. 19	10	
1951	4366	Aug. 28	Sept. 6	Sept. 17	9	20
1953	1164	Aug. 16	Aug. 29	Sept. 7	13	23
1955	9267	Aug. 29	Sept. 1	Sept. 12	3	14
1957	2834	Aug. 14	Aug. 22	Aug. 31	8	17
1959	35,391	Aug. 13	Aug. 29	Sept. 8	16	26
1961	28,759	Aug. 12	Aug. 14	Sept. 2	2	19
1963	16,757	Aug. 13	Aug. 27	Sept. 3	14	21
1965	14,833	Aug. 19	Aug. 26	Sept. 14	7	26
Average	—	Aug. 18	Aug. 23	Sept. 8	9	20

[a] After Ellis 1969:6

some independent evidence to suggest that this estimate may be low by as much as a factor of three.[12]

A reasonable estimate of the amount of fish that one woman could process in a day might be about 100 fish (300 pounds of pink salmon), and, at this rate, the 5.6 females of the productive unit could process the estimated amount of fish in about 6.7 days. The major point to be emphasized is that *at least* 6.7 days of fishing would be necessary to secure the required amount of fish, assuming that daily catches minimally provide 560 fish per day for the housegroup. Obviously, daily catches that fall below this minimum would increase the time necessary to store the required quantity of fish. Thus far, consumer demands of the group have been calculated, and an estimate of the performance capacities of the processors has been made. What remains to be examined is the temporal structure of the fish resource in this particular environment.

Table 5.2 shows the actual temporal patterns of pink salmon migrations into a small stream on Baranof Island in southeast Alaska—the former territory of the

[12] Laguna (1972:400) states, with regard to the Tlingit, "Albin Johnson reports that a large family among the Indians dries and smokes approximately 2,000 to 3,000 salmon." At an average weight of 4 pounds per fish for the most common species (*Oncorhynchus gorbuscha;* Kasahara 1963:48), this would amount to between 8000 and 12,000 pounds (wet weight) utilized by *a single family*. More conservatively, Hewes (1973) estimates that the per capita annual consumption of salmon by the Tlingit was 500 pounds. For a group the size of the housegroup discussed earlier, that would amount to 15,000 pounds of fish. These sources, then, seem to support the contention that the estimate made above is probably somewhat conservative.

Sitka division of the Tlingit. Although no claim is made that these figures represent dependable estimates of the productive capacity of the drainage since these counts include only those fish that have avoided the commercial fishery in the straits, temporal patterning is informative.

This 10-year record of fish entering Sashin Creek indicates that 80% of the total run of pink salmon had passed the counting station in an interval of 14 to 26 days. In 2 years, 1955 and 1961, 40% of the run had passed in less than 3 days. It would be an understatement to say that the productive unit of Tlingit would frequently be hard-pressed to successfully store the necessary amount of fish. This is even more evident in light of additional information.

The pink salmon is the only anadromous species that occurs in any abundance in many of the small streams of southeast Alaska, and this species has a 2-year cycle throughout most of its range. In the streams of southeast Alaska, substantial runs of pink salmon occur only on odd years and during even years few, if any, pinks enter these streams to spawn. This suggests that the amount of stored fish estimated earlier might realistically be doubled to cover periods of *two* winters. Despite the infrequent mention of storage for more than one winter in ethnographic literature (Laguna 1972:51; Teit 1900:234; Jochelson 1908:586), such was probably a necessity in many areas. If the aforementioned situation appeared difficult, it now seems almost impossible. Whether or not any group of Tlingit ever earned a living on Sashin Creek is beside the point. Small, more northerly streams with few species of anadromous fish provide formidable conditions for the storage of the winter food supply.[13]

Other groups of the northern Pacific did not have significantly different fishing situations (e.g., the Haida, Nootka, Kwakiutl, Koniag). It might be expected that the severe demographic changes associated with the introduction of infectious diseases to many aboriginal fishing groups (cf. Cook 1955; Codere 1950:49–61), would have favored a shifting of remnant populations to the more optimal fishing situations offered by larger rivers with more runs of fish and longer periods of availability. In terms of the ethnographic literature related to fishing adaptations then, we might suspect a certain bias largely arising from experience with these less stringent fishing situations.

Having qualified the Tlingit example, we can summarize a number of significant points concerning the importance of a storage strategy and how it influences labor and social organization:

1. Other than the difficulties of procuring fish, the procedure for storing them is critical. Regardless of how abundant a resource may be, its utility for later consumption is dependent upon the success with which it can be processed for

---

[13] Other examples of exceptionally brief salmon runs in more northerly rivers are not uncommon (cf. Straty 1966; Andrew and Geen 1960:31), and this may even be the case for larger drainages. In the Fraser River of British Columbia, for example, nearly an entire run of 2,048,000 sockeye salmon entered the river in a 60-hour period in 1954, with about 1,250,000 entering on the peak day (Andrew and Geen 1960).

storage. A storage strategy is by no means a "fairly simple technique" (Drucker and Heizer 1967:149) in many contexts.

2. As the period of resource availability decreases, the efficiency of the productive unit practicing storage must increase, all other things being equal. Because the period of availability decreases northward, upstream within any drainage, and as river size decreases, one would expect storage to be increasingly difficult in all these contexts.

3. Whatever factors necessitating the storage of larger amounts of fish (e.g., increased population or longer winters) would result in the intensification of the stress upon efficiency.

4. As the temporal congruence of the fishing season with other subsistence activities increases, greater complexity of labor organization would be required. In terms of many terrestrial resources and probably many marine ones as well, the temporal congruence of the fishing season with such resources would tend to be greater toward higher latitudes.

5. It might be expected that the efficient deployment of labor forces necessitated by decreases in temporal availability would tend to favor more centralized control within the productive unit. That is, the greater the stress for efficiency in the performance of various time-constrained activities, the greater the likelihood that these activities would be coordinated by group leaders. The position of "headman" or "chief" might be augmented by those conditions favoring increased efficiency. Where the success or survival of an entire group is dependent upon the integration of all the different activities of its members, more centralized authority is advantageous. It is no coincidence that decision making in combat infantry platoons and football teams is not egalitarian.

6. Specialization in task performance would also be favored where there is stress upon efficiency. As Marian Smith (1940:34) pointed out, the pooling within a productive unit of the different products of specialists not only allows them "to engage in fewer occupations but to spend more time upon them and to become more expert at them." Specialization in task performance within a productive unit, in turn, favors mechanisms for the redistribution of its products within the group that also tends to favor increased authority of a group leader (Fried 1960:718).

7. It is likely that the pressures favoring increased complexity of labor organization and specialization in task performance would favor additional social dimensions along which people might be differentiated. The distinctions of age and sex provide the basis for division of labor among many foragers and, where increasing specialization of task performance occurs, increased social differentiation along other dimensions (e.g., rank, class, clan affiliation, etc.) provides the building blocks for a more complex division of labor.

8. The tightness of group structure and constraints upon membership within a productive unit should vary directly with the intensity of demands upon the organization of the labor force. It is apparent that even the temporary loss of group members during the period of processing for storage could be crippling

where severe temporal constraints prevail. Similarly, weir construction and sein-ing techniques are only possible with some minimal number of workers. It is also evident that the greater the degree of specialization in task performance by individuals or families within the productive unit, the more static group mem-bership must be. Finally, the stewardship of large quantities of stored food for survival during the winter would tend to tighten group structure.

I am suggesting that increasing specialization in task performance within a productive unit, greater discreteness or less fluidity of group structure, increased centralization of authority in the person of group leader, and greater social differentiation could all be viewed as organizational responses to pressures favor-ing increased efficiency in the performance of intensive subsistence activities in shorter periods of time. As the period during which "harvest" activities must be performed decreases, the organization of the cultural system must increase in efficiency accordingly. Heavy dependence upon anadromous fish in environ-ments with short periods of resource availability is a specialist adaptation to an environment in which specialization is opposed by great seasonality in productiv-ity. In addition to increasing seasonality toward the north, year-to-year fluctua-tions in abundance tend to increase north of the broad central zone of anadro-mous fish distributions. In view of these two aspects of the resource, specialization upon anadromous fish should be progressively more difficult as one moves northward. At some point, it is likely that these factors working together would make specialization upon anadromous fish an impossibility for a technology de-pendent upon drying fish for storage. The lower trunks of major drainages in the north may be exceptional in so far as variance in productivity is reduced and temporal availability increased in such areas.

Suttles (1968) has observed that social organization along a north to south transect of the Northwest coast was more formally developed toward the north. He recognizes increasing control of larger labor forces, greater "tightness of structure and size of social unit" (Suttles 1968:64), increased importance of social differentiation, and greater discreteness of social units. To these it might be added that the importance of task specialization and the authority of group leaders seems to increase northward as well. It is asserted that these observed variations must be understood primarily in terms of differences in the demands placed upon cultural systems by variations in the fish resource. Besides the de-creased temporal availability to the north, species diversity is low throughout much of the northern Northwest coast due to geomorphology and its effect upon the structure of rivers. Submerged mountain ranges forming islands (Alexander Archipelago, the Queen Charlotte Islands, Vancouver Island) or rugged moun-tain ranges running closely parallel to the coastline (e.g., the mainland coast of British Columbia) indicate that most rivers are quite small and, therefore, have few species of anadromous fish with accordingly compressed periods of availabil-ity. It is not coincidental that the most "intense" (Kroeber 1939:31) forms of social organization occur in these contexts.

Some of the features of social organization associated with food gatherers dependent upon anadromous fish often seem to be equated with "sociocultural complexity."[14] Before concluding this chapter, it might be useful to briefly explore in just what sense such adaptations are "complex."

Fishing Adaptations as "Complex" Systems

Anthropologists often compare the aboriginal cultures of northwest North America to other "chiefdoms" (cf. Service 1968) or liken them to agriculturalists in terms of sociocultural complexity (cf. Drucker 1965:15; Suttles 1968:56). Murdock (1968:15), for example, states:

> Various other peoples who lack both agriculture and large domestic animals depend not so much on hunting and gathering as on fishing, shellfishing, or the pursuit of aquatic animals. Where they lead an essentially nomadic mode of life, I classify them with hunters and gatherers. Sometimes, however, their marine food supply is so plentiful and stable that they have been able to adopt an exclusively or predominantly sedentary mode of life. Such conditions offer the possibility of attaining a considerable degree of cultural complexity otherwise achievable only with intensive agriculture. The Indians of the North Pacific coast, for example, seem to me to fall well beyond the range of cultural variation of any known hunting and gathering people.

What is generally not reognized in such statements is that, as a group, societies dependent upon anadromous fish and lacking agriculture, are organizationally distinctive from other cultural systems commonly referred to as "complex" (i.e., agricultural "chiefdoms" and "states"). These organizational differences will first be characterized, and then they will be related to differences in the energy base between agriculture and fishing.

The major organizational characteristics that set these fishing societies apart from other cultural systems generally regarded as "complex" are best illustrated in the following statements:

> On the coast from Alaska to California, and East to the Rocky Mountains, the village was the basic political unit with very local exceptions. Villages were strictly autonomous and the chief's power was limited to the village that the represented [Ray 1936:367].

> The extreme of political anarchy is found in the northwest (of California), where there is scarcely a tendency to group towns into higher units, and where even a town is not conceived as an essential unit [Kroeber 1925:830, cited in Ray 1936:112].

> Political separation was carried to a high degree throughout the Pacific slope, the local communities being almost without exception autonomous, or at most grouped for common action within a quite restricted district [Spier 1930:309, cited in Ray 1936:112].

These statements reveals qualities that seem to apply equally well to all food gatherers involved in the systematic exploitation of anadromous fish.[15] The lack of any formal organization extending beyond individual local groups is most

[14] See Tainter (this volume) for a discussion of the difficulties inherent in treating social organization as a unidimensional phenomenon.

[15] This does not mean that individual productive units should be viewed as independent "societies" (cf. Suttles 1963), but it is intended to emphasize the degree of political autonomy that characterizes these fishing groups.

striking when one calls to mind the "chiefdoms" of Polynesia (Sahlins 1958) or the eastern coast of North America (Binford 1964). These agricultural chiefdoms had political and economic systems that linked together many different local groups, all under the hegemony of a single chief. The discreteness and political autonomy of individual local groups among nonagricultural societies dependent upon anadromous fish must be viewed as the evolutionary response to selective forces quite different from those that give rise to complex systems based upon agriculture. On the basis of earlier discussions in this chapter, we might point to three ways in which the energy base of fishing adaptations differs from that of agrarian adaptations.

First, the reduction of ecosystem maturity associated with agriculture results in a decrease in stability of production (Margalef 1968). In temperate and arid environments, this relationship between agriculture and stability might be viewed as the selective context that favors cultural systems that integrate local groups into large-scale economic systems under administrative hierarchies (see Athens, this volume). However, there is little evidence to suggest that increased exploitation of anadromous fish is associated with decreased stability in productivity of the fish resource. To the contrary, there is reason to believe that increasing human predation on anadromous fish populations actually tends to *dampen* year-to-year fluctuations in productivity. For instance, it is believed that heavy fishing on the pink salmon and on the sockeye salmon in the present century has tended to even out the respective 2- and 4-year cycles that occur in these species in Alaska and British Columbia (Jack Van Hyning, personal communication). Also, it is well known that a major cause of fluctuations in anadromous fish populations is the arrival of too many spawners on the spawning grounds leading to overcrowding with resultant competition, destruction of eggs and nests, mortality, and lack of sufficient food for the young fish that do hatch (Foerster 1968:52). This suggests that year-to-year production of anadromous fish may be more stable with a significant amount of predation and perhaps even overfishing. Hence, increased dependence upon anadromous fish may actually be associated with increased stability in production, and there would be little advantage to cultural systems that integrate large areas of the landscape.

Second, there is a marked difference in the spatial predictability of fluctuations in productivity in fishing as opposed to farming adaptations. Although the occurrence of a poor run of fish may be unpredictable temporally, the spatial consequences are highly predictable. Within a single drainage, this is largely the result of the direction of fish migrations. Because all fish that are bound for the upper part of a drainage must first pass through the lower part, it is evident that a poor year on the lower river is almost certain to be a worse year at points upstream. It should be recalled that species diversity, as well as stability of the riverine environment, decrease upstream so that instability of fish productivity should become more pronounced in that direction. It has also been suggested that there are characteristics inherent in the structure of watersheds (e.g., size and storage capacity) that have long-term, predictable consequences for variance in year-to-year productivity of anadromous fish.

Since migrating fish must "run the gauntlet" of human exploitation before reaching groups located further upstream, the latter groups would be at an even greater disadvantage. This is frequently evident in ethnographic literature (cf. Gunther 1927:199; Olson 1936:29; Waterman and Kroeber 1938: Loud 1918:271).

It is maintained that the spatial predictability of fluctuations in productivity is a major distinction between agricultural and fishing economies and that the latter lack the preconditions for the rise of "complex systems." Without going so far as to assert that the spatial correlates of fluctuations in agricultural productivity are totally random, there is reason to expect that they are far more random than fluctuations in anadromous fish. The selective pressures favoring the participation of local groups in a large-scale integrative system must involve a higher degree of unpredictability of fluctuations in space.

A third distinction between agriculture and fishing that should be recognized is that storage is far more demanding in the latter. Plant foods generally do not require immediate processing after being harvested, and processing often lasts for many months *after* the harvest. Due to rapid rates of spoilage, processing of anadromous fish must take place *during* the harvest season, so it might often be difficult for a group to process enough for its own requirements much less an excess for redistribution. While peak years of agricultural production may allow harvesting of a surplus that can be redistributed, such peaks are not as easily exploited in the case of anadromous fish simply as a result of the bottleneck effect of having to harvest *and* process at the same time.

These are some rather fundamental differences between agriculture and the exploitation of anadromous fish. Like nearly all other known hunter–gatherers, the cultural systems of the northern Pacific primarily match consumers to resources, not the reverse. This is particularly significant in terms of the high degree of sedentism and the heavy investment in technology among these groups. Sedentism in the absence of institutionalized redistributive systems creates a bind situation in terms of matching people to fluctuating resources. Social differentiation may be one of the mechanisms whereby basically sedentary populations actually allow for a good deal of demographic flux, and there is good reason to suspect an association between differences in residential mobility and differences in social position (cf. Drucker 1951:278–281; Adams 1973; Hazard, discussed in Harris 1968:306–313, Watanabe 1973:14–15).

Conclusion

It was argued that many of the features of cultural systems that are commonly associated with "complexity" (i.e., increasing social differentiation, specialization in task performance, decreased flexibility of group structure, centralization of group leadership) are features that would be favored by the increased ratio of food procurement to processing per unit time. They are organizational responses for increased efficiency. Storage of large amounts of fish in short periods of time is a specialist strategy that demands greater efficiency from cultural systems as the duration of the harvest season decreases, as the length of time to be overwintered increases, and as the temporal congruency of the resource with other resources increases. This stress would be further accentuated on smaller rivers with low species diversity. The Tlingit example draws attention to the reality of such pressures and brings into focus their major target—those activities associated with storage of the winter food supply.

Storage is the mechanism through which the actual productivity of a fish resource becomes directly relevant to the human carrying capacity of an environment. Fish runs may provide massive surges of energy, but much of that energy may only be harnessed through the storage process. The ease with which that energy can be utilized is a function of *(1)* seasonality, *(2)* stability in year-to-year productivity, and *(3)* productivity itself. These are the major variables that influence the degree of specialization, and increasing seasonality, increasing variance in the resource, and decreased accessible productivity tend to oppose specialization.

In summary, it is useful to reiterate some of the major points discussed in terms of a latitudinal continuum which, for heuristic purposes, will be divided into three fishing regions. These regions exhibit some rather distinctive ways in which hunter–gatherers are expected to interact with anadromous fish populations at these latitudes throughout the Northern Hemisphere.

1. *South of 45° north latitude:* This zone represents the southerly distribution of anadromous fish. Fish runs occur during periods of relatively low terrestrial productivity and are generally long in duration. In the larger rivers of this zone, some fish may be taken almost year round. These conditions of temporal availability mean that significant and systematic exploitation of fish is not dependent upon storage. It is in this zone that the archaeologist should find evidence of the earliest dependence upon anadromous fish. Low-density foragers could be quite dependent upon anadromous fish without the need to store or to make a heavy investment in the technology for capturing and processing large quantities of fish in a short period of time. Population growth in this southern zone should be associated with cumulative change and should not involve significant specialization of anadromous fish.

2. *Between 45 and 60° north latitude:* Seasonality is significantly greater in fish runs in this zone. Although fish migrations may occur to a limited extent throughout much of the year in the larger rivers in this zone, peak runs tend to occur in late summer and fall. The large rivers, particularly to the south within this zone, may also have runs in the spring and summer, but midwinter (approximately November to March) is the season during which fish are either absent or are present only in very small numbers. Potentially high species diversity and low year-to-year variance in productivity are probably most conducive to specialization of anadromous fish in this zone. Dependence on anadromous fish might be rather limited prior to the adoption of storage, and the shift would be quite abrupt and systemic in nature. In the absence of storage, the degree of depen-

dence upon anadromous fish would be determined primarily by duration of availability. The duration of fish runs decreases northward, upstream, and as river size decreases, and related to these trends, decreased dependence on anadromous fish might be anticipated. Implementation of a storage strategy would be increasingly difficult along these same gradients. Specialization of anadromous fish requires increasingly more efficient cultural systems as the storage process becomes more difficult. Because accessible productivity, stability in year-to-year production, and duration of availability all decrease in an upstream direction, it is anticipated that groups will tend to exhibit more generalized adaptations as distance upstream increases.

3. *North of 60° north latitude:* Seasonality in fish migrations in this zone is extreme. Fish runs are very brief—probably less than 2 or 3 weeks in all but the largest rivers—and the runs occur during midsummer. Variance in year-to-year productivity is substantial, and species diversity is low. Dependence on fresh fish should also be slight due to the short duration of the fishing season. Dependence on sea mammals, shellfish, avifauna, and pelagic fish should be more important than anadromous fish. Exceptions to such expectations might occur on lower parts of major watersheds where resource availability would be lengthened and year-to-year production would be more stable.

"Productivity," as the term has often been used, is meaningless as far as human exploitation is concerned if one does not consider the way in which productivity is distributed in space and time and how easily it can be captured and stored. It follows that there is no one-to-one relationship between sociocultural complexity and productivity, as some writers have suggested (Service 1968:143; Baumhoff 1963:230; Fladmark 1974).

It is evident that, in many environments, expansion of the resource base to include anadromous fish would be a last resort, and the impetus to do so would come only from severe demographic pressures in an environment with no other feasible alternatives. It is argued that duration of availability, season of availability, and congruency of fish with other resources would determine the degree to which anadromous fish would be exploited by humans, *regardless of abundance.* This suggests that there is no need to invoke environmental change in efforts to explain the absence of archaeological evidence for exploitation of anadromous fish (cf. Sanger 1969; Fladmark 1974).

Many of the misconceptions concerning subsistence systems based on anadromous fish have arisen from the treatment of the resource as a constant, or even an unknown, in all environments, neither of which is true. The two most commonly cited characteristics of this resource in anthropological literature are high productivity and fluctuation in productivity. Taken alone, these are useless in explaining cultural variability from one region to another; neither is helpful in itself in specifying the nature of selective pressures operating upon cultural systems in different environments. While the Boasians have been criticized for their simplistic notions about unlimited abundance, arguments to the contrary (Piddocke 1965; Vayda 1961; Harris 1968; Weinberg 1965) have seized upon an equally inadequate characterization of the resource base. Since their assertions about fluctuations in productivity are equally applicable to nearly all food resources of northern environments and to agricultural crops almost anywhere, it is necessary to ask: Why the potlatch for the Kwakiutl but not for the Yurok or Kuskokwim? Although this chapter acknowledges the importance of variations in productivity, the notion of randomness, either implicit or as stated in the adaptivist arguments, is challenged.

Despite the focus on Pacific species of anadromous fish in this chapter, I believe that the kinds of structural regularities discussed herein are essentially global patterns. Because the literature of fisheries most often tends to be limited to the perspective of a single drainage or region and is more often biological than ecological, much of this chapter has necessarily amounted to a series of empirical generalizations. But more than that, an attempt has been made to relate the behavior of anadromous fish to ecological variables of general relevance (e.g., species diversity and stability). I maintain that this is necessary in employing such a resource as an independent variable in the environment of diverse cultural systems. Also, some of the material presented may be useful in approaching the archaeological record of areas of the world where anadromous fish were once abundant but for which there will probably never be good biological data.

Finally, it should be emphasized that the approach adopted here is virtually opposite to that of the functionalists (functionalists in terms of the perceived relationship between culture and environment). Taking their interpretations of the potlatch as an example, that approach *assumes* that all cultural phenomena have adaptive functions that can be discovered. The use of environment involves an after-the-fact search for some characteristic of the environment that will accommodate interpretations generated independently of any ecological theory; this is an inductive strategy. In contrast, I am convined that a body of ecological theory is prerequisite to the specification of selective pressures affecting cultural systems in different environments.

ACKNOWLEDGMENTS

For comments on an earlier draft of this chapter or for simply contributing to a stimulating environment, I would like to express appreciation to my adviser, Lewis Binford, and to Steve Athens, Jack Bertram, Greg Burtchard, Greg Cleveland, James Ebert, Robert Hitchcock, Rosalind Hunter-Anderson, Alan Osborn, David Stuart, Richard Taylor, and Hitoshi Watanabe. Also, I am grateful to Burnell Bohn, Bernard Howe, Jack Van Hyning, William Leggitt, and Bill Zook for providing specific information concerning fish ecology.

REFERENCES

Adams, John W.
  1973   *The Gitksan potlatch: Population flux, resource ownership and reciprocity.* Toronto, Can.: Holt.
Andrew, F. J., and G. H. Geen
  1960   Sockeye and pink salmon production in relation to proposed dams in the Fraser River System. *International North Pacific Salmon Fisheries Commission, Bulletin* XI. (New Westminster, British Columbia).

Aro, K. V., and M. P. Shepard
    1967   Pacific salmon in Canada. Salmon of the north Pacific Ocean, Part IV. *International North Pacific Fisheries Commission, Bulletin* 23. Pp. 225–327.
Atkinson, C. E., J. H. Rose, and T. O. Duncan
    1967   Pacific salmon in the United States. *International Pacific Fisheries Commission, Bulletin* 23. (Vancouver, Can.)
Bakkala, Richard
    1970   Synopsis of biological data on the chum salmon, *Oncorhynchus keta* (Walbaum) 1792. U.S. Fish and Wildlife Service, Bureau of Commercial Fisheries, FAO Species Synopsis No. 41, Circular 315.
Banks, J. W.
    1969   A review of the literature on the upstream migration of adult salmonids. *Journal of Fish Biology* **1**:85–136.
Barnett, H. G.
    1968   The nature and function of the potlatch. Reprint of 1938 masters thesis, University of Oregon, Eugene.
Baumhoff, Martin A.
    1963   Ecological determinants of aboriginal California populations. *University of California Publications in American Archaeology and Ethnology* **49**:155–236.
Baxter, G.
    1961   River utilization and the preservation of migratory fish life. *Proceedings of the Institution of Civil Engineers* **18**:225–244.
Benedict, Ruth
    1934   *Patterns of culture.* Boston: Little, Brown. (Edition cited, New York: New American Library, 1960.)
Berg, Leo S.
    1962   *Freshwater fishes of the U.S.S.R. and adjacent countries.* Vol. I, 4th ed. Translated from Russian. Published for The National Science Foundation, Washington D.C.: The Israel Program for Scientific Translations.
Binford, Lewis R.
    n.d.   The Subsistence ecology of hunters and gatherers. Unpublished manuscript.
    1964   Archaeological and ethnohistorical investigations of cultural diversity. Unpublished doctoral dissertation, University of Michigan.
Braun, David P.
    1974   Explanatory models for the evolution of coastal adaptation in prehistoric Eastern New England. *American Antiquity* **39**(4):582–596.
Chapman, D. W.
    1966   Food and space as regulators of salmonid populations in streams. *The American Naturalist* **100**:345–357.
Chard, C.
    1974   *Northeast Asia in prehistory.* Madison: University of Wisconsin Press.
Codere, H.
    1950   Fighting with property, A study of Kwakiutl potlatching and warfare, 1792–1930. *American Ethnological Society Monograph* No. 18. New York: J. J. Augustin.
Colwell, R. K., and D. J. Futuyma
    1971   On the measurement of niche breadth and overlap. *Ecology* **52**:567–576.
Cook, S. F.
    1955   The epidemic of 1830–1833 in California and Oregon. *University of California Publications in American Archaeology and Ethnography* **43**:303–326.
Davidson, Frederick A., and Samuel J. Hutchinson
    1938   The geographic distribution and environmental limitations of the Pacific salmon (genus *Oncorhynchus*). *U.S. Department of Commerce Bulletin* 26, Vol. XLVIII. (Washington, D.C.)

Drucker, Philip
  1951   The northern and central Nootkan tribes. *Smithsonian Institution, Bureau of American Ethnology, Bulletin* 144.
  1965   *Cultures of the north Pacific Coast.* San Francisco: Chandler.
Drucker, Philip, and Robert F. Heizer
  1967   To make my name good: A reexamination of the southern Kwakiutl potlatch. Berkeley: University of California Press.
Egglishaw, H. J.
  1970   Production of salmon and trout in a stream in Scotland. *Journal of Fish Biology* **2:**117–136.
Ellis, Robert J.
  1969   Return and behavior of adults of the first filial generation of transplanted pink salmon, and survival of their progeny, Sashin Creek, Baranof Island, Alaska. *U.S. Fish and Wildlife Service, Bureau of Commercial Fisheries, Special Scientific Report, Fisheries* No. 589.
Elmendorf, W. W.
  1960   Structure of Twana Culture. *Washington State University Research Studies, Monographic Supplement* No. 2. (Pullman, Wash.)
Fladmark, Knut R.
  1974   A Paleoecological model for northwest coast prehistory. Unpublished doctoral dissertation, University of Calgary, Alberta, Canada.
Foerster, R. E.
  1968   The sockeye salmon, *Oncorhynchus nerka. Fisheries Research Board of Canada, Biological Station, Nanaimo, British Columbia, Bulletin* 162. Ottawa, Can.: Queen's Printer and Controller of Stationery.
Fried, Morton
  1960   On the evolution of social stratification and the state. In *Culture in history: Essays in honor of Paul Radin,* edited by Stanley Diamond. New York: Columbia University Press.
Fry, Donald H. Jr.
  1961   King salmon spawning stocks of the California Central Valley, 1940–1959. *California Fish and Game* **47:**55–71.
Fulton, Leonard A.
  1968   Spawning areas and abundance of chinook salmon *(Oncorhynchus tshawytscha)* in the Columbia River Basin—past and present. *U.S. Fish and Wildlife Service, Special Scientific Report, Fisheries,* No. 571. (Washington, D.C.)
  1970   Spawning areas and abundance of steelhead trout and coho, sockeye, and chum salmon in the Columbia River Basin—past and present. *Special Scientific Report, Fisheries,* No. 618, U.S. Department of Commerce. (Washington, D.C.)
Galbreath, James L.
  1966   Timing of tributary races of chinook salmon through the lower Columbia River based on analysis of tag recoveries. *Research Briefs, Fish Commission of Oregon* **12**(1):1–23.
Garfield, Viola, and Paul F. Wingert
  1953   The Tsimshian Indians and their arts. Seattle, Wash.: University of Washington Press.
Gilhousen, P.
  1960   Migratory behavior of adult Fraser River sockeye. *Progress Report International North Pacific Salmon Fisheries Commission* No. 7.
Gunther, E.
  1927   Klallam Ethnography. *University of Washington Publications in Anthropology* **1:**171–314.
Hanamura, N.
  1966   Sockeye salmon in the Far East. Salmon of the north Pacific Ocean, Part III, A review of the life history of north Pacific salmon. *International North Pacific Fisheries Commission Bulletin* 18. Vancouver, Can.)
Hardesty, Donald L.
  1975   The niche concept: Suggestions for its use in human ecology. *Human Ecology* **3**(2):71–85.

Harris, Marvin
1968   The rise of anthropological theory: A history of theories of culture. New York: Crowell.
Hewes, Gordon W.
1973   Indian fisheries productivity in pre-contact times in the Pacific salmon area. *Northwest Anthropological Research Notes* **7**:133–155.
Hoar, W. S.
1953   Control and timing of fish migration. *Biological Review* **28**:437–452.
Hutchinson, G. E.
1957   Concluding remarks. *Cold Spring Harbor Symposium on Quantitative Biology* **22**:415–427.
Hynes, H. B. N.
1970   The ecology of flowing waters in relation to management. *Journal of Water Pollution Control Federation* **42**:418–24.
1969   The enrichment of streams. In *Eutrophication, the ecology of running waters*. National Academy of Science. Liverpool, Eng.: Liverpool University Press.
Ishida, T.
1966   Pink salmon in the Far East. Salmon of the north Pacific Ocean, Part III, A review of the life history of north Pacific salmon. *International North Pacific Fisheries Commission, Bulletin* 18. (Vancouver, Can.)
Jackson, Roy I.
1966   Introduction. Salmon of the North Pacific Ocean, Part I. *International North Pacific Fisheries Commission, Bulletin* 18. (Vancouver, Can.)
Jochelson, W.
1905–1908   The Koryak. *American Museum of Natural History, Memoir* 10, Part II.
Kasahara, Hiroshi
1963   Catch statistics for North Pacific salmon. Salmon of the north Pacific Ocean, Part I. *International North Pacific Fisheries Commission, Bulletin* 12. (Vancouver, Can.)
Krebs, Charles J.
1972   *Ecology—The Experimental analysis of distribution and abundance.* New York: Harper and Row.
Kroeber, A. L.
1925   Handbook of the Indians of California. *Bureau of American Ethnology, Bulletin* 78. (Washingon, D.C.)
1939   Cultural and natural areas of native North America. *University of California Publications in Archaeology and Ethnology* **38.**
Laguna, Frederica de
1972   Under Mt. Saint Elias: The history and culture of the Yakutat Tlingit. *Smithsonian Contributions to Anthropology,* vol. 7. Washington, D.C.: Smithsonian Institution Press.
Leggett, William C., and Richard R. Whitney
1972   Water temperature and the migrations of American shad. *Fishery Bulletin* **70**(3):659–669.
Levins, R.
1968   *Evolution in changing environments.* Princeton, N.J.: Princeton University Press.
Loud, Llewellyn L.
1918   Ethnography and archaeology of the Wiyot territory. *University of California Publications in American Archaeology and Ethnology* **14**(3):221–436.
MacArthur, R. H.
1972   *Geographical ecology: Patterns in the distribution of species.* New York: Harper and Row.
Margalef, Rámon
1960   Ideas for a synthetic approach to the ecology of running waters. *International Review gesamt Hydrobiologica* **45**:133–153.
1968   *Perspectives in ecological theory.* Chicago: University of Chicago Press.
Margolis, L., F. C. Cleaver, Y. Fukuda, and H. Godfrey
1966   Sockeye salmon in offshore waters. Salmon of the north Pacific Ocean, Part VI. *International North Pacific Fisheries Commission, Bulletin* 20. (Vancouver, Can.)

McFarland, William L.
    1925   *Salmon of the Atlantic.* New York: Parke, Austin, and Lipscomb.

Morisawa, Marie
    1968   *Streams: Their dynamics and morphology.* New York: McGraw-Hill.

Mundie, J. H.
    1974   Optimization of the salmonid nursery stream. *Journal of the Fisheries Research Board of Canada* **31:**1827–1837.

Murdock, George P.
    1936   *Rank and potlatch among the Haida.* New Haven, Conn.: Yale University Press.
    1968   The current status of the world's hunting and gathering peoples. In *Man the hunter,* edited by Richard B. Lee and Irven Devore. Chicago: Aldine.

Myers, G. S.
    1949   Usage of anadromous, catadromous, and allied terms for migratory fishes. *Copeia,* No. 2. Pp. 89–97.

Neave, Ferris
    1966   Pink salmon in British Columbia. Salmon of the north Pacific Ocean, Part III, A review of the life history of north Pacific Salmon. *International North Pacific Fisheries Commission, Bulletin* 18. Pp. 71–79.

Neave F., T. Ishida, and S. Murai
    1967   Pink salmon in offshore waters. *International North Pacific Fisheries Commission, Bulletin* 22. (Vancouver, Can.)

Oberg, Kalervo
    1973   The social economy of the Tlingit Indians. *The American Ethnological Society, Monograph* 55. Seattle: University of Washington Press.

Odum, Eugene P.
    1971   *Fundamentals of ecology.* 3rd ed. Philadelphia: Saunders.

Olson, Ronald
    1936   The Quinault Indians. *University of Washington Publications in Anthropology,* Vol. 6, No. 1. (Seattle, Wash.)

Orans, Martin
    1975   Domesticating the functional dragon: An analysis of Piddocke's potlatch. *American Anthropologist* **77**(2):312–328.

Payne, R. H., A. R. Child, and A. Forrest
    1971   Geographical variation in the Atlantic salmon. *Nature* **231:**250–252.

Pianka, Eric R.
    1974   *Evolutionary ecology.* New York: Harper and Row.

Piddocke, Stuart
    1965   The potlatch system of the southern Kwakiutl: A new perspective. *Southwestern Journal of Anthropology* **21:**244–264.

Ray, Verne
    1936   Native villages and groupings of the Columbia Basin. *The Pacific Northwest Quarterly,* **27:**99–152. (Seattle, Wash.)

Rhyther, J. H.
    1963   Geographic variations in productivity. In *The Sea.* Vol. II. edited by M. N. Hill. New York: Interscience. Pp. 347–380.

Ricker, W. E.
    1960   Evidence for environmental and genetic influence on certain characters which distinguish stocks of the Pacific salmons and steelhead trout. *Fisheries Research Board of Canada, Manuscript Report Series (Biological),* No. 695.
    1966   Sockeye salmon in British Columbia. Salmon of the north Pacific Ocean, Part III. *International North Pacific Fisheries Commission, Bulletin* 18. (Vancouver, Can.)

Rostlund, Erhard
    1952   Freshwater fish and fishing in native North America. *University of California Publications in Geography,* Vol. 9.
Roughgarden, J.
    1972   Evolution of niche width. *American Naturalist* **106:**683–718.
Rounsefell, George A.
    1958   Anadromy in North American salmonidae. *U.S. Fish and Wildlife Service, Fishery Bulletin* 131, Vol. 58.
    1958   Factors causing decline in sockeye salmon of Karluk River, Alaska. *U.S. Fish and Wildlife Service, Fishery Bulletin* 130, Vol. 58.
    1962   Relationships among North American salmonidae. *U.S. Fish and Wildlife Service, Fishery Bulletin* 209, Vol. 62.
Royce, William F., Lynwood S. Smith, and Allan C. Hartt
    1968   Models of oceanic migrations of Pacific salmon and comments on guidance mechanisms. *U.S. Fish and Wildlife Service, Fishery Bulletin,* Vol. 66, No. 3.
Sahlins, Marshall
    1958   Social stratification in Polynesia. Seattle: University of Washington Press.
Sanger, David
    1969   Development of the Pacific Northwest Plateau culture area: Historical and environmental considerations. In *Contributions to anthropology: Ecological essays* edited by David Damas. *National Museums of Canada, Bulletin* No. 230:15–23. (Ottawa, Can.)
Saunders, R. L.
    1967   Seasonal pattern of return of Atlantic salmon in the northwest Miramichi River, New Brunswick. *Journal of the Fisheries Research Board of Canada,* Vol. 24. Pp. 21–32.
Service, Elman R.
    1968   *Primitive social organization: An evolutionary perspective.* New York: Random House.
Smith, Marian W.
    1940   *The Puyallup-Nisqually.* New York: Columbia University Press.
Smoker, W. E.
    1953   Fisheries Research Papers 1, 5. Department of Fisheries, Washington State.
Sneed, P. G.
    1972   Of salmon and men: An investigation of ecological determinants and aboriginal man in the Canadian Plateau. In *Aboriginal man and environments on the plateau of northwest America,* edited by Arnoud H. Stryd and Rachel A. Smith. Calgary, Can.: Student's Press.
Spier, L.
    1930   Klamath Ethnography. *University of California Publications in Archaeology and Ethnology* **30.**
Straty, Richard R.
    1966   Time of migration and age group structure of sockeye salmon (Oncorhynchus nerka) spawning populations in the Naknek River system, Alaska. *U.S. Fish and Wildlife Service, Fishery Bulletin* 130, Vol. 58. Pp. 83–169.
Suttles, Wayne
    1962   Variation in habitat and culture on the Northwest Coast. *Akten des 34 International Amerikanistenkongresses,* Wien, 1960. Pp. 522–537.
    1963   The persistence of intervillage ties among the coast Salish. *Ethnology* **2:**512–525.
    1968   Coping with abundance: Subsistence on the northwest coast. In *Man the Hunter* edited by Richard Lee and Irven Devore. Chicago: Aldine.
Teit, James
    1900   The Thompson Indians of British Columbia. *American Museum of Natural History, Memoir* 2.
U.S. Weather Service
    1966   Selected climatic maps of the United States. U.S. Department of Commerce, Environmental Data Service. Pp. 10–11. (Washington, D.C.)

Vandermeer, J. H.
   1972   Niche theory. *Annual Review of Ecology and Systematics* **3:**107–132.
Vayda, Andrew P.
   1961   A re-examination of the northwest coast economic systems. *Transactions of the New York Academy of Sciences* (Series 2)**23**(5):618–624.
Walburg, C. H., and P. R. Nichols
   1967   Biology and management of the American shad and status of the fisheries, Atlantic Coast of the United States, 1960. *United States Fish and Wildlife Service, Special Scientific Report: Fisheries,* No. 550.
Watanabe, Hitoshi
   1973   The Ainu ecosystem: Environment and group structure. *American Ethnological Society, Monograph* 54. Seattle: University of Washington Press.
Waterman, T. T., and A. L. Kroeber
   1938   *The Kepel fish dam.* Berkeley: University of California Press.
Weinberg, Daniela
   1965   Models of southern Kwakiutl social organization. *General Systems* **10:**169–81.

6

Seasonal Phases in Ona Subsistence Territorial Distribution and Organization: Implications for the Archeological Record

DAVID E. STUART

Introduction

Over the past few years, students of hunter–gatherer populations have increasingly revised their focus to accommodate the fact of "flexibility" in subsistence behavior and social organization. Such flexibility in social arrangements has been specifically pointed out for such populations as the Hadza (Woodburn 1968), several Eskimo groups (Damas 1968) including the Dogrib (Helm 1968), and African populations, such as the Mbuti and Ik (Turnbull 1968). In short, with the publication of *Man the Hunter* (Lee and DeVore 1968), a broad spectrum of fairly recent field research solidly documented the high degree of variability in subsistence behavior and group composition within a given population of hunter–gatherers. Perhaps as a consequence, subsequent studies have focused even more on the seasonal nature of subsistence behavior and attendant flexibility in band–group size composition and distribution (Bicchieri 1972).

The legitimacy conferred on "flexibility" and "seasonality" by the publication of such studies has no doubt permitted a more accurate reporting of observations gathered on hunter–gatherer populations in the field. It must have been rather a relief for some in the field to realize that they were not alone in failing to document the clean-cut patrilineality or compositeness they had been trained to expect. Nonetheless, departure from the notion of the band as a generally stable and socially well-patterned entity also left researchers with a plethora of theoretical and methodological problems. Not the least of these was the increasingly unsatisfactory analytical results obtained from the application of generally accepted criteria of residence, descent, and marriage in identifying group structure (Service 1962; Steward 1955). As Woodburn has pointed out:

> The widespread occurrence of this flexibility brings us back to the problem of field method. The analysis of group structure is a crucial area of research, and, if comparative studies are to be of any value, it is essential that the field workers concerned develop a common body of techniques [Woodburn 1968:110].

The subsequent development of such a common body of techniques and the general resolution of difficulties generated by on-the-ground flexibility in hunter–gatherer populations has not proceeded very far. Rather, such terms as "task group" (Helm 1972), "community" (Berndt 1972), and "hunting group" (Rogers 1972:120) are being used to define groups of individuals in fairly specific contexts. A typical contemporary publication will likely include a variety of such terms. The range of criteria thus used to identify groups is broad: type of subsistence activity, family composition, kinship generated groups, territorially defined groups, ritually generated groups, seasonally generated groups, coresident groups, and simply expedient ones. Obviously, the definition of basic social units remains a significant problem. A close inspection of the range of criteria is informative—developing specific labels for a wide variety of groups seems to accommodate the flexibility. Yet, at the same time, the criteria of kinship, residence and descent are applied in certain contexts much as they always were. Reference to the horde is still found (Berndt 1972:193), and patrilineality, at least in Australia, apparently exists. The acceptance of hunter–gatherer flexibility as fact has not displaced the equally compelling fact that stability and pattern also occur. As Peterson (1975:55) has recently pointed out in his article on hunter–gatherer territoriality, there is a substantial basis from which to argue that members of hunter–gatherer populations, like other species, do not wander randomly over the landscape. The problem, then, setting aside questions of definition, would seem to be one of resolving the way in which to deal methodologically with flexibility and recurring pattern within the same system.

Returning to the recent emphasis on seasonality, yearly subsistence cycles, and so on, it would appear that many studies are operating on the assumption that seasonal subsistence behavior generates flexibility in social groupings. Stability and variability, specifically in subsistence behavior, are explained largely in terms of environmental–ecological factors. Flexibility in social groupings is viewed largely in terms of expedient behavior geared to subsistence. On the other hand, nonexpedient social behavior is usually discussed in terms of social organizational features, such as kinship. Significantly, task groups, hunting groups, and so on are usually explained in terms of the context of specific subsistence situations, while horde, patrilineal band, regional band, tribe, and so on are explained in terms of general social organizational principles. It appears implicit that a given population is still considered to have essentially one social organization, but any number of adaptive strategies.

The Ona—A Classic Case?

It seems, in view of this general recognition that hunter–gatherer societies have flexible adaptations, that reevaluations of ethnographic data gathered years ago for populations that are often cited, such as the Ona, would have found their way into the literature. This has not been the case, and the Ona, at least, continue to be accepted as a rather classic example of formal band society. For example, Lathrap has recently maintained that "The Ona bands of Northern Tierra del Fuego survived into the first decade of the present century in an unacculturated condition" (Lathrap 1968:93). He goes on to say that "Here we find people with good hunting territories which they jealously defended from all outsiders" (1968:93). He is not alone in this viewpoint (Gardner 1968:341). The potential point for confusion is real, for Lathrap's statements regarding defense of territory have been cited in a recent and important article by Peterson (1975:57) as perhaps providing the basis for an exception to the more widely (and currently) held view that such groups do not generally engage in armed defense of their territory.

Territoriality is not the only context in which the Ona have been cited recently as supporting the notions of Steward (1955) and Service (1962) with regard to band typology. Lee and DeVore illustrate this point when they say: "The Patrilocal band, however, is not an empty category; cases are presented in which a patrilocal organization was in evidence, including the Ona of South America . . ." (1968:8). More specifically, Baer and Schmitz (1965) present a strong case for the existence of Ona patrilineality in their paper on Ona social organization. For that matter, Steward also continued to support Ona patrilineality (1968:333) in his later publications and his assurances are reproduced implicitly or explicitly in a variety of recent general texts; one such example appears in Bock's revised (1974:279) introduction to the discipline.

In the following passage in *Man the Hunter,* Lathrap adequately summarizes the consensus of recent thinking on the Ona:

> Interestingly enough, all of the classic Stigmata of "hunting peoples," which have been brought into question at this symposium, were strongly developed among the several Ona bands, which were in fact patrilineal. Patrilineages were clearly defined and strictly exogamous. Each held a sharply delineated territory with absolute rights over the included economic resources. The facts of the case are reasonably clear since we have a good account of the culture written by Bridges (1949) . . . [1968:93].

The "included economic resources," according to Lee (1968:42), focused primarily on hunted mammals—guanaco, one assumes. A lack of closer inspection of sources on the Ona might permit one to conclude the matter right here with their documentation of the Ona as a "classic hunting society."

However, even a cursory inspection of the major sources on the Ona reveals their organization and subsistence behavior to be often more variable and less clear-cut than is generally portrayed. For example, in his comparative study of social organization, Lowie (1949:327) asserted that the Ona were a borderline case of patrilineality. He based his conclusion on the absence of a requisite unilateral rigidity. This is not surprising, for, as I have pointed out elsewhere, Lucas Bridges maintained that he was never certain (from terms of address) whether men he had known all his life were brothers, cousins, or even related at all (Stuart 1972:167). I assume that these suspicions caused Murdock to list the Ona as having exogamous (nonclan) communities practicing bilateral descent (1967:230). More dramatically, Lucas Bridges describes a situation in which an old man, his daughter, and his son-in-law (who were all from the same local group) coresided in the territory of the daughter's deceased mother—who was from another local group (1951:350–351, 364). No anthropologist could have even contrived a finer case with which to confuse the issues of exogamy, residence, and territoriality at one blow. Thus, if one considers "flexibility" as a variable rather than a constant in hunter–gatherer systems, it can be argued from these data that there is both stability and variability in Ona organization on a yearround basis. From this theoretical perspective, it is far more useful to monitor changes in Ona flexibility as a response to specified environmental conditions than simply to determine whether they were patrilineal as opposed to flexible.

Subsistence behavior had tended to be oversimplified as well, for they took a wide variety of foods other than large mammals, and the importance of fox, eels, mussels, fish, and geese was noted long ago (Lothrop 1928:32; Cooper 1917:187–188). Other common sources (Steward and Faron 1959) recognize the importance of marine resources and the role women played in obtaining them. Even the most superficial thought on subsistence would lead one to suspect that resources occurred in different parts of the landscape and that some, at least, must be seasonal—ducks and geese being migratory fowl. Bridges also discusses Fuegian seasons and Ona food procurement in many contexts, not the least of which is his assertion that the northern Ona (in reference to Lathrap's earlier comment) subsisted primarily on tuco-tuco, not guanaco (1951). On the other hand, data on Fuegian temperature and rainfall (Wernstedt, 1972) suggest there is less seasonality than in an analogous environment, such as that of the Nunamiut (Binford, personal communication). Since variation in temperature and precipitation in Tierra del Fuego is substantially lower than in most other high latitude environments, the significant question at this stage is what the actual pattern of seasonality is.

I suggest that a careful reevaluation of Southern Ona subsistence, territory, and organization is essential and timely. In order to proceed in a manner consistent with recent treatments of other hunter–gatherers that are not considered "classic" cases, data on the natural environment of Tierra del Fuego will first be presented. Then information with regard to subsistence, population distribution, and organization will be structured for each of the four (fall, winter, spring, summer) traditional seasons of the year. It will be argued that Fuegian environment displays variability that can be treated as seasonal and that patterns of Ona subsistence, population distribution, and social organization were variable on a yearround basis. Thus, Ona response to seasonal subsistence variables required specialized seasonal sets of cultural adaptations or structural poses (Gearing 1958). Unfortunately, this proposition can, at this point, only be based on by secondary ethnographic data as the Ona are now extinct. Therefore, new data on Ona adaptations must be obtained from other sources. The archeological record is suggested as a source that can further clarify Ona ecological adaptations. Thus, ethnographic data will be used to suggest a typology of archeological sites, and implications for the archeological record will be discussed.

Tierra del Fuego—History and Sources

Tierra del Fuego occupies the southernmost part of the South American continent. Since its discovery by Magellan in 1520, it has provided interest and excitement for explorer and scientist alike (Rudolph 1934:251) and has been visited by more than 80 expeditions. A paradox lies in the fact that its early contact with European navigators neither led to settlement nor to a widely disseminated body of accurate information concerning the natural environment and aboriginal inhabitants until the middle of the nineteenth century. At that time, the voyages of the *Adventure* and the *Beagle* ultimately led to the development of regular steamship service between England and Chile through the Straits of Magellan (Butland 1957). The Chilean government established its first settlement on the north shore of the Strait in 1843; in 1849, this colony was permanently relocated to the present day site of Punta Arenas. Later, in the 1870s, Punta Arenas proved to be the primary point of diffusion from which sheep ranchers moved into Northern Tierra del Fuego Island.

The first Europeans to have intensive impact on Fuegian groups were the British missionaries who established themselves in the Beagle Channel area as early as 1859. The most notable of these was Thomas Bridges, whose son, Stephen Lucas Bridges, penetrated and settled the southern Ona country several decades later. Since the northern Ona had been displaced by that time, his firsthand accounts of the Southern Ona are of primary importance for this chapter (Bridges 1938, 1951). Other important and reliable firsthand ethnographic accounts came after the Ona had experienced dramatic population decline (Lothrop 1928; Marett and Penniman 1931; Gusinde 1923, 1924, 1925, 1926, 1928, 1931). The late John Cooper has provided the most reliable secondary sources including his indispensable annotated bibliography (1917, 1946). Other historical notes can be gleaned from the works of Braun-Menendez (1939, 1969).

Environment

Topography

Tierra del Fuego Island is comprised of some 18,600 square miles and lies between 52° and 56° south latitude. Of this area, the southern Ona occupied approximately 6500 square miles in Bridges' time. The relief of the island is quite varied. The northeastern half of the island is a low lying plain broken by hills that generally do not exceed 600 feet in altitude. To the south and west of these plains lies a fairly wide belt of generally rugged hills and secluded valleys; these hills may be as high as 1600–1800 feet. The southern coast and part of the interior are characterized by a high-rugged (usually snow covered) chain of mountains which is a southern extension of the Andean Cordillera.

The entire region is well watered, with rivers, streams, lakes, and springs becoming more numerous as one moves south. The three major river drainages (R. Grande, R. Fuego, R. Ewan) flow north and east to the Atlantic.

Climate

The climate of the region varies from locale to locale, as well as from season to season. The mean July temperature at sea level ranges from 34° F to 38° F as one moves out in all directions from Rio Grande, a central point on the Atlantic Coast. In January (midsummer), the mean temperature is 50° F (Butland 1957:24). The mean annual temperature range in southern Ona territory is roughly 17° F (Wernstedt 1972:95). This mean temperature variation is quite low (partly because of cloud cover) when compared to other regions of similar latitude, yet it is higher than in many tropical zones. For example, Goose, New-foundland (53°15′ N.), has a mean annual temperature range of roughly 59°F. On the other hand, Adak in the Aleutians (51°53′ N.) has approximately the same mean annual temperature (40° F) as Rio Grande, Tierra del Fuego and a similar mean annual temperature variation of 18° F (Wernstedt 1972:395, 412). A recent archeological study of the central Aleutians (Yesner 1975) indicates that significant differences in the effects of seasonality on subsistence operate between the Akun and Umnak Aleuts (approximately 53° N.).

In short, although it has been generally argued that latitude correlates with basic subsistence strategy (Lee and DeVore 1968), apparent variations in subsistence and seasonality at similar latitudes suggest that what is needed is a specific and empirical basis by means of which different environments may be compared with regard to temperature, precipitation, and so on. In such a comparative context, the adaptive behavior of the Ona would assume greater significance.

However, despite a lower annual variation in temperature than might have been expected, the effects of temperature on man, plants, and animals is made the more variable by several other factors. These include altitude, chill factor of

Table 6.1

Seasonal Variation in Wind Strength

Season	Average strength in M.P.H.
Spring	9.6
Summer	10.3
Autumn	8.3
Winter	6.9

the winds, and variance in the length of the day. Due to altitude, the deciduous forest zone (where guanaco are primarily hunted) is significantly more subject to freezing conditions than Rio Grande on the coast. Unfortunately, no climatic data are available for the interior or elevated portions of the island. The whole island lies in a belt of prevailing westerlies, and wind strength shows little variance by season, as is shown in Table 6.1.

Precipitation in southern Ona territory varies from roughly 20 inches yearly in the north (Rio Grande) to 40 inches in the south (Policarpo Cove). In general, precipitation increases as one moves inland (and to higher elevations) from the Atlantic Coast. There are approximately 300 days with significant cloud cover annually. Precipitation generally takes the form of rain and is higher in summer than winter. Central Tierra del Fuego has the greatest snowfall of the island— primarily in late fall through winter, with lesser amounts sometimes falling unexpectedly in summer. Butland (1957) notes the lack of precise precipitation data for central and southern Tierra del Fuego, but *Goode's World Atlas* (Espenshade and Morrison 1974) indicates that there is less than 15% deviation from expected annual precipitation. On the other hand, Lucas Bridges noted two winters during his stay on the island when conditions were dramatically worse than usual, with heavy snowfall, extreme low temperatures, and great numbers of deaths of birds and guanaco (1951:355). All relevant sources, however, note a marked tendency for highly variable and localized weather conditions on a day-to-day basis.

In summary, climatic variability may be highlighted by noting a "winter" season that lasts roughly 6 months and peaks in June and July. Its characteristics are cold temperatures, moderate winds, sleet and snow precipitation, and quite short days. The "summer" season lasts roughly 3 months (December, January, February) and is characterized during its December–January peak by somewhat greater precipitation (primarily rain), moderate temperatures, stronger winds, long days, and marked daily changeability of local weather conditions.

Flora

An outline of flora in the Tierra del Fuego region soon reveals a general trend toward low diversity indices (Godley 1960:466). Basically, there are four types of vegetation zones. These include Magellanic moorland, deciduous forest, ever-

green beech forest, and alpine complexes. In southern Ona country, the Magel-
lanic moorland occurs primarily in a 10–30-mile-wide strip along the Atlantic
Coast. This region is characterized by tussock grasses, matting plants, such as
Donatia, Oreobolus, and *Astelia,* barberry, and a few stunted deciduous beech trees
(Nothophagus). Of importance to the Ona were the seeds of tussock grasses, bar-
berry, arbutus berries, and a "strawberry" *(Rubus geoides)* (Lothrop 1928:29).

As this tussock grass zones fades out toward the interior, the incidence of
deciduous beech increases until a true forest 20–40 miles wide is reached. This
deciduous beech forest corresponds roughly to an altitude range of from 500 to
1500 feet. The trees vary greatly in size, the largest stands measuring over 100
feet in height. Undergrowth is thick, but penetrable, and consists largely of
barberries *(Berberis buxifolia* and *Berberis heterophylla)* (Butland 1957:32). Also of
importance to the Ona are fungi *(Cyttaria darwinii),* which infest the beech, beech
bark, and barberry.

Just north of Lake Fagnano, evergreen beech begins to mix more consistently
with the deciduous variety. The evergreen species predominates the distinctive
forest type between Lake Fagnano and the Beagle Channel between 1500 and
2500 feet in altitude. Bark and some tree fungi were important to the Ona. The
alpine zone (above 3000 feet) was not much occupied and is of passing importance here.

Fauna

The terrestrial zoology of the island is not very impressive from the standpoint
of Mammalia. Of species important to man, the region has only Magellanic deer
(Hippocamelus bisulcus), fox *(Dusicyon culpaeus),* guanaco *(Lama glama guanicoe),*
tuco-tuco *(Ctenomys* spp.*),* and several other species of Rodentia.

The Magellanic deer was extremely rare, at least in historic times (Kuschel
1960) and does not seem to have figured meaningfully in Ona subsistence—it is
not even mentioned by Bridges (1951) or Lothrop (1928). Fox were of considerable importance to the Ona as food during times of scarcity (from winter to early
spring); they were not, however, a preferred species (Cooper 1946:110). According to Bridges, they were very numerous (1951:149–150), unusually large
(1951:156), and occasionally picked to hunt when winters were quite severe
(1951:352).

Guanaco, by all accounts, was the most important large game animal among
the Ona. They were numerous even as late as the first decades of this century and
were available to some degree yearround. According to Lothrop (1928:31–32),
the Ona tool kit was largely oriented toward taking and utilizing guanaco. The
animal itself is an unusual creature—a new world camelid; it is quite large, and a
dressed weight of 200 pounds is not unusual. Guanaco inhabit the upland and
mountainous inland regions of southern Ona country during late summer and
fall (mid-February to mid-May). They are found primarily in the deciduous
forest zone during that period. In winter, they move to lowland valleys near
the coast (Bridges 1951:277); however, a few solitary individuals continue to

winter in the mountains. In general, they move about singly, in pairs, or, at most, in groups of three and four. They are at their prime (both in terms of meat and hide) in fall, when they are fattest.

Tuco-tuco, a small burrowing rodent similar to a guinea pig, was an important food resource. It inhabits grassy areas, primarily the better drained portions of the tussock grass zone near the coast. However, it is also found in substantial numbers within the stunted portion of the deciduous beech zone (northern and eastern fringes) where the trees are leafless for 7 months (March–September) and enough sunlight reaches the ground to support sufficient grass for the animal (Bridges 1951:452). Tuco-tuco were hunted heavily in winter (sometimes at night) when they crossed the sheet ice that formed in lower valleys.

In addition to mammals, a variety of bird species are represented in large numbers. For the present purposes, birds will be broken into water-marine and upland categories. There are six varieties of duck, the most important being the immense streamer (20 pounds) and the loggerhead. Widgeon and teal (five species), snipe (three species), and gull (ten species) were all utilized by the Ona. In addition, the upland goose was especially important, as were several varieties of cormorant (Bridges 1951). Birds of possibly less importance in lake, river, and beach zones were ibis, flamingo, kingfisher, oystercatcher, albatross, and petrel. (As an exhaustive treatment is not possible here, one may wish to consult Goodall *et al.* 1946.)

Birds that inhabit upland and forest zones and are documented as having been eaten include woodpecker, owl, parakeet, woodcock, sparrow, grouse, and wren. Obviously, duck, geese, and other waterfowl are also found to some extent in upland lakes or watercourses.

Nearly all of these birds are migratory and, thus, primarily available in the period from early spring to autumn (September to early March). An exception to this rule is the cormorant, important in fall through winter on the coast (Bridges 1951:333). Some gulls, owls, and small upland birds remain throughout winter.

The third major category of animal life important to Ona subsistence is comprised of littoral-marine species. Of these, southern blue mussels *(Mytilus edulis chilensis)* are the most abundant, available yearround from the beaches on the Atlantic Coast. Also important are several species of limpets and Antarctic crabs similar to Alaska king crabs. Fish and conger eels were quite important from late spring through fall and were obtained chiefly from tidal pools. Large herds of seal (probably elephant) return each spring to the rocky capes on the Atlantic shore, and they were important sources of meat and fat from some time in September to November. Bridges' book (1951: Plate XXXVII) shows pictures of fairly large herds at Cape Peñas taken some time after 1900.

Population and Territory

Estimates for the entire (northern and southern) Ona population vary considerably, and accurate figures may never be available. Steward and Faron suggest a figure of 2000 (1959:406) as does Cooper (1946:108), while Butland estimates 3600 persons in 1850. As the Ona occupied approximately 15,000 square miles of Tierra del Fuego, density was between 4.4 and 8 square miles per individual.

Using Bridges' general information regarding hunting territories, the southern Ona occupied between 6000 and 7000 square miles in 1890–1900. My own (Stuart 1972) "loose" estimate of population at that time is 750, which would yield an approximate density range of from 8 to 9 square miles per person. At that time, there were four functioning "groups" about which Bridges had knowledge: the Northern Group, the Cape San Pablo Group, the Namjisk Group, and the Mountain Group. The data extracted from Bridges do not coincide with Gusinde's attribution of 39 local groups to the island (1931:416, 418) nor with his estimates of 410 square miles per group or band; however, the accelerated population decline of the 1880s could have produced any number of recombinations among remnant populations.

For the present purposes, then, we will have to accept Bridges' testimony at face value and assume four groups, 8 or 9 square miles per individual, and territories that extended from the Atlantic Coast to the interior mountains (Lothrop 1928:84). Significant to the argument that follows is the fact that territories cross-cut the major environmental zones at right angles providing access to the diverse resources available in each (see Figure 6.1) at varying times of the year.

Seasonal Phases

In this section of the chapter, we will present data on Ona subsistence, population distribution, group composition, and social organizational factors. The four major seasons, as we usually perceive them, are applied to the Fuegian calendar (where seasons are reversed) to provide a time frame in which to organize the data. Thus, fall begins in March; midwinter comes the first of July; spring comes the first of October; and midsummer comes on the first of January. This procedure is essential in view of the data presented in the previous section on environment.

We must recall that the patterns of seasonal change in the Fuegian environment have been questioned. If Ona behavior from one "season" to another displays low variability, then the argument for moderate seasonal variability is strengthened. If, as is argued here, behavioral variability is high, this factor supports the proposition that seasonality in the Fuegian environment is sufficient to require behavioral adaptations. This behavioral variability further diminishes the "classic hunting society" characterization and suggests that such variable (or flexible) seasonal adaptive phases may be inconsistent with the notion that one cultural population has one social organization.

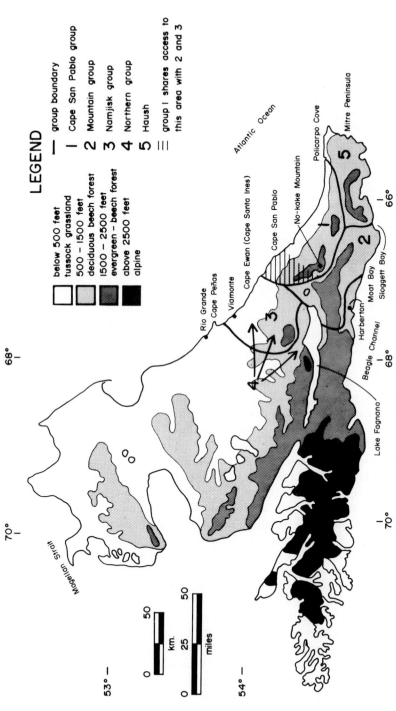

Figure 6.1 Tierra Del Fuego, southern Ona territories—vegetation and relief.

LEGEND

☐	below 500 feet tussock grassland
▨	500 – 1500 feet deciduous beech forest
▨	1500 – 2500 feet evergreen – beech forest
■	above 2500 feet alpine

— group boundary
1 Cape San Pablo group
2 Mountain group
3 Namjisk group
4 Northern group
5 Haush
▥ group 1 shares access to this area with 2 and 3

Magellan Strait

70°

68°

Rio Grande
Cape Peñas
Viamonte
Cape Ewan (Cape Santa Ines)

Atlantic Ocean

Cape San Pablo
No-kake Mountain
Policarpo Cove
Mitre Peninsula

Harberton
Moat Bay
Sloggett Bay
Beagle Channel

Lake Fagnano

53°

54°

68°

70°

66°

50
km.
0   25   50
miles

261

Fall

Subsistence

The fall season finds guanaco in their prime, foraging in the hills and mountain coves of the deciduous beech forest (Bridges 1951:277). It was during this season that the Ona focused primarily on the hunt (Bridges 1951:357). Guanaco were hunted with bow and arrow and stalked to close range if wind noise was sufficient to obscure the human sounds (Lothrop 1928:80). When moving from camp to camp, the women and children walked the valley floors, while the Ona menfolk traveled the hillsides to intercept guanaco forced to flee upward in fear (Lothrop 1928:80–81). This strategy was generally effective when the air was often still at the very beginning of autumn (early March), and hunting groups were still moving up from the coast. Once the hunting season was in full swing, the stalk (by two or three men) seems to have been the norm. Dogs were used to a certain degree, but largely to flush guanaco from thickets and, we presume, were not very useful in association with fall stalking techniques.

A guanaco was partially butchered where killed, to be bundled and carried back to the base camp, where it was cut and divided for the hunter's family and portions were distributed to unlucky hunters. If a hunting party of men butchered in the field, a guanaco was divided into six pieces for carrying (Bridges 1951:218). Binford (personal communication) has suggested this to be a scarce game strategy.

The following implements were carried into the field by such a party: a knife (from an iron barrel hoop or stave), a length of rawhide for tying up the meat, tinder and flint for fire, and a bow, quiver, and arrows (stone or glass points) (Bridges 1951:376). Usually only one or two hearths were made away from base camps, and skin shelters were not carried. Most of the final butchering of guanaco occurred in the base camps and was done by the hunter with homemade iron or stone knives (see Lothrop 1928). Guanaco were cooked by the women over open fires if the men returned to camp. Hide dressing and manufacture of guanaco robes was carried out by the women (for scrapers, see Lothrop 1928). Other camp tools included the flint knappers' equipment, a guanaco bone with jagged end, and a round stone to keep the bone sharp (Bridges 1951:378). Arrows were usually retrieved and touched up after a hunt (Bridges 1951:380), and they were deliberately discarded only after they had been used to kill a man.

Other fall resources were tuco-tuco, which were taken with a pointed stick, primarily from the ecotone where grasses mix with the forest edge. Goslings and adult upland geese, as well as ducks, were caught in upland lakes and either snared or drowned (Bridges 1951:333–334). Lesser game and birds were usually butchered by the women (1951:335). Fall is also the time when barberry is ripe; it was gathered primarily by the women from stands near the eastern edge of the deciduous forest zone. During unsuccessful hunts, men would subsist on tuco-tuco, fungi, fox, small birds, or beech tree sap as circumstances permitted

(Bridges 1951:453–454). Bridges attests to the relative bounty of the fall season and the importance of guanaco (1951:357); other sources do not dispute this contention.

Population Distribution

In fall, the population was definitely concentrated in the highlands (Bridges 1951:483, 453, 519), and the primary occupation was hunting. Some Ona seem always to have remained in the lowlands or near the coast (as in the case of the "specialist" cormorant hunter, Talimeot [Bridges 1951:447]).

References to the size of these groups inhabiting a fall base camp are usually indirect. We can assume by Bridges' reference to men's lodge meetings in the context of guanaco hunting and berry collecting (1951:414) that such groupings occurred in the fall and exceeded in number any one "local group" (1951:410). Bridges refers to 30 adult men (1951:425) at one such gathering, which indicates a group of perhaps 120 Ona, for evidence suggests a ratio of 1 Ona hunter to 4 or 5 dependents (Bridges 1951:211, 300). However, his plates of the same event (1951: Plate XXXIV) show only 12 adult men, indicating a group of perhaps 50–60 individuals.

The population aggregation of immediate concern here is the regular fall hunting–traveling group. Numerous citations suggest an average minimum of 7–10 hunters, yielding base camp sizes of 35–50 persons (Bridges 1951:272, 283). Smaller camps of 2 or 3 hunters and dependents were also common.

These base camps were characterized by clusters of hide windbreaks, /Kowwhi/, usually one per nuclear family, but there are no data on their precise patterns or arrangement. The implements that characterized these camps were iron pyrites and flint for fire making, split wood (barberry) fire tongs, guanaco and fox skin storage bags, a "grease" stone 5 or 6 inches in diameter (for cracking marrow and cooking grass seeds), tussock grass baskets, wood or whalebone combs, knife (stone, later iron), flesher (stone, later glass), awl (bone, later metal), bone chipping tool, stone arrow shaft polisher, and wooden hide beater (Lothrop 1928:64–71). Women used short fish spears tipped by guanaco bone and evidently carried them most of the time (Lothrop 1928:83). From the archeologist's point of view, many of the artifacts that might distinguish base camps from male hunting party camps are perishable. Grease stones, women's bone spear tips, awl, and flesher provide exceptions. The differential use of chipping tool and arrow shaft polisher in different camp types is not clear.

After the introduction of the European ax, according to Lothrop (1928:63–64), the Ona built conical lodges with scooped out floors. Since Bridges mentions no lodges, other than several ceremonial ones, we may assume Lothrop's statement to be more characteristic of the 1920s than of earlier periods.

Other types of fall encampment included those of male hunting parties (three to six) and those of /Klokten/ young male initiates spending a year or two in solitude (one to three boys).

Social Organization

Unfortunately, nowhere does there exist a well-structured and clear-cut body of data on Ona social organization. Nonetheless, in the context of fall subsistence groups, several patterns emerge. The most outstanding feature of the largest fall guanaco-hunting camps was the men's ritual lodge or /Hain/, which carried on the business of inducting young men into adult status.

It emphasized the superiority and cohesion of males as distinguished from females, and it appears to have occurred only in fall (Bridges 1951:405) and never during times of turmoil. Bearing in mind the conflict between Ona groups in the 1880s and 1890s, Bridges citations refer to ceremonies shortly after 1900 and may not be representative of prior conditions. On the other hand, Peterson, who is concerned with the structural implications of ritual behavior among Australian groups, has argued that features such as seating arrangements would be enduring (Peterson, personal communication).

At any rate, the lodges (circular structures of poles), always to the east of the main camp, were "generally placed near a clump of trees, with a wide space separating them from some favorite camping ground" (Bridges 1951:405). Women never participated, but male inductees underwent a 2-year period of trial as solitary hunters before their status was assured. In the lodge ceremony that Bridges describes firsthand, he indicates that the participating men came from a variety of local groups (1951:410), namely, the Namjisk, Cape San Pablo, and Mountain Groups. He (Bridges) was sponsored by one Aneki (of Cape San Pablo) "whose father . . . had been wise and taught his sons . . . much ancient lore" (1951:410). According to Bridges, novitiates who violated the rules were killed, "brother would kill brother, father would kill son" (1951:410). The younger brother of Bridges' sponsor was designated as his (sponsor's) "second." In general, a male agnate of the initiate played an important role in the ceremonies and education of the boy (Bridges 1951:420–421).

Seating arrangements within the lodge were fixed according to descent from either the northern or southern groups, with men of both parentages permitted to choose their position (Bridges 1951:415). This option indicates recognition of both male and female lines. Bridges also points out that the lodge itself was often used as sleeping quarters for male initiates and widowers—one supposes that the use of such sites recurred during a number of fall seasons. In short, there is a strong evidence to suggest the lodge was male centered and stressed the importance of close male kin (brothers, sons, paternal uncles) but made consideration of descent, in both lines, explicit.

Turning to more regular situations in which fall guanaco base camps and lodge activities did not coincide, we find that fathers, sons, and brothers usually constituted the male core of such groups (Bridges 1951: Plates XLI, XXXIX, XXXV, XXXII bottom left). The situation appears to have been the same for male hunting parties away from base camps, for there are literally dozens of Bridges' citations that refer to close relatives in the male line hunting together. Also, at times, sons-in-law of the male core members and nonrelated male companions, from either the same or another local group, were included. It would appear that kinship in the male line was an important, but not exclusive, principle in generating fall groups.

Specifically, even in the context of strong male-centered pursuits, such as lodge activities and hunting, strict patrilocality and jealousy over territorial resources cannot be documented since sons-in-law were present as were unrelated hunters from other regions. The evidence falls far short of documenting strict patrilineal bands, but I have argued elsewhere that a principle of patrifiliation was in operation (Stuart 1972:156).

Midwinter

Subsistence

In midwinter, guanaco become lean and forage either in the lower reaches of the deciduous forest or in the tussock grass zone near the coast (Bridges 1951:217). By winter, the high country is nearly "devoid of life" (1951:289). Guanaco are quite scattered at this time and are difficult to stalk in the open lands near the coast, since sheet ice makes a quiet approach difficult. In all likelihood, it was under these conditions that the dogs were most useful in flushing guanaco from thickets (1951:102). They were hunted, generally, by one or two men with bow and arrow. Other than intensified use of dogs, there is no evidence of specialized devices, techniques, and so on for procuring winter guanaco; hunting implements and butchering techniques as described for fall subsistence were identical.

In winter, tuco-tuco was an important resource found in the frozen grasslands and in pockets within the now leafless deciduous beech forest. They were killed with pointed sticks by both men and boys. Their burrows could be discerned where they had broken through the ice in their nocturnal wanderings, and Bridges claims there was sometimes quite a turnout to hunt them on moonlit winter nights as they crossed the ice (1951:452).

Foxes were also hunted more at this time of year; again, dogs were useful in bringing them to bay in the thickets, where they were shot with bow and arrow. In the 1870s and 1880s, they were quite numerous, but, several decades later, they were becoming scarce due to the extermination programs of sheep ranchers (Bridges 1951:451).

Other resources in the lower forest include dried tree fungi, small birds, such as parakeet and owl, and inner bark from the dwarf deciduous beech tree. Leather shavings were sometimes eaten in times of hardship.

Coastal resources in winter focused primarily on shellfish (mussels and limpets) collected by the women and on such marine birds as remained. The most important of these birds was the cormorant, available in significant numbers from rocky cliffs along the coast. Men often went over the cliffs to kill them at night by biting their heads (Bridges 1951:333). This method appears to have been fairly successful as Talimeot (the shag hunter) often had "scores" of birds hanging in camp. According to Bridges (1951:333), "when they visited him in autumn or winter, less expert hunters could always depend on the gift of a fine, fat bird from the famed Talimeot." Cormorants might also be killed by fair-sized groups (including women and children) frightening hundreds of them from the cliffs at night with torches.

Winter was not a time of plenty for the Ona. Subsistence efforts focused on anything and everything available—resources were not necessarily available in large and dependable quantities in any given locale. Again, with reference to a winter cormorant camp, Bridges writes: "New arrivals were always served first, because their need was usually the greatest" (1951:335). In another, more general, reference Bridges indicates that, for the Ona, fairly long periods without food were not uncommon (1951:336). Some winters might be particularly bad, for, as Bridges recounts, in July of 1908 the temperature was never higher than $-4°$ C (1951:481).

Of interest to the archeologist, winter subsistence behavior was focused on a wide variety of species, likely providing seasonal marking in faunal remains. In addition, the exploitation of shellfish left midden, and women's fish spears were an important implement in the context of littoral exploitation.

In short, in winter, there was still a strong focus on male hunting activity, but it was mixed with littoral resources collected by females and, evidently, "scouring" techniques by young and old alike. There is little evidence to suggest that food storage ameliorated winter resource scarcity.

Population Distribution

In midwinter, population was not concentrated to the extent evident in fall; rather, population was relatively dispersed between the lowland forests and the grass–shrub zones near the coast. Base camps appear to have been significantly smaller than in fall, for Bridges refers to "small hunting parties" during the winter season (1951:294). Specifically, he mentions a winter cormorant hunting camp (which fluctuated in size) of approximately 4 families, or 20 persons (1951:334). Elsewhere, he mentions a group of 8 hunters and their families who wintered at his ranch (1951:216). This suggests a group of 40, but they cannot be considered typical since they had access to Bridges' food supply. Perhaps this further points to a precarious winter subsistence situation. Other references to solitary hunters appear during this season (1951:210). Evidently, it was common at this time of year to find single families encamped. Mobility was somewhat limited by weather conditions (ice and snow).

There is no specific ethnographic evidence that documents either these base camps or hunting camps as having a very different structure from fall camps. However, they appear to have been generally smaller and, of course, lacked the men's lodge activities. Guanaco was still one staple; marrow-cracked bones were thrown in the fires as usual (Bridges 1951:197).

Social Organization

Since the evidence does not suggest a single focus, it is difficult to clarify midwinter organizational patterns. There are no ceremonial or ritual associations described that might provide clues. As was noted previously, in base camps, one found anything from one family to, perhaps, a half dozen. Clearly, these single families were biological units, that is, a man, his wife (or wives), and children. These single family camps account, in part, for the neo-local pattern that has been cited for the Ona (Baer and Schmitz 1965; Murdock 1967:230). Other references regarding the disposition of children also indicate no clear pattern. For example, the widower Kankoat (Ona father and Haush mother) had two sons by different women—one was raised by a distant female relation of his mother and another by the wife of a man with whom he had no blood relationship (Bridges 1951:213, 365, 366). Other references to winter groups suggest that brothers often camped and hunted together, especially if one was unmarried or widowed (Bridges 1951: Plate XXXIX). On the other hand, Bridges often went afield in the winter with several hunting companions who were unrelated and were often from different territorial "groups."

In summary, although some winter groups appear to have had a core of close male consanguines, they might also be drawn together by friendship, adoptive kinship, or affinal relationships. Residence patterns appear to have been rather variable due to small group size and dispersal. Perhaps Peterson's argument for the existence of variably composed social groupings based on both sociological and ecological factors is appropriate in this context (Peterson 1974:23–24).

Spring

Subsistence

Early spring (October) brings an end, haltingly at first, to the rigors of winter as herds of seal return to the rocky capes along the Atlantic. As Bridges notes:

> It had been an age-long custom among the Ona to go from time to time to certain places on the Atlantic Coast and kill seal for the blubber and skins. On one such occasion a considerable number of Ona ventured to Cape Peñas, a prominent headland where the seal came ashore in hundreds . . . the craving for oil and fat seal-flesh was . . . great . . . after living for months on lean guanaco meat [1951:268].

Unfortunately, he does not tell us how many Ona were in this group, only that 14 were murdered by whites, with some survivors escaping (p. 268–269). We can suppose the group to have been quite a bit larger, for nowhere else in his account does he refer to 15 Ona as a large party. Seal were killed with bow and arrow or occasionally netted (Lothrop 1928:81). Mussels were also collected from the coast at sealing time (although not exclusively at this season), as were limpets and conch (Lothrop 1928:33).

Migratory birds return in spring; among these, the several varieties of geese were quite important to the Ona both for eggs and meat (Bridges 1951:447–448). Goose eggs were collected by women and children, as well as by men to sustain them on the hunt. Grown birds were shot with untipped arrows, snared, or drowned. Other birds, of course, returned as well, and a variety of eggs, including those of various duck species, were available—eggs were eaten both fresh and when the embryos were developed (Bridges 1951:448). According to Lothrop (1928:83), birds might also be killed with a sling. Ducks and geese were available most often near the coast where grassy waterways provided feeding grounds. Here elaborate systems of pole "gates" would be set in advance, later, groups camping nearby would set snares and take many birds.

Guanaco were also hunted in the lowlands, especially the young when a few weeks old (Bridges 1951:519). The meat from these young animals was considered a delicacy, and their skins were made into special robes, as were those of yearlings (1951: Plate XXXVI). The meat of older guanaco was lean and of poor quality, hence the emphasis on newborn animals (1951:300), and marrow was eaten as at other times of year (p. 308). Hunting in the higher forest was not always successful during this season (p. 308–309).

Other resources available in spring included the tuco-tuco, more easily taken with the melting of sheet ice and rejuvenation of grasses in the rolling lands near the coast. In the deciduous beech zone, young trees yielded an edible sap, and several kinds of tree fungi were available to unsuccessful guanaco hunters (Bridges 1951:304–305). The sap and tree fungi were collected by the women while searching for firewood (p. 306). Small birds were also available in the forest (p. 307).

There is no ethnographic evidence suggesting that differing features of technology are sufficient to distinguish spring guanaco camps in the low forest from those of other seasons of the year. However, coastal camps at this time of year would probably have had the seal net in addition to other gear already described, and they would be large in relation to littoral camps at other times of the year.

Population Distribution

During spring, encampments seem to have been split between the coast and lower woodlands. This is clear from references to guanaco hunting (forest) and seal hunting. References to specific group sizes are too few to permit an elaborate and well-documented case. From the evidence cited (Bridges 1951:268) and from one reference to a Haush coastal camp of 50 persons, however, groups of 50 to 80 seem likely (Lothrop 1928:108–110). Perhaps archeological evidence could shed more light on this problem. Guanaco hunting camps were smaller, and

Bridges (1951:299) refers to scattered groups of 2 or 3 persons. His explanation of these low numbers is in terms of fear of raids. Nonetheless, it took a few days to gather a party of 50 or 60 individuals to the upland forest, and an aggregation of this size forced hunts at long distances (1951:300). Apparently, this was not the best time of year for large camps in the forest zone (1951:304–305), and guanaco camps were more likely to be in the range of 20–30 persons. In general, population mobility in the uplands was limited during this season by flooded streams.

Social Organization

Spring guanaco camps undoubtedly often displayed the same general core of male consanguines as noted for similar sized camps at other times of year. There are no specific references to any ritual or lodge-type activities during this season.

Although the general concern of this chapter is with regular seasonal patterns, Bridges does give an account of a "whale feast" one spring on the Atlantic Coast near Cape San Pablo. At this gathering, there were more than 150 Ona divided into two nearby encampments. The two encampments focused on the Namjisk and Cape San Pablo Groups, with the Mountain Group (heavily married into the Cape San Pablo Group) absorbed by the latter (Bridges 1951:313–315).

Again, although no references are made specifically to social relationships in the seal-hunting camps, we can gain some clues from the means by which men of the Mountain Group appear to have gained access to coastal resources. One such means was through sisters. Halimink, a hunter of the Mountain Group, had a sister who was married to Tininisk, shaman of the Cape San Pablo Group (Bridges 1951:557). At the "whale feast" just cited, the Mountain Group camped with the Cape San Pablo Group. There are other instances of these two groups (specifically including Halimink and Tininisk) camping on the coast in the latter's territory (Bridges 1951:222, 335). Talimeot, the cormorant hunter from the Mountain Group, closely related in the male line to Halimink, also enjoyed access to the camps of Tininisk (Bridges 1951:217). We cannot be certain, but his wife may also have come from Cape San Pablo.

In another instance, we can trace the marriage of one Ahnikan of the Mountain Group (his father was the brother or half-brother of Halimink; his mother was from Namjisk) to the eldest daughter of Houshken, shaman of the Northern Group being pressed toward the south by sheep ranchers. We should note that, upon the death of Ahnikan's first wife, he should have gotten her younger sister as a replacement. However, the Northern shaman had previously promised the younger daughter to the only son of Tininisk, shaman of the south-coastal Cape San Pablo Group (Bridges 1951:361) which had been trying to gain access to southern territory. This may be an attempt to achieve these ends through affinal relationships. The territorial habits of the Cape San Pablo Group are also pertinent: "The hunting-grounds of this party lay between Nokake Mountain and the Atlantic coast, along which they extended from Cape Santa Ines, past Cape San

Pablo to Policarpo Cove, thus trespassing across the borders of the Aush"
(Bridges 1951:212).

Two of the most important male figures in this group, Tininisk (the shaman)
and Kankoat, claimed no male relation, but they were heavily married into the
Haush (or Aush) on whose coastal territory they trespassed (Bridges 1951:213).
Significantly, we know that it is possible to become a shaman and, thus, a focus of
social power in Ona society without the support of male relatives upon which to
draw. This situation would seem unlikely in a strict patrilineal system in which
the labor–subsistence requirements of status would then have to be met by affines
or unrelated personnel. On the other hand, this situation could also indicate the
importance of access to female labor as a basis for social power. Even though it is
generally accepted that there was a greater subsistence contribution on the part
of males, this possibility should not be dismissed out of hand.

This evidence provides a substantial basis from which to argue that access to
territory could be systematically gained through relationships generated at marriage. Moreover, the available information suggests that, more often than not, this
means of access was focused on coastal resources in terms of which the exploitative role of women was quite important (Bridges 1951:391). A particular base-
camp group on the coast, then, might have been characterized in large part by
affinal relationships (Halimink and sister with her husband). The camp would
likely have displayed patrilocality (Tininisk and son) and uxorilocality and,
perhaps, have included persons who claimed no close relationships with anyone.
It is reasonable to assume that many spring seal camps conformed to this type of
composition. The affinal relationships (because of the greater possible number of
social relationships, especially in the context of polygyny) could, in part, along
with abundant resources, account for the larger size of these groups and their
access to long stretches of coast. I am suggesting that, as a consequence of both
resource and social factors, spring sealing camps were the largest regular Ona
encampments.

Summer

Subsistence

In summer, as in winter, the thrust of subsistence was not focused on the
several most preferred species (guanaco, tuco-tuco, etc.). During this time, the
exploitation of littoral resources became most important.

Mussels may have been the most important single resource and were collected
by women at low tides (Lothrop 1928:32, 111), when as much as a mile of beach
was exposed or under a few inches of water (Bridges 1951:249, 465). Other
shellfish included limpet and conch. Fish and eels were also an important summer resource, collected by women from tidal pools (Bridges 1951:215). Conger
eels and fish were killed with the short spears tipped with guanaco bone (Bridges
1951:250) that were adapted from the Yahgan (Lothrop 1928). Such resources

were evidently quite dependable during those summer months, and women from a group near Bridges' farm on the Atlantic Coast evidently made significant contributions to his diet in addition to that of their own men (1951:358, 391). Crabs provided a smaller contribution to the diet, presumably collected incidentally with fish and shellfish. The importance of women in providing old husbands (or poor hunters) with a diet of fish and shellfish has been generally underestimated (Bridges 1951:391). Although the egg collecting season was past, a great variety of sea birds were hunted along the coast by the men (Bridges 1951:215), in the same fashion as was already described; geese and ducks were also important resources in the lower waterways (1951:357, 451).

In the adjacent grass zones, tuco-tuco were plentiful, and grass seeds were collected. These grass seeds were collected by women and roasted on round stones (Lothrop 1928:67). The seeds were then ground and mixed with water.

Guanaco were scattered in the lower forest and in localities where the forest extended along river valleys to the coast. Although they were generally not available in large numbers in one locale, heavy wind conditions permitted the persevering hunter to make successful stalks. Some hunting, evidently took place in higher forests (1000 feet) as well, for one November Bridges recounts evidence of hunters using dogs in that zone and their success in taking an upland goose (1951:247). In midsummer, such highland hunting probably would not be very productive as guanaco had not yet moved upland in significant numbers. From the archeologist's point of view, summer subsistence activities would not generate base and hunting camp sites distinct from those already discussed (in the context of other seasons) on the basis of specialized implements; rather, the distinguishing features would be faunal remains, location, and general camp size.

Population Distribution

In summer, the Ona ranged further than at any other time of the year (Bridges 1951:212, 215). There was no single geographic focus to their subsistence activities, but a strong tendency to exploit the coastal zones and lowland forests over a wide area is evident. There was also some scattering throughout, and mobility was fairly high.

The size of summer subsistence groups was highly variable. In the summer of 1901, a "party" of 20 Ona visited at Harberton on the Beagle Channel, but, since Bridges gave them work and food, it is uncertain how many would have been together otherwise (1951:317). If anything, access to European food supplies made a larger encampment possible. In late summer, a group of 5 or 6 families (25–30 individuals) camped in the deciduous forest zone north of the Beagle Channel (Bridges 1951:321). They too had come to seek Bridges at work in the forest to gain satisfaction in a dispute with him—again, one suspects that extra onlookers were attracted. On the other hand, Bridges accidentally ran into a camp of 10 or 11 Ona men and their families (50 individuals) on a high tableland south of Lake Fagnano on December 29, 1897 (1951:248). This camp had "plenty of guanaco meat" and is the largest cited during the summer season.

Despite these instances of fairly large camps, smaller groups may have been more the norm during the summer. Several parties of one or two families encamped are specifically mentioned (Bridges 1951:267, 269), and general references are made to the many "small" parties stopping near Beagle Channel for periods of a week or 10 days (p. 212).

In short, a reasonable average range of base camp size during summer would have been 10–25 persons. Evidence of this tendency for population to concentrate in the coastal zone is strengthened by reference to many summer visits at the Bridges' coastal farms of Harberton (Beagle Channel) and Viamonte (Atlantic Coast). Furthermore, the lesser importance of male hunting pursuits at this time is indicated by the inclination of Ona men to work on the various Bridges farms in the summer (when wives were supplying food) but not in the fall. For it was fall during which the Ona returned to the highlands again, hunting guanaco and carrying on their lodge activities.

Social Organization

With the greater range of territory exploited during summer, utilization of the coast and exploitation of marine resources by females was heightened. As was argued for the spring season, affinal relationships must have played one of the more important roles in joining families together at coastal camping sites. It seems likely that the majority of summer encampments, although not as large, were similar in composition to the spring sealing camps. In addition, single biological families moving about on their own seem to have been a common feature of this season, while the larger father-son-brother–oriented (patrifilial) guanaco hunting camps also occurred to some degree. Such summer groups were likely quite short lived and "chameleon-like" in their social arrangements.

Seasonal Phases: Summary and Discussion

It seems evident from the data presented for each of the seasons that there were significant differences in Ona subsistence, population distribution, and organizational behavior from one season to the next (see Figure 6.2). Specifically, the range of largest average encampment sizes varied as follows: fall, 40–60; winter, 10–20; spring, 50–80; and summer, 10–25. While a large margin of error is possible due to the nature of available data, the general pattern is clear.

The focus on most exploited resources also varies significantly from season to season as follows: fall—guanaco, geese, ducks, tuco-tuco; winter—guanaco, tuco-tuco, mussels, fish, cormorant; spring—seal, birds and birds' eggs, fish, mussels; summer—mussels, eels, fish, marine birds, guanaco. Guanaco, tuco-tuco, mussels, and some birds were exploited yearround, but their quantity and loca-

EXPLANATION: Dependence indicates whether major thrust of subsistence activity is specifically male-centered, female-centered or not clearly sex defined (mixed). Population size indicates largest regular group sizes during given period. Smaller groups may occur concurrently. Distribution indicates geographic focus of population at given time. (focus = majority) Scattering may be throughout several zones simultaneously. Species utilized are listed in order of importance. An italicized species indicates that it is a focal resource and far outweighs the other species in importance. A cross-section or profile of Tierra del Fuego Island from mountains to Atlantic coast is superimposed in gray to indicate the general pattern of seasonal mobility through the various altitude zones.

Month:	JANUARY (mid-summer)	FEBRUARY	MARCH (first autumn)	APRIL (fall)	MAY	JUNE (mid-winter)
Dependence:	mixed	male + mixed	male	male	male	male + mixed
Population size:	10 – 25	30 – 40	40 – 60	40 – 60	30 – 40	10 – 20
Distribution:	midlands and scattered	uplands and scattered	upland/mountains	upland/mountains	uplands to midlands	midlands to coast (low mobility and scattered)
Species utilized:	*guanaco, mussels,* eel, tuco-tuco, fish, birds (geese), limpets, crabs	*guanaco,* mussels, geese, ducks, tuco-tuco, fungi, berries	*guanaco,* upland goose, tuco-tuco, ducks, mussels, limpets, berries	*guanaco, small birds, tuco-tuco,* mussels, other, berries	*guanaco, tuco-tuco, upland birds,* mussels, other	guanaco, tuco-tuco, *mussels, fish,* fox, fungi, leather, bark, small birds

Month:	JULY	AUGUST	SEPTEMBER (spring)	OCTOBER	NOVEMBER	DECEMBER
Dependence:	mixed	mixed	male + female	male + female	female + mixed	mixed
Population size:	5 – 15	5 – 15	20 – 40	50 – 80	20 – 30	10 – 25
Distribution:	midlands to coast (low mobility and scattered)	midlands and scattered	split: coast and midlands, some scattered	coast	coast and midlands	coast to midlands and scattered
Species utilized:	birds, tuco-tuco, *fox, guanaco,* fish, mussels, limpets, other	tuco-tuco, marine birds, fox, fungi, fish, mussels, guanaco	*seal, guanaco,* birds + bird *eggs,* mussels, tuco-tuco, other	*seal,* birds and bird *eggs,* mussels, fish, guanaco	*mussels, crabs, eel, limpets,* birds, fish, guanaco, seal	*eel, limpets, mussels, birds,* fish, tuco-tuco, guanaco

Figure 6.2 Ona resource utilization and seasonality, Tierra Del Fuego Island.

273

tion in catchable form varied with the season. It does seem clear, however, that, in accordance with traditional accounts, guanaco *was* the most important single species on a yearround basis.

Although few zones were virtually uninhabited at a given time, the locus and distribution of population definitely varied with the seasons as follows: fall—lower to upper reaches of deciduous forest zone and aggregated; winter—lower forest to coast and dispersed; spring—split between coast and lower forest and aggregated; summer—coast and adjacent zones with greatest extent of range and generally dispersed.

Social organizational features display both variability and stability. There does seem to have been a certain consistency in that close male relatives gathered for the pursuit of guanaco. On the other hand, distinct social features can be related to seasonal changes: fall—patrifiliation and ceremonial lodge; winter—flexible social groupings; spring—tendency to utilize affinal relationships; summer—affinal relationships and other variable groupings. These data are summarized in Figure 6.2.

The evidence for environmental variability is considered adequate to support the proposition that seasonality in the Fuegian environment was sufficient to have required distinct (not discrete) sets of adaptive cultural behavior. These adaptive responses in subsistence, population distribution, and social features assumed a certain amount of internal consistency by season. For this reason, they are considered here as adaptive phases.

Due to the habits of guanaco in fall, the Ona males intensively exploited the most compressed (see Figure 6.1) part of their annual range. One would expect the combination of geographical "compression" in the mountain areas and the male hunting core's need to prevent others from disturbing guanaco in the region they intended to hunt to have generated the strongest expression of territoriality during this season of the year. Competition for undisturbed hunting territory in the mountains appears to have been keen; by focusing on the narrower (than affinal ties from plural wives) network of close male relatives, the Ona could amass enough skilled personnel to exploit guanaco intensively in a given locale. This intensive exploitation and its associated large camps of women, children, and dogs, rather than force of arms, kept outsiders away. Such a base camp made hunting in near proximity impossible. This is another reason why dependents and dogs were lumped into one camp, for, if small family groups were scattered at short distances over the mountains, guanaco would have been disturbed over a large area. Thus, the practice was to aggregate as many dependents and dogs as could be provided for and to let the men disperse quietly in small parties. The degree to which unrelated personnel were brought in would depend partly on the size of the initial male core and partly on the point at which feeding a huge mass of dependents would mean hunting and carrying game from too far afield. Within this context, some reciprocity in access to resources brought members of the coastal Cape San Pablo Group (and others) to the highlands each fall. As has been argued elsewhere (Stuart 1972), the patrifilial pattern was also probably altered by a tendency to distribute the subsistence benefits provided by the most skilled hunters among different social groups without primary reference to kinship.

It would appear from the evidence that 30 or 40 dependents in one mountain valley was about right. If 10 hunters was an average size for a patrilineal "core" (Baer and Schmitz 1965) before heavy population decline set in (1880s), then conceivably few unrelated hunters might have been in such camps. However, this was not the case in contact times, and affines or unrelated personnel were encamped together. Access to membership in the male lodge may have functioned to regulate the size of a group in a given area; in addition, it certainly provided a social focus for fall hunting activity.

Winter encampments, due to scarcer resources and weather conditions, were limited in size, relocated less often, and more isolated. Since weather and resources varied from locale to locale, it is not surprising that a fixed pattern of group composition has not emerged. This variability in subsistence situation, in combination with variable access to social relations because of uncertain traveling conditions, provides a convincing argument for variability in group composition from locale to locale. Simple difficulties in the availability of firewood and tree fungi in deep snow would tend to keep population from aggregating even if conditions (foodwise) were equally poor everywhere.

In spring, access to coastal resources was important, and littoral resources were plentiful. Although the Ona female's role in subsistence activities has generally been minimized, I suggest that her importance was great on a seasonal basis. At this time, it appears that economic ties with females were emphasized. The exploitation of seal herds and an occasional stranded whale likely provided more calories in one place than at any other time of the year. In such instances, it appears that individuals gathered together from a wider social network. Since males exploited the seal herds, one might argue that an extension of the social network was along male lines were it not for specific evidence suggesting that access to such resources was often gained through wives. This social reaching out to affines may have "set the stage" for the composition of many groups in the summer season.

During the summer, we find a situation similar to spring—a recurring interest in affinal relations plus a heightened emphasis on or interest in the exploitative potential of female labor. One might ask how affinal relationships in spring generated larger social groupings, while, in summer, smaller groups were the norm. There are two likely reasons. First, females were providing a major portion of the summer diet. Thus, a highly renowned and successful fall guanaco hunter who reinforced his position by means of a "large" (relative to unsuccessful hunters) entourage of dependents would have needed access to more than one female's exploitative potential during the summer season. By custom, such a male might gain additional female subsistence labor by demanding as a second wife a younger sister of his first wife, that is, by activating an option granted by affines. Second, a group generated in this fashion was easily limited, for relationships with affines were easier to abrogate or ignore when convenient than relationships with male consanguines. Thus, the group size variability of summer camps could be "managed" by using affinal relations. Interesting, in this context, is the variety of ways in which second wives might be obtained: by a younger sister "helping" the older sister, by demanding a younger sister of her father, by abducting a woman unrelated to the first wife, or by taking as a wife the daughter (if fathered by someone else) of the first wife (Bridges 1951:359–361). Mathematically, the various means of obtaining a wife coupled with polygyny must have provided a tempting array of social networks, both large and small, to manipulate.

In conclusion, there is serious doubt whether or not an ethnologist stationed in a fall guanaco base camp (with lodge) would have ascribed to the Ona the same on-the-ground organization as would one studying a spring sealing or summer fishing camp. This again demonstrates that a dynamic view of Ona social organization is necessary, for the two hypothetical ethnologists would certainly be observing variations in organizational flexibility between fall and spring. Although this appears to be the case, the actual mechanics of these changes in "structural pose," or adaptive phase, will not be forthcoming from existing data. Thus, we should turn our attention to other potential sources of information.

An Ethnographic Typology of Sites and Implications for the Archeological Record

This section explicitly abstracts available ethnographic information to suggest several types of sites that might one day be documented in the archeological record. The purpose here is twofold: first, to direct attention to potential archeological research and, second, to suggest that such research can profitably seek to test and refine the notions presented herein with regard to the seasonal nature of Ona adaptations. This description of sites is arranged primarily according to the expected degree of focalization (attention to one species) in subsistence behavior as suggested by the ethnographic data. The intention is to provide general models for such sites that the archeologist may use in identifying initial hypotheses for field research. Moreover, I do not intend to formally define visibility for the archeologist but, rather, simply to suggest what is plausible from ethnographic evidence gathered between 1880 and 1928.

Specialized Sites

Fall Guanaco Hunting Lodge Camp

These encampment sites should occur primarily in association with the deciduous forest zone, concentrated within an altitude range of from 650 to 1600 feet above sea level. To the south of Lake Fagnano, these sites may occur up to an altitude of 2000 feet. These camps represent an occupation period averaging from 2 to 6 weeks, with recurring use over many years. Specific situations would most likely be in elevated, grassy areas with fairly dense surrounding woods and in association with springs or seeps as sources of water (rather than rivers or slow streams) (Bridges 1951:334). Based on an average camp size of 40–60 persons, 8 to 12 fire hearths are expected at a given time—with recurring use, this number might be multiplied many times, and distinct isolated cooking areas might not be evident. The precise arrangements of family units is not known. Activities definitely associated with this area of the camp would be final butchering, bone marrow processing, hide processing, and processing of any vegetable food. The locus of primary guanaco butchering remains to be documented, as does primary tool preparation, including bow and arrow preparation as indicated by wood scrapers, arrow shaft polishers, and so on (see Lothrop 1928).

The lodge, a three-fourths circle pole "tipi" measuring roughly 16–20 feet across (Bridges 1951: Plate XL; Lothrop 1928: Figs. 38–39), should be located to the east at an average distance of 100 to 200 yards. Activities definitely associated with the lodge are processing of ceremonial paraphernalia and cooking of guanaco. Flint and glass tool preparation is suspected, but not documented. There was one fire hearth within the lodge.

Artifact assemblages in this type of camp have already been noted under fall subsistence. Since hide processing was a female activity, differential tool use in the lodge and camping areas is expected. Specifically, a higher frequency of hide scrapers in the encampment area is likely, but other differences require documentation.

Faunal remains identifying such a site should include those of guanaco (especially cracked and burnt bone of adults in hearth areas) and geese, especially goslings. Secondarily, evidence of duck, other bird species, tuco-tuco and barberry in small quantity may be present.

Guanaco Hunting Base Camps

These encampment sites are similar to the lodge camp described earlier with several exceptions. Specifically, in situations in which no lodge is present, these sites may be smaller on the average, the majority having six to eight fire sites. Since male activities were not directed away from the main camp, the full range of activities and associated artifact usage would probably have taken place within the main camping area. The frequency of hide processing tools should be higher than in generalized subsistence camps. There should be evidence of basic tool preparation. Length of occupation at a given time was probably shorter—1 to 2 weeks—and recurring use over the years would not have been as systematic as with the lodge camp. Site situation and faunal remains would be likely indicators of the season of occupation. Higher elevations are expected in fall and the lowest elevations in midsummer or midwinter. Adult guanaco remains, subadult birds, and berry seeds are indicators of fall; adult guanaco bones and an absence of migratory birds would indicate winter; the bones of adult or very young guanaco would be found in spring along with geese; in summer, there would be bones of adult and subadult guanaco and indications of migratory birds.

Guanaco Hunting Camp

Camps of this type can be expected to occur yearround scattered throughout the deciduous forest zone (600–1600 feet). They represent the hunting activities of three to six men on an average. One or two hearths are likely. Length of occupation would range from 1 to 3 or 4 days, and the degree of recurrence in occupation is not known but is suspected to be low. Activities would include some butchering of guanaco into large units and, during longer occupations, some final butchering as well. Evidence of vegetable food processing and hide processing (scrapers) should be minimal or nonexistent. Some retouching (bone chipper) of arrow points is likely, but basic tool preparation is not expected.

The artifact assemblage expected for this type of camp is noted under fall subsistence. Artifactual evidence of hide processing (scrapers) or marrow processing (grease stones) is not likely. Some retouching of points (bone chipper) is expected. But arrow and bow making activities are not expected; nor are arrow shaft polishers and so on (see Lothrop 1928).

Faunal remains would be limited; relatively few cracked guanaco bones are expected in the fire pit, and other remains of birds, tuco-tuco, and so on would likely be greatest when no guanaco have been taken—the mark, perhaps, of an unsuccessful hunt. Again, site occurrence in different altitude zones and associated faunal remains could, together, be taken as basic indicators of season. Although these sites were ethnographically quite visible, the degree of archeological visibility is questionable.

Spring Sealing Base Camps

These specialized subsistence camps occur within a mile or so of areas characterized by rocky capes and headlands, primarily on the Atlantic Coast. The data are not clear, but they quite likely represent an occupation period in excess of several weeks. Based on suspected camp sizes of 60–80 persons or more, 12 to 20 fire hearths are expected. Recurring occupation in specific localities is likely, due to habitual location of seal herds. The incidence of burnt, cracked guanaco bone in the fire hearths should be quite low. Although there is no specific ethnographic evidence, seal bone should replace the guanaco in these camp fires, for one purpose of throwing bones into the fire was to keep the splintered remains from the camp dogs.

Site setting is expected to be generally in high, fairly open hill areas near the coast (Bridges 1951:334). The internal structure of these camps is nowhere documented in detail, but, as with the whale feast described earlier, one might find several discrete clusters of family hearth areas.

A nearly complete representation of the Ona artifact assemblage should occur in such sites. Activities would include tool preparation, arrow point retouching, butchering, and some associated fish spearing nearby. Thus, women's guanaco-bone fish spear tips are likely to be more highly represented than in other resource focalized sites. It is not known whether or not specialized fleshers and scrapers were used for seal processing—it would be quite useful to have that archeological information.

Faunal remains should show a high proportion of seal. Other possible remains found in much smaller proportions would include adult geese, ducks, bird egg fragments, mussels, and fish.

Finally, due to short distances between camps and the sea, we do not expect to find special male seal hunting camps, but no specific ethnographic information is available, and future research is required.

Generalized Sites

Generalized Littoral Resource Camps

These sites may occur to some degree throughout the year near the Atlantic or Beagle Channel shores. However, if the general model of seasonal subsistence presented in the first section of this chapter is accurate, occurrence should be primarily in summer and secondarily in winter. As these camp sizes vary from 10 to 30 individuals, 2 to 6 hearths are expected. We suspect a high degree of variability in the length of occupation.

I propose that the smallest of these camps were utilized for the longest periods of time. This is deduced from ethnographic references indicating that old men and incompetent hunters are fed on fish by their wives. A test of this hypothesis might be documentation of a higher depositional rate for mussel shells, cormorant bones, fish bone, and so on within a given area than in the larger, more generalized and supposedly shorter term camps. Secondarily, more "blurring" of hearth and other features could be expected in the larger, short-term reoccupations. This hypothesis would be further supported by the documentation of a lower incidence of guanaco bone and bones of large bird species for the smaller camps (of incompetent hunters). Finally, the artifactual assemblage, in the camp of an incompetent or aged hunter, could be expected to show a lower frequency of fleshers, hide scrapers, or bow and arrow making artifacts than the assemblage of the larger, more generalized camp.

Faunal remains are expected to include (fairly visible) shells of mussels, some limpets, and conch. Other remains indicating a winter encampment would include a high proportion of cormorant and some fish. In summer, seasonal indicators would include remains of migratory fowl and eel.

Generalized Subsistence Camps

In midwinter and midsummer, ethnographic evidence suggests, but does not formally confirm, the occurrence of encampments in the lower deciduous forest and broken grassland zones that do not focus on any one or two species to the degree evidenced at other seasons of the year in these same biotic zones. Group size is expected to vary, on an average, between 10 and 20 individuals yielding 2 to 4 hearths. Period of occupation is not known, but a few days to, at most, several weeks seems probable. These sites should be similar in most ways to the smaller guanaco hunting base camps with several important exceptions. The variety of faunal remains (with no one or two species predominating) should be greater than at other similar sites in these zones, and, artifactually, a lower incidence of hide fleshers and scrapers and points is expected when compared with guanaco base camp assemblages.

/Klokten/ Camp Sites

These encampments are known ethnographically to be occupied by one or two (one hearth) young males for periods of one to a few days. They occur throughout the year and in all biotic zones; such camps are located so as to avoid other ordinary encampments. Known activities include butchering and preparation of large and small game and vegetable resources. Suspected (but not documented) activities run the full gamut of tool preparation, hide processing, and so on. Since they emphasize initiates learning how to make out on their own, these small, ephemeral camps may be generally below the threshold of archeological visibility.

The intention of this section has been to direct attention to future archeological research, and the archeologist reading this will, no doubt, be left with many questions regarding preservation, visibility, deposition, specialization in the Ona tool kit, and so on. However, the difficulty encountered here in outlining descriptively distinct types of sites may be significant itself, since the preceding outline of archeological sites, abstracted from ethnographic data, suggests lower archeological visibility for variation in Ona sites than was initially expected. Intersite variability in internal site structure from one season to the next may not prove to be dramatic as, for example, in distinct winter versus summer house types. Thus, the difficulty in determining the season of occupation for Ona sites based on internal site features would have to be overcome by reliance on sometimes subtle information about faunal remains and geographical distribution. This suggests a specific research problem central to the argument presented in this chapter.

Since intersite variability is generally expected to increase with the magnitude of seasonal variation, archeological field verification of low intersite variability in the Ona case could cast doubt on *(1)* the degree of seasonal variation in Fuegian environment suggested in this chapter or *(2)* the use of seasonal variation to explain intersite and, presumably, behavioral variability. In Tierra del Fuego, the relationship between seasonal variation and intersite variability could be initially tested in a quite straightforward manner: Since one can expect the magnitude of seasonal variation to correspond to altitude differences, intersite variability should be greater in southern Ona sites where the altitude of site location ranges from approximately 0 to 2500 feet than in northern Ona sites where site altitude ranges from 0 to 600 feet. At this point, an accurate assessment of seasonal variations in Fuegian environment simply requires much more field data than is available.

Conclusion

As an ethnologist, I might prefer to suggest that the case for seasonal phases in Ona behavior has been tested and rests on the available ethnographic evidence. Yet, this is not so, for all that has been established is an apparent correlation between variability in environment and variability in Ona subsistence, population distribution, and social–organizational features. Although this may be sufficient to set aside the "classic patrilineal hunting society" characterization in the literature and to point out variations in the degree of on-the-ground organizational flexibility during the yearly subsistence cycle, it is not sufficient to permit a statement of causality. The basic question is to what degree Ona flexibility is, when compared to rigidity at a given point in time, a function of flux in the environment. Since European influx resulted in dramatic changes in the environment during the period for which ethnographic information is available, it must be determined, first, whether the subsistence cycle outlined here was typical and a function of long-term patterns in the Fuegian environment or the immediate result of ecological circumstances induced by the introduction of a foreign population. As no new independent body of ethnographic data (against which appropriate hypotheses can be tested) is likely forthcoming, such data and the testing process will have to be produced by the archeologist.

REFERENCES

Baer, G., and C. A. Schmitz
    1965   On the social organization of the Ona (Selk'nam). *Journal de la Societe des Americanistes de Paris* (n.s.) **54**:23–29.
Berndt, Ronald M.
    1972   The Walmadjiri and Gugadja. In *Hunters and gatherers today,* edited by M. G. Bicchieri. New York: Holt. Pp. 177–216.
Bicchieri, Marco G.
    1972   *Hunters and gatherers today.* New York: Holt.
Bock, Philip K.
    1974   *Modern cultural anthropology.* 2d ed. New York: Knopf.
Braun-Menendez, A.
    1939   *Pequeña historia Fuegiña.* Buenos Aires: editorial Francisco de Aguirre.
    1969   *Pequeña historia Magallanica.* 5th ed. Buenos Aires: editorial Francisco de Aguirre.
Bridges, E. Lucas
    1938   Burying the Hatchet. *Man* **38**:4–7.
    1951   *Uttermost part of the earth.* London: Reader's Union (Hodder and Stoughton).

Butland, Gilbert J.
    1957   *The human geography of Southern Chile. Institute of British Geographers Publication* No. 24. (London)
Cooper, John M.
    1917   *Analytical and critical bibliography of the tribes of Tierra del Fuego. Bureau of American Ethnology Bulletin* No. 63. Washington, D.C.: Smithsonian Institution.
    1946   The Ona. In *Handbook of South American Indians,* edited by J. H. Steward. *Bureau of American Ethnology Bulletin* No. 143, Vol. 1, Washington, D.C.: Smithsonian Institution. Pp. 107–125.
Damas, David
    1968   The Diversity of Eskimo Societies. In *Man the hunter,* edited by Richard B. Lee and Irven DeVore. Chicago: Aldine. Pp. 111–117.
Espenshade, Edward B., and Joel L. Morrison (Eds.)
    1974   *Goode's world atlas.* 14th ed. Chicago: Rand McNally.
Gardner, Peter
    1968   Discussion 35 b. In *Man the hunter,* edited by Richard B. Lee, and Irven DeVore. Chicago: Aldine. Pp. 339–344.
Gearing, Fred
    1958   The structural poses of 18th century Cherokee villages. *American Anthropologist* **60**(6):1148–1157.
Godley, E. J.
    1960   The botany of southern Chile in relation to New Zealand and the Subantarctic. *Proceedings of the Royal Society,* Series B **152:**457–475.
Goodall, John D. *et al.*
    1946   *Las aves de Chile.* Buenos Aires: Platt Establecimientos Gráficos.
Gusinde, Martin
    1923   Vierte Reise zum Feuerlandstamm der Ona. *Anthropos,* Vol. 18–19. Pp. 966–977.
    1924   Cuarta expedicion a la Tierra del Fuego. *Publicaciones del Museo de Etnologia y Antropologia de Chile* **4:**7–67.
    1925   Elemente aus der Weltanschauung der Ona and Alakaluf. *International Congress of Americanists, session* 21, Vol. 1. Pp. 123–147. (Goteborg)
    1926   Die Eigentumsverhaltnisse bei den Selk'nam auf Feuerland, *Zeitschrift für Ethnologie,* Vol. 58. Pp. 398–412. (Berlin)
    1928   Das hochste Wesen bei den Selk'nam auf Feuerland. In *Festschrift: P. W. Schmidt,* edited by Koppers. Vienna: Mechitharisten. Pp. 269–274.
    1931   *Die Feuerland Indianer.* Vienna: Modling.
Helm, June
    1968   The nature of Dogrib socio-territorial groups. In *Man the hunter,* edited by Richard B. Lee and Irven DeVore. Chicago: Aldine. Pp. 118–125.
    1972   The Dogrib Indians. In *Hunters and gatherers today,* edited by M. G. Bicchieri. New York: Holt. Pp. 51–89.
Kuschel, G.
    1960   Terrestrial zoology in southern Chile. *Proceedings of the Royal Society,* Series B **152:** 540–550.
Lathrap, Donald W.
    1968   Discussion 9a. In *Man the hunter,* edited by Richard B. Lee and Irven DeVore. Chicago: Aldine. Pp. 93–94.
Lee, Richard B.
    1968   What hunters do for a living, or how to make out on scarce resources. In *Man the hunter,* edited by Richard B. Lee and Irven DeVore. Chicago:Aldine. Pp. 30–48.
Lee, Richard B., and Irven DeVore (Editors)
    1968   *Man the hunter.* Chicago: Aldine.

Lothrop, Samuel K.
    1928   The Indians of Tierra del Fuego. *Contributions,* Vol. 10, Museum of the American Indian. New York: Heye Foundation.

Lowie, Robert H.
    1949   Social and political organization of the tropical forest and marginal tribes. In *Handbook of South American Indians,* edited by J. H. Steward. *Bureau of American Ethnology Bulletin* No. 143, Vol. 5. Washington, D.C.: Smithsonian Institution. Pp. 313–350.

Marret, R. R., and T. K. Penniman
    1931   *Spencer's last journey: Being the journal of an expedition to Tierra Del Fuego by the late Sir Baldwin Spencer.* Oxford: Clarendon Press.

Murdock, George P.
    1967   Ethnographic atlas. *Ethnology* **4:**343–348.

Peterson, Nicolas
    1974   The importance of women in determining the composition of residential groups in aboriginal Australia. In *Woman's Role in aboriginal society,* edited by Fay Gale. Canberra, Australia: Australian Institute of Aboriginal Studies. Pp. 16–27.
    1975   Hunter–gatherer territoriality: The perspective from Australia, *American Anthropologist* **77**(1):53–68.

Rogers, Edward S.
    1972   The Mistassini Cree. In *Hunters and gatherers today,* edited by M. G. Bicchieri. New York: Holt. Pp. 90–137.

Rudolph, W. E.
    1934   Southern Patagonia. *Geographical Review* **24:**62–79.

Service, Elman R.
    1962   *Primitive social organization.* New York: Random House.

Steward, Julian H.
    1955   *Theory of culture change.* Urbana, Ill.: University of Illinois Press.
    1968   Causal factors and processes in the evolution of pre-farming societies. In *Man the hunter,* edited by Richard B. Lee and Irven DeVore. Chicago: Aldine. Pp. 321–324.

Steward, Julian H., and Louis C. Faron
    1959   *Native peoples of South America.* New York: McGraw-Hill.

Stuart, David E.
    1972   Band structure and ecological variability: The Ona and Yahgan of Tierra del Fuego. Unpublished doctoral dissertation, University of New Mexico.

Turnbull, Colin M.
    1968   The importance of flux in two hunting societies. In *Man the hunter,* edited by Richard B. Lee and Irven DeVore. Chicago: Aldine. Pp. 132–137.

Wernstedt, Frederick L.
    1972   *World climatic data.* Lemont, Pa.: Climatic Data Press.

Woodburn, James
    1968   Stability and flexibility in Hadza residential groupings In *Man the hunter,* edited by Richard B. Lee and Irven DeVore. Chicago:Aldine. Pp. 103–110.

Yesner, David R.
    1975   Maritime hunter-gatherers: Demographic and biogeographical models. Paper presented to the Society for American Archeology, Dallas, Texas, May 1975.

Space: Its Organized Use and Analysis

7

A Theoretical Approach to the Study of House Form

ROSALIND L. HUNTER-ANDERSON
University of New Mexico

Introduction: Comments on the Role of Archaeology

Traditionally the role of archaeology has been to discover the past as if it were a chronological series of events occurring in three major domains: geographic regions, ethnic or nationalistic groups, and the human species in general. Archaeological materials were seen as the remnants of previously complete pictures of past events in a specific region, associated with particular ethnic groups or with the history of mankind as a whole. The basic problem was—and is—how to reconstruct these pictures of the past when only a fragmentary record remains. Historical archaeologists partially solve this problem by referring to written records. Similarly, prehistorians have turned to ethnographies.

In the absence of written records describing historical events, on the one hand, and with the availability of ethnographic descriptions, on the other hand, prehistoric archaeologists have developed a mixed mode of interpretation. Pictures of the past are descriptions both of ways of life derived from ethnographies and of postulated historical events. The latter serve to account for abrupt changes that can be observed in the archaeological record (e.g., invasions, migrations, collapses).

Historical and prehistoric archaeology, history, and ethnography have been primarily concerned with description. Much effort has been spent in finding out what, when, and where, rather than why and how. Working within a primarily inductive philosophy of knowledge, workers in these fields expected cause and effect relationships to be manifested once a large body of observations had accumulated. But, since archaeological remains, regardless of their absolute volume, never compose a truly large body of observations as compared to the potential observation volume of past events themselves, archaeology, by definition, has had an inferior status to that of ethnography–ethnology and history.[1] Within the inductive framework, archaeological interpretation has thus been "dependent" on historical and ethnographic sources.

The dependence of prehistory on ethnographies has resulted in a mode of archaeological interpretation known as the *ethnographic analogy*. Ethnographic analogy has been used in such a way as to imply the following concept of knowledge. First, one must know what happened, when, and where. Description of events can be accomplished with considerable safety and high standards of accuracy, namely, scientifically. One can know why and how events happened only *after* the task of description has been completed. Since archaeology can never fully accomplish this task, it cannot contribute much to the answering of why and how questions. In practice, to use an ethnographic analogy has been to cite ethnographic cases that have components similar to those excavated and then to argue that the rest of the past picture, which was not preserved, was similar to the remaining components of the ethnographic picture cited.

In contrast to this view, we do not see the role of archaeology as providing descriptions of ways of life and events of the past, nor do we see the role of ethnography–ethnology as describing the cultural present. Both anthropological subdisciplines should be geared to the explanation of what they observe. To explain means to specify the conditions under which classes of symptoms occur. More precisely, to explain is to suggest models in which certain conditions, by virtue of their specific consequences, cause the observed symptoms to occur regularly. There are no restrictions on what factors in the researcher's experience might function as clues to ignite the cognitive processes that eventually result in an explanatory model. The wealth of observations made by ethnographers and archaeologists may or may not serve as sources of clues or for testing hypotheses.

The components forming the bases of explanatory models are entities "outside" the system or class of phenomena to which the symptoms being explained belong. For instance, consider the symptoms of an illness that today we know is "caused" by germs. Part of the explanation of the symptoms of a particular illness involves certain physiological processes, such as chemical reactions, that eventually lead to the observed symptoms. One may think of these processes as occurring "within" the same system as the symptoms. Germs, however, may not; they

---

[1] It was never contended that archaeology is inferior in terms of the ability to make original observations on human culture. Indeed, in a descriptive framework, in which the actual revelation that something exists or existed is in itself worthwhile knowledge, archaeological "discoveries" are highly prized. However, the weakness of observing nonperishable remnants rather than complete pictures of the past remains.

have an independent existence. In the case of human cultural systems, the "environment" is a general term covering a host of measurable variables whose configurations constitute conditions relevant to the occurrence of cultural symptoms, conditions that are outside the system under study.

Since the majority of ethnographic and archaeological observations have been collected for the purpose of accurate description at the symptom level, most ethnographic accounts do not include systematically recorded data on causal conditions. It is also true that observations and measurements that are sought as test implications derived from theory do not always conform to the confines of a given descriptive orientation. In other words, they may not have been collected at all, or only insufficiently.

Compared to the cultural pictures they represent, archaeological remains are "partial" observations. But, in terms of theory and tested explanations, observation-rich ethnography–ethnology has done rather poorly, judging by rigorous scientific criteria. The meager theory and explanation in ethnology is supporting evidence of the ineffectiveness of descriptive collections of observations in generating scientific knowledge. As anthropologists, both ethnographers and archaeologists make observations about cultural systems, and, in terms of the view adopted here, they are obliged to explain them. Both kinds of researchers may undertake to suggest explanatory models, to derive test implications from them, and to strive to gain access to relevant data. These observations may be the kind made by ethnographers, by archaeologists, or by others, such as climatologists or zoologists. In a deductive explanatory framework, we may find explanations offered for ethnographically observed phenomena tested against archaeological remains and vice versa. In the former case, we could say that it is ethnography–ethnology that "depends" on archaeology.

The Subject of House Form

This chapter presents the results of an attempt to discover the principles explaining one aspect of house variability—the basic shape or form. We suggest specific variables whose consequences are capable of "causing" certain preferences for different house forms, and, ultimately, the different house forms actually observed. Our discussion also includes a few suggestions regarding the adaptive contexts in which the variables may attain the high values that influence a shift to a new house form. As yet, we do not have a complete explanation for house form variations. We feel, however, that our ideas are moving in the right direction and, if pursued further, will eventually lead to a better understanding of the occurrence of different house forms. The subject of house form was chosen for study because it is an aspect of adaptation that can be observed both ethnographically and archaeologically and, as such, it is of interest to both kinds of anthropological research.

Evaluation of Previous Studies of House Form

Descriptive Findings

Although it is possible to view variability in house form as being infinite, it has been observed directly and documented in many ethnographies that some cultures use round houses and others use rectangular ones, while still others use both forms. Archaeological observations have added an evolutionary dimension to the problem. Robbins' (1966) study of correlations between house form and the relative permanence of settlement pattern notes a temporal shift from round to rectangular floor plan of houses in aboriginal North America. This shift is documented in the Mogollon and Anasazi of the southwestern United States and in the eastern United States from ca. 8000 B.C.E. to 1200 C.E. Flannery (1972) documents a similar change in house form in the Near East ca. 7000–5500 B.C.E. The subject of house form was studied by Robbins (1966) and later by Whiting and Ayres (1968). Both of these studies used a mechanical procedure to establish correlations between house form and other cultural traits.

The Correlations

The scientific status of findings in the context of correlational studies should be identified at the outset. The phrase "correlation is not causation" should be familiar to most readers, but no one could dismiss correlations as totally irrelevant to causation. In everyday experience, we are aware of many correlations. Most of them could be measured and expressed in statistical language. The statistical form does not constitute new information in itself. Indeed, a person who statistically expresses the knowledge that rain is related to clouds is at no practical advantage. If we compare the correlational knowledge that clouds are related to rain with what is known today by climatologists, we can see how low the scientific status of some correlations can be. One qualification must be made, however. The low status of this correlation is a function of at least two factors. First, both rain and clouds are equally accessible for direct observation by our natural senses. We have no sense for barometric pressure, and, as a result, we assign a higher status to the correlation between low barometric pressure and rain. Second, both rain and clouds are of a very similar order, namely, they are both aspects of a larger phenomenon, stormy weather. Correlations between symptoms of a similar order always have a lower status than if each belonged to a class of entities of separate systems. The role of correlations noticed during the initial, observational stage of research is to function as clues. The clues point to restricted areas of study in which further investigation may lead to the discovery of those relevant variables whose consequences generate the phenomenon in question.

The correlations found by Robbins are: *Round houses* are associated with small community size, a relatively impermanent settlement pattern (high residential mobility), and the absence or casual practice of agriculture; *rectangular houses* are associated with the converse—large community size, relatively permanent settlement pattern, and intensive agriculture. The Whiting and Ayres (1968) findings are similar in some respects. Rectangular houses are associated with a sedentary settlement pattern, but an impermanent settlement pattern is *not* correlated only with round houses.

It is not possible to compare directly the results of the two studies because each differently classified the observations in the Ethnographic Atlas (Murdock 1967). Whiting and Ayres classified rectangular, quadrilateral, and elliptical houses as "rectilinear," and circular and semicircular houses as "curvilinear." They classified relative permanence of settlement pattern as sedentary, seminomadic, and nomadic (Robbins used only sedentary versus nomadic categories). Unlike Robbins, Whiting and Ayres found that nomadic peoples have almost equally round and rectangular houses. Seminomadic groups were found to have either type, and some had both types. There were also some sedentary cases with both house forms. The latter study found a positive correlation between curvilinear houses and polygyny.

In general, the nomadic category lumps hunters and gatherers with pastoralists. The seminomadic category lumps the cases of hunting and gathering that exhibit lapses of movement, either due to the exploitation of an abundant seasonal resource or the periodic practice of cultivation, with pastoralism that is also associated with lapses in movement and swidden horticulture. Both studies showed that the rectangular form prevails over the round as we move from hunting and gathering to the more complex forms of adaptation.

Traits like "intensive practice of agriculture" and "large community size" are aspects of this general increase in the complexity of adaptation. The broad facts described by these correlational studies match the archaeological record. Since, in many cases, the change through time in a region involves increased complexity and a shift from hunting and gathering to agriculture, the observed change in house form as expressed by floor plans is from round to rectangular.

The findings of the two studies do not tell us *why* different house forms are chosen. The categories are very broad and cannot be used in an explanation since it is not possible to point to any consequences, even if we had treated them as conditions that should generate house form in a cause and effect manner. The authors suggest that their work is valuable because it allows anthropologists to infer one observed trait from another, with a limited degree of confidence (Whiting and Ayres 1968:132; Robbins 1966: 3). Thus, an archaeologist excavating a round house floor may infer at least part of the past ethnographic picture as that of a seminomadic or nomadic settlement pattern, with a given probability of error. This is reasoning of the type, "All swans observed thus far have been white, so the next swan to be observed will be white." For archaeologists, the reasoning goes, "All swans observed thus far have been white, so the swan whose skeleton was just excavated used to be white."

Our argument with this approach does not so much concern the validity of the conclusion for each specific case but, rather, the scientific worth of the knowledge achieved. If we already know that swans are white, why should we hear it again from someone who just excavated a swan's skeleton? An alternative kind of reasoning might be: "There are conditions under which organisms attain a white color. These conditions have been observed in all cases in which swans were observed to be white. Since there is evidence that these conditions prevailed at the time the swan (whose skeleton was just excavated) lived, it too must have been white." The best alternative reasoning would be as follows: "We are puzzled by the fact that all swans observed thus far have been white. To find out why, we undertake research aimed at discovering the conditions whose consequences generate white swans. Since these conditions are not yet known, we do not automatically assume that all swans whose skeletons we have excavated were once white. When the relevant conditions are known and when there is evidence that they occurred when our swans were alive, then we may confidently say that these past swans were white." The process by which relevant conditions are discovered is not mechanical; it is both imaginative and systematic. Clues may be found in a variety of contexts, including those involving excavation of skeletons. In fact, test implications may lead to observation of things that can be seen only through excavation, while others may lead to nonarchaeological observations.

Explanatory Statements about House Form

The literature contains a few attempts to explain variations in house form, that is, round versus rectangular shape. Robbins (1966) quotes several authors (Clark, Fitch and Branch, Hoebel, Ascher, and Driver). These explanations tend to be determined by clues derived from the relative permanence of settlement pattern, namely, from the mobility–semimobility–sedentary dimension. They can be summarized in the following abstract argument: "The mode of subsistence determines the relative permanence of settlement pattern. Both hunting and herding require some mobility. Mobility dictates that houses be light and dismountable. These features are found in the tent." Unfortunately, a tent does not need to be circular, and, indeed, in the majority of cases listed in the Ethnographic Atlas (Murdock 1967), tents are rectilinear.

Another explanation offered by Fitch and Branch (quoted in Robbins 1966) relates dome-shaped houses to maximum wind resistance and to the least exposure of surface area. The authors cite the dome's merit of enclosing the largest volume per unit of surface area. This explanation, however, does not *exclude* the possibility that a dome-shaped house can be used in a sedentary settlement pattern. In fact, it probably would best serve its purpose in the case of a permanent settlement where the necessary house location may not be optimal in terms of winds. The explanation may hold in some specific cases, but it cannot account for the general decrease in the proportion of dome-shaped houses that is correlated with an increase in sedentism and adaptive complexity. One might add that, in general, ethnographically observed tents are not dome shaped; they are conical or rectilinear with angled or flat roofs. Even in Mongolia where the dome-shaped *yurt* is used, other nomadic house forms have been observed as well (Carruthers 1914). Although we will not pursue that topic in this chapter, there is the possibility that house form (as in other facilities) may incorporate symbolic expression, such as ethnicity.[2] In any case, dome-shaped tents are rare, and their general pattern appears to be independent of the occurrence of winds.

In addition to their correlational study, Whiting and Ayres (1968) offered an explanation that was tested with negative results. They directed attention to the problem of mobile people having to carry their houses with them. The logic was simple: "If it is true that round houses can be built from lighter material than that used to build rectangular houses, then the association of round houses with mobility can be explained as a consequence of attempts to minimize the weight that people must carry."

It is simply not true that rectangular houses cannot be built from the same kinds of light-weight materials that are used for round houses. This error in the proposition was revealed in the negative test results. Of the nomadic cases, 8 of 15 had rectilinear houses. It was also suggested that the use of round or rectangular houses by sedentary people depends on whether or not there are trees in the environment. If there are trees available (i.e., heavy building materials), then houses will be rectangular. If there are not, the houses will be circular. The results of the test were negative:

> Sedentary societies were predicted to construct curvilinear houses when heavy building materials were not available, but all of these societies, in fact, build rectilinear houses despite this difficulty. Equally surprising is the fact that all of the sedentary peoples who build curvilinear houses live in an environment where they could easily have built rectilinear dwellings [Whiting and Ayres 1968:125].

As was noted earlier, the dimension of impermanent–permanent settlement pattern predominated over other aspects of human adaptation in capturing the interest of authors trying to explain variability in house form. The use of the mobility dimension may have been due to its easily apparent measurability. The categories, "hunting and gathering," "pastoralism," "horticulture," and "agriculture," are of a nominal character. It is somehow easier to work with a continuous variable that can be measured on an ordinal or interval scale. Relative permanence is cognitively satisfying, and it appears to underlie these nominal categories. The question is whether or not the data in the Ethnographic Atlas justify the selection of the mobility dimension as the one having the greatest potential for furnishing clues about house form variation. It is significant that,

---

[2] Some of the variation in house forms among nomadic peoples in Mongolia may be due to this factor. The Navajo *hogan* may be another case in which ethnicity is symbolized in house form. According to Kluckhohn *et al.* (1971:144), the traditional houses were conical, similar to other Athabascan groups, while the hexagonal, cribwork type is post-Fort Sumner. This coincides with a rise in ethnicity among all southwestern groups associated with conflicts over land.

out of about 750 cases, only 19 were built of materials that unequivocally can be dismounted and transported. Thjese materials are bark, felt, other fabric, and hides and skins (Murdock 1967:168). Of the 19 cases in which houses were built of these materials, 14 were rectangular, while only 5 were circular. The overwhelming majority of round houses actually could not be dismounted. Furthermore, in societies that use both types of houses (round and rectangular), the houses are built of the same wall materials.

Exceptions

The correlational studies of Robbins (1966) and of Whiting and Ayres (1968) revealed a number of exceptional cases in which round houses were associated with sedentary settlement, with agriculture, and with large population size or in which rectangular houses were associated with nomadic groups that practice little or no agriculture, and so on. Almost all research into natural phenomena involves cases in which expectations are not met. We again distinguish between research that does not go beyond the descriptive level (exemplified by the correlational studies mentioned earlier) and research involving tests of explanatory models. In the latter, the variables that are expected to correlate with symptoms should possess attributes whose consequences generate the symptoms in a regular cause and effect manner. In both types of research, exceptions have the potential for providing clues about causal factors.

In the case of descriptive research, exceptions may hint at the existence of variables that are closer to the exact cause than the one used in the correlation, which simply *masked* the more relevant variable(s). In the case of explanatory research, exceptions may hint at the existence of variables that *inhibit* the effect of the variables used in the correlation. Research following the specification of exceptional cases should have the structure of the Method of Difference, beginning when effects are known (Mill 1950:215). In this research design, the cause is under control and the effect, which is initially unknown, is measured at the end of the experiment. In its converse (beginning at the other end), the differential effect *is* initially known, and the cause is sought. In our example, the usual case has rectangular houses, and the exceptional case has round houses. Control is provided by the variables used in the correlational study. Both groups of cases are sedentary, practice agriculture, and so on, while the cause is initially unknown. In Mill's Method of Difference research design, the causal factors must be confined to those variables that exhibit contrasting measurements in the two groups. In the converse, exceptions may provide clues to the existence of causal factors that inhibit or reverse the effect of the variable used in the correlation.

Exceptional cases can be highly informative. Had the strategy here been to probe further, in the absence of an explanatory model, we would continue where Whiting and Ayres left off. We would examine the exceptional cases, contrasting them with the normal ones. We did not adopt this strategy, however, for the following reasons. First, the data in the Ethnographic Atlas do not justify the heavy emphasis on mobility. We do not regard the mechanical correlational study as either the only or the best way to derive stimulating clues from a body of observations. By examining the ethnographic and archaeological records and from a familiarity with western industrialized cultures, we find that an increase in the frequency of rectangular houses is correlated with an increase in the complexity of adaptation. We assume also that residential structures are one type of functionally definable facility. We are unsure whether or not the laws that govern forms of one class of facilities are the same as those governing more general classes of facilities. Earlier studies were guided by an a priori assumption, which we do not share, that residential houses are a class of phenomena governed by laws unique to itself. Certain consistencies in the forms that are chosen for different kinds of facilities suggest to us that the kinds of functions facilities fulfill provide the key to the question of form. Finally, it is an epistemological preference on our part to evaluate observed facts in the light of an explanatory model, at any level of clarity. In other words, in order to fruitfully pursue a given topic, an explanatory model need not be immediately perfect, but one must exist to guide research.

House Form

Form is one aspect of houses, as it is of other facilities. There are, however, many other aspects or properties no less important than form, such as permeability, rigidity, or size. We doubt the epistemological appropriateness of directing research toward one aspect of a phenomenon in the absence of a broad theory about the nature of the phenomenon in general. A better approach is to study houses as such.

The Place of Houses within a Theoretical Framework for Material Culture

Among the material aspects of human culture, houses belong to a general class, facilities (as distinguished from implements). The term facility is used here after Wagner (1966). Facilities are devices that contain or restrain the motion of matter. Familiar examples of facilities are houses, elevators, roads, tubes, and pots. Within this broad class, houses and containers, such as pots, appear to be functionally closer to each other than either is to roads or tubes, although the latter do constrain the motion of matter.

The difference between houses and containers, in general terms, is that containers function to prevent matter from dispersing into the environment. Houses, on the other hand, prevent their contents from the external environment. Structural elements (walls, roof, floor) and the properties that they exhibit, such as permeability, shape, and so on, reflect, among other things, the kinds of environmental interference anticipated *and* the contents housed. Thus, two lines of investigation into the house phenomenon are possible. One is concerned with the *nature of the housed contents* and the other with the *nature of interfering environmental agencies.* Previous explanations for house form differences ignored the contents housed. The following discussion explores the possibility of a causal relationship between content housed and house form. We begin with a discussion of containers for which the relationship between the content and the form of a facility is most easily perceived.

Containers

Relevant Content Characteristics of Bins

We observe that a large proportion of containers are round (see Figure 7.1). Containers, unlike houses, function primarily to prevent dispersal of matter. In addition, many containers allow for intact transportation of the contained matter. Container contents may vary along several dimensions. One such dimension is the *degree of content homogeneity–heterogeneity.* Examples of completely homogeneous contents are water or grain in bulk. We will call containers of homogeneous contents *bins.* An important characteristic of binned contents that affects the way in which they are introduced and retrieved is that all content components have an "equal target value." For instance, it does not matter *which* water molecule is poured into or out of a jug first, in any one introduction or

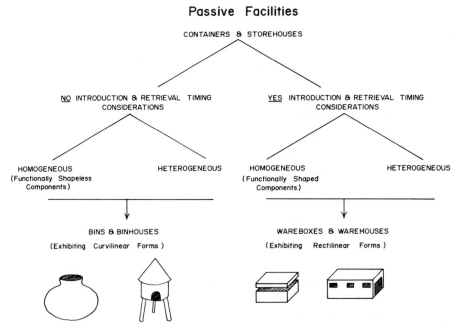

Figure 7.1 Subclasses of facilities for passive contents: Relevant content characteristics and associated forms.

retrieval event. The significance of this characteristic for container form is that there is no need for a structural separation of content components. On the other hand, heterogeneous content components may or may not have equal target values. Having an equal target value implies, in general, that there is *no differential timing* for introduction and retrieval of individual content components.

A good example of the difference between a situation in which internal differentiation is associated with different target values of components and one in which it is not is the laundry bag. While being carried to the laundry, all pieces to be washed have equal target values. Their introduction and retrieval do not involve differential timing. On the way back from the laundry, each item has its own target value. This change in the situation is manifested in the ways in which the clothes are treated as contained contents. Before washing, the pieces are grouped together without being treated individually. Their positions within the container are equivalent to individual grains or water molecules. After washing and drying, they are sorted and folded. Through the process of sorting and folding, the items gain functional shapes (stacks) that allow for their separation into an order reflecting their differential target values. The two different contained states of the same items are associated with different container forms. Unsorted and unfolded laundry items are more frequently carried in sacks or bags with an overall shape approximating a sphere. Sorted and folded ones tend to be carried in less flexible containers whose shape approximates a rectangular box.

Relevant Content Characteristics of Wareboxes

In many cases, heterogeneous contents *are* associated with different target values for different components and, accordingly, with differential introduction and retrieval timing. Containers for such contents usually involve a structural solution to the need to keep components separated. Familiar examples of structurally differentiated containers are tool boxes, fishing tackle boxes, and so on. We will call this kind of container a *warebox* by analogy with warehouses, to be discussed later (see Figure 7.1).

Why Bins Are Curvilinear and Wareboxes Are Rectangular

Of all the aforementioned considerations, differential introduction and retrieval timing associated with different content components is the most important constraint on container form. The retrieval and introduction of homogeneous contents may be gradual or immediate, and, such content is usually *consumed* after retrieval, rather than put back. A gradual accumulation and depletion of contents is actually a series of introduction and retrieval events. The bin that contains this content is often larger than is necessary for the quantities involved in a single introduction or retrieval event.

Once we think of matter, whether homogeneous or heterogeneous, placed in a bin, kept together, and then retrieved as bulk, we can ask what would be the most economical form such a container could take. The ideal shape is a sphere. To explain the predominance of curvilinear bins, we make use of the propositions that *(1)* the sphere is the best form in which matter can be economically contained and *(2)* much human behavior is governed by economic considerations or by the principle of least effort (Zipf 1949). To the degree to which demands made by other factors are incompatible with the spherical form, there will be deviations from this shape. The number of other factors (such as a need for bin stability, giving rise to a flat bottom) is enormous. They include mechanical–physical and stylistic constraints. Thus, we can view the many curvilinear containers whose contents are introduced and retrieved *without* differential timing for each component as deviations from the sphere due to specific considerations to be explored in each case.[3]

Wareboxes (e.g., tool boxes and fishing boxes, etc.) are examples of facilities whose main function is to contain. Their heterogeneous contents are components that, unless separately contained, would easily disperse into the environment. Like other portable containers, these boxes allow for transportation of their contents intact. The housing function of wareboxes may be simply a by-product and may be secondary to the main containing function. Wareboxes are usually rectangular. This shape will be explained later, after we have made a few more observations.

Tool boxes, suitcases, and fishing tackle boxes all perform functions that otherwise are accomplished by containers: prevention of dispersal. They also perform the function of a house: to protect contents from the environment. In contrast to bins, in which the contents are kept in bulk, the contents of wareboxes are not usually associated with consumption but, rather, with *temporary use and replacement*. The heterogeneous components of the content, which are groups of items with identical or similar functions, are placed in separate compartments within the facility. These are subcontainers in that they prevent dispersal and intermingling of grouped items. Wareboxes are usually made with internal partitions. In many cases, heterogeneous contents involve different finished products, while binned contents are usually raw materials or simply shapeless matter. In some cases, finished products are of a size and shape that actually prevent intermingling, in which case, there is no need for physical partitioning by means of built-in subcompartments. We may ask now what is the most economic shape that containers of this type should have—for those with subcompartments and for those without subcompartments.

---

[3] The formlessness of the content allows for great flexibility in the design of such containers, especially in the small size ranges when the weight of materials is not limiting. Given the possibilities of form variation in bins, it is not surprising that symbolic information, such as the culturally prescribed attributes of formal dining crystal, signifying their specific uses and the social status of the users, is not limited to surface decoration but is incorporated into the actual *form* of the vessels.

Subcompartmentalized Wareboxes

A warebox with built-in compartments is a structure in which a number of subcontainers are packed. For economic packing purposes, a sphere or cylinder is not practical. First, walls cannot be shared and the container still have subdivided spaces with regular dimensions; there would be some unusable spaces between the curvilinear boundaries of the packed subcontainers. Second, the ratio of both wall material and total facility volume to potentially contained volume is quite high. When cubic subcontainers are packed, however, they can share walls in all directions, leaving no unusable spaces. Thus, a container subdivided into cubic forms is more economic than one subdivided into curvilinear forms.[4]

The shape of a container closely approximates the shape of its total contents. When the contents are packed in subcontainers of cubic form, the entire content package is also cubic, as is the shape of the container. This proposition also accounts for the rectilinear shape of containers of differentiated contents *without* structural partitions, as will be argued later.

Noncompartmentalized Wareboxes

Nonsubdivided boxes of various sizes, such as simple suitcases, assume a rectangular shape for the same reasons that subdivided containers do: The contents are arranged in some order—such as for sequential use—and this order is expressed in lineal rows and stacks of items. Each group may be composed of items having a form that prevents easy intermingling with other forms. When they are stacked vertically or laid out in rows, these items can be contained most economically within a rectilinear cubic shape, as long as groups can be packed closely as blocks. Rectilinear laundry baskets may represent a solution to the problem of economically packing sorted clothing within a portable facility.

A Model for Predicting Relative Dimensions of Wareboxes as Containers of Heterogeneous Contents

We may explain preference for a rectangular box over a square one as follows. A rectangular box has the same economic advantage as the square cube. The

[4]It could be argued mathematically that hexagonal forms are the most economic packing units, giving an even lower structure to volume ratio. But hexagonal forms are difficult to build. Furthermore, in most human use contexts, horizontal flooring is required; therefore, in these cases, the hexagon proper is not usable. The Navajo *hogan* (see Footnote 2) is the only ethnographically observed case of a hexagonal house (other than in our own society) known to this writer. Since it always occurs in isolation from other such structures, it is unlikely that its form is the result of any packing considerations. The fact that the actual form of the Navajo house is apparently free to vary without significant interruption of internal activities, however, suggests that activities within the *hogan* are probably not strictly partitioned.

difference between the two is that the rectangular box provides for an arrangement of internal compartments with one dimension greater than the others. Let us call this dimension *width*. In a rectangular box, width increases as the number of compartments in the row increases. The advantage of a lateral row arrangement is the ease it provides in reaching content components. The greatest reaching range of the arms is achieved by extending the arms laterally, while the reaching range straight ahead is the shortest. The range up and down is also great. Its potential can be exploited by adjusting the position of the body from a kneeling posture to an erect one. The reaching range factor predicts that compartmentalized containers will vary from the square cube in width first, in height second, and in depth (forward from the body) last.

Facilities that function both as containers and as houses not intended to be used in transportation, such as closets, storage chests, and dressers, tend to vary in this manner. We do find a regular exception when retrieval and introduction of contents are critically dependent on visual discrimination. We see more comfortably in a forward rather than a lateral direction. As a result, a large proportion of file drawers are deep. This depth is limited to the length of the arms in many cases. The overall form of a file cabinet tends to attain the expected dimensions—width and height greater than forward depth—as the number of drawers it accommodates increases.

Another consideration in the design of such subcompartmentalized containers is the degree of "mental effort" necessary in accomplishing successful introduction and retrieval of differentiated content components. The more alternative places in which an item may be located, the more mental effort involving memory is required to locate it properly within the facility. From the least effort standpoint, the order of increasingly more difficult arrangements is from a single compartment to a row, to a row of rows, and finally to a row of rows in a three-dimensional cubic arrangement.

Our expectations are based on the effect of the mental factor, namely, that an increase in the complexity of compartmentalization by using more dimensions will occur only after the capacity of a simpler arrangement, involving fewer dimensions, is fully utilized. Beyond a single compartment, the effect of this factor begins to generate rectangular containers in which expansion starts either laterally or vertically, then moves in both dimensions (although not necessarily in equal measure), and finally moves in all dimensions, including depth. Only in this last case and when expansion in all directions is the same, do we obtain a square cubic form. In all other cases (obviously the majority), the form must be rectangular.

Houses

Having gained some understanding of the relationship between the contents and the form of containers, we move on to another kind of facility—houses. Since *functions* can be defined in mutually exclusive terms while *actual cases* may be combinations of them, we designate as *houses* facilities whose dominant function is housing. *Housing* is the prevention of environmental interference with contents by means of a protective structure. This function does not require that the walls of the facility touch the contents. The function of housing provides not only for protection of passive matter but also for protection of contents whose components move, with respect to one another and to the housing structure itself. Unlike containers, houses are not generally associated with the transportation of contents intact. They are permanent structures in the sense that their structural elements do not change position vis à vis the outside. For example, one usually cannot roll a house around on the ground or swing it through the air.

Storehouses

The link between containers and houses is the storage facility (see Figure 7.1). *Storehouses* seem to perform both functions: to prevent dispersal into and interference with the environment. The term storehouse actually refers to the outermost, surrounding structure that accomplishes the function of housing with respect to the various facilities and other kinds of contents within it. A complete analysis of storage itself is not directly relevant to the present subject. It is sufficient to point out that to store means to keep matter in an *idle state (a)* between periods of use in a production system, which is a kind of custodial function, and *(b)* between procurement and consumption, enabling the regulation of rates of inputs such that they accommodate rates of consumption. The contents of storehouses are generally passive. We can ask: Do the relationships suggested between certain features of content and form of containers also hold in the context of storing?

Storage of Homogeneous Contents

Making the same distinctions among different kinds of contents, we find that, when content components are functionally shapeless units of matter, such as grain or water, and they are stored in bulk, then indeed many storehouses designed to protect them look like enlarged containers (see Figure 7.1). With storage, the distinction between solid and nonsolid contents becomes relevant. Liquid or gaseous matter must be contained under any circumstances. The walls of the structures designed to house such material must touch it. The principles that govern container shape also apply to houses when the content is not solid. As was suggested earlier, the sphere is the most economic form, given the high ratio of volume to surface area. The curvilinearity of containers is what remains of the ideal form after additional considerations lead to deviations from it. A simple deviant form is the cylinder, and many storehouses for formless matter, such as silos, are cylindrical.

Nonliquid matter, which is physically stable, does not have to be contained in order to be stored. It can be kept in piles. When there are no other considerations, the elementary form that a pile of functionally shapeless, stable particles takes is a conical one. As the units or particles enlarge, deviations from the cone are feasible. A common deviant is the dome-shaped pile. The most economic structure that can be designed to protect piled matter in these two forms (the cone and dome) is the one that approximates the pile form. That solids do not need to be contained in the sense of support does not exclude the possibility that they might be contained. Solids, therefore, may be protected by either container-like structures that shape the contents, or by dome- or cone-shaped structures.

Storage of Differentiated Contents

The storage function is a temporal one. Storehouses, as do other facilities, involve content introduction and retrieval. These events may result in gradual accumulations and depletions. One simple accommodation to the need for differential rates of introduction and retrieval of contents in portions of various sizes is to store them in containers of different sizes. The size of such containers depends on a variety of factors, such as the typical volume associated with a retrieval event and a match between the strength of the handler and the weight of the portion handled (contained) at a time. For our purpose, it is important to note that a storehouse may harbor containers as intermediary facilities, between the storing structure and its contents. These intermediary containers can be viewed as large chunks of solid matter having a standardized shape. It is at this level of organization of contents that we begin to see a justification for a rectangular storehouse form.

Some solid matter occurs naturally as large chunks of consistent shape, or it can be prepared as such for storage, that is, given an artificial storage shape. Functionally, this situation is analogous to that in which contents are kept in containers within the storehouse. The form of such containers or storage chunks will deviate from the sphere to meet the requirements of packing, should this be a consideration in their storage. One can expect the shape of the storehouse to approximate the overall shape of the orderly grouping of chunks or containers within it. In general, a pile's shape is related to the shape of its components. The large number of rectangular storehouses observable today may reflect the proportion of cases in which shapes of storage chunks have allowed for orderly vertical and horizontal stacking.

Two Kinds of Storehouses

Among storehouses, we have distinguished between those designed to store contents in bulk and those designed to store differentiated contents. The components of contents stored in bulk have no differential timing associated with introduction and retrieval. Differentiated contents do have this characteristic. In the previous discussion of containers, we distinguished between two kinds (bins and wareboxes), based on similar content distinctions. As can be seen in Figure 7.1, *binhouses* correspond to bin containers, and *warehouses* to wareboxes.

The same factors that cause wareboxes to be rectangular work in the case of warehouses. In addition, warehouses proper must include access routes within them. Warehouse designers (Dodge Corporation 1957:54) specify the optimal shape of a warehouse to be a rectangular structure with the length approximately three times the width. This design formula takes into account not only the issue of sharing walls in the context of differentiation of content items, but also the economy of distance traveled in order to reach various points in the facility. The energy expenditure (translated into time cost) associated with movement within a warehouse is a sufficiently critical factor in the commercial world to take priority over the memory problem (see p. 300) in the design of these large structures. Thus, the dimension of depth is kept proportional to length rather than allowed to be independent of it and minimized to facilitate memory.

Activityhouses

After discussing storehouses, which harbor passive materials, we proceed to a discussion of residential houses, which are a subclass of *activityhouses*. In the abstract, activityhouses harbor only activities. That is, they house active contents whose components move within the house space and in relation to each other. Residential houses are a subclass of activityhouses, on the basis of the domestic nature of the activities they harbor. The word activity implies movement, but, if we are concerned with residential houses, we encounter activities in which movement is not really great. For the purposes of this chapter, the term *activity* will be restricted to any behavioral aspect of a living organism, ignoring nonliving activities, such as the movements of machines.

Human beings engage in two major classes of activities. One we call *living aspects,* which consist of biological functions, such as eating and sleeping. The other we call *role aspects,* which consist of activities performed in the context of a person's role(s) in society. In general, activities are housed only if they are performed locally. Spatially wide-ranging, long-distance movement is a behavioral aspect of certain societal roles, such as hunting or gathering, but these are rarely housed.

The most elementary kind of activityhouse is a structure designed to harbor a single living or role aspect of one living unit (person or animal). Even in our own society, not all living and role aspects are housed. The number of living and role aspects housed increases with the complexity of adaptation. There are two ways in which this increase can be accomplished practically. It is possible to build different structures for limited numbers of living and role aspects, such as sleeping houses, cooking houses, eating houses, and so on. The other possibility is to "pack" several aspects into one structure. We need to investigate the conditions under which decisions are made to separate or to combine the various living and role aspects housed. We can observe that housing several aspects in one structure tends to occur in private contexts of activity, while separation of aspects in single structures tends to occur in public contexts. Another observation is that functionally related aspects tend to be packed or nested together in one structure first; therefore, the combination of aspects whose functional relationship is weak occurs at a higher level in the hierarchical structure of adaptive complexity. These observations are merely clues that could be used in an intensive investigation of the causes of differences in aspect housing strategies. We are looking here for relationships between the fact of separation or combination of aspect housing and the forms that this housing takes.

Three Variables Relevant to House Form

We are interested in the variables that are responsible for any elaboration of the most elementary form of activityhouses. As can be seen in Figure 7.2, the first variable is the *number of living or role aspects* a structure is designed to harbor. A house may serve one living unit and, at the same time, be designed to harbor progressively more living and role aspects performed by this unit. A familiar example would be a house in which an artisan lives and works.

The second variable is *aspect heterogeneity* of the activities performed by the

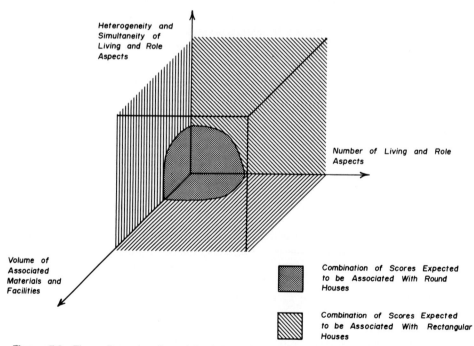

Figure 7.2 Three-dimensional model of the effect of number of living and role aspects, heterogeneity and simultaneity of living and role aspects, and the volume of associated materials and facilities on house form. Higher values make rectangular house form more likely.

units sharing the house. A house may be designed to harbor more than one living unit. As long as the living and role aspects are identical among living units sharing the house, the only expected difference is in size of the facility. When, however, a house is designed to harbor several living units that do not hold identical societal roles such that different role aspects are housed within the structure, we have heterogeneity in the aspects housed. This variable denotes the number of different role-related activities harbored by a structure. Simultaneity of activity performance is associated with a high degree of aspect heterogeneity. Some role and living aspects, depending on the specific case, are performed at the same time. This simultaneity creates problems of mutual disturbance and interference among aspects. There are architectual solutions to these problems, as will be seen later.

The third variable is the *volume of associated materials and facilities.* The performance of living and role aspects can be associated with various materials and facilities. Again, the issue of when and under what conditions we expect to see an increase in or sophistication of aspect-associated materials and facilities is beyond the scope of this chapter. It is sufficient to say that materials and facilities associated with living and role aspects can be observed readily in many societies. They may be permanent or portable features and are often taken into consideration in house design. To simplify the discussion, we will ignore the differences in effect due to portable facilities, although use of another independent variable, permanence of associated materials and facilities, might allow for more accurate prediction of house form. Normally, permanence of materials and facilities is associated with larger volumes of these features; therefore, we will restrict our focus to the volume variable.

The Central Figure Model

In order to see how the three variables contribute to house form, let us begin with the simple case in which each adult has a structure where he performs very few living aspects, such as resting and sleeping. Let us say that the structure scores low on all three variables: no aspect heterogeneity, few living and role aspects, and no associated materials or facilities. We can view the individual in this case as a *central figure moving freely in all directions.* The form of the area that this figure would cover is roughly circular. A similar circular situation would exist if a structure associated with the aspect of cooking had been built around a central hearth. The most economic way of enclosing such situations is by a round structure. If the number of living aspects housed is increased, they need not be performed at the same time; so, again, one can expect the circular enclosure. The number of facilities and materials associated with an increase in living aspects may themselves increase. Since the person is the center around which the facilities can be organized in space (as long as the critical point at which the number and volume become so great that they require more efficient packing is not reached), there is no need to deviate from the economical circular shape. Once the volume of materials and facilities reaches the critical point, considerations similar to those discussed in the case of warehouses will gain priority over those of economy in enclosing an acting central figure. These considerations give rise to a rectangular structure.

The Row Model

If the number of housed persons increases, will the house form change? We have seen that it will, if an increase in the values of our three variables accompanies the increase in living units housed. The central figure model holds in cases in which the pattern of use of the house involves low values on the three variables. It should also hold when the number of persons housed increases, as long as the activities housed are unpredictable, that is, when each person uses the house on an irregular basis. But, if all users perform activities at the same time, the mental factor mentioned earlier will have an effect on house form. To facilitate access to one's place within the facility, communication between individuals, and so on, a *row arrangement* would be preferable. Again, expansion is expected to be lateral first, in height second, and depthwise third. The row order would give rise to an elongated structure. If the volume of facilities and materials associated with activities increases, and especially if these are permanently installed, the rectangular form will have an advantage. The arguments for this advantage are the same as those given earlier for rectangular warehouses and wareboxes.[5]

As the heterogeneity of living and role aspects housed increases, the problems of coping with simultaneity of activity performances results in architectural differentiation of localities within the house. The need to prevent mutual interference and disturbance among the different activities and their associated materials and facilities, leads to a structural solution involving rooms, or *subhouses*. These are equivalent to the subcontainers in the wareboxes discussed earlier. Again, we have the same advantages. Round houses can tolerate simple subdivision, such as a fence or wall cutting the circular floor in two. This solution is common when the number of persons housed is small. As the number of persons or living units associated with *different* living and role aspects increases, however, the rectangular form will be used.

As we saw earlier, an increase in any one of the variables gives rise to a situation in which a rectangular house is the most economic solution. Since there are only three main variables, it is possible to represent their effects geometrically. In Figure 7.2, as values get higher, they are located further away from the corner where all scores are zero. In the area furthest from the zero point, we have

---

[5] The lineal windbreaks of desert groups in Australia are a simple example of a row order that is "housed." Persons are aligned for sleeping, separated by small hearths (Binford, personal communication). The smallest conjugal groups have semicircular shelters (in abstract terms, a short line with rounded ends), while larger groups of persons, such as adolescent males, have rectilinear ones (see Tindale 1972:243 for an illustration of the row effect of increased numbers of living units housed in one structure).

conditions that should theoretically generate rectangular houses. In the restricted area near the zero point, we expect houses to be round.

The relationships presented thus far work in theory. We hope, of course, that the theoretical expectations will closely approximate empirical observations. The cases directly observed in the real world are manifestations of different combinations of causal variables, involving hierarchical priorities given to the different factors that we have considered, as well as to others. The variables and their suggested relationships with house form can serve as analytical tools when an attempt is made to explain specific cases.

We will take a familiar example to demonstrate how the theoretical models can be applied in the real world. Many churches observable today are rectangular. It is generally believed that churches are designed to house one major activity (one role aspect in our terminology). This activity is participated in, more or less equally, by all the church members. Thus, the structure should score low on number of living and role aspects housed and on aspect heterogeneity. Given these low scores, we would expect a round form, an expectation that is contradicted by the observed facts. As we examine the case further, however, we find that a church houses much more than religious activity. For instance, it provides quarters for some permanent staff, which means an increase in the heterogeneity of role and living aspects housed. The church also functions as a storehouse for heterogeneous and functionally shaped chunks of content (ritual paraphrenalia). In addition, the religious activities are performed at fixed intervals and are associated with permanently installed facilities, such as pews and lofts. According to our row model, all these observations would favor the rectangular shape that is frequently observed in churches.

Analysis of a Specific Case Involving Factors Other Than Content Characteristics

Thus far, we have concentrated on the contents of houses. We have explored their potential for causing variation in house form. The concentration on one set of factors should not be misinterpreted as a denial of the potential causal power of other factors. We cannot disregard the possibility that other factors, such as symbolic expression (see previous footnotes 2 and 4) or geographical conditions, may contribute to house form. We will briefly investigate the effects of the latter set of factors in a specific case: the winter houses of the Central Eskimo (Boas 1964). *Geographical conditions* are all the environmental features, from landscape characteristics and naturally available materials to climatic and weather conditions. Such features are *external* to housed content, as opposed to being part of it. We feel, however, that an investigation of the role of external factors will benefit from the control provided by a knowledge of the relationships between house form and features of the content housed. The interaction among factors belonging to different domains in the causation of house form variation is a matter of the order of priorities attributed to those problems that are critical in a given situation. The following example demonstrates how house form can be explained as a solution to critical problems that are associated primarily with geographical conditions.

The Central Eskimo Winter Houses

According to Boas (1964), the Central Eskimo used two types of winter house. One, the dome-shaped snow house, was built on the ice floe. It was constructed of spirally aligned snow blocks. Curvilinear sections of various sizes were appended (see Figure 7.3) to the main dome-shaped chamber. Access to some of these appendages was from the outside. The adaptive context in which these houses were built and used—and here we must rely on Boas' general descriptions—was to maximize the total yearly seal procurement. This included hunting the seals when they were neither abundant nor aggregated.

The activities harbored by the snow house were sleeping, eating, and small equipment production and repair. The appended "vaults" were used to store meat (Boas does not say how much or for how long) and gear (see Figure 7.3). According to Boas' illustrations, some activities were partitioned within the house, but without the use of walls. The division of space was social and determined by living aspect. The house was occupied by two families. The communal bed was in back, and on each side was a "woman's area"—a bench with a fireplace, consisting of a stone lamp and a framework for hanging pots (see Figure 7.4).

On the basis of Boas' general descriptions of domestic activities and the illustration of the snow house interior, we would predict an almost equal probability for either a round or a rectangular form. Although the few different activities associated with living and role aspects might benefit from internal partitioning structures, the case is probably below the threshold at which the need for protection by enclosure is critical. The activities could easily be scheduled for minimal simultaneity. Furthermore, adult males must have spent a large part of their waking hours out on the ice, leaving the living space free for females and children. In short, whatever content circumstances justifying a rectangular house

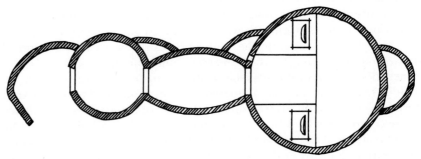

Figure 7.3   Ground plan of snow house of Davis Strait tribes. [After Boas 1964: Fig. 102.]

Figure 7.4 Section and interior of snow house. [After Boas 1964: Fig. 104.]

form may have existed, they were not critical. The final decision, therefore, must have depended on *external factors,* in this case, geographical conditions.

The strongest geographical factor affecting house building decisions under these circumstances is temperature. The function of the snow house is to prevent external interference with the temperature necessary for comfortable functioning of the living units housed. The ice floe lacks building materials other than snow. Heating fuel (blubber) is provided by the kill; therefore, its availability is a function of hunting success. Since the hunting circumstances are not favorable, availability of heating fuel is generally low. Conservation of heat and heating material is, therefore, critical.

The dome shape is an ideal architectural solution for both problems: lack of building materials other than snow and heat conservation. Although the Eskimo could conceivably bring other kinds of building materials with them to the ice floe, the principle of least effort would prevail in the absence of any pay-off for further effort investment in house building. Given the use of snow, the spiral

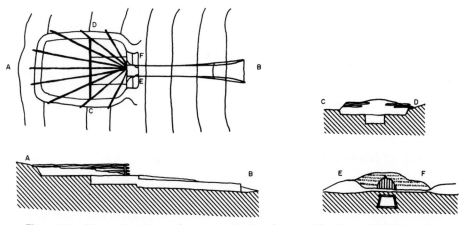

Figure 7.5 Plan and sections of garmang or stone house. [After Boas 1964: Fig. 109.]

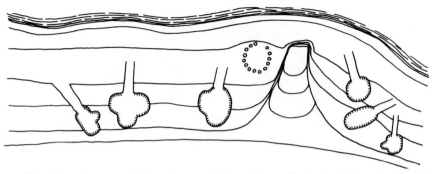

Figure 7.6 Plan of group of stone houses in Pangnirtung, Cumberland Sound. [After Boas 1964: Fig. 112.]

alignment of snow blocks allows for thick, insulating roofing without the need for scaffolding. The dome gives the best ratio of volume to (heat radiating) surface. Within the house, space volume decreases from the floor upward. As a result, living space diminishes with use, so that no heat is "spent" on unused space. Since stored materials need not be heated, they are kept in the outer compartments.

The other type of winter house described by Boas was not built on ice. It was cut into the slope of a hill, and its walls were lined with large slabs of stone. The long entrance passage sloped up to the house opening. The roof was formed from an arc of whale bone at the entrance with poles running from the arc to the back and sides of the house, forming the "rafters" (see Figure 7.5). The floor plan of these houses varied. Some were circular, some were lobed (each lobe was a two-family room), and others were rectangular or square (see Figure 7.6). According to Boas the layout of activities was the same as in the snow house.

The impression that one gets from Boas' general description of subsistence rounds is that the stone house was used in the context of seal and walrus hunting when the animals were more abundant and more aggregated. This would indicate that success in hunting was more likely and a higher volume of meat was procured in comparison to that associated with snow house occupation. It also indicates that the certainty of introduction of resources into a family consumption system was relatively higher as well. While the domestic activities taking place in the two types of houses may have been similar, a readily apparent difference between them is in terms of the amount of effort invested in building the houses. The stone houses were permanent structures, the result of much greater initial investment of building effort.

The Issue of Differential Effort Investment in Facilities

The studies discussed earlier suggested that more effort is necessary to build rectangular houses than round houses. The question of effort investment pertains not only to differences in house form but also to facilities in general. Even erecting a brush shelter requires some effort. The variables offered earlier (see

Figure 7.2), especially the volume of associated materials and facilities, are them-selves by-products of decisions to invest effort. We need to know the adaptive conditions under which decisions to invest effort are made. Pursuit of this topic is not within the scope of this chapter, but we will offer a suggestion as to the relevant conditions in the case of the Eskimo stone versus snow houses, since these conditions may have relevance for understanding facility form and use in general.

The Central Eskimo case involves different amounts of initial effort in build-ing. The snow house was associated with procurement activities under conditions of *low* certainty of resource introduction into the house. The stone house was associated with a *higher* certainty of resource introduction. We suspect that there is a regular relationship between the *certainty of procurement* of large amounts of resources and the *amount of effort invested* in facilities. Facilities are constructed when the availability of the contents that they will contain or house is to some degree predictable. Lack of contents makes the facility useless and a waste of effort. Therefore, we expect expedient solutions for accommodating contents to be replaced by preplanned ones as certainty about content availability and use increases. High content volume associated with certainty of availability (and, thus, of introduction) may give rise to stronger, permanent facilities such that cost of maintenance and repair is minimized.

The issue of energy investment required to build a house is probably spurious. The stone houses of the Central Eskimo were reused, while the snow houses had to be rebuilt (in different places) each winter or more often. In the long run, there was probably more effort invested in the snow houses. High volume and certainty of contents introduction may result in more "expensive" facilities, but they represent less effort invested when the cost is spread over the entire time of use.

Another aspect of house design that is affected by the probability of success in procurement and, eventually, the certainty of content introduction is the critical point at which the increase in the relevant variable(s) triggers a new response. A *high* probability of success and its associated certainty of content intro-duction would cause the threshold to occur at a lower point for our three variables. A *low* probability of success would tend to push the threshold up, that is, to occur when scores on the three variables are higher. In other words, under conditions characterized by *low* predictability of success and *low* certainty of content introduction, no shift to a rectangular house form should occur, despite some degree of role heterogeneity. Under conditions of low probability of suc-cess, inconveniences stemming from mutual interference of unrelated activities should be tolerated longer and be accommodated by other means than a shift to a rectangular house form.

The relationship between probability of success and certainty of content intro-duction, on the one hand, and the threshold for a shift to a rectangular house form is presented here as an idea or hypothesis in the formative stage. It was generated in the context of examining a specific case. Probability of success and certainty of content introduction are not the only conditions associated with a shift to rectangular house forms. In other adaptive contexts, other factors, such as the volume and the specific nature of the resources procured, which would affect the way in which they were processed, might contribute to house form decisions. The best strategy for discovering factors and their relationships to house form is to examine and compare specific cases. Once examination and comparison results in hypotheses concerning factors and their interrelationships, there may be a place for correlational research, in the testing phase. The hypotheses would indicate what should be controlled for, such that correlational runs would have a good chance of providing unambiguous results. In reality, the task of performing such correlational studies is difficult, due to a lack of sufficiently specific ethnographic documentation. This insufficiency exists both qualitatively and quantitatively.

Previous Studies of House Form Reevaluated

We began with reference to the correlational studies of Robbins (1966) and Whiting and Ayres (1968) and to Flannery's (1972) article on the rise of the "village" as a settlement type. It might now be appropriate to briefly reevaluate their findings in the light of our suggestions concerning the relationships that are relevant to house form.

The results of the correlational studies were that full-time sedentism, large community size, and intensive agriculture are all associated with rectangular houses. These general descriptive categories include high scores on the three variables in Figure 7.2. For example, large communities of agriculturalists are often characterized by role differentiation and high volumes of materials and facilities, especially when food and other resources are stored. Along with these conditions occur the housing of many role and living aspects in one structure. Flannery's characterization of the "village settlement type" conforms to this description, as will be seen later.

The relationship of house form to mobility, as depicted by the correlational studies, is ambiguous (see pp. 290–292). A partial explanation for the ambiguity may be due to the way in which nonsedentary cultures were classified. The issue is complex, and to cover it properly would require another paper. For the present purposes, it is sufficient to note that the categories that were used lumped together very different adaptive systems, if judged from the perspective of the variables we suggested. For example, certain forms of hunting and gathering may be analogous to grazing and predation. This kind of adaptation involves exploitation of resources by means of nearly continuous movement throughout the foraging range. Another kind of nonagricultural adaptation involves "harvesting" resources that occur periodically in large quantities at restricted locations (e.g., migrating caribou, salmon). When the occurrence of each resource is associated with a different time and place, the settlement pattern might be a series of sedentary periods and periodic moves. The differences between these two kinds of nonagricultural adaptations—continuous foraging and periodic harvesting—in terms of processing procured resources for storage and consumption, the organization of labor, and the use of facilities, when analyzed according to our theoretical framework, could account for differences in house forms.

In nonsedentary cases, we expect to find round houses when values on our three variables are low and rectangular ones when they are high. Because hunting and gathering usually involves little role differentiation, and many role-related activities are performed away from camp and/or are not housed, the number of role aspects housed and their associated heterogeneity is generally low. The few role aspects that are housed, that is, manufacturing and maintenance of clothing and hunting gear, can be housed in two alternative ways: They may be housed in a communal structure, such as the *karigi*, or "men's house," as described for the north Alaska Eskimo (Spencer 1959), or they may be housed on an individual basis, that is, together with domestic activities in family structures. In the former case, the low value of the heterogeneity variable associated with residential structures is obvious. The residential structure houses domestic services and few role aspects (other than those that are housed in a communal structure). These activities could be executed sequentially; therefore, simultaneity is also very low. In terms of our variables, the housing circumstance associated with the former case is one in which we would expect round houses. In the latter case, more role aspects are housed per structure so that heterogeneity and simultaneity are higher. There is, however, no associated significant increase in the volume of permanent facilities. Despite higher values of the heterogeneity and simultaneity variables, the increase is not significant enough to generate a shift to a rectangular house form. Manufacturing and maintenance of clothing and hunting gear are activities that do not usually follow a predictable course, since they are often dependent on accidental breakage. They can, therefore, be interspersed among the sequences of the domestic activities so as not to cause problems of simultaneity. We expect the housing circumstance associated with the latter case to be one of simple subdivision, such as halving the round floor area, where maintenance and manufacturing activities are accommodated expediently within the domestic-activities-dominated residential structure. It might be added that, in general, round houses in many different adaptive contexts, including nomadic herders, shifting cultivators, and hunter–gatherers, are enclosures for the activities of a central figure plus some sporadic or sequential activities of additional figures.

The central figure and row models are compatible with the ethnographic and archaeological data summarized by Flannery (1972). He describes two types of settlement: the *compound* of small, circular houses or huts and the *village* of larger, rectangular houses, often with patios and courtyards. Both settlement types are associated with permanent settlement, illustrating again that mobility is not the important factor in determining house form.

The round huts of the compound are "designed to house only one, or at most two, persons" (Flannery 1972:8). This is compatible with the acting central figure model of housed contents. The rectangular houses of the village are "designed to accommodate *families*" (Flannery 1972:39). Flannery suggests that at least three or four persons (a man, his wife, unmarried children, and occasionally more distant relatives) were housed in the rectangular houses. This corresponds to our row model with high values of role heterogeneity and simultaneity in role and living-aspect-related activities. Flannery notes that there are a considerable number of facilities attached to or within rectangular houses. In contrast, the few facilities found in the compound are separate, round structures located in the open between the huts. Finally, he says that the village is associated with a higher volume of input of resources (due to the "intensification of production at the family level") than the compound. This kind of organization of labor and consumption in which each family is a relatively self-sufficient production–consumption unit is feasible when the certainty of introduction of large volumes of resources is high. And housing these materials and facilities in the family living space would probably result in a rectangular form.

Closing Remarks

The purpose of the correlational studies mentioned in the beginning of this chapter were to furnish archaeologists with "interpretive tools." For example, upon observing a round or a rectangular floor plan of a house, archaeologists could describe the past adaptive system as either nomadic or sedentary, with a specified probability of being wrong. However, the contributions of these studies to the explanation of why houses are round or why nomadic people use them remains negligible.

By using our suggested variables and their relationships to house form, and our few suggestions concerning the general adaptive conditions under which these variables may have high or low values, archaeologists now have a guide for further investigation. This investigation might lead to discoveries of underlying causes for archaeologically and ethnographically observed variability. For instance, given a round floor plan, independent evidence for low values on our variables could be sought in other classes of archaeological remains at the site. More specifically, independent evidence could be sought for the model of a central acting figure around whose limited number of activities the house was built. The archaeologist could then offer propositions about the specific conditions under which a cultural system is expected to house only one or a few living units, a limited number of sequentially performed activities, low volumes of facilities, and so on, using clues provided at the site and elsewhere. These propositions could be tested wherever possible.

With this approach, the archaeologist would be participating in, and even making, original contributions both to discovering the facts about the past and to explaining anthropological phenomena in general.

ACKNOWLEDGMENTS

I would like to thank my husband, Yigal Zan, for his valuable help and encouragement in the writing of this chapter.

REFERENCES

Boas, Franz
    1964   *The central Eskimo.* Lincoln, Neb.: University of Nebraska Press.
Carruthers, Douglas
    1914   *Unkown Mongolia.* London: Hutchinson.
Dodge Corporation
    1957   *Buildings for industry.* F. W. Dodge Corporation.
Flannery, Kent V.
    1972   The Origins of the village as a settlement type in Mesoamerica and the Near East: A comparative study. In *Man, settlement and urbanism,* edited by Peter J. Ucko, Ruth Tringham, and G. W. Dimbleby. London: Duckworth.
Kluckhohn, Clyde, W. W. Hill, and Lucy W. Kluckhohn
    1971   *Navaho material culture.* Cambridge, Mass.: Belknap Press of Harvard University Press.
Mill, John S.
    1950   *Philosophy of scientific method.* New York: Hafner.
Murdock, George P.
    1967   Ethnographic Atlas. *Ethnology* **6**(2).
Robbins, Michael C.
    1966   House types and settlement patterns: An application of ethnology to archaeological interpretation. *Minnesota Archaeologist* **28**(1):3–26.
Spencer, Robert F.
    1959   The North Alaskan Eskimo. *Bulletin of the Bureau of American Ethnology* No. 171. Washington, D.C.: U.S. Govt. Printing Office.
Tindale, Norman B.
    1972   The Pitjandjara. In *Hunters and gatherers today,* edited by M. G. Bicchieri. New York: Holt.
Wagner, Philip
    1966   *The human use of the earth.* Glencoe, Ill.: Free Press.
Whiting, John W., and Barbara Ayres
    1968   Inferences from the shape of dwellings. In *Settlement archaeology,* edited by K. C. Chang. Palo Alto, Calif.: National Press Books.
Zipf, George K.
    1949   *Human behavior and the principle of least effort: An introduction to human ecology.* Reading, Mass.: Addison–Wesley.

8

Dummy Data Distributions and Quantitative Methods: An Example Applied to Overlapping Spatial Distributions

ROBERT K. VIERRA
Northwestern University

RICHARD L. TAYLOR
University of New Mexico

In the past decade, archaeologists have paid increasingly more attention to patterned distributions in the archaeological record. This has been coupled with an increased emphasis on the use of quantitative methods as an aid to discerning distributional patterns. This emphasis is clear when one examines the nature of the articles published in *American Antiquity* over the last 10 years.

However, it is all too easy to jump on the "bandwagon" of quantitative methods to demonstrate that we are being scientific by using more objective and rigorous methods in our analysis of archaeological materials. In such a context, the potential for misusing statistical techniques is high, particularly when the assumptions underlying the statistical measures are not well understood. Mismatching is one result: The statistical measures used are not designed to handle the kinds of questions being asked of the data.

There is also a tendency to use quantitative methods as a means of facilitating the analysis of large data sets. Statistical measures in this context are often applied as a search technique; for example, in the early stages of analysis, an investigator may use statistics to discover whether or not there is any structure or redundancy in the data matrix. Sometimes the result is a "shotgun approach" in which a variety of statistical measures are applied in the hope of finding some pattern in the data. A not uncommon result is contradictory sets of analyses. This problem can be avoided by clearly specifying the kinds of structures being looked for: for example, nondirectional associational patterning or covariant patterning. With this kind of specificity, the investigator can use only those statistical methods that are designed to measure the structures for which he is looking.

This is not to say that even the most careful investigator can avoid methodological problems. The methodological "revolution" in archaeology, defined by Freeman as "the use of statistics in the discernment and explanation of occupation residue patterning at the supra-artifactual level" (1973:1), is still in its infancy. Methodological problems are still very much with us, as Freeman himself admits while trying to cope with the constraints imposed by his data on his statistics. Whallon has recently devoted several articles to an attempt to develop the appropriate methodological tools for spatial analysis of occupation floors (1973a, b, 1974).

The purpose of this chapter is to illustrate the aforementioned concerns by discussing an analytical and methodological problem that bears directly on distributional studies of occupation floors. One of the authors, in the course of his own research in Ayacucho, Peru, became very concerned, from an analytic standpoint, with the spatial distributions of approximately 120 occupation floors from a dozen or more sites. Some of these occupation floors had incredibly dense artifact distributions, averaging around 500 artifacts in an area of 85 square meters. Based on the depositional history and the number of hearths, he began to suspect that these could very well be multiple short-term occupations. If specific tasks had been performed in specific areas and their by-products had been superimposed over previous short-term task-specific occupations, the resulting overlapping spatial distributions would be very difficult to isolate.

Such overlapping distributions are probably not an unusual phenomenon. Yellen (1974:209) has recently reported that, in !Kung Bushman camps, many of the daily activities are restricted to a small area around each household hearth; the remains of these varying activities are not, therefore, spatially discrete. Although it is recognized, this problem of overlapping distributions has not been dealt with very adequately in the archaeological record.

The problem in using quantitative methods to measure suspected overlapping spatial distributions concerns knowing which methods are appropriate. This is a measurement problem in the sense that we would like a method that allows us to isolate and recognize the presence and extent of these distributions. It is often useful, when one is exploring new methods of processing data, to create an idealized dummy data set. The properties of such a set are well understood, of course, before the data are processed. Results of new methods of analysis can then be compared to what is already known about the hypothetical data in order to validate the new methods. In adopting this approach, an investigator feels more confident in arguing for the utility and applicability of a particular research or statistical method—provided, of course, that his data set approximates reality. Without employing such a strategy, he can never be sure whether his results actually reflect the structure in his data or the limitations and/or constraints of his statistical measures.

This problem is becoming increasingly pressing as we rely more and more on high-powered multivariate statistics, not only because parametric statistics are robust, but also because the resulting analyses are often so abstract that it is difficult to relate the results to empirical reality. When we do not know the character of a distribution before we employ a statistical technique, particularly if we are experimenting with new techniques, we are more likely to be misguided by the results of such abstract techniques. The utility of generating expected data sets in such a context was tested in the following manner.

In an attempt to develop a methodology for isolating both discrete and overlapping spatial distributions, we created a dummy occupation floor consisting of 100 square meters. Within this area, 16 dummy "tool types" were distributed in the following manner: tool types 1–4 in the northwest corner; types 5–8 in the northeast corner; and types 9–12 in the south-central portion of the "site." These distributions represent three spatially discrete areas. To create an overlapping distribution, additional tool types 13–16 were directly superimposed on the four tool types previously placed in the south-central area (see Figure 8.1).

Each category of four tool types can be thought of as a tool kit made up of covariant tool types. Random combinations of all 16 types were distributed throughout the remainder of the site as a noise component. This was done to bring our ideal distribution closer to reality.

Next we imposed a 1-×-1-meter grid over the occupation. This was not an arbitrary grid selection, but rather one that would most accurately map onto the exact locations of the dummy distributions. This was done to control for any departure in expected results that could be attributed to grid size. It also increased our confidence that the following analysis would be capable of retrieving both kinds of distributions.

Within each grid square, counts were tabulated for each tool type present. The result was a matrix of 100 cases by 16 variables. This matrix was then subjected to an R-mode common factor analysis. This model was chosen because it is designed to elicit patterning of covariation—in our case, covariant tool types. Squared

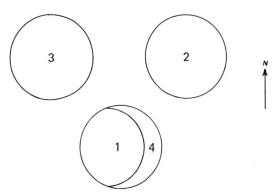

Figure 8.1 Dummy distributions (numbers indicate factor dimensions).

multiple correlations were used in the diagonal. This treatment of the diagonal accords with the use of common factor analysis, which is concerned with the dimensions of the space of common parts of the variables and thus avoids the problem of lumping common, specific and random error variances (Rummel 1970: 112). We also settled on oblique rather than orthogonal rotation, since oblique rotation generates additional information from the analysis. Given the real world and the interrelationships that exist in adaptive sociocultural systems, it cannot be realistically assumed that the underlying factor dimensions are always operating independently of each other. With oblique rotation, the factors are allowed to become correlated. If the clusters of variables are, in fact, uncorrelated, then oblique rotation will result in orthogonal factors.

The factor analysis provided us with some interesting results. A 4-factor solution was extracted, accounting for 97% of the total variance. Variables 13–16 loaded under factor 1, variables 5–8 under factor 2, variables 1–4 under factor 3, and variables 9–12 under factor 4. These results were most encouraging, since our factors coincided exactly with our hypothetical tool type distributions. But most important was the fact that tool types 9–12 and 13–16, representing the overlapping distribution, were separated out into factors 4 and 1, respectively. Our confidence in the use of factor analysis for this purpose was increased considerably since all four variable clusters were isolated.

The next question was whether or not the variable clusters have a spatial referent. In answering this question, we found it useful to use the factor scores from the factor analytic solution. Factor scores are computed by multiplying a case's datum on each variable by the factor weight for that variable. The sum of these weight-times-datum products for all the variables yields the factor score for each case. The weighted summation will give cases high (or low) scores if their values are high (or low) on the variables involved with a factor (Rummel 1970: 150). Those cases containing any or all of the variables within our previously defined clusters should then be associated with higher scores on the factors representing those clusters. Since our cases represented one square meter grid units, we could ultimately return to the occupation floor to determine if the variable clusters do, in fact, cluster spatially.

One further computation was necessary, however, before we could proceed to that step. Each column of factor scores had to be rank ordered in descending magnitude. If the variables defining a factor have positive factor loadings, then the rank ordering of that factor begins with the highest positive factor score. The highest negative factor score should be used when the factor-defining variables have negative factor loadings. For bipolar factors, the rank ordering should be done twice—once for positive factor scores and one for negative scores—so as not to lose any information.

In an attempt to examine whether or not the variable clusters do, in fact, cluster spatially, we used a departure of contiguity criterion. This was based on the assumption that distributions, such as activity areas, are bounded in space and their partitions are adjacent to one another. After rank ordering the factor scores for factor 3, the case associated with the highest factor score was marked on the occupation floor. Each succeeding case was marked in the same manner if it was contiguous to the previous case or cases, or within one square meter of them. This process was continued until we observed a noticeable spatial departure after 16 cases. All 16 cases were contiguous in the northwestern part of the floor; this coincided precisely with our dummy distribution. In this example, we isolated the entire area and its boundaries. We should mention one note of caution pertaining to the departure of contiguity criterion at this point. It is possible that a departure might lead to a second similar distribution spatially distinct from the first. Therefore, we suggest the plotting of as many cases as necessary beyond the initial departure to determine whether or not there are additional spatial distributions for a given factor.

We repeated the same procedure on the factor scores for factor 2. This time, the isolation of an entire area and its boundaries coincided with the distribution in the northeastern part of the floor. Using the factor analytic model, these two spatially discrete distributions were easily recovered and delineated.

Although the spatially discrete distributions were interesting, we were more concerned with the problems of overlapping distributions, which can be brought about by multiple occupations. Given a large inventory of tool types, unless one knows exactly what one is looking for, overlapping distributions will not be as readily observable as the two discrete distributions described earlier.

Factors 4 and 1 represent the overlapping distributions. When the factor scores for factor 4 were rank ordered and plotted, we isolated 81% of the dummy area, which included its entire boundary. This percentage was better than we had expected, and it certainly was sufficient to allow us to draw an iso-factor circumscribing the spatial distribution.

Tool types 13–16, loading under factor 1, were the types that we had superimposed within the area represented by factor 4. When we rank ordered the factor scores for factor 1, we observed that the highest ranked cases were those that were also included under factor 4. Using the departure of contiguity criterion and plotting these cases on our grid layout, we were able to draw an iso-factor that circumscribed 89% of the overlapping distribution, all within the larger area outlined by factor 4. It is possible then, using this method, to isolate and recognize overlapping spatial distributions as well as spatially discrete ones.

It should be obvious that, up to this point, we controlled not only for the placement of the distributions, but also for the grid size that would allow maximum recovery. As we mentioned earlier, this was done to test the accuracy and validity of using a factor analytic model as an inductive search technique. When the technique is used on real data, however, problems present themselves. What is the proper grid size to use, and how do we know that we have extracted all the significant factors?

There can be little disagreement with the statement that there is no proper analytic grid size for dealing with spatial distributions. The proper grid size obviously is dependent on the nature and distribution of the spatial clusters; the latter are always an unknown set of parameters. In an attempt to get around this problem, we employed an expanded grid system, as was suggested by Whallon (1973a). Using the same body of data, we tabulated counts per square while varying the size of the grid. In all, we used four different grid sizes: ½ × 1 meter, 1 × 1 meter, 1 × 2 meters, and 2 × 2 meters. We then reran the factor analysis on each of the three new grid sizes. It should be noted that, for each grid size, we always had more cases than variables, thereby eliminating any severe asymetrical matrix problems.

We rank ordered the factor scores for the three new grid sizes and plotted their distributions. For each new grid size, the areal distribution was not as precise as it was in the 1 × 1 meter case. More important, however, the factor solutions were different. With each of the last three grid sizes, only three factors were extracted. Factors 4 and 1, which represented the overlapping distribution in the 1 × 1 meter example, were now combined into one factor. In each of the additional examples, then, we reduced our spatial and dimensional resolution.

The number of factors extracted for each example was based on an eigenvalue greater than 1.0. This assures that the common factors extracted define a certain level of variance among the variables. Since the variance of a variable is unity, such a cutoff rejects factors that do not account for at least the variance of one variable (Rummel 1970:356). The application of an across-the-board cutoff may, however, be difficult to justify in some cases, particularly in situations in which the first rejected eigenvalue is slightly less than 1.0. Instead of adhering strictly to a cutoff value such as 1.0, we suggest that the relative relationships between eigenvalues is a more meaningful assessment of the number of significant factors. A relative measure of the strength of the break between eigenvalues should reflect the relative importance of each eigenvalue vis-a-vis its adjacent values.

To establish such a measure, the eigenvalue ratios must be computed for each grid size; that is, the first eigenvalue is divided by the second, the second divided by the third, and so on. The desired goal of these computations is what we will call the "ledge effect." A ledge is characterized by a steep dropping off between adjacent eigenvalues. This corresponds numerically to the highest ratio value. When plotted against the number of factors, the ledge will be that portion of the curve with the largest negative slope. In principle, the ledge effect should be the juncture between information and noise. Eigenvalues beyond the ledge will be equated with noise, and those eigenvalues preceding the ledge should represent the number of significant factors.

The ratios for the expanded grid units were tabulated and are presented in Figure 8.2. The ratios were tabulated against grid size and against the numbers of factors that include those factors below the 1.0 cutoff. The results were both provocative and exciting. The highest ratio or ledge effect, 34.4, occurs at the intersection of the 1 × 1 meter row and the column of factors 4 and 5; this means that the optimal solution, in this case, is to use a 1 × 1 meter grid with four significant factors. It should be noted that this solution corresponds exactly to the

Numbers of Factors

Grid size (sq. m)	(1–2)	(2–3)	(3–4)	(4–5)	(5–6)	(6–7)
.5	1.6	1.7	2.7	2.3	1.4	2.5
1.0	1.5	1.7	2.6	34.4	1.5	3.8
2.0	1.6	1.9	5.2	12.0	2.0	3.8
4.0	1.6	2.0	11.1	5.5	4.0	1.8

Figure 8.2 Eigenvalue ratios.

number of activity areas and their spatial boundaries as described in the dummy data set. This appears to be a method, then, not only for selecting the best grid size, but also for determining the number of significant factors irrespective of any across-the-board eigenvalue cutoff.

It is hoped, however, that the isolation and recognition of spatial distributions will not be ends in themselves. The presence or absence of these distributions should be a starting point from which to move into a higher order of analysis, one that encompasses not only inter- and intrasite variability, but also, more importantly, the organizational dynamics and adaptive strategies that underlie the presence or absence of these distributions.

In summary, the factor analytic model discussed here seems to be very appropriate for discerning both discrete and overlapping spatial distributions as well as specifying the grid size and the number of significant factors for maximum recovery. More important, we feel that the strategy of generating a known data set with expected results is most profitable for testing the accuracy and validity of potentially useful multivariate search techniques.

Whether we are using quantitative methods as a search technique or for deductive testing purposes, the point is that any such methods should be used as instruments for measurement. In any analysis, the investigator is obligated to specify the rationale for selecting some variables and ignoring others. We expect the researcher to explicitly state what is being measured and how it is being measured, that is, what is the instrument of measurement. Furthermore, we are always faced with the problem of knowing whether or not we are, in fact, measuring what we think we are, such as inherent patterns of covariation. We argue here that the construction of expected data sets, such as the one discussed earlier will allow us to assess whether or not our instruments are actually measuring what we want them to measure. In doing so, we ultimately increase our degree of confidence in the results of any such analysis.

We are encouraged by the fact that some researchers are moving in similar directions (e.g., Lewis Binford's recent research on faunal analysis [this volume] and the work of Ammerman and Feldman [1974] on stone tool assemblages).

It must be remembered that any evaluation of whether or not a discipline can be considered a science is based, to a large extent, on the accuracy of its instruments of measurement.

REFERENCES

Ammerman, A. J., and M. W. Feldman
    1974   On the "making" of an assemblage of stone tools. *American Antiquity* **39**:610–616.
Freeman, L. G.
    1973   The analysis of some occupation floor distributions from Earlier and Middle Paleolithic sites in Spain. Paper read at the IXth International Congress of Anthropological and Ethnological Sciences, Chicago.
Rummel, R. J.
    1970   *Applied factor analysis.* Evanston, Ill.: Northwestern University Press.
Whallon, R., Jr.
    1973a Spatial analysis of occupation floors I: Application of dimensional analysis of variance. *American Antiquity* **38**(3):266–278.
    1973b Spatial analysis of Palaeolithic occupation areas. In *Models in prehistory: The explanation of culture change,* edited by C. Renfrew. London. Pp. 115–130.
    1974   Spatial analysis of occupation floors II: The application of nearest neighbor analysis. *American Antiquity* **39**(1):16–34.
Yellen, J. E.
    1974   The !Kung settlement pattern: An archaeological perspective. Unpublished doctoral dissertation, Harvard University.

Modeling and Monitoring Change in Relatively Complex Prehistoric Systems

9

Modeling Change in Prehistoric Social Systems*

JOSEPH A. TAINTER
University of New Mexico

Introductory Remarks

One of the characteristics of archaeology today is a proliferating body of literature dealing with the social organization of past populations. The studies that make up this body of literature present a variety of research goals and analytical methods, reflecting the diversity of research interests that can be served in the investigation of past social systems. This variety of research interests makes it difficult to characterize and evaluate the archaeological study of past societies in anything but the most general terms. On the other hand, a discussion of this area of investigation might be approached, not from the perspective of past research, but from the viewpoint of the subject matter itself. Such a perspective will prove useful.

The study of prehistoric societies may be approached with either of two goals in mind: the study of social *features* and the investigation of social *systems*. It should be understood at the outset that these research goals are in no sense mutually exclusive. Nevertheless they are conceptually distinct. The study of social features proceeds when a research question has been formulated dealing with a single feature or characteristic of a past society, or with several characteris-

* This research was financially supported by the National Science Foundation (GS-42606) and by the Foundation for Illinois Archeology.

tics that can be treated independently. At a very basic level, the archaeologist may ask such questions as: Were there discrete residential units in this settlement? Was the mode of postmarital residence with the wife's natal group? Was this society egalitarian or ranked? Given such a question, research proceeds in a direction that emphasizes analytical procedures appropriate for dealing with each individual social characteristic. The research goal is met when the nature of each characteristic has been ascertained to the archaeologist's satisfaction. The important point to emphasize in the study of social features is that each feature is approached and treated independently.

In contrast, the study of social systems deals with patterns of interaction among social features. In this instance, research may focus on the manner in which sets of social features function interdependently as a system. Research topics may range from the very specific to the highly abstract, depending in part upon the number of interacting social features that are investigated. The important point to note is that the study of social systems requires substantially more than the independent specification of the characteristics of each social feature. The reason for this is clear. A system can never be characterized merely by describing the attributes of its parts. A system is, by definition, a holistic entity, and the characteristics of a system are not equivalent to the summed characteristics of its individual parts (cf. Bertalanffy 1968:55). In order to characterize a system, social or otherwise, archaeologists must develop the ability to isolate and measure dimensions that compositely reflect both the constituent parts of a system, as well as the patterned relationships among these parts. In essence, the analysis of social systems requires the isolation and measurement of variables that are at a level of abstraction beyond such commonly considered features as residence, ranking, and so forth.

The abstract, composite dimensions that allow for the characterization of a social system are the *structure* and the *organization* of the system. The meanings of these two terms, as they are used here, are most closely approximated by definitions derived from the fields of systems theory and cybernetics. The *structure* of a system is meant to indicate the number, nature, and arrangement of its articulated subsystems and components. A *subsystem* of a system is defined as a unit that carries out a distinct, specific process; *process* is defined as change over time of matter–energy or information. A *component,* on the other hand, is a unit of the system that is distinguishable as an arrangement in three-dimensional space (Miller 1965:209, 218). *Organization* is most basically defined as the constraints imposed upon the ranges of behavior that may be pursued by the elements of a system (Rothstein 1958:34–36). The source of such behavioral constraint originates in the patterns of interaction among a system's elements, for it is only through patterned, constrained behavior that a system may successfully function.

These definitions illustrate why a social system can be characterized as a system by specification of its structure and organization. The nature of a system derives from both the nature of its constituent parts and the patterned interaction among these parts. The former characteristic is what has been referred to as structure; the latter attribute, patterned interaction, is what is termed organization. It should be apparent from these definitions that the determination of prehistoric social structure is an essential first step in archaeological research, for the analysis of organization becomes meaningful only when considered in relation to explicitly defined structures.

When viewed in this perspective, the goal of studying past social systems is to specify the structure and the organization of a set of interacting social components. The set of social components that is selected will ordinarily vary with the research topic under investigation. The purpose of this study is to demonstrate the usefulness of both the concepts and the analytical methods that are presented here. To this end, there are four characteristics to be considered: the structural complexity of a social system, the nature of structural differentiation, the amount or degree of organization, and the nature of organization. The first and third of these characteristics, the degree of structural complexity and the amount or degree of organization, are quantitative variables and must be modeled as such.

The goals of the present study have definite implications concerning the types of data that are most appropriate for the analysis. In dealing with variables such as the structural complexity of a social system, it is necessary to acquire information about the number of structural components that constitute a system. Perhaps the single category of data that is best suited for this purpose is mortuary remains. Arthur Saxe (1970:6) has noted that the occasion of death calls for the participation in mortuary ritual of individuals who had engaged in identity relationships with the deceased person. Mortuary activity incorporates the symbolic representation of a greater range of the deceased individual's social identities than any occasion during life. Since individuals acquire their social identities through membership in the structural components of a social system, the representation in mortuary ritual of the deceased's social identities simultaneously conveys information concerning the structural components in which the individual held membership. Indeed, to the extent to which a mortuary population contains individuals who held membership in the various structural components of a system, one can expect the mortuary population to reflect the structure of the extinct society. There is no other category of archaeological data for which this claim might be so confidently advanced. Thus, mortuary data are expected to best reflect the structure of past social systems, and mortuary data will, therefore, serve as the basis for development of methods of social inference in the following pages.

Sociometric Techniques in Archaeology

In this section, the analysis of structure and organization in past social systems is made operational by the development of techniques for the isolation and measurement of these dimensions in mortuary data.

By far the most common approach used in the archaeological study of mortuary practices is to attempt to assign a past society to an appropriate slot in an evolutionary typology (see Stickel 1968; King 1970; Tainter 1971; Brown 1971; Peebles 1974). Unfortunately, no archaeological study has yet given detailed consideration to the logic or limitations of this approach. A brief analysis of evolutionary typologies, and their role in archaeology, will illustrate the drawbacks of this research method.

The ethnologists who have attempted to develop evolutionary typologies have largely, although of course not exclusively, conceptualized social variables as dichotomous entities: for example, the presence–absence of pan-tribal sodalities, the presence–absence of redistribution, the presence–absence of differential access to resources, the presence–absence of occupational specialization, and so on (see Service 1962; Fried 1967.) It is interrelated combinations of such dichotomous attributes that are used to define evolutionary stages. Presumably, the means by which a newly discovered society, whether ethnographic or archaeological, can be assigned to a proper evolutionary slot is by keying the society on its various dichotomous attributes until the final combination of elements indicates its appropriate designation.

This keying procedure logically implies a specific strategy for archaeological research. Since combinations of dichotomous attributes designate societal types, the approach to modeling past social systems would be to specify archaeological indicators for the presence or absence of a large list of binary attributes. Armed with such a list of indicators, the archaeologist would then proceed to determine the presence or absence of each dichotomous character, eventually combining the results into a key that would indicate the appropriate evolutionary label for the society in question. This method of analysis, which is logically intrinsic to evolutionism, might be termed the *checklist* approach to social modeling. In fact, archaeologists working within the framework of evolutionary typologies have generally abridged this checklist procedure by identifying only a limited number of social characteristics, most often rank differences, and by inferring from these the appropriate typological designation for the society under consideration (but see Renfrew 1973). The implicit assumption in this approach is that the dichotomous attributes defining societal types are so strongly associated and so highly redundant that the identification of one implies the presence of all the others, as well as the abstracted societal form that they collectively designate. This assumption has never been subjected to rigorous testing, and so must be viewed with caution.

A primary drawback of this checklist approach is that it tends to mask the nature of societies as adaptive systems, leading instead to a view of societies as mere lists of traits. Adherence to evolutionary typologies will hinder the study of change in social systems as complex, integrated entities, rather than simply as lists of attributes. What is perhaps more fundamental, evolutionary typologies suffer from a failure to provide a finely differentiated scale against which to measure variation and change. The gross nominal categories that are the hallmark of evolutionism are simply inadequate for the purpose of meaningful comparative analysis. When diverse political forms, such as those that existed on the Northwest Coast and in aboriginal Hawaii, are condensed within the category of chiefdoms (Service 1962:153), then not only can this category have little meaning, but it is also of little utility in monitoring variation and change.

It should be understood that this discussion is not intended to urge a particularistic approach to research. Rather, the purpose is to underscore the limitations inherent in squeezing archaeological data into rigid, monothetically defined evolutionary slots. While such nominal categories can be of some value in research, particularly in facilitating description and communication, the goal of archaeological endeavor must transcend such categorizations and extend further than the mere labeling of prehistoric systems. Given the drawbacks to evolutionary typologies, alternative approaches to modeling social systems must be developed. Such approaches must be truly quantitative in nature in order to permit the study of social variation and change.

Measuring Structural Complexity

In any social system, from the simplest to the most complex, there will be at least several dimensions of structural differentiation. Peter Blau (1970:203–204) has provided a definition and characterization on the concept of dimensions of differentiation.

> A dimension of differentiation is any criterion on the basis of which the members of an organization are formally divided into positions, . . . or into ranks, . . . or into subunits. . . . A structural component is either a distinct official status . . . or a subunit in the organization. . . . The term differentiation refers to the number of structural components that are formally distinguished in terms of any *one* criterion. [Emphasis in original.]

For the analysis of prehistoric social systems, it is possible to abstract two dimensions of structural differentiation that are of general significance: These might be termed the *vertical* and the *horizontal dimensions*. The former clearly refers to the structure of rank grading in a society. The horizontal dimension, on the other hand, encompasses structural components that are equivalent on identical hierarchical levels and between which there are no major, institutionalized differences in rank. Examples of such horizontally differentiated components might include sodalities, individual descent units of segmentary descent systems, task groups, territorial bands, and the like.

To isolate structural differentiation along the vertical dimension, an objective and cross-culturally valid criterion for interpreting mortuary data can be developed. This interpretive principle is based on Arthur Saxe's (1970:6) observation that the occasion of death calls for the participation in mortuary ritual of the range of individuals who had entered into social relationships with the deceased. It follows from this observation, as Lewis Binford (1971:17, 21) has suggested, that there are generally two components of social significance that participate in structuring the form of mortuary ritual. The first is what in anthropological role theory (Goodenough 1965) has been called the *social persona* of the deceased, a term that refers to the range of social identities characterizing a person for any given interaction. The second is the size and internal composition of the social unit recognizing status responsibilities to the individual. In any system of hierarchical ranking, increased relative ranking of status positions will positively covary with increased numbers of persons recognizing duty–status relationships with individuals holding such status positions. Lewis Binford (1971:21) proposes that such a larger array of status relationships, which is characteristic of persons of high rank, entitles the deceased to a larger amount of corporate involvement in the act of interment, and to a larger degree of disruption of normal community activities for the mortuary ritual. Expanding upon this proposal, we may observe that both the amount of corporate involvement and the degree of activity disruption will positively correspond to the amount of human labor expended in the mortuary act. Directionally, higher social rank of a deceased individual will correspond to greater amounts of corporate involvement and activity disruption, and this should result in the expenditure of greater effort in the interment ritual. Labor expenditure should, in turn, be reflected in such features of burial as size and elaborateness of the interment facility, method of handling and disposal of the corpse, and the nature of grave associations.

This proposition linking labor expenditure in mortuary ritual to the rank of the deceased has been tested on a large ethnographic sample (103 cases). In this sample, there was not a single case that contradicted the labor expenditure argument (documentation in Tainter 1975). Such strong results suggest that the analysis of labor expenditure is essential for identifying patterns of rank grading in mortuary data. It must be stressed, however, that the evaluation of labor expenditure does not provide a panacea for all problems of mortuary analysis and should not be considered as a substitute for careful study of individual data sets. The labor expenditure argument simply provides an objective criterion for social inference that, if carefully applied, can yield comparable evaluations concerning rank differentiation in prehistoric societies.

Ultimately, the goal of studying labor expenditure is to quantify the amount of human energy expended in mortuary behavior. The attainment of this goal must await physiological studies documenting the quantities of energy human beings expend on the activities that comprise a mortuary ritual. For the present, degrees of labor expenditure must be evaluated on an ordinal scale by assessment of such factors as *(1)* the complexity of body treatment (for example, simple inhumation as opposed to cremation or skeletal manipulation), *(2)* the form and/or location of the interment facility (whether, for example, the body is interred in a simple earthen grave or in an elaborate, labor-consuming tomb), and *(3)* material contributions to the ritual (evaluated in terms of the effort required to produce or replace an item lost through inclusion in the grave).

Reversing our earlier reasoning, when sets of mortuary data cluster into distinctive levels of labor expenditure, this signifies distinctive levels of social involvement in the mortuary act and reflexively indicates distinctive levels or grades of ranking. As Blau (1970:203–204) has noted, such distinctive levels of ranking may be viewed as structural components of a social system. The number of such components will mark the degree of structural complexity along this dimension. The analysis of labor expenditure may, therefore, be used as a method for specifying the degree of structural differentiation along the vertical dimension in past social systems.

Unfortunately, no objective and cross-culturally valid criterion has been developed for monitoring structural differentiation along the horizontal dimension. Actually, however, this conceptual void presents no obstruction. In an analysis of structural differentiation in modern economic organizations, Blau (1970) found that the size of an organization correlates strongly with the number of hierarchical levels, the number of occupational divisions, and the number of functional divisions. In short, the size of an organization covaries with both its degree of vertical differentiation and its degree of horizontal differentiation. Blau divided segments of the organizations with which he dealt into functionally discrete types, thus making it possible to analyze structure while controlling function. Among these separate divisions, the same results obtained: The size of an organization correlates with its degrees of both vertical and horizontal differentiation. This result suggests that the observations obtained are independent of an organization's function (Blau 1970:204, 206) and pertain instead to structural characteristics of organizations in general. This finding indicates that Blau's results may be considered applicable to any type of organization, including the prehistoric social systems with which archaeologists deal.

The demonstration that the size of an organization covaries with its degrees of both vertical and horizontal differentiation is significant for archaeological research. The strength of the observed correlations (see Blau 1970) suggests that any one of these characteristics of a social system may be used to monitor not only itself, but the state of the other two as well. Thus, structural differentiation along the vertical dimension can serve as an index of the total structural complexity of a past social system.

Measuring Organization

Organization has been defined previously as the constraints imposed upon the ranges of behavior that may be pursued by the elements of a system (Rothstein 1958:34–36). Since organization is basically related to constraint on behavior, the measurement of organization must be approached through the measurement of behavioral constraint. The field that provides techniques for the measurement of organization is information theory.

Information theory, as Kullback (1959:1) has noted, "is a branch of the mathematical theory of probability and statistics. As such, its abstract formulations are applicable to any probabilistic or statistical system of observations." Information theory is closely linked with the field of communication theory and is often mistakenly referred to as another label for this field. The concept of information in communication theory focuses on the existence of a set of messages, from which one is selected for transmission (Shannon 1949:31). Information, then, can be considered a measure of one's freedom of choice to select a particular message from this set (Weaver 1949:9), as well as a measure of the amount of surprise one registers at receiving a particular message (Goldman 1953:1–2; Theil 1967:3; Young 1971:18–19).

The concept of information is closely linked with that of entropy, which is a measure of disorder, disorganization, lack of patterning, or randomness. In communication systems, the entropy of a message ensemble is at a maximum when all possible messages have an equal probability of occurrence and decreases when some messages are more likely a priori candidates for transmission than others (Shannon 1949:51). In such communication systems, both information and entropy directly covary. If information is conceptualized in terms of the freedom of choice to select a given message, then information is at a maximum under conditions of statistical equilibrium, when all messages are equally probable; in this case, no probability constraints decrease the degree of freedom in selection (Weaver 1949:12–13). Similarly, the information derived when a particular message is transmitted is at a maximum when all messages were a priori equally probable and, hence, the occurrence of any specific message unpredictable (cf. Theil 1967:3). Since a condition of statistical equilibrium (when all messages are equally probable) is a situation of maximal entropy, and since statistical equilibrium is also a condition under which the maximum information may be conveyed when a particular message is sent, entropy and information in communication systems are analogous concepts. Entropy, being a measure of disorganization, will, of course, vary inversely with the organization of a system. Since organization is defined as constraint, decreases in the entropy of a message ensemble will occur when probability constraints limit the freedom to select certain messages for transmission.

The concepts of entropy and organization in communication theory are analogous to the concepts underlying the use of information theory to measure organization in social systems. To illustrate this, let us consider a hypothetical social system structurally differentiated into a number of components. In the total absence of *any* organizational constraints arising from the interaction among these components, the process by which individuals acquire membership in the components would be purely random. In the long run, such a random process would result in a situation in which the proportion of the population selecting affiliation with each component would be a fraction equal to $1/N$, where N is the number of components. Such a proportional distribution, of course, corresponds to a situation of statistical equilibrium and, hence, to a condition of entropy.

But, of course, no social situation totally lacks constraints of one form or another. To the extent that either social or demographic pressures limit the freedom to acquire membership in certain components, there is constraint and, thus, organization. In the presence of such constraints, the proportion of the population affiliated with certain components will no longer result from random processes and will correspondingly depart from a condition of statistical equilibrium. It is precisely such departures from equilibrium that the mathematical techniques of information theory may be used to measure.

It can be seen from this discussion that information theory, as applied here, can be used to measure certain types of constraints that function in a demographic context, constraints that operate to *organize* a population into membership in the components of a social system. In societies characterized by hierarchical ranking, such demographic constraints will in part measure restrictions on access to positions of high rank. Organizational constraints on access to such positions will be directly associated with other organizational constraints affecting a system's behavior, because, in hierarchically ordered societies, major decision-making processes are often localized in the upper rank grades. This last point indicates that the measurement of demographic organization should indirectly measure a social system's requirements for centralized decision making and for centralized control of behavior. One would expect that systems placing extensive constraints on access to positions of high rank would be systems that require centralized decision-making by individuals possessing critical, but rare, capabilities or by persons (or groups) controlling crucial, but limited, resources.

Information measures can assess organizational constraint in societies with either achieved or ascribed positions of rank. In systems of achieved ranking, the measures will directly reflect constraints on the acquisition of positions of rank. In societies with ascribed ranking, the information measures will reflect constraints on the segment of the population within which positions of high rank are inherited.

The formula for measuring information, as developed by Shannon (1949:50–51), is

$$H = -K \sum_{i=1}^{N} p_i \log p_i$$

where K is a positive constant, and p_i is the probability of occurrence of the ith message (or, for our purposes, the ith structural component). Since the constant K merely amounts to a choice of a unit of measure and is commonly set at 1.0, the formula, for practical purposes, becomes

$$H = - \sum_{i=1}^{N} p_i \log p_i$$

or

$$H = \sum_{i=1}^{N} p_i \log 1/p_i$$

which is the entropy (information) of a set of probabilities. The logarithm used in the equation is usually taken to the base 2, but logarithms taken to any other base obviously provide comparable results. This information measure ranges from 0 (no entropy) to $\log N$, when all messages or components are equally probable (maximum entropy, referred to as H_{max}).

This formula leads directly to a measure of organization. Rothstein (1958:36) has proposed that organization be measured as the excess of the maximum entropy a system may potentially exhibit, less the entropy it actually does exhibit, as in the following equation. Gatlin (1972:35–36) refers to this measure as the Divergence from Equiprobability, symbolized as D_1. The formula for organization, which can range from 0 (maximum entropy) to a value that converges on H_{max} (maximum organization), is

$$D_1 = H_{max} - H$$

H_{max} is, of course, $\log N$, where N is the number of structural components.

At this point, an important distinction must be introduced. It is obvious from the calculation of the D_1 measure that the amount of organization a system may potentially exhibit increases with its degree of structural complexity. Since the maximum D_1 value is equal to H_{max}, or $\log N$, increases in the number of components (that is, increases in H_{max}) will lead to increases in the maximum possible organization in a system. This point is note-worthy: As a system increases in structural complexity, its capacity for organization changes correspondingly. Yet, in the study of prehistoric social organization, it may prove enlightening to investigate not only the amount of organization, but also the extent to which any system maximizes its organizational potential within the confines of its structural limits. In the latter instance, we are asking how much constraint (organization) is imposed on a population's distribution among the components of a system relative to the amount that might be imposed. In other words, we are making the distinction between the *amount* and the *degree* of organization. D_1 measures the former; to compute the latter, we can use the simple ratio D_1/H_{max}. This measure can be referred to as the degree of organization, or relative organization, and will be symbolized as RD_1. This ratio, which is equivalent to the standard information–theoretic measure of redundancy, $1 - (H/H_{max})$, will range between 0 (maximum relative entropy) and a value that approaches 1.0 (maximum relative organization).

One might legitimately raise the question of how seriously these measures could be skewed by such common archaeological factors as sampling variations, poor preservation, missing data, and so forth. In fact, the use of information measures provides a partial solution to these typical problems. Quastler (1955:78–82) has demonstrated that information measures will not be significantly skewed by moderate fluctuations in probability. Random variations in probability will not significantly alter the value of an entropy measure, and, therefore, probably will not cause inaccurate interpretations concerning the organization of social systems.

Measuring Rank Differentiation

Rank differentiation is included in the variables of a social system to be measured because it includes elements of both structure and organization. Levels of ranking may be viewed as structural components of a system, while organization, and hence behavioral constraint, is clearly an element of rank differentiation.

Kemeny and Snell (1962:104) have suggested that a measure of the status of individuals in an organization must satisfy several requirements. For the status measure $s(P)$ of a person P in a social system, three of these requirements are:

1. If P has no subordinates, then $s(P) = 0$.
2. If, without otherwise changing the structure, we add a new person subordinate to P, then $s(P)$ increases.
3. If, without otherwise changing the structure, we move a subordinate of P to a lower level (relative to P), then $s(P)$ increases.

In essence, then, the status measure of an individual should be based upon two interacting factors: the number of persons subordinate to the individual and the number of rank grades separating these subordinates from the person of higher status.

Frank Harary (1959:23–25) has proposed a measure that fulfills these requirements. This measure was developed from the field of graph theory and is designed to evaluate what Harary terms "structural or positional status." In a ranked hierarchy, for any person P who has n_k subordinates at rank level k (rank levels are numbered downward from any given rank level, so that the first level down is 1, the second is 2, etc.), and where M is the number of rank levels below P, the status $s(P)$ of person P can be measured by the formula

$$s(P) = \sum_{k=1}^{M} k(n_k).$$

Expressed verbally, the status $s(P)$ of a person P in an organization is the number of the individual's immediate subordinates, plus twice the number of their immediate subordinates, plus three times the number of their immediate subordinates, and so fourth. By constructing a graph of a hierarchical organization, one can illustrate the reasoning behind this measure. Figure 9.1 presents a graph of a hierarchical organization consisting of four levels. To assess the status of A in this hierarchy, we note that A has two subordinates in level B, four in level C, and eight in level D. The status relationship to individual A of persons in levels C or D, however, cannot be the same as the relationship of the persons in level B to A. In addition to the gross number of A's subordinates, the distance from A to B, A to C, and A to D must be considered in the status measure of A. The status of A is then calculated as the sum for all levels of the number of subordinates in each level times the number of links in the graph that separate that level from A.

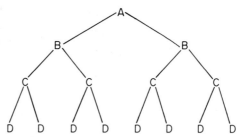

Figure 9.1 Graph of hierarchical organization.

In archaeological analysis, it is, of course, quite impossible to determine the number of individuals who were subordinate to a person of paramount rank at any point in time. It is possible archaeologically to determine the number of levels of ranking in a past social system and to ascertain the number of persons in an entire mortuary population who were members of each rank grade. To compute the $s(P)$ measure, we need only to consider subordinate rank levels as multiples (or fractions) of the number of persons in the paramount rank grade. The formula used to compute these multiples would simply be N_k/N_1, where N_k refers to the number of persons in rank level k, and N_1 indicates the number in the highest rank level. With this transformation, the paramount rank grade will always be associated with the value 1.0, and the remaining levels will become appropriate multiples (or fractions) of 1.0. This transformation will render mortuary data suitable for the calculation of $s(P)$ values. The degree of rank differentiation in a hierarchy can then be expressed as the difference between the highest and lowest levels. Since the status of the lowest level is always zero, the degree of rank differentiation can be expressed as $s(1)$, the status measure of the highest level.

A Test Case for the Analysis of Social Change

The usefulness of the framework developed thus far can be illustrated by applying it to an enduring research problem: the nature of social change between the Middle and Late Woodland periods in the Midwest.

The Middle Woodland, or Hopewell, period is widely known for the degree of cultural complexity that is reflected in the archaeological record. Perhaps the best known of the features defining the Middle Woodland period are systems of elaborate mortuary ritual. These systems are of obvious interest to the present study. Other Middle Woodland characteristics that have been detailed include highly ornate artifact styles, long-distance trade in exotic raw materials and perhaps in finished artifacts, and, in many locations, the construction of large-scale earthworks (Griffin 1967; Prufer 1964; Struever 1964; Struever and Houart 1972).

The Late Woodland period, while less well documented, can be contrasted with the Hopewellian features just outlined on a number of dimensions. There appears to have been a marked degree of attenuation in mortuary ceremonialism and a constriction in the elaborateness and diversity of artifact forms. Correspondingly, there was a severe curtailment of extraregional trade relationships and an end to the construction of extremely large earthworks (cf. Prufer 1964; Griffin 1967). The Late Woodland period, then, is associated with archaeological indications of a cultural system that has undergone a shift away from earthwork constructions requiring relatively large-scale labor organization, away from elaborate mortuary ceremonialism, and away from certain forms of economic interaction among social units. Therefore, the archaeological record seems to indicate alterations that can best be described as reflections of major cultural change.

The region of the Midwest that is of most immediate interest is the portion of west-central Illinois that includes the Illinois River and Mississippi River drainages. In this area, the Middle Woodland period dates between 150 B.C. and A.D. 400 (Struever 1968:141), while the succeeding Late Woodland period extends until around A.D. 900. After A.D. 900, there is evidence of the development of the complex types of cultural systems that existed during the Mississippian period (Fowler and Hall 1972:4). The problem of Woodland social change has been considered by investigators working in this area, albeit in a very cursory manner. Previous research has suggested a decrease in status differentiation and social complexity between the Middle and Late Woodland periods (McGregor 1958:188–190; cf. Wray *et al.* 1961:66; Morse 1963:11, 113), followed by increases in these variables during the initial Mississippian period (Harn 1973:10; Fowler and Hall 1972:4).

Although vague and qualitative, these suggestions provide a background for the quantitative analysis of Woodland social change. A total of six sets of mortuary data are available from this region. These span the time interval between ca. A.D. 200 and 800. Each data set includes the total recovered mortuary population from a single mound group. These mound groups are, for the most part, well dated, and every effort has been made to ensure that each individual data set is temporally homogeneous. The archaeological characteristics of these mound groups, radiocarbon determinations, methods of data coding and analysis, and other pertinent information have been discussed elsewhere (Tainter 1975) and need not be covered at length here.

The Middle Woodland mortuary system considered in this study appears to contain six distinctive levels of labor expenditure. These may be described on an ordinal scale.

Level 1. This level is composed of individuals placed in, or processed through, large tombs that formed the central node in most Middle Woodland mounds. These tombs regularly display log roofs, as well as log or limestone walls, and are surrounded by ramps of loaded earth. Individuals placed in these tombs were periodically removed and reburied nearby as bundles of disarticulated bones, while subsequent individuals were interred in the feature (Perino 1968:38; Buikstra 1972:33–34). Individuals placed in these tombs were associated with nearly all of the exotic, imported materials found with mortuary remains. This mode of disposal reflects greater amounts of labor expenditure than any other Middle Woodland form of interment.

Level 2. The second level of labor expenditure is reflected in graves arranged peripherally about the central tombs. These particular graves displayed log coverings over the grave but were substantially smaller and less elaborate than the central log tombs.

Level 3. The third level of labor expenditure includes burials with limestone slabs placed in the grave, occasionally as specific arrangements around the body (e.g., Perino 1968:35).

Level 4. The set of individuals comprising this level were identified by the placement of locally produced sociotechnic items (see Binford 1962) in the grave. The most common items thus included were Hopewell series pottery vessels. Struever and Houart (1972:74–75) have suggested that these vessels were produced in the Illinois Valley and occasionally distributed to other areas of the Midwest.

Level 5. The individuals in this level were interred in mounds in simple subfloor graves, with little effort expended on the construction of the facility.

Level 6. The lowest amount of labor expenditure was allocated to persons in this level. These individuals were merely deposited on accretional surfaces of the mound, and small amounts of earth were piled over them. This mode of disposal required less effort than the excavation of subfloor graves for individuals in Level 5.

In terms of the arguments presented earlier, these distinctive levels of labor expenditure can be viewed as reflecting distinctive levels of social involvement in the mortuary act. These distinctive levels of social involvement reflexively indicate distinctive grades of hierarchical ranking. Therefore, the Middle Woodland social system appears to have been characterized by six grades of ranking.

Of the five Late Woodland data sets analyzed, the Schild mound group (Perino 1973) may be selected to illustrate levels of labor expenditure in Late Woodland mortuary systems. The other Late Woodland mound groups display mortuary patterns that are basically similar to the Schild group. While the Middle Woodland mortuary system included six levels of labor expenditure, only five levels are evident in the Schild data.

Level 1. The greatest amount of labor in the Schild mortuary system was expended on persons buried in large, log-roofed tombs. Some of these tombs were, in turn, used as crematories. The log tombs in this mound group were substantially less elaborate than the ones in Middle Woodland mounds.

Level 2. The second level of labor expenditure included a degree of custodial care and skeletal manipulation that resulted in the final interment of a disarticulated bundle of bones.

Level 3. This level is identified as a set of interments accorded the placement of limestone slabs over the grave.

Level 4. The fourth level in the Schild system includes individuals associated with certain forms of sociotechnic items. These items, like the Late Woodland technological system in general, were noticeably less elaborate than the grave associations found in Middle Woodland mounds. While sociotechnic items in Middle Woodland mounds might include copper ornaments, Gulf Coast shells, and other exotic materials, in Late Woodland mounds, ornamental grave associations are limited to items such as *Anculosa* shell beads.

Level 5. This level includes the largest segment of the population and consists of persons merely interred in a flexed position, in otherwise unpretentious graves.

This discussion suggests that the Late Woodland social system that is reflected in the Schild data was structurally differentiated into five levels of ranking.

In both the Middle and Late Woodland data sets, the rank levels that have been identified generally display population profiles in which all age grades, from infant to 50+ years, are represented. The expenditure of identical amounts of effort on the interment of infants and full adults indicates that the level of social involvement in the mortuary act was not linked to age-graded distinctions. This suggests that the status positions involved were not acquired by means of passing through age grades and were not dependent upon the performance of age-linked activities. One might interpret these status positions, therefore, as largely inheritable (cf. Saxe 1970:8). There are exceptions to this pattern, and at least a minority of the status levels in Woodland social systems were achieved positions. In all cases, however, the paramount rank level seems to have been a hereditary, ascribed status.

Table 9.1 shows the distribution of the mound group populations among the rank levels identified in the data sets. This table provides the basic information that is used to calculate the measures of organization and rank differentiation. Actual calculation of these measures is illustrated for the Middle Woodland data in Tables 9.2 and 9.3. Structurally, the Middle Woodland social system comprised six levels of ranking. As Table 9.2 shows, the entropy (H) of the population distribution among these levels is 1.8354 bits. Since the maximum possible entropy for six structural components (H_{max}) is 2.58496 bits, the amount of organization in the system (D_1) is $(2.58496 - 1.8354)$ .7496. The degree of organization (RD_1), on the other hand, amounts to $(.7496/2.58496)$ .29. These figures measure both the amount and the degree of constraint on the distribution of the population among rank levels. The rank differentiation in the Middle Woodland data is calculated in Table 9.3. The status measure of the paramount rank grade, $s(1)$, amounts to 13.671, a figure that may be used to indicate the degree of rank differentiation in the system.

Two of the dimensions that were specified earlier as essential components of this model of past social systems may be eliminated from further discussion.

Table 9.1

Population Distribution among Rank Levels in Mound Groups

Rank levels	Klunk-Gibson		Joe Gay		Koster		Klunk L. W.		Homer Adams		Schild	
	N	%	N	%	N	%	N	%	N	%	N	%
1	91	20.5	27	14.6	5	1.9	29	47.5	33	23.9	35	12.5
2	58	13.1	4	2.2	95	36.1	6	9.8	50	36.2	7	2.5
3	11	2.5	7	3.8	7	2.7	3	4.9	3	2.2	3	1.1
4	5	1.1	51	27.6	12	4.6	5	8.2	8	5.8	4	1.4
5	241	54.4	96	51.9	7	2.7	18	29.5	44	31.9	230	82.4
6	37	8.4			137	52.1						
Totals	443	100.0	185	100.1	263	100.1	61	99.9	138	100.0	279	99.9

342

Table 9.2

Entropy of Middle Woodland Rank System

Rank level	p	$\log_2 1/p$	$p \log_2 1/p$
1	.205	2.28630	.4687
2	.131	2.93236	.3841
3	.025	5.32193	.1330
4	.011	6.50635	.0716
5	.544	.878321	.4778
6	.084	3.57347	.3002
			$\Sigma = 1.8354$

These are the *nature of structural differentiation* and the *nature of organization.* In the data sets used here, the social system was structurally differentiated along the vertical dimension and was organized correspondingly. Middle and Late Woodland societies in this region were distinctively hierarchical in nature. This attribute appears to have been an immutable constant, and, therefore, it does not enter into a consideration of social change.

Changes in the other dimensions that we have isolated are noticeable and significant. Table 9.4 specifies the values for these dimensions. In this table, the dates given for mound groups represent either weighted averages for a series of radiocarbon determinations (although, for the Middle Woodland data set, only one radiocarbon date is available) or midpoints of estimated temporal ranges. In all cases, the temporal ranges for these mound groups was small, and, therefore, it was possible to average radiocarbon determinations to obtain a mean date for a mound group. The largest standard deviation for the averaged radiocarbon dates is 85 years, while the maximum range for the mound groups that have been cross-dated by artifactual inclusions is estimated to be ±100 years (see Tainter 1975). With the information in this table, it is possible to outline the trends of Woodland social change.

Table 9.3

Middle Woodland Rank Differentiation

Rank level	N	N_k/N_1	$s(1)$
1	91	1.000	13.671
2	58	.637	
3	11	.121	
4	5	.055	
5	241	2.648	
6	37	.407	

Table 9.4
Dimensions of Variation in Woodland Social Systems

Mound group	Date	R.L.[a]	D_1	RD_1	$s(1)$
Middle Woodland					
Klunk-Gibson	A.D. 180	6	.7496	.2900	13.671
Late Woodland					
Joe Gay	A.D. 650	5	.6125	.2638	20.446
Koster	A.D. 650	6	.9710	.3756	171.600
Klunk L.W.	A.D. 700	5	.4546	.1958	3.413
Homer Adams	A.D. 700	5	.4125	.1777	7.756
Schild	A.D. 790	5	1.4260	.6141	26.998

[a] Number of structurally differentiated rank levels.

Changes in Structural Complexity

Perhaps the most constant distinction between the Middle and Late Woodland social systems was the lower degree of structural complexity that characterized the later systems. While the Middle Woodland system displays six hierarchical grades of ranking, Late Woodland data sets generally reflect five structural levels. The exception to this pattern is the Late Woodland Koster mound group. Nevertheless, this exception appears to have been unique, or at least unusual. The majority of data sets suggest that Late Woodland social systems were structurally less complex than their Middle Woodland counterparts.

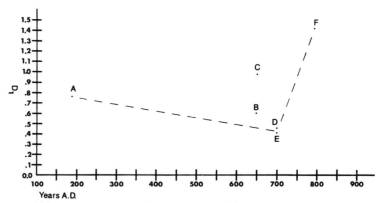

Figure 9.2 Changes in the amount of organization in Woodland social systems. Dimension D_1 indicates the divergence from equiprobability, the measure of the amount of organization. The dashed line indicates the pattern of change in this dimension. *Key:* A. Klunk-Gibson; B. Joe Gay; C. Koster; D. Klunk Late Woodland; E. Homer Adams; F. Schild.

Changes in the Amount of Organization

With the exception of the Koster mound group, Late Woodland social systems during the time period ca. A.D. 650–700 were characterized by a lower amount of organization than is evident during the Middle Woodland period (Figure 9.2). As with all other social variables, the Koster mound group appears to be an exception to this general trend in organizational change. There are, however, substantial reasons for doubting the reliability of the recovered Koster sample (see Tainter 1975:186), and, therefore, this anomaly is not considered significant.

Toward the end of the Late Woodland period, there was a marked increase in the amount of organization in social groups. In fact, so great was this increase in organization that the Late Woodland system represented in the Schild mound group displayed a far higher amount of organization than the Middle Woodland system.

Changes in the Degree of Organization

Changes in the degree of organization characterizing Woodland social units parallel changes in the amount of organization (Figure 9.3). This dimension shows a small, but general, decrease between the Middle Woodland system and the Late Woodland systems of ca. A.D. 650–700. (The anomalous exception to this trend is, again, the Koster mound group.) However, toward the end of the Late Woodland period, the degree of organization rose markedly to the highest value evident in any of the data sets. The Schild mound group, which is temporally the most recent data set considered in this study, reflects a social system that was demographically organized at close to the maximum level possible for a system with five hierarchical components.

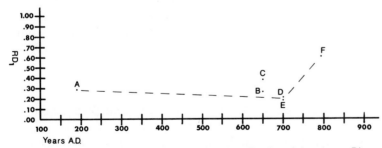

Figure 9.3 Changes in the degree of organization in Woodland social systems. Dimension RD_1 indicates the relative divergence from equiprobability, the measure of relative organization. The dashed line indicates the pattern of change in this dimension. Key: A. Klunk-Gibson; B. Joe Gay; C. Koster; D. Klunk Late Woodland; E. Homer Adams; F. Schild.

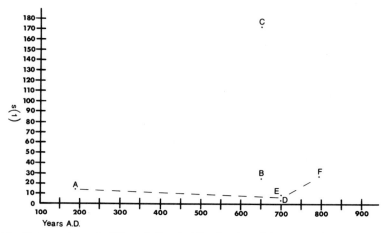

Figure 9.4 Changes in rank differentiation in Woodland social systems. Dimension $s(1)$ indicates the degree of rank differentiation in each system. The dashed line indicates the general pattern of change in this dimension. Key: A. Klunk-Gibson; B. Joe Gay; C. Koster; D. Klunk Late Woodland; E. Homer Adams; F. Schild.

Changes in Rank Differentiation

Changes in this dimension generally, although not entirely, mirror the changes that took place in the organization of Woodland social systems (Figure 9.4). There was a general decrease in rank differentiation in localized social units between the Middle Woodland period and the earlier Late Woodland systems. The Joe Gay system, however, appears to be an exception to this general trend, for, in this data set, a slightly greater degree of rank differentiation is evident than what is apparent in the Middle Woodland data. The Koster mound group is noticeably anomalous, displaying a strikingly high degree of rank differentiation. As was noted earlier, there are substantial reasons for questioning the reliability of the Koster sample.

As in the other social dimensions, the degree of rank differentiation increased toward the end of the Late Woodland period. The Schild mound group displays a higher value for this variable than is evident even in the Middle Woodland series.

Woodland Social Change: Summary and Discussion

The Middle to Late Woodland transition seems, from the data analyzed, to have involved a number of distinctive social changes. The most constant of these was a decrease in the structural complexity of social units. Correspondingly, there were decreases in both the amount and degree of organization characterizing Woodland social groups. The degree of rank differentiation also generally decreased between the Middle and Late Woodland periods, although the Joe Gay mound group did display a somewhat higher value on this dimension than the Middle Woodland system.

This trend appears to have altered after A.D. 700. Between A.D. 700 and perhaps 800, the Late Woodland social system underwent changes that resulted in both a higher amount and degree of organization and in a higher degree of rank differentiation. This pattern of change suggests that later Late Woodland cultural systems were formulating an adaptive social posture that led to the highly organized and highly differentiated social systems characterizing the succeeding Mississippian period.

It is possible to suggest relationships between this pattern of social change and other elements of change that occurred during the Late Woodland period. There was a sharp and continued rise in population density in the region (DeRousseau 1973) that forced major population resettlement from the Illinois Valley trench to the upper reaches of drainages tributary to the Illinois (cf. Farnsworth 1973:17–18). This population increase may have caused subsistence stress and nutritional deterioration, which were reflected in a more severe mortality pattern (Cook 1974) and in a lower childhood growth rate (Cook 1972) in Late Woodland and early Mississippian populations. This subsistence stress may have precipitated competition and conflict among groups, for Late Woodland mounds display a noticeable frequency of violent deaths. The response to this situation, during the earlier Late Woodland period, was to maintain a generalized hunting and gathering subsistence system (cf. Munson et al. 1971). Sometime after A.D. 800, a point was reached at which this system could no longer be maintained, and a shift to maize agriculture ensured (Cutler and Blake 1969; Munson 1971:10–12, 1973:110; Harn 1971:33).

The mortuary data yield evidence indicating that the Late Woodland response to stress was not limited to changes in the settlement location and subsistence strategies. Adaptive responses occurred in the social system as well. Although the structural complexity of the system remained constant, changes occurred in the direction of increased organization and increased rank differentiation. These types of changes are basically related to the integrative capacity of a social system. A more highly organized system, characterized by greater rank differentiation, would have been increasingly capable of regulating task performance, allocating personnel to task units, directing energy flows, and coping with competition. In essence, the later Late Woodland response to stress involved alterations in the subsistence strategy and may also have involved greater centralized control of both task units and their output. This centralized control would have resulted in greater regularity in subsistence-related behavior, and, correspondingly, in decreased uncertainty concerning energy flows. The fact that this strategy of increased social complexity proved successful is indicated by the long duration of complex social systems during the succeeding Mississippian period, not only in Illinois, but also throughout many areas of the Eastern Woodlands.

Concluding Note

In summary, the concepts and quantitative methods developed in this study have proven useful in an archaeological study of social change. The concepts underlying this approach have successfully guided the investigation to the isolation of social variables that are significant for the study of change. The quantitative methods have revealed patterns of social change that parallel the qualitative suggestions of earlier research (McGregor 1958:188–190; Harn 1973:10), and which provide evidence of organizational responses to conditions of nutritional stress and competition. These concepts and quantitative methods may, therefore, be considered valuable tools for modeling change in prehistoric social systems.

ACKNOWLEDGMENTS

I would like to express my gratitude to Gregory Perino, Della Cook, and Jane Buikstra, who generously made available the unpublished data that forms the basis for much of this study.

REFERENCES

Bertalanffy, Ludwig von
  1968   *General system theory.* New York: George Braziller.
Binford, Lewis R.
  1962   Archaeology as anthropology. *American Antiquity* **28:**217–225.
  1971   Mortuary practices: Their study and their potential. In *Approaches to the social dimensions of mortuary practices,* edited by James A. Brown. *Society for American Archaeology Memoir* 25. Pp. 6–29.
Blau, Peter M.
  1970   A formal theory of differentiation in organizations. *American Sociological Review* **35:**201–218.
Brown, James A.
  1971   The dimensions of status in the burials at Spiro. In *Approaches to the social dimensions of mortuary practices,* edited by James A. Brown. *Society for American Archaeology Memoir* 25. Pp. 92–112.
Buikstra, Jane E.
  1972   *Hopewell in the lower Illinois River Valley: A regional approach to the study of biological variability and mortuary activity.* Unpublished doctoral dissertation, University of Chicago.
Cook, Della C.
  1972   Human growth rate as a measure of subsistence base changes in Middle and Late Woodland Indians. Paper presented at the 1972 meeting of the Canadian Archaeological Association, St. John's, Newfoundland.
  1974   Mortuary practice: An assessment of sources of error in paleodemography. Paper presented at the 1974 meeting of the American Association of Physical Anthropologists, Amherst, Mass.
Cutler, Hugh C., and Leonard W. Blake
  1969   Corn from Cahokia sites. In *Explorations into Cahokia archaeology,* edited by Melvin L. Fowler. *Illinois Archaeological Survey Bulletin* No. 7. Pp. 122–136.
DeRousseau, C. Jean
  1973   A model of population change in the lower Illinois River Valley: 150 B.C.–1200 A.D.

Paper presented at the 1973 meeting of the American Anthropological Association, New Orleans.

Farnsworth, Kenneth B.
  1973   An archaeological survey of the Macoupin Valley. *Illinois State Museum Reports of Investigations* No. 26. *Illinois Valley Archaeological Program Research Papers,* Vol. 7.

Fowler, Melvin L., and Robert L. Hall
  1972   Archaeological phases at Cahokia. *Illinois State Museum Research Series, Papers in Anthropology* No. 1.

Fried, Morton H.
  1967   *The evolution of political society, an essay in political anthropology.* New York: Random House.

Gatlin, Lila L.
  1972   *Information theory and the living system.* New York: Columbia University Press.

Goldman, Stanford
  1953   *Information theory.* New York: Dover.

Goodenough, Ward H.
  1965   Rethinking "status" and "role": Toward a general model of the cultural organization of social relationships. In *The relevance of models for social anthropology,* edited by Michael Banton. *A.S.A., Monographs* 1. London: Tavistock. Pp. 1–24.

Griffin, James B.
  1967   Eastern North American archaeology: A summary. *Science* **156:**175–191.

Harary, Frank
  1959   Status and contrastatus. *Sociometry* **22:**23–43.

Harn, Alan D.
  1971   An archaeological survey of the American Bottoms in Madison and St. Clair counties, Illinois. *Illinois State Museum Reports of Investigations* No. 21.
  1973   Cahokia and the Mississippian emergence in the Spoon River area of Illinois. Paper presented at the 1973 meeting of the Central States Anthropological Society, St. Louis. Mo.

Kemeny, John G., and J. Laurie Snell
  1962   *Mathematical models in the social sciences.* Waltham, Mass.: Blaisdell.

King, Thomas F.
  1970   The dead at Tiburon: Mortuary customs and social organization on northern San Francisco Bay. *Northwestern California Archaeological Society Occasional Papers,* No. 2.

Kullback, Solomon
  1959   *Information theory and statistics.* New York: Wiley.

McGregor, John C.
  1958   *The Pool and Irving villages.* Urbana, Ill.: University of Illinois Press.

Miller, James G.
  1965   Living systems: Basic concepts. *Behavioral Science* **10:**193–237.

Morse, Dan F.
  1963   The Steuben village and mounds: A multicomponent late Hopewell site in Illinois. *University of Michigan, Museum of Anthropology, Anthropological Papers* No. 21.

Munson, Patrick J.
  1971   An archaeological survey of the Wood River terrace and adjacent bottoms and bluffs in Madison County, Illinois. *Illinois State Museum Reports of Investigations* No. 21.
  1973   The origins and antiquity of maize–beans–squash agriculture in eastern North America: Some linguistic implications. In *Variation in anthropology: Essays in honor of John C. McGregor,* edited by Donald W. Lathrap and Jody Douglas. Urbana: Illinois Archaeological Survey. Pp. 107–135.

Munson, Patrick J, Paul W. Parmalee, and Richard A. Yarnell
  1971   Subsistence ecology of Scovill, a terminal Middle Woodland village. *American Antiquity* **36:**410–431.

Peebles, Christopher S.
  1974   *Moundville: The organization of a prehistoric community and culture.* Unpublished doctoral dissertation, University of California, Santa Barbara. (University Microfilms, Ann Arbor.)
Perino, Gregory
  1968   The Pete Klunk mound group, Calhoun County, Illinois: The Archaic and Hopewell occupations. In *Hopewell and Woodland site archaeology in Illinois,* edited by James A. Brown. *Illinois Archaeological Survey, Bulletin* No. 6. Pp. 9–124.
  1973   The Late Woodland component at the Schild sites, Greene County, Illinois. In *Late Woodland site archaeology in Illinois I,* edited by James A. Brown. *Illinois Archaeological Survey, Bulletin* No. 9. Pp. 90–140.
Prufer, Olaf H.
  1964   The Hopewell complex of Ohio. In *Hopewellian studies,* edited by Joseph R. Caldwell and Robert L. Hall. *Illinois State Museum Scientific Papers* No. 12. Pp. 35–84.
Quastler, Henry
  1955   Comments on "Tables for computing informational measures" by E. T. Klemmer. In *Information theory in psychology: Problems and methods,* edited by Henry Quastler. Glencoe, Ill.: Free Press. Pp. 78–83.
Renfrew, Colin
  1973   Monuments, mobilization, and social organization in neolithic Wessex. In *The explanation of culture change: Models in prehistory,* edited by Colin Renfrew. London: Duckworth. Pp. 539–558.
Rothstein, Jerome
  1958   *Communication, organization, and science.* Indian Hills, Colo.: Falcon's Wing Press.
Saxe, Arthur A.
  1970   *Social dimensions of mortuary practices.* Unpublished doctoral dissertation, University of Michigan. (University Microfilms, Ann Arbor.)
Service, Elman R.
  1962   *Primitive social organization, an evolutionary perspective.* New York: Random House.
Shannon, Claude E.
  1949   The mathematical theory of communication. In *The mathematical theory of communication,* by Claude E. Shannon and Warren Weaver. Urbana: University of Illinois Press. Pp. 29–125.
Stickel, Edwin Gary
  1968   Status differentiations at the Rincon Site. *Archaeological Survey Annual Report* No. 10. Pp. 209–261. University of California, Los Angeles.
Struever, Stuart
  1964   The Hopewell Interaction Sphere in riverine-western Great Lakes culture history. In *Hopewellian studies,* edited by Joseph R. Caldwell and Robert L. Hall. *Illinois State Museum Scientific Papers* No. 12. Pp. 85–106.
  1968   *A re-examination of Hopewell in eastern North America.* Unpublished doctoral dissertation, University of Chicago.
Struever, Stuart, and Gail L. Houart
  1972   An analysis of the Hopewell interaction sphere. In *Social exchange and interaction,* edited by Edwin N. Wilmsen. *University of Michigan, Museum of Anthropology, Anthropological Papers* No. 46. Pp. 47–49.
Tainter, Joseph A.
  1971   Salvage excavations at the Fowler Site: Some aspects of the social organization of the northern Chumash. *San Luis Obispo County Archaeological Society Occasional Papers* No. 3.
  1975   *The archaeological study of social change: Woodland systems in west-central Illinois.* Unpublished doctoral dissertation, Northwestern University. (University Microfilms, Ann Arbor.)
Theil, Henri
  1967   *Economics and information theory.* Amsterdam: North-Holland.

Weaver, Warren
    1949   Recent contributions to the mathematical theory of communication. In *The mathematical theory of communication*, by Claude E. Shannon and Warren Weaver. Urbana: University of Illinois Press. Pp. 1–28.
Wray, Donald E., Richard S. MacNeish, and Warren L. Wittry
    1961   The Hopewellian and Weaver occupations at the Weaver site, Fulton County, Illinois. *Illinois State Museum Scientific Papers* **7**(2).
Young, J. F.
    1971   *Information theory* New York: Wiley Interscience.

10

Theory Building and the Study of Evolutionary Process in Complex Societies

J. STEPHEN ATHENS
University of New Mexico

Introduction

There has been no adequate general explanation for the evolution of complex societies. A perusal of the literature, both recent and past, gives the impression that no single idea or theory has dominated the discussion. Wright (1970) and Flannery (1972) have both offered summaries of these ideas along with their chief proponents. My own somewhat informal summary is presented in Table 10.1. The list could be expanded, and it goes without saying that endless discourse could proceed on the subjects of intellectual antecedents, relative merits, author's intention, later modifications and permutations, and other aspects. But I think most observers will agree that these ideas exhibit the range of explanatory phenomena utilized. As Wright (1970:18) and Flannery (1972:404–408) have indicated, most arguments consider causation to reside ultimately in a single variable or "prime mover" which, depending on the complexity of the theory, may interact with a number of other variables to produce a complex form of social organization. That the purported explanations of Table 10.1 lack universal applicability (or are untestable, e.g., psychological explanations) and, thus, cannot be considered explanations at all is recognized by both Wright and Flannery. Apparently, while taking note of this failure and, at the same time, seeing some validity in certain of the prime mover arguments for particular cases (Wright

Table 10.1

Ideas Used as Causal Factors in Complex Society Formation

Elaborate waterworks	Steward 1955; Wittfogel 1955
Integrating power of great religions	Willey 1962
Regional symbiosis and cooperation and competition	Sanders 1968; Sanders and Price 1968
Technological improvement and economic surpluses	Childe 1951
Monopolistic control of critical resources	Flannery et al. 1967
Environmental diversity and redistribution	Fried 1960; Sahlins 1958
Population growth, circumscription and warfare	Carneiro 1970; Webster 1975
Sociological differentiation	Adams 1966
Trade	Polanyi et al. 1957; Rathje 1971
Risk dividing in agriculture and redistribution	Chmurny 1973
Population growth	Harner 1970; Smith 1972
Diffusion	Meggers 1975
Psychological variables (i.e. individual motivations for power and dominance)	Service 1975
Cybernetic processes and multivariate causality	Flannery 1972; Wright 1970; Wright and Johnson 1975

Note: Many of these ideas are not mutually exclusive but are interrelated in varying degrees.

1970:1), they propose that causality must be multivariate (Wright 1970: 5,17; Flannery 1972:407–408). Systems theory, they seem to indicate, provides the integrating corpus of dynamic principles that have universal applicability, a feature necessary for scientific explanation (Flannery 1972:409–412; Wright 1970:18). For Flannery and Wright (and others, cf. Salmon 1975:464), systems theory constitutes an adequate explanatory orientation, with causality attributable to nonuniversal phenomena. It is my feeling, however, that such a position is not really informative, nor does it permit insight into the development of complex societies. What is worse, it is a research strategy that foregoes all possibility of inquiry into how and why complex forms of social organization have evolved.

In this chapter, besides discussing the system theory approach of Wright and Flannery, I develop several ideas related to the nature of the energy base found in many complex societies—that of agriculture.[1] In brief, I argue that the differential constraints imposed by the internal functioning of varying levels of agricultural intensification, along with the varying character of meteorological variables, give rise to a range of problems in the maintenance of a stable flow of energy to the cultural system. These problems call for different strategies in their solutions and, therefore, different forms of complex social organization. Thus, by monitoring variables related to the functioning of agricultural systems, it should be possible to develop a series of expectations regarding the character of specified dimensions of complex cultural systems.

[1] See Schalk (this volume) for a discussion of social complexity and anadromous fish exploitation.

These ideas, I hope, will be worthy of further development. The methodological problems concerned with hypothesis formation, developing units of measurement, and analytical procedures will not be discussed. Indeed, these questions are not resolved and comprise an ongoing facet of research. Thus, my arguments will not (and cannot yet) be tested. In point of fact, another problem with testing and evaluation is the "theory building" nature of this chapter, in which I acknowledge the fact that the following arguments are only partially developed. This is not to imply, however, that, on an informal comparative basis, the ideas have not proven useful, even exciting. But, until the methodological problems have been worked out and possibly further elaboration and refinements to the theory are made, hypothesis testing cannot proceed in a strictly analytical manner. Meanwhile, the foregoing discussion will serve to focus research efforts as well as guide the selection of appropriate methodological procedures.

Before continuing, I believe it worthwhile to make a distinction between "prime mover" arguments (usually regarded as processual by their proponents) and what I regard as a processual argument. The confusion is largely a matter of not understanding the difference between statics and dynamics. To use a very popular explanatory concept as an example, many of these problems may be readily observed in the "environmental diversity" argument. First, how can environmental diversity be defined? What constitutes a diverse environment? There are a number of dimensions that can be used, (such as between habitat diversity and within habitat diversity), but I do not know of any anthropologist making this argument who has defined and measured environmental diversity. Second, even if we can, in some intuitive way, agree upon what constitutes a diverse environment, it is apparent that there are any number of areas in the world with environments analogous to Polynesia, the type case (Sahlins 1958), that do not have complex societies. Clearly, the concept is static in the sense that it does not accurately specify those variables that differentially interact to produce a complex form of social organization. What we have is a primitive label, masking a potentially useful idea (if it could be operationalized), which is applied differentially by the investigator to only those areas of the world having complex forms of social organization.[2] This brings me to the third problem: The concept of environmental diversity does not allow one to understand or predict the organizational variability found in complex socieities. A familiarization with the literature (see Table 10.2) leaves no doubt that all complex societies are not the same on a number of important dimensions. These may include population size, population density, territorial size, stability of system with regard to a number of attributes, population distribution patterns, settlement types, social structure, and so on. Again, I believe the failure of explanation lies in differentially specifying a concept, rather than the conditions under which variables interact. In short, the idea of environmental diversity is not being used as a variable, but as a static, natural entity. Likewise, the dependent variable, the complex society (usually specified as

[2] For this reason, practically every environment found on this planet has been considered "diverse" by those employing this concept.

Table 10.2

Selected Listing of Complex Societies Known from Archaeology, Ethnohistory, and Ethnography

South America
    1. Inca   Mason 1957; Métraux 1969; Morris 1972;
                              Morris and Thompson 1970; Murra 1958, 1975
    2. Chimu   Keatinge and Day 1973; Moseley 1975
    3. Lupaka   Murra 1968
    4. Moche   Donnan 1973; Willey 1971
    5. Chavin   Lumbreras 1971
    6. Chibcha   Broadbent 1964, 1966; Kroeber 1946; Pérez 1950
Central America
    7. Aztec   Brundage 1972; Davies 1973
    8. Teotihuacan   Millon 1973; Parsons 1974
    9. Monte Alban   Acosta 1965; Bernal 1965, Winter 1974
  10. Maya   Culbert 1973, 1974; Hammond 1972, 1974;
                              Marcus 1973
  11. Kaminaljuyú   Kidder, Jennings, and Shook 1946;
                              Michels and Sanders 1973
  12. Olmec   Benson 1967; Meggers 1975
  13. Nicarao and Chorotega   Lothrop 1926
North America
  14. Cahokia—Middle Mississippi   Fowler 1974, 1975
  15. Poverty Point   Gibson 1973, 1974
  16. Powhatan   Binford 1964
  17. Calusa   Goggin and Sturtevant 1964
  18. Tlingit   de Laguna 1972; Schalk (this volume)
  19. Nootka   Drucker 1951
  20. Coast Salish   Suttles 1951
Europe
  21. Neolithic Wessex   Renfrew 1973
  22. Aegean area   Renfrew 1972
Asia
  23. Mesopotamia   Adams 1970, 1972; Adams and Nissen 1972;
                              Wright and Johnson 1975
  24. Indus   Allchin 1968; Malik 1968; Singh 1971, Wheeler 1966
  25. Khmer   Audric 1972; Briggs 1951; Coe 1961
  26. Shang   Chang 1968, 1974; Meggers 1975
Africa
  27. Egypt   Edwards 1971; Hayes 1971; Kemp 1972;
                              O'Connor 1972, 1974; Smith 1971; Wilson 1951, 1960
  28. Lozi   Gluckman 1951
  29. Buganda   Kottak 1972; Roscoe 1911
Pacific
  30. Tonga   Sahlins 1958
  31. Tahiti   Oliver 1974; Sahlins 1958
  32. Hawaii   Cordy 1974; Sahlins 1958

Note: In regard to references, an attempt was made to list basic studies as well as more recent investigations that would tend to have up-to-date bibliographies. In some cases, only the more recent studies seemed appropriate, and this was partly determined by my own biases as to the kind of data that is useful. There are many additional references that can be consulted, but a complete listing is beyond the scope of this chapter.

being either a chiefdom or state), is not used as a variable, but also as a static, natural entity. Thus, it seems hardly surprising that such "prime mover" arguments are doomed from the beginning. These problems are to be found in every idea listed in Table 10.1, with the exception of the systems theory arguments.

My own ideas concerning processual theory should be clear by now. Processes are concerned with dynamics. These dynamics are subsumed under a concept by means of which variable dimensions of selected empirical phenomena may be accounted for. This concept is generally referred to as a theory, which is composed of a body of interrelated assumptions, warranted, to a greater or lesser extent, by empirical experience and observation, but independent of the empirical phenomena or dimensions to which they may be referred. These interrelated assumptions specify the conditions governing relationships between variables. It is important to note that one can never select the appropriate dimensions and measurements for any kind of absolute test of the validity of the theory. We can only gain confidence in our theory through the process of hypothesis formation (relating dynamic processes to the behavior of empirical phenomena), testing, and confirmation. The more comprehensive the theory proves to be, the greater our confidence. A disproof of a hypothesis, however, does not necessarily affect the validity of the theory, as the error may be in the incorrect formation of the hypothesis, thereby fostering an illegitimate test. Thus, a theory comprises only half the problem of scientific investigation. Relating theoretical concepts to empirical phenomena for testing may even be more difficult than theory formation and may require a great deal of care. As was mentioned earlier, however, the advantage of having a theory to work with is that it can direct inquiry into potentially appropriate areas for empirical analysis. These points are more fully discussed by Binford (this volume).

In summary, the purpose of this chapter is twofold: (1) to demonstrate the failures of past attempts to explain the origin of complex societies and (2) to provide a new conceptual framework—that of the ecology of agricultural systems—in which to pursue these investigations.

Systems Theory and Multivariate Causality—A Critique[3]

Identifying the relevant domain for investigation of state formation, Wright (1970:7–8) conceptualizes a state "as a socio-cultural system in which there is a differentiated, internally-specialized decision-making subsystem which regulates varying exchanges between other subsystems and with other systems." Thus, the institutional character of a state and its regulatory function is regarded as being of fundamental significance. According to Wright (1970:8), this focuses the study

---

[3] This critique does not concern systems theory as discussed by Ashby (1956), Bertalanffy (1962), and others who have made many interesting and useful advances within this frame of reference. Rather, I question the appropriateness of using an epistemological procedure as scientific theory.

of state origins on the analysis of information flow (matter and energy exchanges) as an essential factor in the dynamics of institutional development. The prinicple of channel capacity (Quastler 1956), in which information flow is related to institutional growth and elaboration, is cited as a possible mechanism (Wright 1970:8). For Wright, then, the major problem in the investigation of state origins centers on defining "the subsystem operating in a given case of state development and [in devising] some means of measuring the major flows into, within, and between these subsystems during this period of development" (1970:8–9).

Flannery's article (1972) is very similar to Wright's in that it identifies institutional development as the primary domain in the problem of state origins: "An explanation of the rise of the state then centers on the ways in which the processes of increasing segregation and centralization take place" (1972:409). Accordingly, he sees institutions as information processors that serve as homeostatic regulators (1972:409–412). If existing institutions are incapable of maintaining a steady state due to perturbation by variables exceeding their regulatory capacity, evolutionary advance may be brought about by means such as "promotion" and "linearization" (Flannery 1972:411–412). The end result is manifest in the increased segregation and centralization of the social system. In addition, as "more highly evolved systems may be less stable" (Flannery 1972:411), a pathology, such as "hypercoherence," may eventually interrupt the evolutionary feedback process (Flannery 1972:414).

As does Wright (1970:5,17,18), Flannery believes that causality is multivariate and that there are no prime movers with regard to a single universal factor initiating the development of all complex societies (1972:407–408) Flannery, for example, has stated:

> The socio-environmental stresses are not necessarily universal, but may be specific to particular regions and societies. It is in this latter category that I place the "prime movers" already discussed, and this categorization helps explain why, although important, they cannot be shown to operate everywhere in the world [1972:409].

Earlier in this chapter, while discussing the difference between statics and dynamics, I gave more substantive reasons why the prime mover arguments have been so unsuccessful. It is not because causes per se are nonuniversal, but because the various factors attributed to origins of complex society have been treated as static, nonvariable concepts rather than dynamic processes. The outgrowth of the "multivariate causality" concept may be attributed to this misconception, which denies the possibility of universal causation. It is probably for this reason that the subject of cause (those multiple factors, particular to the complex society under investigation, that initiate institutional development) receives so little attention by either Wright or Flannery.

What Wright and Flannery do focus on, however, is a concern with the regulatory function of institutions, with information flow as the dynamic agent in their development. Thus, processual theory, for Wright and Flannery, is concerned with an inquiry into the *internal* dynamics of system states. This view is succinctly expressed by Renfrew, who treats the origin of civilization in the Cyclades and the Aegean:

> Changes in culture can meaningfully be explained in terms of the continuous operation of factors within the culture, which are continually inter-acting [1972:17 citing Flannery 1967:119]. The explanation then involves the choice of a mechanism, a notion of how these factors interact [1972:17].

It is my feeling that this kind of endeavor will never lead to an understanding of *why* complex social systems have evolved. Even granting the arguments of Wright and Flannery, there is no way such a theoretical orientation could ever *predict* the evolution of complex social systems. Prediction of variable phenomena, in this case complex social systems (demonstrated by the empirical evidence of Table 10.2), can only occur when the conditions of the differential interaction of relevant variables are known. This means that inquiry must extend beyond (or be external to) the system under investigation. Until research efforts are directed in this mannner, the failure to arrive at an explanation will be a forgone conclusion. Wright and Flannery's narrow and special interpretation of what constitutes an explanation, especially as seen in their notion of multivariate causality, avoids confrontation of the problem of generating a causal theory. To dismiss the problem as being unsolvable or irrelevant begs the question. I fail to see how there can be much headway in the study of origin of complex society until a conscious effort is made at processual and predictive theory building.

Before continuing, I would like to refer to data presented by Wright and Johnson (1975) in order to be explicit about several points concerning our discussion. Briefly, they have postulated that local exchange was a crucial factor predicating administrative specialization in Mesopotamia (Wright and Johnson 1975; Johnson 1973). Ample documentation is provided to demonstrate the sudden increase in volume of local exchange in pottery and, perhaps, cereal grains from centralized production areas (Wright and Johnson 1975:279–283). A mathematical model dealing with service industry distribution is cited as theoretical support for the idea "that unpredictable fluctuation in demand would select for such a centralized shop pattern" (Wright and Johnson 1975:283). The cause of such market fluctuation were possibly "the periodic appearance on the lowland plains of large groups of specialized nomads in need of goods" Wright and Johnson 1975:283). The data, according to Wright and Johnson, argue against population increase (1975:276) or the need for interregional trade (1975:279) as causative factors.

The dynamics of Wright and Johnson's argument rests upon the notion that the structure of institutional organization is responsive to information flow patterns. This may indeed be the case, but we are led to believe that this *is* the explanation, that is, the identification of a cybernetic process. The fact that nomadic herders may be involved (a largely unsupported hypothesis; Wright and Johnson 1975:283) is apparently an interesting and necessary topic for consideration in that, if true, it would have been a sufficient condition for the initiation of the cybernetic process. We can only surmise that this factor is not attributed theoretical importance because nomadic herders were obviously not involved with the evolution of states everywhere. It is one of the "multivariate causes" that may consist of any number of factors, some in co-occurrence, in different times and places of state formation.

Besides failing to meet the criteria of explanation, Wright and Johnson also do not show how a systems theory orientation can account for variability of institutional organization in complex societies outside of Mesopotamia. It is acknowledged that comparative analysis is not their stated purpose, but, even if their criteria of explanation could be accepted, the usefulness of their approach would be in doubt. For example, it is not shown how systems theory could account for the presumed differences in institutional organization between Late Classic Maya (a time for which state organization is postulated; cf. Culbert 1974:74) and the Uruk period state of southern Mesopotamia Wright and Johnson 1975:268–274). In short, I do not see how there can be general principles about the internal dynamics of systems that could account for this variabiltiy. To assume that the institutional organization of all "state" level societies is structurally the same, a seeming requirement of the systems theory orientation, is asking a bit much.[4]

To summarize, while Wright, Johnson, and Flannery have presented stimulating discussions in many respects, I am of the opinion that their theory is not theory in the scientific sense of the word (cf. Binford, this volume). What they consider to be theory really amounts to "descriptive mechanics" or the study of internal dynamic processes of system states. They have suggested ways in which various types of information flow can overload a social system and select for higher levels of controls to overcome the stresses. But we have no scientific idea (i.e., principles of universal applicability) of why these channels become overloaded in certain cases and not in others, nor why there is so much variability among complex social systems. Once again, simply stating that the causes are multiple does not really address the problem. The theories of Wright, Johnson, and Flannery, in many ways the most sophisticated treatments of the origin of complex societies, are unsuccessful because they cannot *predict* state formation. This is symptomatic of an inability to address adequately the problem of causation, which is related to a failure to provide a body of explanatory principles operative from outside the system under investigation.

Definitions and Variables

Wright and Johnson define a state as a "society with specialized administrative activities" (1975:267). Other definitions have also been employed, and usually

---

[4] The problem of variability is greatly reduced if only cases of "pristine" state development are considered, of which just two are recognized (Wright and Johnson 1975:267–268, and Footnote 3). I regard this as being unduly restrictive, as the problem of explanation is being limited to a practically unique event, a rather undesirable situation for scientists.

they are fairly similar to one another (e.g., Fried 1967:229; Krader 1968:13). I believe, however, that there are two basic problems with the use of the term state with regard to the focus of complex society studies. Firstly, the frame of reference is overly restrictive, and, secondly, it encourages the kind of thinking that takes for granted states as natural static entities, which they are not (the same can be said for the use of the terms *chiefdom, urbanism,* and other terms of reference typically associated with the study of complex societies).[5] Regarding the first problem, I feel that these terms are overly restrictive because they assume an unrealistic boundedness of the phenomenon of interest. Often, it appears, the distinction between state and nonstate is a matter of degrees on a continuum. Here, the distinction between Early and Late Classic Maya may be cited (cf. Culbert 1974). Additionally, although the cutoff between prestate and state occupations may be more readily apparent in some cases, as with the Susa period and Early Uruk period occupations of southwestern Iran (Wright and Johnson 1975), the restriction of analysis to only the state occupation may also be seen as rather arbitrary. Thus, comparative analysis with the earlier periods is discouraged; otherwise, this could expand the scope and enrich the investigator's perspective on the explanatory problem.

On the second issue, I have already made comments, but, to reiterate, we must frame our analysis in terms of the relevant variable dimensions of the phenomena under study. It is my conviction that complex societies are highly variable, and it will never be possible to measure and explain the assumed variability if the use of static concepts and dimensions persists. Furthermore, the use of variable dimensions of analysis naturally lends itself to comparative investigation, as is argued earlier.

I would like to emphasize that the use of a definition is heuristic. Although it may be scientifically informed, a definition tends to be little more than a statement expressing the user's cognitive outlook, serving to identify and place boundaries on the phenomenon under consideration. It is a static concept and, thus, is not informative concerning dynamic processes, nor is it amenable to evaluation. Intuition and experience are probably the principal guideposts in definition formation. The only criteria to justify its acceptance and use is its utility in the job of focusing inquiry. For my purposes, use of a term with broad implications seems most appropriate; therefore, I will use the designation "complex society" to indicate the focus of research. I define this as a cultural system having a social heirarchy as a permanent institutional feature. As a matter of scale, it may be observed that such social systems generally have direct control over a larger fixed territory and populace than noncomplex systems.

A social hierarchy refers to the vertical partitioning of individuals in a society into status differentiated groups. The upper echelon of the hierarchy, occupied by persons with high status, is usually concerned, to some degree, with administrative tasks. Apparently, this often involves hereditary continuity and is accompanied by economic and social priviledges.

---

[5] This is not to deny that, in other kinds of endeavors, these terms may be appropriate.

This definition is inclusive of a broad range of social variability that can be considered complex (see Table 10.2). Obviously, however, it does not solve the problem of theory building, nor does it necessarily indicate the dimensions that may be relevant for analysis. For this, I will now turn to a discussion of agriculture, ecology, and energy subsidies.

Agriculture, Ecology, and Energy Subsidies

I would first like to make two statements concerning what agriculture is and does:

1. It is the deliberate caring for, manipulation of, or cultivation of plants so as to enhance their utility for human consumption or use. This may involve genetic change of the plants, in which case domestication may be said to have occurred. The immediate and most far-reaching effect of agriculture is that it concentrates usable productivity, increasing consumable yield per unit area of land.
2. Agriculture involves human intervention in the ecosystem process. I will term this action the maintenance of an artificial ecosystem.

I will return to the first statement a little later. For the present, I would like to comment on some of the implications of maintaining an artificial ecosystem.

The most basic consideration is the factor of energy cost. One aspect of energy cost is labor effort. Therefore, my initial interest focused on documenting the notion that work effort increased between hunter–gatherers and the varying levels of agricultural intensification (M. Harris 1971:218; Boserup 1965). The principle of least effort has been cited as the underlying assumption of this model (Bronson 1972:190–191), whereby increases in productivity between subsistence levels require proportionally larger increases in the labor effort. Thus, production will tend to stabilize at the lowest possible level (given resource needs) to maximize labor effort. This seems like a reasonable assumption, especially for nonindustrial egalitarian societies, in which the accumulation of personal wealth tends to be neither practical nor advantageous (except in limited circumstances, such as bride payments). In my analysis of work effort (Table 10.3), I might have predicted that the real world would not be as simple as anthropologists had supposed. Empirically, there is no evidence for the supposed unilineal progression in quantity of work effort and subsistence types.[6]

---

[6] Bronson (1972) arrived at a similar conclusion using a measure of productivity per unit of work effort. I did not learn of his article until after Table 10.3 was complete. His other conclusion concerning the possibility of the evolutionary priority of intensive forms of agriculture (1972:217) seems untenable. This idea is based on data indicating increased productivity per unit labor input for intensive forms of agriculture and some evidence that individual farmers with extensive agricultural systems will intensify without hesitation, given the opportunity to do so. I do not doubt Bronson's data, but, at the same time, it seems that such changes occurred within the milieu of a complex and

Work effort among hunter–gatherers is highly variable, depending on the type of subsistence economy. Littoral collecting, for example, demands much more labor time than Bushman foraging (Table 10.3). Another difficulty, perhaps more substantial, is that certain hunter–gatherers may have a higher per capita work effort than some horticulturalists (Table 10.3). To make matters worse, the single case of hoe agriculturalists (an intensified form of short fallow agricultural production) indicates a lower work effort than several of the swidden cases and one of the hunting–gathering cases (Table 10.3).[7]

At first, this discrepancy between fact and theory was most disturbing. Although the data were limited, they had been very meticulously collected, making it difficult to question the figures. Does this mean that the principle of least effort is a mistaken notion? I would answer "probably not." It is my feeling that the aforementioned analytic problems rest with the mistaken assumption of environment as a constant. I believe it can be rather easily demonstrated that labor usage for subsistence operates under very different kinds of constraints in differing environments and, furthermore, that this will have a pronounced effect on social and technological evolution. The importance of Table 10.3 is not that it proves or disproves the principle of least effort, but that it has helped to bring to the forefront some potentially useful new considerations in understanding labor effort.[8]

Among tropical swidden horticulturalists, there is a great deal more work effort expended per hectare than for the single group of hoe cultivators in a savanna environment (Table 10.3). The primary reason has to do with seasonality—in the tropics, garden activities do not tend to be sharply constricted by seasonal changes in temperature and water supply. Under such conditions, food supplies may be increased by either expanding the amount of land under cultivation or by more intensively cropping a single swidden throughout the year. Under both

---

often modern economic and political situation. Productivity may have actually increased per unit of labor for the farmer, but it must be remembered that he is relying on a whole range of specialized services such as systems for credit procurement, labor procurement, marketing, distributing, storing, specialized tools often made of metal, scientific aids for improving production, and other supportive mechanisms and institutional features. These all have an energy cost. If it were possible to quantify them, it would almost certainly be seen that productivity declines substantially with respect to *total* energy input. Thus, dependence on the more intensive cultivation practices probably could not occur in arid and temperate environments outside the context of a complex form of social organization. In tropical environments, in those areas that can sustain intensive cultivation practices, this would happen only in the context of a proportionally larger increase in labor investment, but not necessarily in the context of a complex form of social organization. The reason will hopefully become clear as my discussion of argiculture proceeds.

[7] Another interesting factor brought out by these data, although not one I wish to pursue here, concerns the great differences in the amount of cultivated land and labor needed per capita to sustain groups not dependent on seed crops as opposed to those groups who are dependent in the tropics.

[8] It is possible that other cross-cutting considerations could override the principle of least effort once complex societies have formed (see Bronson 1972:200–201 for a listing of several potential factors).

Table 10.3

Work Effort for Selected Groups of Hunter–Gatherers and Agriculturalists

Group	Location	Environment	Subsistence strategy	Population	Percentage seed crops	Percentage other crops[a]	Hours/Hectare per year	Hectare/person	Hours per day per capita
1. Bushman	Kalahari Desert	desert–savanna	hunting–gathering	30.9	—	—	—	—	1.23
2. Hemple Bay	Arnhemland, Australia	littoral	littoral collecting and fishing	13	—	—	—	—	3.12
3. Yukpa	Colombia–Venezuela	tropical	swidden	8	26	74	2013	.39	2.15
4. Hanunóo	Mindoro, Phillipines	tropical	swidden	141	34	66	3000	.42	3.45
5. Bomagai-Angoiang	New Guinea	tropical	swidden	154	1	99	2038	.15	.83
6. Kapauku	West Irian	tropical	81% swidden 19% hoe	181	1	99	2471	.09	.61
7. Genieri Village	Gambia, West Africa	savanna	hoe	494	100	0	926	.61	1.54

[a] These include mostly vegetatively reproducing cultigens.

References:

Group 1: Lee 1966.
Group 2: McCarthy and McArthur 1960 (duration of time–motion studies was 7 days).
Group 3: Ruddle 1974 (data are from a single family of traditional horticulturalists).
Group 4: Conklin 1957.
Group 5: Clarke 1971.
Group 6: Pospisil 1963.
Group 7: Haswell 1953.

circumstances, the work effort is increased, and this may result in longer working days, use of formerly marginal help (such as children), continuous employment in cropping activities throughout the year, or all three. Contrary to Boserup (1965), however, a shortening of the fallow cycle may not accompany increases in labor intensification (or perhaps only minimally) in the tropics, except in special circumstances. These special circumstances are primarily related to areas where paddy rice is a possible cropping strategy, although other kinds of examples may be found.[9] Thus, the need to augment food supplies in the tropics takes place by means of a simple intensification of labor effort. Cropping activities remain largely at a swiddening level because edaphic conditions cannot support the short fallow agricultural practices found in arid and temperate zones (Janzen 1973). Even in those cases in which very intensive cropping practices are found in the tropics, as among the Ifugao (Barton 1922), there is often little correspondence with the level of social and technological development usually associated with analogous practices in temperate and arid environments. This is not to imply that there can never be an impetus toward social evolution in the tropics. Societal change obviously does occur, but the reason appears not to be related directly to changes in subsistence strategies. This will, perhaps, be more apparent in the following discussion of arid and temperate environments. Anticipating a later conclusion, however, I believe that tropical complex systems evolve in the context of intragroup competition, predicated primarily by a population–resource imbalance.

The conditions and consequences surrounding labor intensification are markedly different in arid and temperate environments. Food production at whatever level of labor investment must be undertaken within the constraints of seasonal climatic changes. It is for this reason that the work effort per hectare of Genieri Village is so low (Table 10.3). In higher latitude environments, the number of months available for agricultural production would be much fewer. An additional environmental constraint involves the unpredictable nature of rainfall and temperature patterns. Thus, agriculturalists must cope not only with a short growing season, but also with uncertain meteorological variables. Exact timing is, therefore, critical for a successful crop (further implications of unpredictable meteorological variables will be discussed later). It is my belief, therefore, that augmenting food supplies in arid and temperate environments is not merely a problem of putting more labor to work, but one of overcoming the difficulties of having all the activities of field preparation, planting, maintenance, and harvesting occur at the same time. A real bottleneck in labor utilization develops at certain critical periods in the cropping cycle during which time is of the essence. The leeway for attending to a particular activity may be only a matter of days, after which time, the risk of total failure becomes very high.

It seems clear, then, that, unlike tropical swidden systems, cultivation in arid

---

[9] For example, the New Guinea highlands, such cases often appear to be related to the presence of nutrient rich volcanic soils.

and temperate environments does not permit cycling of plantings in such a way as to equalize the labor requirement throughout the year. Should limits to the growth of food supplies occur, a major area of stress would conceivably be related to the problem of labor shortages for particular time-specific tasks (given the capability of the land to sustain more intensive cultivation practices). For this reason, I feel that these environments tend to select for technologies and organizational structures that maximize or extend the capabilities of the labor supply. In short, stresses to augment food supplies call for an "efficiency response." Thus it may be expected that complex social systems in arid and temperate environments will be of a different character from those of the tropics. Time constraint on labor utilization, however, is not the only adaptive problem that confronts these systems. Although they are related to labor utilization, these other problems are concerned with the maintenance of security or stability in the flow of energy to the cultural system. We turn to them now, after a brief speculative comment on the possible effect of seasonal labor shortage on population dynamics.

Given these arguments, the potential for seasonal labor shortage found in arid and temperate environments may provide the context for expanding the size of the labor force through an increase of population. This is because the easiest and most obvious way for the individual producer, who actually feels the burden of labor shortage, to overcome the problem is to increase his family size by having more children. In the short run, increases in the producer labor force solve the immediate labor shortage problem. But, in the long run, total population grows as does the need to continually augment food supplies. Thus, selective pressures for efficiency in the productive effort would not abate, and changes in social and technological systems would continue in this direction. In tropical environments, on the other hand, the positive advantages accruing to increased family size are probably absent. Agricultural intensification is generally not possible, and advance planning by the cultivator can forestall the possibility of a critical labor shortage. This is not to suggest that population does not grow in the tropics but, rather, that the dynamics may be different in arid and temperate regions.

Although the topic of labor cost is an interesting and potentially fruitful area for investigation in all types of subsistence economies, there is another aspect of cost accounting associated with maintaining agricultural systems. This is stability, and it is basic to what I mean by saying that agriculture involves the maintenance of an artificial ecosystem. The "cost" of stability, of course, has its ultimate expression in labor effort, but I believe it would be useful to specify how these costs arise and also how they relate to the process of agricultural intensification. Again, the implications for social and technological evolution appear enormous.

It is important to make a distinction between two aspects of stability—one having to do with processes internal to the ecosystem and the other with variables external to the ecosystem. Their relation may be best understood through a discussion of ecological succession, which Odum (1971:251) has described as follows:

> 1) It is an orderly process of community development that involves changes in species structure and community processes with time; it is reasonably directional and, therefore, predictable. 2) It results from modification of the physical environment by the community; that is succession is community-controlled even though the physical environment determines the pattern, the rate of change, and often sets limits as to how far development can go. 3) It culminates in a stabilized ecosystem in which maximum biomass (or high information content) and symbiotic function between organisms are maintained per unit of available energy flow.
>
> In a word, the "strategy" of succession as a short-term process is basically the same as the "strategy" of long-term evolutionary development of the biosphere, namely, increased control of, or homeostasis with, the physical environment in the sense of achieving maximum protection from its perturbations.

Where successional advance has occurred, ecosystems are referred to as "mature." If the process has not taken place, they are called "immature" or simple ecosystems. Table 10.4 contrasts a number of attributes found in these successional states. In this table, we see that there are different types of selective pressures for the developmental stages as opposed to the mature stage (items 18 and 19). The particular attributes found in ecosystems may be viewed as a function of these selective pressures, as will be discussed later. Margalef (1968) notes that these pressures operate within the framework of ecological succession, which he describes as incorporating the features of a cybernetic system, and from which he is able to deduce many of the properties of ecosystems. As such, his discussion is particularly useful in that ecosystem development is conceptualized as a general process.

If evolution could be said to have an objective, it would be the maintenance of life (see Odum 1971:251). Since conditions of the natural environment can be enormously variable, it may be expected that security problems and the means to overcome them will vary with the environmental setting of the organism. Thus, security is always a problem defined by the environmental setting, and it follows that, as the environmental setting changes, the strategy for security in energy capture must also change. In this sense, a survival strategy may also be called an adaptation. As was mentioned earlier, however, the primary context in which adaptation occurs is the setting presented by the successional stage of the ecosystem. This is why there are so many congruencies in the adaptive strategies of organisms found in different kinds of environmental settings. Since the structural properties of these ecosystems are alike, similar adaptive strategies are necessary to insure survival. The external environment, however, may exert a strong influence on the rate of successional change, on its limits, and also on certain formal aspects of community structure. Thus ecosystems of similar successional stages at different latitudes may appear to be superficially different but may have similar structural properties (such as those listed in Table 10.4 under "ecosystem attributes"). These general characteristics of ecosystems may be related to the struc-

Table 10.4

A Tabular Model of Ecological Succession: Trends to Be Expected in
the Development of Ecosystems[a]

Ecosystem attributes	Developmental stages	Mature stages
Community energetics		
1. Gross production/community respiration (*P/R* ratio)	greater or less than 1	approaches 1
2. Gross production/standing crop biomass (*P/B* ratio)	high	low
3. Biomass supported/unit energy flow (*B/E* ratio)	low	high
4. Net community production (yield)	high	low
5. Food chains	linear, predominantly grazing	weblike, predominantly detritus
Community structure		
6. Total organic matter	small	large
7. Inorganic nutrients	extrabiotic	intrabiotic
8. Species diversity—variety component	low	high
9. Species diversity—equitability component	low	high
10. Biochemical diversity	low	high
11. Stratification and spatial heterogeneity (pattern diversity)	poorly organized	well-organized
Life history		
12. Niche specialization	broad	narrow
13. Size of organism	small	large
14. Life cycles	short, simple	long, complex
Nutrient cycling		
15. Mineral cycles	open	closed
16. Nutrient exchange rate, between organisms and environment	rapid	slow
17. Role of detritus in nutrient regeneration	unimportant	important
Selection pressure		
18. Growth form	for rapid growth ("*r*-selection")	for feedback control ("*K*-selection")
19. Production	quantity	quality
Overall homeostasis		
20. Internal symbiosis	undeveloped	developed
21. Nutrient conservation	poor	good
22. Stability (resistance to external perturbations)	poor	good
23. Entropy	high	low
24. Information	low	high

[a] Reprinted from Odum 1969: 265.

tural properties of agricultural systems, thereby providing a basis for discussion of the dependencies that must necessarily be generated between them and their human exploiters.

Before discussing agricultural systems, I would first like to remark briefly on several aspects of energy dynamics of ecosystems. I will move from the more general level of community development to the level of particular organisms.

Energy utilized by living organisms ultimately derives from the sun. It is made available to them through the chemical process of photosynthesis in green plants, known as "primary producers" (autotrophs). Organisms obtaining energy either directly from primary producers (herbivores) or indirectly by means of predation (predators) are said to be "consumers" (heterotrophs). Organisms of a third group found in ecosystems are generally referred to as "decomposers," which consume detritus or the dead remains of production. It is through the efforts of this group, which assumes increasing importance as succession advances, that inorganic nutrients can be recycled for continuing use in the ecosystem. The dependency links between different classes of consumers (as found between primary producers–herbivores–carnivores–secondary carnivores) are referred to as "trophic levels." These form a pyramidal arrangement depending on the amount of productivity capable of being sustained at each level. The farther removed the consumer's trophic level is from the primary producer level, the less energy will be available for those organisms. This is because there is only a 10–20% efficiency rate of energy transfer between trophic levels.

When referring to the total amount of energy fixed in an ecosystem, ecologists use the term "gross productivity." This is expressed as a rate and is generally measured in terms of dry organic matter formed per unit area per unit time (calories/m²/year). However, in order to investigate ecosystem dynamics, it is necessary to know something about the way in which this energy is partitioned. To begin with, an ecosystem requires a certain portion of the energy "budget" for its respiration, that is, for use in sustaining its life processes. The energy remaining is utilized in new tissue growth and is called "net production." Gross production, net production, and respiration may be measured at the level of a single organism or at the level of the entire ecosystem. Just as a single plant requires a certain portion of the energy budget for respiration, other consumers participating in the ecosystem utilize energy for respiration. The distinction between primary producers (or green plants) and consumers, however, is that the latter do not contribute to the energy budget. Consumers, therefore, are totally dependent upon the net production of primary producers for their respiration. Any leftover energy not utilized by either the consumers or the primary producers is termed "net ecosystem production." Logically, this leftover energy is potentially available for the respiration of additional consumer populations. External constraints not withstanding (unpredictable or fluctuating environmental conditions, generally, climatic variables), we may expect that, when there is net ecosystem production, additional consumers will move into the system until its value approaches zero. When this happens, there exists what ecologists call a climax or mature ecosystem.[10]

To understand the energy dynamics involved in the adaptive strategies of particular organisms, it is convenient to contrast *"r"* and *"K"* selection and the associated ramifications for successional development. Following MacArthur (1955, 1972), I would like to characterize the resulting strategies of these selection processes as the difference between generalists (*r*-strategy) and specialists (*K*-strategy).

Generalists are associated with uncertain or fluctuating environments, which is a feature of the internal structure of immature ecosystems, although it may also characterize the external physical environment. In order to maximize the probability for evolutionary success, therefore, an adaptive premium will tend to be placed on opportunism (the capacity to utilize a variety of resource forms) as well as the production of many offspring. In terms of energy utilization by particular organisms, the greatest expenditure is made directly in the reproductive effort (relative to specialists). With regard to community development, this creates a situation in which energy, in the form of net production, is available within the ecosystem. Therefore, given stable conditions in the external environment (especially such factors as rainfall and temperature), succession may proceed in the direction of increased biomass, species diversity, symbiotic function, and the other attributes listed in Table 10.4. This eventually means that selection will begin to favor a reproductive strategy emphasizing "quality" rather than "quantity." As a greater variety of organisms enter the community structure, competition for the finite energy supply held within the system (ultimately deriving from primary producers or green plants) becomes increasingly severe. Specialization, or exploitative efficiency, is the result. In this new selective context, energy expenditure is now partitioned by the particular organisms; therefore, there tends to be few offspring produced so that the energy available may be channeled into any of various facets of developmental growth, as needed for successful competition.

Thus, whatever the adaptive strategy—be it generalist or specialist—there is an energy cost to insure evolutionary success. In the model just presented, a species cannot choose both "quantity" and "quality" in reproduction (Cody and Diamond 1975:4–5; MacArthur 1972:229–230 citing Odum and Pinkerton 1955). The particular strategy used depends on the state of the ecosystem with respect to community structure and environmental variables. With regard to the focus of this chapter, one may ask: What happens when organisms, such as cultivated plants of an agricultural field, are removed from their successional context? The answer, of course, has to do with energy.

All agricultural systems are removed from the normal processes of ecosystem

[10] Much of this information can be found in basic ecology textbooks (e.g., Emlen 1973; Odum 1971; Pianka 1974; Phillipson 1966; Whittaker 1975). The articles by Odum (1969) and Woodwell (1970) are also useful.

development; the degree of interruption depends on the intensity of the cultivation practice. In effect, there is an attempt on the part of agriculturalists to make an immature community structure (the agricultural system) stable over the period of time that production is being sustained. Thus, man is imposing his own survival strategy on plants, and this renders the plants' adaptive mechanisms inoperative. The organisms (most plant cultigens and especially seed crops) that were originally adapted to unstable environmental conditions are now forced to become stable communities. This is because man's strategy is to concentrate consumable yield in time and space. Given this unnatural state of affairs, it is hardly surprising that a host of problems arise, all of which are related to the maintenance of a stable community structure of the plants under cultivation. Now, however, the organisms (cultigens) must rely on artificial maintenance of their "ecosystem" (the agricultural plot), rather than on their own adaptations acquired through the course of their evolution. As will be seen later, the stability problem become increasingly severe with the intensity of the cultivation practice. Furthermore, problem solving, as with the adaptations of organisms in their natural settings, has an energy cost, and this is also a function of the intensity of the cultivation practice.

It is convenient to use Nye and Greenland's (1960) listing of the general problem areas of maintaining agricultural systems. These are *(1)* deterioration in the nutrient status of the soil, *(2)* deterioration in the physical status of the soil, *(3)* erosion of top soil, *(4)* changes in the numbers and composition of soil fauna and flora, *(5)* increase of weeds, and *(6)* multiplication of pests and diseases. Although conditions vary with the geographic setting, these factors arise as a result of a constriction of the natural process of ecosystem development, of which soils are an integral part. Regarding the importance of the latter, Witkamp (1971:105) has observed that:

> The emerging picture is one of soils as habitats of interacting biota, which are the prime agents in maintaining and elevating local levels of fertility and thus of perpetuating species composition and the level of activity of the ecosystem.

He has further observed that this occurs as a part of the process of ecosystem succession and, thus, is fundamental in determining levels of fertility and nutrient cycling (Witkamp 1971:85). This, in fact, is well documented in Nye and Greenland's (1960) thorough study of shifting cultivation. Thus, there is increasing recognition of the importance of interactions between soil, soil biota, and plant and animal communities as linked subsystems. As Whittaker observes:

> The soil of a natural community is not an inert substrate, it is part of the ecosystem. There is an interactive, complementary relation between the soils that support the community and affect its character of the soil [1975:261–262; reprinted by permission of Macmillan Publishing Co., Inc.].

The practice of agriculture destroys this interaction largely by interfering with the process of nutrient cycling. Decline of the productive capability of the soil

Table 10.5

Percentage of Global Losses Preharvest Due to Weeds,
Insects, or Diseases[a]

Cause of loss	Crop		
	Maize	Wheat	Rice
Weeds	37	40	23
Insects	36	21	58
Diseases	27	39	19
Total loss (L) preharvest (million tons)	121	86	207
Harvested crop (H) (million tons)	218	266	232
$\dfrac{L}{L+H} \times 100$	35.7	24.4	47.1

[a] Spedding 1975: 174.

becomes inevitable. Witkamp summarizes this process and the possible severity of the problem as follows:

> Mineral pools can be reduced in size by removal of minerals with the harvested crop in excess of natural inputs and by manmade additions such as fertilization or eutrophication. Mineral pools may also be depleted by leaching of minerals upon destruction of the biological buffer by man-made biocides or loss of the colloidal buffer by accelerated humus decomposition upon defoliation, clear-cutting, or fire.
>
> Loss of nutrient minerals in general leads to decreased productivity for long periods of time. Most of the factors listed that cause loss of nutrients are the direct or indirect results of human action. Thus there is a threat that the increasing human population will increasingly interfere with the environment and that this intervention will lead to reduced productivity [1971:86].

Interruption of nutrient cycling is also the prime factor behind deterioration of the physical status of the soil and in its erosion.

That weeds, pests, and diseases can have a limiting effect on agricultural production is amply illustrated in table 10.5. The figures in Table 10.5 are *averages*, however, and they do not indicate the possible magnitude of destruction that can occur on individual plots.[11] Outbreaks are characteristic of immature systems, and they can be as unpredictable as they are devastating, thereby adding to the problem of maintaining stability in crop production (Margalef 1968:45–46; Pianka 1974:242–244). It seems probable that the severity of the problem increases with the intensity of cropping activities.

[11] It is important to note that the figures of Table 10.5 were derived at a time when the use of chemicals to control weeds, pests, and diseases is widespread. These problems must often have been especially acute for preindustrial societies, which did not have such methods available.

The exception to this, which, in effect, proves the point, concerns the agricultural system of shifting cultivation or swiddening. The distinctive feature of this highly variable practice is that it makes use of an extended fallow period. Cultivation takes place for several years (usually 1 to 3 years); after which time, the vegetation is generally allowed to revert to its normal successional pattern before cultivation is attempted again. This is a highly effective means of achieving stability of agricultural production from an inherently unstable form of community structure.[12] In a sense, this is because it enables the cultigens to behave as organisms of an immature community, which participate in the normal process of succession. The cultigens are analogous to the pioneer species initiating and imitating the early stages of ecosystem development. They are gradually overtaken and out-competed by wild plants, but the whole process proceeds virtually uninterrupted. Thus, the shifting cultivator avoids the problem of artificially maintaining stability by integrating his system of production with the normal process of successional development. Chances of severe problems arising from any of Nye and Greenland's factors are minimized (although the cultivator may face certain problems particular to local conditions).[13]

On the other hand, when fixed-plot, short-fallow systems of agriculture are utilized, problems in almost all the areas listed by Nye and Greenland become manifest in varying degrees. If production is to be secure, these must be resolved. although, again, the particular problems will depend on a number of factors. These may include length of fallow period, local geography, past history of land use, types of crops under production, and so on. As the writing of this chapter is undertaken during the spring, the obvious analogy for the suburban anthropologist is the work entailed in preparing the lawn for another summer of production. Preparation will certainly include energy and nutrient subsidizing through fertilization, either chemically or with manure. It is possible that plowing or hoeing and the addition of other chemicals to enhance nutrients response also will be involved. Weed and pest control will undoubtedly become problems once summer is in full swing, and more fertilizer may well become necessary. Those who make the effort know this can add up to a substantial monetary expenditure as well as labor investment; and, generally, those with the finest lawn in the neighborhood will also have made the greatest expenditure in labor and money. The maintenance of agricultural systems is no different, and greater levels of intensification will mean increased costs to insure stability of production. The amount spent depends on how intensive the producer either wants to be or has to

[12] Perhaps it would be best to speak of stability only in the short run. See Smole (1976:199–211) for an example of the way in which swiddening can degrade an environment through the cumulative effect of many generations of cropping.

[13] I disagree with the commonly cited analogy between the ecology of swidden systems and tropical rain forests (Geertz 1963; D. Harris 1971, 1973; Rappaport 1971). Not all swiddens have a multiplicity of plants, community structure of swiddens is not at all developed, and the stability of swiddens has nothing to do with crop diversity. In short, there is no resemblance to a tropical rain forest. Swiddens, as with more intensive forms of cultivation, contain very immature communities of plants.

be. There are implications for social evolution, but, before discussing them, I would like to present another factor that is critical to the stability of agricultural production.

This factor deals with meteorological variables, especially temperature and rainfall. In temperate environments, where seasonality is pronounced, temperature and rainfall fluctuations are often marked. This is also true for arid environments, where unpredictable rainfall patterns can be quite extreme (cf. Noy-Meir 1973). It is obvious that they may constitute major limiting factors in agricultural production, although the kinds of strategies used to cope with these problems have, in many cases, only recently come under investigation. In the arid American Southwest, for example, these strategies may include technological methods, such as water control techniques (Plog and Garrett 1972), sociological and ideological methods, such as time-dependent ritual cycles that are hypothesized to have an important food redistribution function (Ford 1972), and multiple field locations to divide crop loss risks, such as those described for the Hopi (Hack 1942). Other strategies may include the building of storage facilities and, perhaps, even ceramic ware to reconstitute food grains dried for use during non-food-producing months. These examples, it should be emphasized, pertain only to local environmental conditions in the Southwest. With a different physical environment, a different level of agricultural intensification, different types of cultigens, a different population density, and the presence of other interacting cultural systems, different kinds of stability problems may be expected. Variation in forms of adaptation would, therefore, be anticipated. The American Southwest as a region is quite heterogeneous, and even here there are local variations meeting the various environmental constraints (cf. Plog and Garrett 1972; Hack 1942).

When agriculture is considered from the perspective of energy costs that are required to maintain stability of production in an artificial ecosystem, it may be expected that there will be different kinds of subsidies operating at different levels within the system. Subsidies are here considered to be those inputs that, in some manner, promote security of energy flow to the cultural system. For this reason, I would argue, many of the activities found in cultural systems dependent upon agriculture (even though they may not be directly involved with food production and consumption) are related to the maintenance of a secure energetic source. Energy subsidies, then, are part of the cost of plant cultivation; the amount and kind are specific to the local environmental setting and the level of agricultural intensification. These costs, it may be reiterated, are divided between those pertaining to internal ecosystem maintenance (nutrients, soils, pest control, etc.) and those factors external to the system (meteorological variables).

Complex Cultural Systems—Some Expectations

To return to the statement made earlier in this chapter, agriculture has the effect of concentrating usable productivity. As cultivation practices are intensified, productivity becomes further concentrated in both time and space. However, because agriculture involves the maintenance of an artificial ecosystem, which presupposes the need for energy subsidies, it is doubtful that more intense forms of agricultural production would be developed or become adopted unless there was a compelling reason to do so. The only reason sufficiently pervasive to account for agricultural intensification must be related to a disequilibrium between population and available food resources.[14] Production, of course, must be sufficient to maintain the energy supply during periods of fluctuation.

In arid and temperate environments, fluctuations in agricultural production can be severe and locally unpredictable. This is becuase of the potential for pest and disease outbreaks and the uncertain meteorological conditions, both of which can have highly devastating effects. Energy subsidies (which can be expressed in terms of total work effort), by means of which these factors may be stabilized, may also increase as land becomes more intensively cultivated. These may be expressed in any of a number of ways, depending on local conditions. Examples include more extensive irrigation, larger canals from more predictable water sources, closer attention to crops for controlling pests and isolating diseased plants, terracing, and land leveling. With more intensified agricultural systems, closer attention must be paid to proper soil preparation, fertilizing, protection from erosion, and so on. Energy subsidies obviously add substantially to the work effort. As was indicated at the beginning of this chapter, however, seasonality of the productive cycle sharply circumscribes the available time in which to do this work. Thus, in these environments, there would always be a great deal of pressure to use labor efficiently through technological and sociological means. Regarding the latter, it can be anticipated that, under conditions of agricultural intensification, there will be increasing specialization in the kinds of tasks performed for purposes of labor efficiency. When labor needs require a level of efficiency beyond that which can be supplied by productive specialization in the local household or residential group, an organizing principle based on the hierarchical partitioning of the society may arise. The hierarchy, a specialized work force concerned with administration, serves to organize and direct energy exchanges between the increasingly specialized segments of the society. Otherwise, there would be very little security for individuals producing only a limited range of goods to satisfy their needs. In addition, the power and authority that usually accompany hierarchical systems make it possible for those holding such positions to require that work critical to agricultural production be completed within the time constraint allowed by environmental factors, thereby insuring the stability of production. This power of compulsion may be particularly necessary as labor becomes more specialized due to further reasons. In this regard, it seems possible that individual motivations for production might decline, which would run counter to the maintenance of the security of the system as a whole. A hierar-

---

[14] This has been Boserup's (1965) argument, although my emphasis on energy subsidies provides a more comprehensive treatment of underlying causes.

chy would potentially have the means to prevent from happening. There are many unknown conditions regarding the character of hierarchical organization, power, and authority within cultural systems in arid and temperate settings. These unknowns and the kinds of dimensions appropriate in analysis, however, remain questions for further research.

The particular ecology of agriculture in arid and temperate environments also seems to have implications for the way in which space is used by complex cultural systems. Specialization within a complex society may lead to a settlement pattern highly differentiated functionally and hierarchically. Another factor may relate to the territorial size of the cultural system. If production is locally unpredictable due to climatic and internal ecosystemic perturbations, territorial extension of the cultural system would minimize the effect of a drop in productivity in any one area. In this way, energy flow to the system as a whole would remain stable. In addition, the hierarchical organization of the cultural system is the most effective way in which to monitor matter and energy exchanges and deviations of relevant organic and inorganic variables over a large area. Potential problems may be detected, and compensating adjustments made. This is probably why complex systems of arid and temperate environments are generally so much larger in territorial area than their tropical counterparts. Other dimensions in the use of space may refer to stability in the location and offices of political authority, stability in the settlement hierarchy, and population aggregation. Tropical complex systems, usually having what is referred to as a chiefdom type of social organization, are often politically very unstable (Service 1962:142–143). Furthermore, tropical complex systems usually do not have large aggregations of population or settlements that might be considered urban (cf. Coe 1961). Again, I believe the differences between complex cultural systems in arid and temperate environments and those of the tropics can be attributed to variation in the agricultural ecology of these zones. The suggestions concerning the kinds of differences that may be expected in space use of complex societies should be regarded as rather informal propositions that await testing. Other propositions could certainly be deduced; perhaps some are more suitable for testing. This remains a subject for future study.

Another facet in the evolution of complex societies appears to be related to competition between social groups, as was postulated earlier for the tropics. The ecology of agricultural systems in the tropics does not appear to have the problem of perturbations nor the need for efficiency responses to maximize labor effort. Thus, organizational features of these complex societies cannot be related, in any direct sense, to factors of stability in food production. It may be surmised that such systems, which always have relatively dense populations, arise primarily as a response to intragroup competition. The need for additional crop land may be a principal factor, although territorial expansion is not always evident for these systems. When particular problems or threats arise, it seems that a charismatic leader is able to organize a local populace for defensive or aggressive purposes. Once the immediate problem is solved, however, there is very little to hold the system together, although perhaps a strong religious establishment functions to counter this tendency. It often seems that conquered territories become independent and competition resumes again. As the severity of the competition grows, especially through intensive warfare and feuding, larger complex systems may be expected, but the political structure will remain relatively unstable. These comments are admittedly speculative, although they do seem to fit a lot of the data involving a temporal perspective on the complex system. Sahlins' study of political types in Melanesia and Polynesia (1963) has been a useful source for some of these ideas. These propositions, of course, must be more rigorously defined, warranted, and tested, thereby permitting evaluation of the theory.

Thus far, I have indicated some of the dimensions for analysis of complex cultural systems, and, in a general way, I also have indicated how they should vary according to the environment. I would like emphasize, however, that my use of the environmental types—arid, temperate, and tropical—has been only for ease of contrast. They are not suitable as analytical dimensions, and comparison of societies on such a gross level would not account for all the variability. We have yet to decide what would be a good measure of environment for investigating complex systems. I have considered using either a scale based on length of growing season or perhaps that of climatic equability. There are problems involved with using both measures. It will be necessary to experiment before we can decide what works best, either one of these measures or something else.

Conclusion

In conclusion, an understanding of the evolution of complex social systems can only proceed through an examination of factors relating to the stability of agricultural production and the use of relevant variable dimensions of analysis. This orientation is quite different from that of the "systems theorists" in a number of respects. Flannery makes this point clear when he states:

> Looked at in this way, the most striking differences between states and simpler societies lie in the realm of decision-making and its hierarchical organization, rather than in matter and energy exchanges. Herein lies another problem faced by those "cultural ecologists" who place such emphasis on the way that civilized peoples get their food [1972:412].

On the contrary, I believe that a strong case has been made for the importance of subsistence, as well as matter and energy exchanges, in investigating why complex social systems with particular kinds of attributes have evolved. This chapter represents only a preliminary effort in advancing these studies.

ACKNOWLEDGMENTS

I owe the inspiration for this chapter, and probably much of what is in it, to Lewis Binford. His instruction has been not only very influential but, perhaps more importantly, a source of motivation. I would especially like to thank him for his encouragement during the various drafts of this chapter. In addition, useful comments, criticisms, and discussion were provided by S. Beckerman, J. Bertram, G. Burtchard, M. Harlan, H. Harpending, R. Hunter-Anderson, L. Jorde, W. J. Judge, R. Schalk, and K. Schwerin. Any deficiencies, of course, are the result of my own failings.

REFERENCES

Acosta, Jorge R.
  1965   Preclassic and Classic architecture of Oaxaca. In *Handbook of American Indians,* Vol. 3, *Archaeology of southern Mesoamerica,* Part 2, edited by Gordon R. Willey. Austin, Tex.: Univeristy of Texas Press. Pp. 814–836.
Adams, Robert McC.
  1966   *The evolution of urban society: Early Mesopotamia and Prehispanic Mexico.* Chicago: Aldine.
  1970   The study of ancient Mesopotamian settlement patterns and the problem of urban origins. *Sumer* **25:**111–124.
  1972   Patterns of urbanization in early southern Mesopotamia. In *Man, settlement and urbanism,* edited by Peter J. Ucko, Ruth Tringham, and G. W. Dimbleby. London: Duckworth. Pp. 735–749.
Adams, Robert McC., and Hans J. Nissen
  1972   *The Uruk countryside: The natural setting of urban societies.* Chicago: University of Chicago Press.
Auchin, Bridget, and Raymond Auchin
  1968   *The birth of Indian civilization: India and Pakistan before 500* B.C. Harmondsworth, Eng.: Penguin Books.
Ashby, W. R.
  1956   *An introduction to cybernetics.* London: Chapman and Hall.
Audric, John
  1972   *Angkor and the Khmer Empire.* London: Hale.
Barton, R. F.
  1922   Ifugao economics. *University of California Publications in American Archaeology and Ethnology* **15:**385–446.
Benson, Elizabeth P.
  1968   *Dumbarton Oaks Conference on the Olmec.* Dumbarton Oaks Research Library and Collection, Washington, D.C.
Bernal, Ignacio
  1965   Archaeological synthesis of Oaxaca. In *Handbook of Middle American Indians,* Vol. 3, *Archaeology of southern Mesoamerica,* Part 2, edited by Gordon R. Willey. Austin, Tex.: University of Texas Press. Pp. 788–813.
Bertalanffy, Ludwig von
  1962   General system theory—a critical review. *General Systems* **7:**1–20.
Binford, Lewis R.
  1964   Archaeological and ethnohistorical investigations of cultural diversity. Unpublished doctoral dissertation, Department of Anthropology, University of Michigan.
Boserup, Ester
  1965   *The conditions of agricultural growth: The economics of agrarian change under population pressure.* Chicago: Aldine.
Briggs, Lawrence Palmer
  1951   The ancient Khmer Empire. *Transactions of the American Philosophical Society* **41:**1–295.
Broadbent, Sylvia M.
  1964   Los Chibchas: Organización socio-política. *Serie Latinoamericana,* No. 5, Facultad de Sociologiá, Universidad Nacional de Columbia, Bogotá.
  1966   The site of Chibcha Bogotá. *Ñawpa Pacha* **4:**1–13.

Bronson, Bennet
    1972   Farm labor and the evolution of food production. In *Population growth: Anthropological implications,* edited by Brian Spooner. Cambridge, Mass.: M.I.T. Press. Pp. 190–218.

Brundage, Bun Cartwright
    1972   *A rain of darts: The Mexican Aztecs.* Austin, Tex.: Univeristy of Texas Press.

Carneiro, Robert L.
    1970   A theory of the origin of the state. *Science* **169:**733–738.

Chang, Kwang-chih
    1968   *The archaeology of ancient China.* (revised ed.) New Haven, Conn.: Yale University Press.
    1974   Urbanism and the king in ancient China. *World Archaeology* **6:**1–14.

Childe, V. Gordon
    1951   *Man makes himself.* (revised ed.) New York: New American Library.

Chmurny, William Wayne
    1973   The ecology of the Middle Mississippian occupation of the American Bottom. Unpublished doctoral dissertation, Department of Anthropology, University of Illinois, Urbana–Champaign.

Clarke, William C.
    1971   *Place and people: An ecology of a New Guinean community.* Berkeley, Calif.: University of California Press.

Cody, Martin L., and Jared M. Diamond
    1975   Editors introduction. In *Ecology and evolution of communities,* edited by Martin L. Cody and Jared M. Diamond. Cambridge, Mass.: Belknap Press of Harvard University Press.

Coe, Michael D.
    1961   Social typology and the tropical forest civilizations. *Comparative studies in Society and History* **4:**65–85.

Conklin, Harold C.
    1957   *Hanunóo agriculture: Report on an integral system of shifting cultivation in the Philippines.* Food and Agriculture Organization of the United Nations, Rome.

Cordy, Ross H.
    1974   Complex rank cultural systems in the Hawaiian Islands: Suggested explanations for their origin. *Archaeology and Physical Anthropology in Oceania* **9:**89–109.

Culbert, T. Patrick (Ed.)
    1973   *The Classic Maya collapse.* Albuquerque, N.M.: University of New Mexico Press.

Culbert, T. Patrick
    1974   *The lost civilization: The story of the Classic Maya.* New York: Harper and Row.

Davies, Nigel
    1973   *The Aztecs: A history.* London: MacMillan.

Donnan, Christopher B.
    1973   *Moche occupation of the Santa Valley, Peru.* Berkeley, Calif.: University of California Press.

Drucker, Philip
    1951   The northern and central Nootkan tribes. *Smithsonian Institution, Bureau of American Ethnology Bulletin* 144. Washington, D.C.: United States Government Printing Office.

Edwards, I. E. S.
    1971   The Early Dynastic Period in Egypt. In *The Cambridge ancient history.* Vol. 1, Part 2. *Early history of the Middle East* (3d ed.), edited by I. E. S. Edwards, C. J. Gadd, N. G. L. Hammond. Cambridge: Cambridge University Press. Pp. 1–70.

Emlen, J. Merritt
    1973   *Ecology: An evolutionary approach.* Reading, Mass.: Addison-Wesley.

Flannery, Kent V.
    1967   Culture history versus culture process: A debate in American archaeology. *Scientific American* **217:**119–122.
    1972   The cultural evolution of civilizations. *Annual Review of Ecology and Systematics* **3:**399–426.

Flannery, Kent V., Anne V. T. Kirkby, Michael J. Kirkby, Aubrey W. Williams, Jr.
  1967   Farming systems and political growth in ancient Oaxaca. *Science* **158**:445–453.
Ford, Richard I.
  1972   An ecological perspective on the eastern Pueblos. In *New perspectives on the Pueblos,* edited by Alfonso Ortiz. Albuquerque, N.M.: University of New Mexico Press. Pp. 1–17.
Fowler, Melvin L.
  1974   Cahokia: Ancient capital of the midwest. *Addison-Wesley Module in Anthropology* No. 48. Menlo Park, Calif.: Cummings.
  1975   A pre-Columbian urban center on the Mississippi. *Scientific American* **233**:92–101.
Fried, Morton H.
  1960   On the evolution of social stratification and the state. In *Culture in History: Essays in honor of Paul Radin,* edited by S. Diamond. New York: Columbia University Press. Pp. 713–731.
  1967   *The evolution of political society: An essay in political anthropology.* New York: Random House.
Geertz, Clifford
  1963   *Agricultural involution: The process of ecological change in Indonesia.* Berkeley, Calif.: University of California Press.
Gibson, Jon Lee
  1973   *Social systems at poverty point: An analysis of intersite and intrasite variability.* Unpublished doctoral dissertation, Department of Anthropology, Southern Methodist University.
  1974   Poverty point: The first North American chiefdom. *Archaeology* **27**:97–105.
Gluckman, Max
  1951   The Lozi. In *Seven tribes of central Africa,* edited by Elizabeth Colson and Max Gluckman. London: Oxford University Press. Pp. 1–93.
Goggin, John M., and William C. Sturtevant
  1964   The Calusa: A stratified non agricultural society (with notes on sibling marriage). In *Explorations in cultural anthropology: Essays in honor of George Peter Murdock,* edited by Ward H. Goodenough. New York: McGraw-Hill. Pp. 179–219.
Hack, John T.
  1942   The changing physical environment of the Hopi Indians of Arizona. *Papers of the Peabody Museum of American Archaeology and Ethnology, Harvard University,* Vol. 35, No. 1. *Reports of the Awatovi Expedition* No. 1. (Cambridge, Mass.)
Hammond, N. D. C.
  1972   Locational models and the site of Lubaantún: A Classic Maya centre. In *Models in archaeology,* edited by David L. Clarke. London: Methuen. Pp. 757–800.
  1974   The distribution of Late Classic Maya major ceremonial centers in the central area. In *Mesoamerican archaeology: New approaches,* edited by N. Hammond. Austin, Tex.: University of Texas Press. Pp. 313–334.
Harner, Michael J.
  1970   Population pressure and the social evolution of agriculturalists. *Southwestern Journal of Anthropology* **26**:67–86.
Harris, David R.
  1971   The ecology of swidden cultivation in the upper Orinoco rain forest, Venezuela. *Geographical Review* **61**:475–495
  1973   The prehistory of tropical agriculture: An ethnecological model. In *The explanation of culture change: Models in prehistory,* edited by Colin Renfrew. London: Duckworth. Pp. 391–417.
Harris, Marvin
  1971   *Culture, man, and nature: An introduction to general anthropology.* New York: Crowell.
Haswell, M. R.
  1953   Economics of agriculture in a savannah village. *Colonial Research Studies* No. 8. London: Her Majesty's Stationary Office for the Colonial Office.

Hayes, William C.
  1971   The Middle Kingdom in Egypt. In *The Cambridge ancient history*, Vol. 1, Part 2. *Early History of the Middle East* (3d ed.), edited by I. E. S. Edwards, C. J. Gadd, N. C. L. Hammond. Cambridge: Cambridge University Press. Pp. 464–531.
Janzen, Daniel H.
  1973   Tropical agroecosystems. *Science* **182**:1212–1219.
Johnson, Gregory Alan
  1973   Local exchange and early state development in southwestern Iran. *Anthropological Paper* No. 51. Museum of Anthropology, University of Michigan, Ann Arbor, Michigan.
Keatinge, Richard W., and Kent C. Day
  1973   Socio-economic organization of the Moche Valley, Peru, during the Chimu occupation of Chan Chan. *Journal of Anthropological Research* **29**:275–295.
Kemp, Barry J.
  1972   Temple and town in ancient Egypt. In *Man, settlement and urbanism,* edited by Peter J. Ucko, Ruth Tringham, and G. W. Dimbleby. London: Duckworth. Pp. 657–680.
Kidder, A. V., J. D. Jennings, and E. M. Shook
  1946   Excavations at Kaminaljuyu, Guatemala. *Carnegie Institution of Washington, Publication* No. 561. (Washington, D.C.)
Kottak, Conrad P.
  1972   Ecological variables in the origin and evolution of African states: The Buganda example. *Comparative Studies in Society and History* **14**:351–380.
Krader, Lawrence
  1968   *Formation of the State*. Englewood Cliffs, N.J.: Prentice-Hall.
Kroeber, A. L.
  1946   The Chibcha. In *Handbook of South American Indians,* Vol. 2, edited by Juliean H. Steward. Washington, D.C.: United States Government Printing Office. Pp. 887–909.
Laguna, Frederica de
  1972   *Under Mount Saint Elias: The history and culture of the Yakutat Tlingit,* Part 1. Washington, D.C.: Smithsonian Institution Press.
Lee, Richard B.
  1969   !Kung Bushman subsistence: An input–output analysis. In *Environment and cultural behavior: Ecological studies in cultural anthropology,* edited by Andrew P. Vayda. Garden City: Natural History Press. Pp. 47–79.
Lothrop, Samuel Kirkland
  1926   *Pottery of Costa Rica and Nicaragua,* Vol. 1. Museum of the American Indian, Heye Foundation. (New York)
Lumbreras, Luís Guillermo
  1971   Towards a re-evaluation of Chavín. In *Dumbarton Oaks Conference on Chavín,* edited by Elizabeth P. Benson. Dumbarton Oaks Research Library and Collection. Pp. 1–28. (Washington, D.C.)
MacArthur, Robert H.
  1955   Fluctuations of animal populations, and a measure of community stability. *Ecology* **36**:533–536.
  1972   *Geographical ecology: Patterns in the distribution of species.* New York: Harper and Row.
Malik, S. C.
  1968   *Indian civilization: The formative period.* Indian Institute of Advanced Study, Simla, India.
Marcus, Joyce
  1973   Territorial organization of the lowland Classic Maya. *Science* **180**:911–916.
Margalef, Ramón
  1968   *Perspectives in ecological theory.* Chicago: University of Chicago Press.
Mason, J. Alden
  1957   *The ancient civilizations of Peru.* Harmondsworth, Eng.: Penguin Books.

McCarthy, Frederick D., and Margaret McArthur
    1960   The food quest and the time factor in aboriginal economic life. In *Records of the American-Australian scientific expedition to Arnhem Land,* Vol. 2. *Anthropology and nutrition,* edited by Charles P. Mountford. Melbourne, Australia: Melbourne University Press. Pp. 145–194.
Meggers, Betty J.
    1975   The transpacific origin of Mesoamerican civilization: A preliminary review of the evidence and its theoretical implications. *American Anthropologist* **77:**1–27.
Métraux, Alfred
    1969   *The history of the Incas.* New York: Random House.
Michels, Joseph W., and William T. Sanders (Eds.)
    1973   The Pennsylvania State University Kaminaljuyu Project—1969, 1970 seasons, Part 1—Mound Excavations. *Occasional Papers in Anthropology* No. 9. Department of Anthropology, Pennsylvania State University, University Park, Pennsylvania.
Millon, René
    1973   *The Teotihuacán map,* Vol. 1, Part 1. Austin, Tex.: University of Texas Press.
Morris, Craig
    1972   State settlements in Tawantinsuyu: A strategy of compulsory urbanism. In *Contemporary archaeology: A guide to theory and contributions,* edited by Mark P. Leone. Carbondale, Ill.: Southern Illinois Press. Pp. 393–401.
Morris, Craig, and Donald E. Thompson
    1970   Huanuco Viejo: An Inca administrative center. *American Antiquity* **35:**344–362.
Moseley, Michael Edward
    1975   Chan Chan: Andean alternative of the preindustrial city. *Science* **187:**219–225.
Murra, John V.
    1958   On Inca political structure. In *Systems of political control and bureaucracy in human societies,* edited by Vern F. Ray. Seattle, Wash.: University of Washington. Pp. 30–41.
    1968   An Aymara kingdom in 1567. *Ethnohistory* **15:**115–151.
    1975   *Formaciones económicas y políticas del mundo Anido.* Lima, Peru: Instituto de Estudios Peruanos.
Noy-Meir, Imanuel
    1973   Desert ecosystems: Environment and producers. *Annual Review of Ecology and Systematics* **4:**25–51.
Nye, P. H., and D. J. Greenland
    1960   The soil under shifting cultivation. *Technical communication* 51, Commwealth Bureau of soils, Farnham Royal, Bucks, England.
O'Conner, David
    1972   The geography of settlement in ancient Egypt. In *Man, settlement and urbansim,* edited by Peter J. Ucko, Ruth Tringham, and G. W. Dimbleby. London: Duckworth. Pp. 681–698.
    1974   Political systems and archaeological data in Egypt 2600–1780 B.C. *World Archaeology* **6:**15–38.
Odum, Eugene P.
    1969   The strategy of ecosystem development. *Science* **164:**262–270.
    1971   *Fundamentals of ecology.* 3d ed. Philadelphia: Saunders.
Odum, Howard T., and Richard C. Pinkerton
    1955   Time's speed regulator. *American Scientist* **43:**331–343.
Oliver, Douglas L.
    1974   *Ancient Tahitian society.* Honolulu, Hawaii: University press of Hawaii.
Parsons, Jeffry
    1974   The development of a Prehistoric complex society: A regional perspective from the Valley of Mexico. *Journal of Field Archaeology* **1:**81–108.
Pérez de Barradas, Jose
    1950   *Los Muiscas antes de la conquista.* Consejo Superior de Unvestigaciónes Cientifíras, Instituto Bernadino de Sahagún, Madrid.

Phillipson, John
1966 *Ecological energetics.* London: Arnold.
Pianka, Eric R.
1974 *Evolutionary ecology.* New York: Harper and Row.
Pimentel, D.
1961 Species diversity and insect population outbreaks. *Annals of the Entomological Society of America* **54:**76–86.
Plog, Fred T., and Cheryl K. Garrett
1972 Explaining variability in Prehistoric southwestern water control systems. In *Contemporary archaeology: A guide to theory and contributions,* edited by Mark P. Leone. Carbondale, Ill.: Southern Illinois Press. Pp. 280–288.
Polanyi, Karl, Harry Pearson, and C. M. Ahrensburg
1957 *Trade and market in the early empires.* Glencoe, Ill.: Free Press.
Pospisil, Leopold
1963 Kapauku Papuan economy. *Yale University Publications in Anthropology* No. 67. Department of Anthropology, New Haven, Conn.
Quastler, Henry
1956 Studies of human channel capacity. In *Information theory,* edited by C. Cherry. New York: Academic Press. Pp. 361–371.
Rappaport, Roy A.
1971 The flow of energy in an agricultural society. *Scientific American* **224:**116–132.
Rathje, William L.
1971 The origin and development of lowland classic Maya civilization. *American Antiquity* **36:**275–285.
Renfrew, Colin
1972 *The emergence of civilisation: The Cyclades and the Aegean in the third millennium* B.C. London: Methuen.
1973 Monuments, mobilization, and social organization in neolithic Wessex. In *The explanation of culture change: Models in prehistory,* edited by Colin Refrew. London: Duckworth. Pp. 539–558.
Roscoe, John
1911 *The Baganda.* London Macmillan.
Ruddle, Kenneth
1974 The Yukpa cultivation system: A study of shifting cultivation in Colombia and Venezuela. *Ibero-Americana* No. 52. Berkeley, Calif.: University of Califormia Press.
Sahlins, Marshall D.
1958 *Social stratification in Polynesia.* Seattle, Wash.: University of Washington Press.
1963 Poor man, rich man, big man, chief: Political types in Melanesia and Polynesia. *Comparative Studies in Society and Hisotry* **5:**285–303.
Salmon, Merrilee H.
1975 Confirmation and explanation in archaeology. *American Antiquity* **40:**459–464.
Sanders, William T.
1968 Hydraulic agriculture, economic symbiosis, and the evolution of states in central Mexico. In *Anthropological archaeology in the Americas,* edited by B. J. Meggers. Washington, D.C.: The Anthropological Society of Washington. Pp. 88–107.
Sanders, William T., and Barara J. Price
1968 *Mesoamerica: The evolution of a civilization.* New York: Random House.
Service, Elman R.
1962 *Primitive social organization: An evolutionary perspective.* New York: Random House
1975 *Origins of the state and civilization: The process of cultural evolution.* New York: Norton.
Singh, Gurdip
1971 The Indus Valley culture. *Archaeology and Physical Anthropology in Oceania* **6:**177–188.
Smith, Philip E. L.
1972 Land-use, settlement patterns and subsistence agriculture: A demographic perspecitve.

In *Man, settlement and urbanism,* edited by Peter J. Ucko, Ruth Tringham, and G. W. Dimbleby. London: Duckworth. Pp. 409–425.

Smith, W. Stevenson
  1971   The Old Kingdom in Egypt and the beginning of the First Intermediate Period. In *The Cambridge ancient history,* Vol. 1, Part 2, *Early history of the Middle East,* edited by I. E. S. Edwards, C. J. Gadd, and N. C. L. Hammond. Cambridge: Cambridge University Press. Pp. 145–207.

Smole, William J.
  1976   *The Yanomamö Indians: A cultural geography.* Austin, Tex.: University of Texas Press.

Spedding, C. R. W.
  1975   *The biology of agricultural systems.* New York: Academic Press.

Steward, Julian H.
  1955   Development of complex societies: Cultural causality and law: A trial formulation of the development of early civilizations. In *Theory of culture change,* edited by Julian H. Steward. Urbana, Ill.: University of Illinois Press. Pp. 178–209.

Suttles, Wayne
  1951   The economic life of the coast Salish of Haro and Rosario Straits. Unpublished doctoral dissertation, Department of Anthropology, University of Washington, Seattle.

Webster, David
  1975   Warfare and the evolution of the state: A reconsideration. *American Antiquity* **40:**464–470.

Wheeler, Mortimer
  1966   *Civilizations of the Indus Valley and beyond.* New York: McGraw-Hill.

Whittaker, Robert H.
  1975   *Communities and ecosystems.* (2d ed.) New York: Macmillan.

Willey, Gordon R.
  1962   The early great styles and the rise of the Pre-Columbian civilizations. *American Anthropologist* **64:**1–14.
  1971   *An introduction to American archaeology,* Vol. 2, *South America.* Englewood Cliffs, N.J.: Prentice-Hall.

Wilson, John A.
  1951   *The culture of ancient Egypt.* Chicago: University of Chicago Press.
  1960   Egypt through the New Kingdom, civilization without cities. In *City invincible,* edited by C. Kraeling and R. McC. Adams. Chicago: University of Chicago Pres.

Winter, Marcus C.
  1974   Residential patterns at Monte Alban, Oaxaca, Mexico. *Science* **186:**981–987.

Witkamp, Martin
  1971   Soils as components of ecosystems. *Annual Review of Ecology and Systematics* **2:**85–110.

Wittfogel, Karl A.
  1955   Irrigation civilizations: A comparative study. Social Science Monographs, Department of Cultural Affairs, Pan American Union, Washington, D.C.

Woodwell, G. M.
  1970   The energy cycle of the biosphere. *Scientific American* **223:**64–74.

Wright, Henry T.
  1970   Toward an explanation of the origin of the state. Paper delivered at the School of American Research Symposium, "The explanation of prehistoric organizational change," 1970, Santa Fe, New Mexico.

Wright, Henry T., and Gregory A. Johnson
  1975   Population, exchange, and early state formation in southwestern Iran. *American Anthropologist* **77:**267–289.

11

Precipitation Cycles and Cultural Buffering in the Prehistoric Southwest

L. B. JORDE
University of New Mexico

Recently, some attempts have been made to clarify and expand concepts of cultural buffering of environmental inputs. Harpending and Bertram (1975) have provided mathematical models, some of which relate to buffering, and Jorde and Harpending (1976) elaborated these models and conducted a synchronic study to demonstrate empirically some aspects of the dynamics of cultural buffering. The purpose of this study is to extend and to develop further some ideas concerning buffering. By making use of the diachronic perspective that archaeological data provide, exploration and explanation of the *evolution* of buffering mechanisms can be carried out. Statistical analysis of annual precipitation (as indicated by tree rings) is performed in an attempt to demonstrate climatic changes that brought about an increase in buffering mechanisms (food storage, irrigation, aggregation) in the United States Southwest between approximately A.D. 1000 and 1100. These climatic changes include a longer rainfall periodicity after 1050 (demonstrated by spectral analysis) and a decrease in rainfall variance. The employment of cultural buffers, while damping the effects of high-frequency fluctuation in precipitation, tends to bring about a condition of instability that renders the system more susceptible to the effects of low-frequency (long-term) fluctuation. This condition apparently is associated with the collapse of many settlements in the Southwest during the thirteenth century A.D.

Past statements concerning the evolution of cultural buffering are infrequent and poorly developed. Steward (1955) and Kroeber (1963), for example, have asserted, without elaboration, that cultures become "freer of their environment" as they evolve toward increasing complexity. Historians interested in evolutionary questions have made similar statements (Spengler 1926, Toynbee 1974). Kaplan (1960) briefly disagreed with this view, but he, like his predecessors, chose not to explore the question in greater detail.

Much of the theoretical foundation of the approach adopted here has been provided by Harpending and Bertram (1975). They view the cultural buffering system as a "black box" (see Figure 11.1) that can be modeled mathematically. As an example of one such modeling equation, an exponentially weighted 5-year moving average process, we can consider the food storage component of the buffering system:

$$F(k) = \sum_{t=N-k-5}^{k} e^{-c(k-t)}F(t)$$

where $F(k)$ is the amount of food collected in a given year k; N is the total number of years in the sequence; t is the index for summation of the present year and four preceding years; and c is an arbitrary weighting constant.

This equation is probably a fairly realistic, though simplistic, model of food storage. Figure 11.2 diagrammatically depicts the effect of this equation: It simply "smooths" the input process, resulting in a more dependable output.

Jorde and Harpending (1976) examined the effects of these buffers, using a small sample of nonindustrial and industrial populations. They treated yearly rainfall as the input to the system; the output was annual birth rate, which was expected to vary in response to precipitation variation. The central proposition was that, as populations achieve increased technological complexity, they are able to damp out the effects of high-frequency (2–3 year) periodicities in precipitation. Mechanisms, such as irrigation, food storage, and trade, smooth the effects of this variation.[1] Response to low-frequency input should still be observable, however, since it is not possible to damp out completely these effects. Cross-spectral analysis of time series data for precipitation and birth rate confirmed our

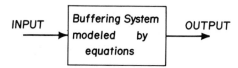

Figure 11.1 The black box system.

[1] Another mechanism that Jorde and Harpending do not consider is the use of nonrenewable resources, which do not respond to changes in climate, as buffers in trade (e.g., trading U.S. wheat for Russian oil).

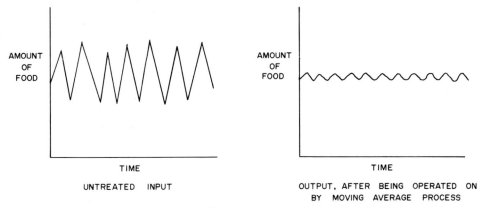

Figure 11.2 The effect of the moving average process on food input.

expectations: Groups with relatively low technological complexity, such as Ramah Navajo and San Juan Pueblo, showed peak response to high-frequency precipitation periodicity (2 and 3 years, respectively). Groups with greater complexity, such as England, Scotland, and Italy, showed peak responses to lower-frequency oscillations (8–10 years).

A concept that Jorde and Harpending developed only partially in their paper concerns the increase in ecological instability brought about by technological complexity. It must be recognized that mechanisms that buffer short-term oscillations require additional energy, as well as (probably) a higher population density. To procure this energy, ecosystems that might previously have been ecologically stable (e.g., a temperate woodland) are converted to a disclimax condition (e.g., a wheat field) in order to increase the edible portion of the net aboveground productivity. Pianka (1974), among others, has pointed out that this lowers the stability of the ecosystem. Thus, populations that have successfully damped short-term climatic oscillations have done so at the expense of increased instability, which, in turn, increases susceptibility to long-term changes in climate. Therefore, such populations are more likely to "crash" when faced with climatic fluctuations that are beyond their buffering capacity. (See Athens, this volume, for a complementary approach to instability and buffering.)

The purpose of this study is to explain why buffers became important in much of the United States Southwest ca. A.D. 1000–1100. Several buffering mechanisms show a marked increase in development at this time:

1. *Food surplus.* Hill (1970), Martin and Plog (1973), and Lipe (1970) have demonstrated an increase in food storage facilities.
2. *Irrigation.* Woodbury (1961) notes an increase in this buffering mechanism over much of the Southwest at this time.
3. *Aggregation along permanent drainages.* Hill (1970), Longacre (1970), Martin and Plog (1973), and Zubrow (1975) have documented this event. This

aggregation plays two roles: It provides the high population density that is needed to support the buffering mechanisms, and the permanent drainages help to insure a more constant water supply in the face of increased rainfall fluctuation.

Several other explanations have been offered an explanation of the widespread aggregation that occurs ca. A.D. 1000–1100. These include war (Jett 1964), disease (Titiev 1944), and inner cultural tendency (Kroeber 1953). Those who favor a climatic causation for this phenomenon usually cite a shift from winter-dominant to summer-dominant precipitation patterns (Schoenwetter and Dittert 1968). The apparent effect of this shift was to increase erosion and arroyo cutting, thus lowering the water table and necessitating settlement along permanent drainages.

In this study, changes in year-to-year precipitation patterns are examined in an effort to explain the increase in buffering mechanisms. Tree-ring widths provide a good indication of annual precipitation, with correlation coefficients between these two variables ranging from .70 to .85 or more for southwestern series (Schulman 1954), as well as for tree-ring series from various other parts of the continent (e.g., Hawley 1937). More recently, multivariate studies have shown that up to 85% of the variance in tree rings is due to precipitation (Fritts *et al.* 1971) and that, in several case studies, precipitation and temperature together account for up to 87% of the tree-ring variance (Fritts, Smith, and Stokes 1965).

Martin (1963), however, has criticized the use of tree rings for this purpose, claiming that they represent only winter precipitation. Fritts, Smith, and Stokes (1965), in a series of careful studies, have shown that Douglas fir, the most reliable species for tree-ring analysis, does, in fact, respond to both winter and summer precipitation.

Spectral analysis was used to detect changes in precipitation periodicity. Since this is a technique that is unfamiliar to most anthropologists, a brief description of the procedure and its application will be presented (detailed discussion can be found in standard texts on the subject, such as Anderson 1971; Jenkins and Watts 1968; Koopmans 1974; Otnes and Enochson 1972).

We begin with a time series X_t, $t = 1,2,\ldots,N$, where N is the number of data points in the series. One of the most common methods of spectral analysis commences with the computation of an autocovariance function:

$$c(k) = \frac{1}{N} \sum_{t=1}^{N-k} (X_t - \overline{X})(X_{t+k} - \overline{X}) \qquad 0 \leq k \leq L - 1$$

where $\overline{X}$ is the arithmetic mean of the time series; k is a lag value; and L is the maximum lag value.

A lag is the number of units of displacement between the original series X_t and the portion of $X_t(X_{t+k})$ whose covariance with X_t we wish to know. This measure, then, is nearly identical to the standard statistical measure of covariance. The only difference is that, while covariance measures the association between two different variables, autocovariance measures the association between a times series and *itself*, displaced by k units. The result is a series of autocovariance coefficients, $c(k)$, which give the autocovariance of the series at each lag value.

Often, an autocorrelation estimate is preferable; this is obtained by dividing the autocovariance estimates at each lag by the variance of the time series, resulting in a standardized autocorrelation function, $r(k)$.

Next, the power spectral density function is computed. This function expresses "power" (or variance, or amplitude) at various frequencies. A large estimate of power at a frequency of .25, for example, indicates that a "wave" exists in the times series that has a period (i.e., repeats itself) of 4 years (since period is the reciprocal of frequency). The power spectral density is derived by computing the Fourier transformation of the autocorrelation function:

$$\overline{C}(f) = 2\left[1 + 2 \sum_{k=1}^{L-1} r(k)w(k) \cos 2\pi fk\right] \qquad 0 \leq f \leq \tfrac{1}{2}$$

where L represents the maximum lag value; f is the frequency at which the spectral density estimate is being computed; $r(k)$ is the autocorrelation function; $w(k)$ is a spectral window, a statistical device used to derive a smoothed (and, hence, more accurate) spectral density function (see any of the texts cited earlier for a full explanation of spectral windows).

Spectral density functions were computed for the periods A.D. 750–1049 and A.D. 1050–1349 for standardized tree-ring indices from Mesa Verde (Navajo Canyon) (Schulman 1947), Flagstaff (Douglass 1947), Navajo National Monument (Tsegi) (Schulman 1948), Wetherill Mesa (Nichols and Harlan 1967), and Chaco Canyon (J. S. Dean, personal communication). Chaco Canyon tree rings were available only through A.D. 1129. Spectral density functions were computed for each 300-year period. In addition, the data were divided into 100-year sections for spectral analysis. A maximum lag of 20 years was used for the 100-year sections, while a maximum lag of 30 years was used in computing spectral density estimates for the 300-year sequences. Smoothed spectral estimation was carried out, using a Tukey spectral window. Also, raw (unsmoothed) spectral estimation, followed by Hamming smoothing of the estimates (see Blackman and Tukey 1958), was performed.

There was very close agreement between the power spectra obtained using the two different methods. Figures 11.3–11.7 show the power spectral densities plotted against frequency) for each of the tree-ring series. The three 100-year divisions prior to 1050 showed patterns that were essentially similar to the 750–1049 series; those after 1050 were also quite similar to the 1050–1349 300-year series. The close correspondence among the Mesa Verde, Flagstaff, Wetherill Mesa, and Chaco Canyon spectra supports the conclusion that we are dealing with climatic phenomena general to much of the Southwest. This agrees with the results obtained by Schulman's (1948) correlation analysis of tree-ring indices in various parts of the Southwest, as well as Fritts' (1963) more extensive analysis of areal

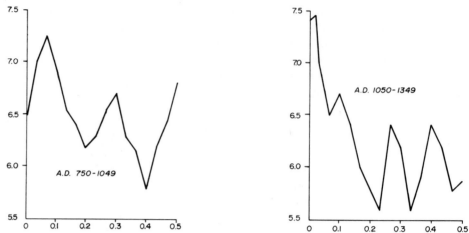

Figure 11.3   Mesa Verde (Navajo Canyon). Log$_e$ of power spectral density (y axis) plotted against frequency (x axis).

correlation of tree-ring series, which showed significant correlations between series from locations up to 700 miles apart.

Figures 11.3, 11.4, 11.6, and 11.7 show, in the high-frequency range, a peak at a period of 2 years (frequency of .5) for the 750–1049 sequence. For the 1050–1349 sequence, there is a peak at periods of 2.5–3 years. In the lower frequency range (0–.2), a similar shift of peaks from higher to lower frequencies is seen.

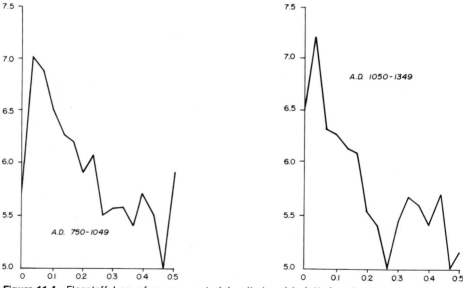

Figure 11.4   Flagstaff. Log$_e$ of power spectral density (y axis) plotted against frequency (x axis).

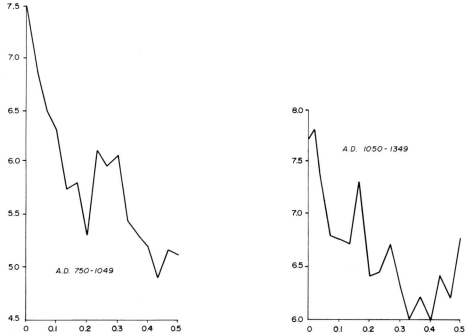

Figure 11.5 Tsegi. Log$_e$ of power spectral density (*y* axis) plotted against frequency (*x* axis).

The anomalous behavior of the Tsegi sequence is disappointing; it is encouraging, however, that Dean (personal communication) has detected visually a shift similar to that of Figures 11.3, 11.4, 11.6, and 11.7 for 23 different Southwest tree-ring sequences. This again supports the notion that the change was a fairly general occurrence throughout much of the Southwest.

Table 11.1 summarizes the values of statistical variance for the two time periods. Four of the five sequences show a decrease in variance after A.D. 1050. Again, the Tsegi sequence behaves differently.

Table 11.1

Tree-Ring Variance in the Two Time Periods

Location	750–1049	1050–1349[a]
Mesa Verde	2201	1747
Flagstaff	1376	1242
Tsegi	1373	2525
Wetherill Mesa	2335	2162
Chaco Canyon	1228	1128

[a] Extends only through 1129 for Chaco Canyon sequence.

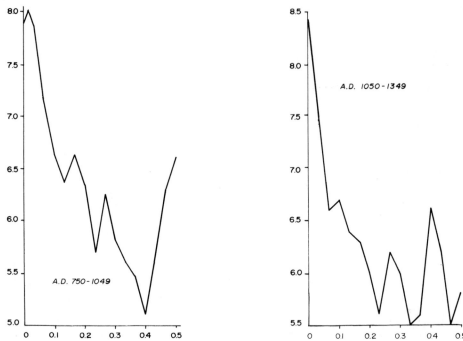

Figure 11.6 Wetherill Mesa. Log$_e$ of power spectral density (y axis) plotted against frequency (x axis).

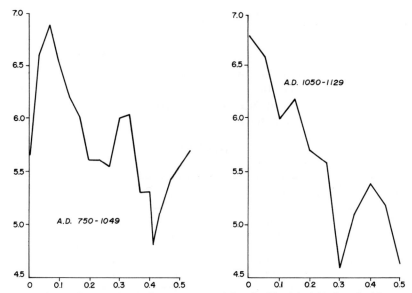

Figure 11.7 Chaco Canyon. Log$_e$ of power spectral density (Y axis) plotted against frequency (x axis).

The shift to a longer periodicity in rainfall tends to increase the probability of two or more dry years occurring consecutively. Ethnohistoric evidence indicates that two consecutive dry years created much hardship among Pueblo farmers (Titiev 1944). Faced with this shift, prehistoric populations appear to have responded with more elaborate buffering mechanisms to control water and food supply.

The decrease in rainfall variance would have enabled the adoption of the less diverse subsistence strategy that an increase in buffering necessitated. Martin and Plog (1973) have noted that the diversity of Anasazi technology decreased significantly during this time period, and Zubrow (1975) has documented the shift from occupation of many diverse ecozones to occupation principally of only one ecozone. Gumerman (1975) points out that flooding would have been important in damaging prehistoric crops. A decrease in rainfall variance would diminish the seriousness of flooding and concomitant disturbances for populations farming along permanent drainages.

It appears, then, that these changes in precipitation pattern brought about some important changes in settlement and subsistence patterns in the Southwest. Several buffering strategies were initiated that significantly increased the general level of complexity of these cultures. Once begun, it seems that this subsistence adaptation formed a positive feedback relation with population growth in much the same manner as suggested by Young (1972) for Mesopotamian populations with the advent of agriculture. Increased buffering, sedentism, and intensity of agriculture demand higher population density; higher population density, in turn, demands increased buffering and agricultural intensity. Meanwhile, the stability of the ecosystem is being lowered in order to supply needed energy and materials (e.g., all the trees in the vicinity of Chaco Canyon are cut down for building materials and firewood). This continued for about 200 years. Then, population that had successfully damped high-frequency oscillations in precipitation were exposed to the ill effects of a major low-frequency climate cycle. In the Southwest, the trough of this cycle is seen in the "Great Drought" of A.D. 1276–1299. Winkless and Browning (1975) claim that the Great Drought is the trough of a proposed 800-year climate cycle. While they document this cycle fairly well, the popularized style of their book forces one to adopt a skeptical view of their proposal. The Great Drought could also be the trough of one of several other well-documented low-frequency climate cycles (e.g., Borchert 1971; Dansgaard et al. 1971), and its severity could well be due to the superposition of more than one of these cycles.

The effect of the Great Drought was catastrophic in many areas. By the end of it, virtually all the major Pueblo III settlements were adandoned in favor of the Hopi, Zuni, and Rio Grande areas. In other words, the system crashed.

At this point, a note of caution must be inserted. It is well known that not all Pueblo III settlements crashed during the Great Drought. Their crashes, if and when they took place, may have been due to other climate cycles, or perhaps to different influences altogether. In addition, the regional variability of climate in the Southwest cannot be ignored, as the spectral density plots for Tsegi demonstrate well.

Conclusion

Some ideas on the dynamics and origins of cultural buffering mechanisms have been explored, and empirical evidence has been assembled to show that buffers can originate in response to environmental shifts. In the Prehistoric Southwest, these shifts consisted of a lengthened periodicity and a decreased variance in precipitation. The buffers that were employed in response to these changes enabled populations to damp the effects of high-frequency climatic oscillations. In doing so, local ecosystems were destabilized in order to meet increased energy requirements, thus bringing about a condition in which a long-term shift could precipitate a total collapse of the system. Such a collapse is documented for the Prehistoric Southwest.

ACKNOWLEDGMENTS

I am grateful for the aid and advice of Greg Burtchard, Linda Cordell, Henry Harpending, Mark Henderson, and W. James Judge. Robert Roosen provided useful information on climate cycles, and Jeffrey S. Dean provided tree-ring data and much valuable criticism of an early draft of the manuscript.

REFERENCES

Anderson, T. W.
    1971   *The statistical analysis of time series.* New York: John Wiley.
Blackman, R. B., and J. W. Tukey
    1958   *The measurement of power spectra from the point of view of communications engineering.* New York: Dover.
Borchert, J. B.
    1971   The dust bowl in the 1970s. *Annals of the Association of American Geographers* **61**:1–22.
Dansgaard, W., S. J. Johnsen, H. B. Clausen, and C. C. Langway
    1971   Climatic record revealed by the Camp Century ice core. In *Late Cenozoic glacial ages,* edited by K. K. Turekian. New Haven, Conn.: Yale University Press. Pp. 37–56.
Douglass, A. E.
    1947   Photographic tree-ring chronologies and the Flagstaff sequence. *Tree-Ring Bulletin* **14**(2):10–16.
Fritts, H. C.
    1963   Computer programs for tree-ring research. *Tree-Ring Bulletin* **25**(3–4):2–7.
Fritts, H. C., T. J. Blasing, B. P. Hayden, and J. E. Kutzbach
    1971   Multivariate techniques for specifying tree growth and climate relationships and for reconstructing anomalies in paleoclimate. *Journal of Applied Meteorology* **10**:845–864.
Fritts, H. C., D. G. Smith, and M. Stokes
    1965   The biological model for paleoclimatic interpretation of Mesa Verde tree-ring series. In *Contributions of the Wetherill Mesa Archaeological Project,* edited by D. Osborne. *Society for American Archaeology Memoir* No. 19. Pp. 101–121.

Gumerman, G. J.
   1975   Alternative cultural models for demographic change: Southwestern examples. In *Population studies in archaeology and biological anthropology: A symposium,* edited by A. C. Swedlund. *Society for American Archaeology Memoir* No. 30. Pp. 104–115.

Harpending, H. C., and J. B. Bertram
   1975   Human population dynamics in archaeological time: Some simple models. In *Population studies in archaeology and biological anthropology: A symposium,* edited by A. C. Swedlund. *Society for American Archaeology Memoir* No. 30. Pp. 82–91.

Hawley, F. M.
   1937   Relationship of southern cedar growth to precipitation and runoff. *Ecology* **18:**398–405.

Hill, J. N.
   1970   Broken K Pueblo: Prehistoric social organization in the American Southwest. *Anthropoligical Papers of the University of Arizona* No. 18. Tucson: University of Arizona Press.

Jenkins, G. M., and D. G. Watts
   1968   *Spectral analysis and its applications.* San Francisco: Holden-Day.

Jett, S. C.
   1964   Pueblo Indian migrations: An evaluation of the possible physical and cultural determinants. *American Antiquity* **29:**281–300.

Jorde, L. B., and H. C. Harpending
   1976   Cross-spectral analysis of rainfall and human birth rate: An empirical test of a linear model. In *The demographic evolution of human populations,* edited by R. H. Ward and K. M. Weiss. London: Academic Press. [Also in *Journal of Human Evolution* **5:**129–138.]

Kaplan, D.
   1960   The law of cultural dominance. In *Evolution and culture,* edited by M. D. Sahlins and E. R. Service. Ann Arbor, Mich.: University of Michigan Press. Pp. 69–92.

Koopmans, L. H.
   1974   *The spectral analysis of time series.* New York: Academic Press.

Kroeber, A. L.
   1953   *Cultural and natural areas of native North America.* Berkeley, Calif.: University of California Press.
   1963   *An anthropologist looks at history.* Berkeley, Calif.: University of California Press.

Lipe, W. D.
   1970   Anasazi communities in the Red Rock Plateau, southeastern Utah. In *Reconstructing Prehistoric Pueblo societies,* edited by W. A. Longacre. Albuquerque, N.M.: University of New Mexico Press. Pp. 84–139.

Longacre, W. A.
   1970   Archaeology as anthropology: A case study. *Anthropological Papers of the University of Arizona* No. 17. Tucson: University of Arizona Press.

Martin, P. S.
   1963   *The last 10,000 years: A fossil pollen record of the American Southwest.* Tucson: University of Arizona Press.

Martin, P. S., and F. Plog
   1973   The archaeology of Arizona: A study of the southwest region. Garden City, N.Y.: Doubleday/Natural History Press.

Nichols, R. F., and T. P. Harlan
   1967   Archaeological tree-ring dates from Wetherill Mesa. *Tree-Ring Bulletin* **28**(1–4):13–40.

Otnes, R. K., and L. Enochson
   1972   *Digital time series analysis.* New York: Wiley.

Pianka, E. R.
   1974   *Evolutionary ecology.* New York: Harper and Row.

Schoenwetter, A., and A. E. Dittert
   1968   An ecological interpretation of Anasazi settlement patterns. In *Anthropological archeology in*

the Americas, edited by B. J. Meggers. Washington, D.C.: Anthropological Society of Washington. Pp. 41–66.

Schulman, E.
1947   An 800-year Douglas fir at Mesa Verde. *Tree-Ring Bulletin* **14**(1):2–8.
1948   Dendrochronology of Navajo National Monument. *Tree-Ring Bulletin* **14**(3):18–24.
1954   Dendroclimatic changes in semiarid regions. *Tree-Ring Bulletin* **14**(3-4):26–30.

Spengler, O.
1926   *The decline of the West.* New York: Knopf.

Steward, J. H.
1955   *Theory of culture change.* Urbana, Ill.: University of Illinois Press.

Titiev, M.
1944   Old Oraibi: A study of the Hopi Indians of Third Mesa. *Peabody Museum of American Archaeology and Ethnology,* Vol. 22, No. 1.

Toynbee, A. J.
1974   *A study of history.* (abridged ed.) London: Oxford University Press.

Winkless, N., and I. Browning
1975   *Climate and the affairs of men.* New York: Harpers Magazine Press.

Woodbury, R. B.
1961   Prehistoric agriculture at Point of Pines, Arizona. *Society for American Archaeology Memoir* No. 17.

Young, T. C.
1972   Population densities and early Mesopotamian urbanism. In *Man, settlement and urbanism,* edited by P. J. Ucko, R. Tringham, and G. W. Dimbleby. London: Duckworth. Pp. 827–842.

Zubrow, E. B. W.
1975   *Prehistoric carrying capacity: A model.* Menlo Park, Calif.: Cummings.

Author Index

We acknowledge with gratitude the preparation of the indexes by Richard L. Taylor.

Subject Index

SUBJECT INDEX